The Morphos
of Complement-Head *equences*

Recent Titles in
OXFORD STUDIES IN COMPARATIVE SYNTAX
Richard Kayne, General Editor

The Morphosyntax of Complement-Head Sequences

Clause Structure and Word Order Patterns in Kwa

Enoch Oladé Aboh

OXFORD

UNIVERSITY PRESS

2004

OXFORD
UNIVERSITY PRESS

Oxford   New York
Auckland   Bangkok   Buenos Aires   Cape Town   Chennai
Dar es Salaam   Delhi   Hong Kong   Istanbul   Karachi   Kolkata
Kuala Lumpur   Madrid   Melbourne   Mexico City   Mumbai   Nairobi
São Paulo   Shanghai   Taipei   Tokyo   Toronto

Published by Oxford University Press, Inc.
198 Madison Avenue, New York, New York 10016

www.oup.com

Oxford is a registered trademark of Oxford University Press

Library of Congress Cataloging-in-Publication Data
Aboh, Enoch Oladé.
The Morphosyntax of complement-head sequences :
clause structure and word order patterns in Kwa / Enoch Oladé Aboh.
p. cm.
Based on the author's thesis—doctoral (1998, University of Geneva).
Includes bibliographical references and index.
ISBN 0-19-515989-6 (cloth) — ISBN 0-19-515990-X (pbk.)
1. Kwa languages—Syntax. I. Title.
PL8424 .A66 2003
496'.337—dc21   2002072346

2 4 6 8 9 7 5 3 1

Printed in the United States of America
on acid-free paper

To Marc Sessinou and Hope Assiaba

Preface

This book is based on my 1998 Ph.D. dissertation (Université de Genève). It discusses aspects of the Gbe languages (Kwa) in the light of Kayne's (1994) universal specifier-head-complement hypothesis. In this respect, the discussion in the following chapters shows that even in a theory that assumes the directionality parameter, only an analysis in terms of the specifier-head-complement captures better the Kwa data. This renders the directionality parameter theoretically superfluous and undesirable. The discussion on the Kwa languages is therefore extended to other Niger-Congo (e.g., Mandekan, Kru) and to certain Indo-European language families (e.g., Germanic, Romance). For instance, a parallel is established between word order variations in the Gbe and Kwa languages (i.e., the OV vs. VO asymmetry) and the Germanic SOV languages. In this respect, a fine structure of the I- and C-systems suggests that word order variations result from the interaction between movement of the complement (i.e., 'object shift') and movement of the head (e.g. verb movement). On the other hand, the study of the Gbe nominal sequence and certain constructions that involve the clausal left edge leads to a clearer parallelism between D and C as two manifestations of the same system: the left periphery. D selects for a nominal sequence, that is, an articulated predicative structure that is void of finiteness, while C selects for a structure that is specified for finiteness.

Most of the conclusions reached in this book would have not been possible without the help of various linguistic scholars. I'm grateful to Liliane Haegeman and Luigi Rizzi for making this work possible. I'm also greatly indebted to Houkpati B. C. Capo, Chris Collins, Rose Marie Déchaine, Cinque Guglielmo, Richard Kayne, Victor Manfredi, and Anne Zribi-Hertz for encouraging the publication of this book. My warmest thanks also go to Felix Ameka, Hans den Bensten, Anna Cardinaletti, James Essegbey, Thierry Etchegoyhen, Eric Haeberli, Séverin Kinhou, Christopher Laenzlinger, Peter Muysken, Nedzad Leko, Genoveva Puskás, Lucienne Rasetti, Ur Shlonsky, Norval Smith, and Michal Starke. I apologize to any I have forgotten.

I would not have been able to come to Geneva and start my research program without the help of my sisters and brothers, Jocelyne, Luc, Seth, Inès,

Alvine, Frieda, and Ethel. Thanks also to Da-Silva Urbain for believing in me. I'm also grateful to Raoul Gomez for helping. Special thanks go to Jean-Claude and Renée Dauvergne and to Véronique and Cyrille Delaye for providing a home and a second family away from home.

Needless to say I owe the greatest debt of gratitude to Anne, Aniola, Fèmi, and Orê for loving me and opening my eyes to a new and better world, *mí dó kpé.*

Contents

List of Abbreviations

ACC	Accusative
Agr	Agreement
Asp	Aspect
AspP1	Habitual Aspect Phrase
AspP2	Imperfective Aspect Phrase
AspP3	Prospective Aspect Phrase
Aux	Auxiliary
Cond	Conditional
Coord	Coordination
Dem	Demonstrative
DemP	Demonstrative Phrase
Def	Definite
Det	Determiner
F	Feminine
Fin	Finiteness
FinP	Finiteness Phrase
FM	Focus Marker
Foc	Focus
FocP	Focus Phrase
Fut	Future
GEN	Genitive
Hab	Habitual
Imperf	Imperfective
Indef	Indefinite
Inj	Injunctive
InjP	Injunctive Phrase
Inter	Interrogative
InterP	Interrogative Phrase
INSTR	Instrument

Irr	Irrealis
Loc	Locative
Neg	Negation
NOM	Nominative
NomP	Nominalizing Phrase
NR	Nominalizer
Nral	Numeral
NralP	Numeral Phrase
Num	Number
NumP	Number Phrase
P	Postnominal Morpheme
Pas	Past
Part	Particle
Perf	Perfective
Pl	Plural
Poss	Possessive
P	Prepositions
*P*P	Postnominal Phrase
Pres	Present
Prosp	Prospective
QM	Question Marker
RED	Reduplicated
S-sg	Strong Pronoun Singular
S-pl	Strong Pronoun Plural
SpfP	Specificity Phrase
Spf	Specific
Subj	Subjunctive
TM	Topic Marker
Top	Topic
TopP	Topic Phrase
W-sg	Weak Pronoun Singular
W-pl	Weak Pronoun Plural

The Morphosyntax
of Complement-Head Sequences

1

Introduction

1.1 PURPOSE AND ORGANIZATION OF THE BOOK

This book discusses different aspects of the syntax of the Gbe languages and seeks to figure out how the explanations proposed for these languages can cast some light on our understanding of the grammar of the Kwa languages and more generally of Universal Grammar (UG). Under the unified analysis for the Gbe languages, I propose that even though these languages may manifest head-final structures in certain contexts, they uniformly involve head-complement structures. This would mean that the head-complement versus complement-head asymmetry that is found in these languages does not reflect their mixed structures. Instead, word order variations arise from the interaction between leftward complement movements on the one hand and head movement on the other. In this respect, the Gbe languages provide empirical evidence for Kayne's (1994) universal spec-head-complement hypothesis.

Although some aspects of the Gbe languages have been widely studied (see Ansre 1966a, b; Clements 1972; Bole-Richard 1983; Ameka 1991; da Cruz 1993; Ndayragije 1993, 2000; Tossa 1993, 1994; Collins 1993, 1994a, b, 1997), less attention has been given to the architecture of these languages. The challenge of this study is thus to consider the D-, I-, and C-systems of Gungbe, bearing in mind the similarities or dissimilarities that may arise internally to Gbe and across Kwa languages. This book argues that the Gungbe D-, I-, and C-systems involve a highly articulated structure where each set of the features that realize D, I, or C is the syntactic head of a functional projection which projects within the D-, I-, or C-systems. The Gbe languages provide strong evidence for this analysis. For instance, Gungbe manifests different sets of markers, each of which encodes a feature that is associated with the head of the corresponding functional projection within the D-, I-, or C-systems (e.g., Abney 1987; Pollock 1989; Rizzi 1997; Cinque 1999 and subsequent work).

Chapter 2 is an outline of the grammar of the Gbe languages. It is an informal discussion of morphological and syntactic aspects of Gungbe, Fongbe, Gengbe, and Ewegbe. These languages branch from three subgroups of the Gbe cluster: Vhe (Ewegbe), Gen (Gengbe), and Fon (Gungbe, Fongbe) (see Capo 1988, 1991).

Chapter 3 investigates the Gungbe nominal system. On the basis of the head-initial hypothesis, I propose an analysis of the Gungbe D-system, where the specificity marker encodes D° and the number marker realizes Num° (see Ritter 1991, 1992, 1995). Under the split-D hypothesis, I suggest that these two functional heads project within the D-system as the nominal left periphery. Like certain Gungbe left peripheral markers, the specificity and number markers occur to the right edge because they force movement on their complement to their specifier positions.

Chapter 4 shows that the split-D hypothesis correlates with the existence of two sets of pronouns in Gungbe: those that manifest D and those that express Num. A careful analysis of the Gungbe pronominal system leads us to refine this characterization in terms of strong, weak, and clitic pronouns.

Chapter 5 focuses on certain Gungbe markers that occur in the middle field, that is, between the subject and the verb. In the light of Pollock's (1989) split-I hypothesis, I propose a sentence-internal structure where the Gungbe tense and aspect markers are the morphological realizations of the features [±future], [±habitual], [±imperfective], [±prospective] associated with the tense and aspect phrases TP, AspP1, AspP2, and AspP3, respectively. Assuming Rizzi's (1997) split-C hypothesis that each of the force and finiteness features associated with C is the syntactic head of a functional projection within the C-system, I further argue that the Gungbe counterpart of the English *if* and the Gungbe injunctive marker are the morphological realizations of the heads Force° and Fin° that project as the topmost and lowest frontiers of the C-system. The former occurs sentence-initially while the latter always surfaces in a position to the right of the subject.

Building on the analysis of the Gungbe tense and aspect markers, chapter 6 proposes a new analysis for the Gungbe imperfective and related clauses in terms of a biclausal structure. In so doing, I suggest that the Gungbe imperfective marker selects for a small clause headed by a nominalizer 'quasi null morpheme'. This morpheme encodes the feature [+n] associated with a nominalizing functional head that projects as the left-periphery of the small clause. The subject position of this clause represents the specifier position of the prospective aspect phrase AspP3. Under the EPP, this position is filled either by object shift (a typical property of imperfective and related constructions) or verb reduplication: a process that licenses a null expletive in [spec AspP3]. The occurrence of the nominalizer head in sentence-final position is regarded as a reflex of the leftward movement of the sequence Object-(Prospective)-verb-(Clitic)-(Indirect Object) to the specifier position of the nominalizing phrase. Granting object and verb movements, I further postulate that non-imperfective constructions differ from imperfective clauses in that they do not involve a small clause. This would mean that non-imperfective constructions are monoclausal. The object must move to [spec AgroP] to be licensed for case. On the other hand, the verb moves past the object to some aspect head position, where it checks its aspect features.

Assuming that both state and dynamic verbs follow the same path in syntax, I argue that the default present tense reading assigned to state verbs as opposed to the default perfective reading associated with dynamic verbs does not result from difference in structure. Instead, the difference in interpretation (i.e., perfective versus present state reading) may follow from certain semantic properties inherent to each class of lexical verbs.

Chapters 7 and 8 discuss the Gungbe CP-markers that are not involved in mood specification. Following Culicover (1992), Ndayiragije (1993), Aboh (1995, 1996a, b, 1998, 1999), Puskás (1995, 1996), Rizzi (1997) and subsequent work, I demonstrate that Gungbe provides strong evidence in favor of the split-C hypothesis. In the theory developed here, each of the Gungbe CP-markers, the topic marker, the focus marker, and the question marker, is the overt realization of a functional head Top°, Foc°, and Inter° that projects within the C-system. Given that these markers co-occur in a fixed order, I assume that their ordering manifests the underlying hierarchy of the C-system whereby Force° precedes Inter°, which in turn precedes Top°, which precedes Foc°, which precedes Fin°. The brief discussion in the appendix shows that the so-called clausal determiner naturally falls in the class of the Gbe left peripheral markers. This implies that the C-system probably involves a more complex structure than we might think a priori.

1.2 THEORETICAL BACKGROUND

The aim of this section is to provide a short discussion of the theoretical background underlying this study. The basic concern of generative grammar is to determine and characterize the speaker's knowledge of a language. The language faculty involves an initial state that evolves in the course of development to achieve a relatively stable state that reflects the speaker's ability to evaluate linguistic expressions of the target language. The initial state is genetically determined and is common to the human species. It represents UG: the core of grammar characterizing universal properties of languages. The final state attained derives from the interaction of the initial state with linguistic experience and corresponds to a language-specific grammar. A fairly standard assumption is that "(i) UG contains a set of absolute universals, notions and principles which do not vary from one language to the next. (ii) There are language-specific properties that are not fully determined by UG and vary cross-linguistically. For these properties a range of choices is made available by UG" (Haegeman 1994: 15).

The Principles and Parameters Theory seeks to formalize these two aspects of the language faculty. Language-invariant properties are principles that may be associated with a set of parameters (where UG offers a range of possibilities), and language-particular properties are specifications of particular values of parameters (see Chomsky & Lasnik 1993). In this regard, Chomsky (1995: 1) suggests that the Minimalist Program is motivated by two related questions: (1) what are the general conditions that the human language faculty should be expected to satisfy? And (2) to what extent is the language faculty determined by these conditions, without special structure that lies beyond them? The first question in turn has two aspects: what conditions are imposed on the language faculty by virtue of (A) its place within the array of cognitive systems of the mind/brain, and (B) general considerations of conceptual naturalness that have some independent plausibility, namely, simplicity, economy, symmetry, nonredundancy, and the like?

As a general introduction to this book, the following sections discuss certain theoretical implications that derive from the Principles and Parameters framework and the Minimalist Program.

1.2.1 Clause structure

Generative syntax is guided by the fundamental idea that syntax is structure-determined. Clauses consist of different types of phrases that are hierarchically organized around a head. The head determines the properties of the phrase and the structure of the phrases results from a number of rigid principles that are summarized by the X-bar theory.

1.2.1.1 The X-bar theory

X-bar theory is seen as the module of the grammar that regulates the structure of phrases. According to this theory, all phrases are headed by one head. The head, say X, is a zero-level category that projects a phrase. XP is the projection of X: it is a maximal projection. The head X combines with its complement YP, a maximal projection, to form an intermediate projection X'. The latter in its turn combines with ZP, the maximal projection in the specifier of the phrase, to form the maximal projection XP as represented in (1), but see Kayne (1994) and Chomsky (1995) for new developments.

(1)

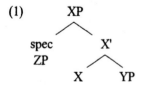

Under fairly standard assumption, it is often proposed that a maximal projection, FP, can adjoin to another one as illustrated in structure (2), but see Kayne (1994) and Chomsky (1995, 1999, 2001) on a restrictive analysis of adjunction. In structure (2), the base XP is combined with FP to form a higher projection of XP.

(2)

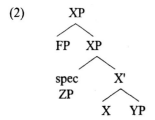

The basic syntactic relations between the projections are expressed in terms of c-command:

(3)   a node X c-commands a node Y iff
       (i) X does not dominate Y;
       (ii) Y does not dominate X;
       (iii) the first branching node Z dominating X dominates Y.

When Z is a maximal projection, the relation is identified as **m-command**.

1.2.1.1.1 Word order

Representations (1) and (2) clearly show that the X-bar theory determines the internal hierarchy of phrases, that is, the relationship between a head and its specifier and that between a head and its complement. Languages vary considerably with respect to the linear order of phrases in the sentence. For instance, the English embedded clause in (4a) manifests VO order, unlike the German sentence in (4b), which exhibits OV order. On the other hand, languages of the Gbe-type display both VO and OV orders. Contrast the Gungbe non-imperfective construction in (4c) to the imperfective sentence in (4d).

(4)   a.   ...that John   buys   [the book]
       b.   dass Hans   [das   Buch]   kauft
            that Hans   the   book   buys
            '...that Hans buys the book'
       c.   ...ɖɔ̀ Ján   xɔ̀   wémá   lɔ́
            that John   buy   book   Det
            '...that John bought the book'
       d.   ...ɖɔ̀ Ján   tò   wémá   lɔ́   xɔ̃́
            that John   Imperf   book   Det   buy-NR
            '...that John is buying the book'

In order to account for cross-linguistic variation, it is traditionally assumed that X-bar theory defines only the hierarchy of phrases. The linear ordering of constituents in the sentence is subject to parametric variation as represented in (5), where the semi-colon indicates that linear order varies.

(5)   a.   XP → spec; X'   b.   X' → X; YP

In other words, (5a) allows for situations where the specifier precedes or follows the head, while (5b) expresses situations where the complement follows or precedes the head. Under (5), word order variation is determined by a fixing parameter of UG. In the literature, this parameter is known as the directionality parameter. In terms of this approach, the orders VO and OV are made available by UG and the child has to set the word order parameter for his language. In head-initial languages VO is the base order, unlike head-final languages, where the base order is OV. It is traditionally assumed that case is assigned to the right in VO languages, but to the left in OV languages. It has also been claimed that other languages (e.g., Gbe and other Kwa) have the two options since they manifest both VO and OV characteristics.

A drawback of this system is that it gives rise to several linear word orders that are not generally found in human languages. For example, the OV order found in the West Germanic languages and the Gbe languages is limited to specific contexts: embedded clauses in Germanic and imperfective clauses in Gbe. Recently, this inconsistency has led to a reanalysis of the standard X-bar theory in terms of a more restricted analysis where only one base order (VO) is adopted (see Zwart 1993, 1997a, b; Kayne 1994, and references cited there).

1.2.1.1.2 Kayne (1994)

In his antisymmetry theory, Kayne (1994) abandons the idea, expressed in (5a–b), that linear order is parametrically determined. He proposes the Linear Correspondence Axiom (LCA) to derive the linear order of terminal nodes, from the hierarchical relations between the non-terminal nodes dominating them. This leads to a highly restricted theory where precedence relations reproduce asymmetric c-command relations. If X asymmetrically c-commands Y in a sequence, then X precedes Y in the structure. Asymmetry c-command is defined as follows:

(6)   X asymmetrically c-commands Y iff X c-commands Y and Y does not c-command X (Kayne 1994: 4)

A major consequence of Kayne's theory is that only specifier-head-complement (S-H-C) linear order is possible. Situations where the complement precedes the head cannot reflect the base order. If the complement precedes the head, then the surface ordering must be a derived order where the complement moves to an asymmetric c-commanding specifier position. Movement always targets a c-commanding position, and no rightward movement is allowed by the grammar because asymmetric c-command implies precedence. In addition, Kayne's approach eliminates the intermediate level X'. There is only one projection level, which allows for only one adjoined maximal projection at most.

In terms of Kayne's analysis, the West Germanic SOV languages should be analyzed as involving head-initial underlying structures. Similarly, the S-H-C versus S-C-H contrast manifested by the Gbe non-imperfective constructions versus imperfective and related clauses on the one hand (see chapters 5, 6) and by prepositional phrases versus postnominal phrases on the other hand (see chapter 3, appendix) cannot be taken as an indication that the Gbe languages manifest both head-initial and head-final structures. Instead, they must be analyzed on the basis of a universal underlying head-initial structure. In this respect, Kayne (1994: 47) suggests that "if UG unfailingly imposes S-H-C order, there cannot be any directionality parameter in the standard sense of the term. The difference between so-called head-initial languages and so-called head-final languages cannot be due to parametric setting whereby complement positions in the latter type precede their associated heads." I show in the following chapters that an analysis that assumes such a restricted structure accounts for the Gbe and Kwa languages in a straightforward manner. In addition, that the S-H-C hypothesis is empirically motivated in Gbe suggests that only the SVO base order could be maintained for these languages, even if we were to adopt classical GB analysis and allow for parametric variation in base order (see chapter 2, section 2.5).

1.2.1.2 Argument structure

Under standard X-bar theory, it is assumed that the features of the head of a phrase determine the features of the phrase. Similarly, it is proposed that the components of a sentence are dependent on the type of verb it contains. Consider sentences under (7).

(7)   a.   Mary will probably invite John
        b.   *Mary will probably invite
        c.   *will probably invite John

In the grammatical sentence (7a), *Mary* and *John* are the arguments of the verb *invite*. The ungrammatical sentences (7b–c) show that these two arguments, that is, the participants in the event, must be realized in the sentence on a par with the verb *invite*. Within the principles and parameter framework, this relation is expressed in terms of the theta criterion. Under the assumption that lexical heads (e.g., verbs, nouns, adjectives, and prepositions) bear thematic information, it is proposed that they are associated to a number of arguments to which they assign thematic roles. The theta criterion is formulated as follows:

(8)   Theta criterion
        a. each argument is associated with one and only one theta role
        b. each theta role is associated with one and only one argument

One consequence of the theta criterion is that there is a locality constraint on the realization of arguments: all the thematic roles must be assigned within the maximal projection of the lexical head. It follows that the verb *invite* assigns all its thematic roles VP-internally. This is consistent with Sportiche's (1988) proposal that the subject originates from the VP (see, among others, Zagona 1982; Kitagawa 1986; Kuroda 1986; Koopman & Sportiche 1991; Alexiadou & Anagnostopoulou 2001). This need not mean, though, that arguments are not subject to movement operations. For example, the intervention of the adverb *probably* between the subject and the verb suggests that the subject is not realized VP-internally. That arguments may occur outside the maximal projection where they receive thematic roles is also confirmed by example (9b)—derived from (9a)—where the wh-phrase *who* is extracted from the VP-internal position. As shown by ungrammatical (9c), the extraction site is not available for another argument, suggesting that the position is filled by an empty category (ec).

(9)   a.   Mary invited John
       b.   Who did Mary invite ec ?
       c.   *Who did Mary invite Paul ?

In the principles and parameters framework, it is argued that whenever an argument of a head X is realized outside the projection XP, the argument moves to some c-commanding position in the structure, leaving an empty category in its extraction site. The Empty Category Principle regulates the distribution of empty categories.

1.2.1.3 The Empty Category Principle (ECP)

A movement operation leaves an empty category in the extraction site. Assuming the distinctive features [±pronominal , ±anaphor], four types of empty categories obtain:

(10)   [-pronominal, +anaphor]   =   NP-trace
        [-pronominal, -anaphor]   =   wh-trace
        [+pronominal, -anaphor]   =   pro
        [+pronominal, +anaphor]   =   PRO

Certain empty categories cannot be arbitrarily generated in the sentence, as they must be associated with an overt antecedent. Accordingly, they are subject to specific licensing conditions. One formal licensing condition on nonpronominal empty categories is the ECP, which requires that:

(11)   A nonpronominal empty category must be properly head-governed,

where head government is defined as follows:

(12)   X head-governs Y iff
        (i) X ∈ {A, N, P, V, Agr, T}
        (ii) X m-command Y

(iii) no barrier intervenes

(iv) Relativized Minimality is respected (Rizzi 1990: 30)

Given that empty categories must be interpretable, they are also subject to an identification requirement that is achieved either by binding or by antecedent-government. Under Rizzi (1990), binding is restricted to elements that are associated with a theta role, that is, arguments. Being arguments, these elements are referential and can therefore be thought of as bearing a referential index that helps to identify the empty category they are linked to. Binding is defined in (13).

(13)   X binds Y iff

      (i) X c-commands Y

      (ii) X and Y have the same referential index

Since elements like adjuncts do not have a referential index, the empty category they are associated with is subject to antecedent-government, a more local relation that enables one to identify elements without referential indices. The antecedent-government is defined in (14).

(14)   X antecedent-governs Y iff

      (i) X and Y are non-distinct

      (ii) X c-commands Y

      (iii) no barrier intervenes

      (iv) Relativized Minimality is respected.

The licensing conditions in (12) and (14) distinguish between head-governors (i.e., lexical and functional heads, e.g., A, N, P, V, Agr, T) and antecedent-governors (i.e., coindexed categories) (see Rizzi 1990: 6). Head-government is a local process between a head and an empty category. Antecedent-government, however, appears a property of the chain that arises through movement. The chain consists of the antecedent and the empty category that occupies its extraction site (including possible intermediate empty categories signaling movement through intermediate positions). It is generally assumed that movement operations trigger three types of chains: A-chains result from NP-movement, A'-chains are created by wh-movement and X°-chains are formed by head-movement. The question now arises whether these different chains interact with each other.

1.2.1.4 Relativized minimality

In his account for minimality effects that might arise between chains, Rizzi (1990) proposes a symmetric analysis in terms of relativized minimality that restricts the types of possible interveners that may block government (i.e., head-government or antecedent-government). Relativized Minimality is defined in (15).

(15)   X α-governs Y only if there is no Z such that:
     (i) Z is a typical potential α-governor for Y
     (ii) Z c-commands Y and does not c-command X (Rizzi 1990: 7)

Under Rizzi's (1990) relativized minimality, head-government and antecedent-government do not interfere with each other as they involve two separate or parallel chains. In this respect, relativized minimality blocks antecedent-government from X when Z is a potential antecedent governor. Relativized minimality, though, cannot block antecedent-government from X if Z is a potential head governor (Rizzi 1990: 2). This amounts to saying that minimality effects are triggered only by similar elements:

1.   Potential governors block head-government between a head and the governee,
2.   A'-elements are potential interveners for antecedent-government in an A'-chain,
3.   A-elements are potential interveners for antecedent-government in an A-chain,
4. X°-elements are potential interveners for antecedent-government in an X°-chain.

Property 2, for instance, helps account for the contrast between sentences (16a–b).

(16)   a.   Why$_i$ did you think $[_{CP}$ t'$_i$ that $[_{IP}$ Louise called John t$_i$]]
       b.   *Why$_j$ did you wonder $[_{CP}$ who$_i$ $[_{IP}$ Louise called t$_i$ t$_j$]]

In sentence (16a), *why* is extracted from the embedded clause. Being an adjunct, it does not bear a referential index and its trace is subject to antecedent-government. This is made possible due to the intervening trace in the embedded CP-layer and the sentence is grammatical. In (16b), instead, long construal is impossible because the potential antecedent *who* blocks antecedent-government between *why* and its trace. Accordingly, sentence (16b) can be interpreted as involving only wh-extraction of *why* from the matrix clause to the sentence initial position as illustrated in (17).

(17)   Why$_j$ did you wonder t$_j$ $[_{CP}$ who$_i$ $[_{IP}$ Louise called t$_i$]]

Recent developments have led to a formulation of relativized minimality in terms of a general condition on economy of derivations: movement operations must construct the shortest or minimal link (see Chomsky 1995; Collins 1996). In this framework, syntax is economy-driven: overt movement operations are costlier than abstract movement (or feature movement). Movement is always a last resort phenomenon that is delayed as late as possible (i.e., till LF). In the minimalist framework, this process is formulated in terms of the condition Procrastinate that prefers covert movement to overt movement (see Chomsky 1992, 1995). This means that overt movement applies if otherwise the derivation would lead to ungrammaticality (or would crash in Chomsky's term). In the light of this, Chomsky then proposes that the minimality effects expressed by Rizzi's relativized minimality can be reanalyzed in terms of 'Minimize chain link', a condition which requires that movement must always target the shortest potential landing site. In this respect, sentence (16b) is ungrammatical because the legitimate target of movement is already occupied by the wh-phrase *who* and the "minimal link condition" is violated. Chomsky (1995: 331) defines the minimal link condition as in (18) (see also Collins 1996 on local economy conditions).

(18)   Minimal Link Condition
       K attracts α only if there is no β, β closer to K than α, such that K attracts β.

1.2.1.5 The structure of sentences

Under X-bar theory and the discussion in previous paragraphs, sentences can be attributed the general structure represented in (19). Here, the clause consists of a verb projection VP that combines with a functional projection associated with inflection (i.e., tense and agreement features) labeled as IP; and CP, the functional projection representing the left periphery. The latter hosts the complementizer and its specifier position represents the landing site of wh-phrases and other scope elements.

(19) $[_{CP} [_{C^\circ} [_{IP} [_{I^\circ} [_{VP}\ldots]]]]]$

1.2.1.5.1 The split-I hypothesis: Pollock (1989)

In analyzing the structure of English and French sentences, Pollock (1989) postulates a more articulated IP structure where each of the tense and agreement features is associated with a maximal projection, TP and AgrP, respectively, within the inflectional system. Extending the same reasoning to negation, Pollock (1989: 397) suggests that the structure of negative sentences involves a maximal projection NegP that projects between TP and AgrP as illustrated by (20). TP dominates NegP, which in turn dominates AgrP.

(20) $[_{TP} [_{NegP} [_{AgrP} [_{VP} \cdots]]]]$

Partial justification for Pollock's analysis is based on the distribution of adverbs and negative elements in regard to the position of the verb in French and English. Consider the following sentences:

(21)   a.   Jean embrasse souvent Marie
       b.   *Jean souvent embrasse Marie
       c.   John often kisses Mary
       d.   *John kisses often Mary

Granting that adverbs occupy a fixed position in the sentence, the only explanation for the fact that *souvent* 'often' intervenes between the verb *embrasse* 'kiss' and the DP-object *Marie* in the French sentence (21a) but not in the English example (21c) is to assume obligatory verb movement to T° in French but not in English. The same situation obtains in (22) with respect to the negative elements *pas* and *not* in French and English, respectively.

(22) a. Jean ne mange pas de chocolat
      b. Jean does not eat any chocolate
      c. *John eats not any chocolate

In sentence (22a), negation is expressed by means of the elements *ne* and *pas*. On the assumption that *ne* is a clitic element, it must move to some head position (say T°), while *pas*, being a maximal projection, can stay in a fixed specifier position (e.g., [spec NegP]). That the verb precedes the negative adverbial elements *pas* in the French sentence (22a) but must follow *not* in the English negative sentence (22b) is interpreted in terms of verb movement to T° in French followed by clitic movement of *ne*, as opposed to a static situation in English where movement of the lexical verb is impossible and tense features are encoded by *do*.

A slightly different distribution of the verb in French non-finite clauses, as opposed to English non-finite clauses, leads Pollock (1989) to conclude that in this particular context, verb movement in French targets a lower position than T°. Consider, for example, the French sentences in (23a–b), compared to their English counterparts in (24a–b).

(23) a. A peine parler l'italien après cinq ans d'étude dénote un manque de don ...
          to hardly speak Italian after five years of study denotes a lack of gift ...
      b. Parler à peine l'italien après cinq ans d'étude dénote un manque de don ...
          to speak hardly Italian after five years of study denotes a lack of gift...
(24) a. to hardly speak Italian after years of hard work means you have no gift for languages
      b. *to speak hardly Italian after years of hard work means you have no gift for languages

That the verb may precede or follow the adverb in French (23a–b) but not in English (24a–b) is interpreted as a manifestation of verb movement past adverbs in French, unlike English where no such strategy is available. The contrast in example (25a–b) clearly shows that verb movement in French does not move past the negation element *pas*.

(25) a. ne pas regarder la télévision consolide l'esprit critique
          ne not to watch television strengthens one's independence
      b. *ne regarder pas la télévision consolide l'esprit critique
          ne to watch not television strengthens one's independence

In Pollock's (1989) approach, the fact that the infinitive verb may move past the adverb but occurs in a position lower than the negative element indicates that there are intermediate positions, such as Agr°, which may host the verb. Since the verb never moves in English, it necessarily occurs to the right of both adverbs and the negative element *not*. Pollock then proposes that the contrast observed in French and English with respect to verb movement results from the properties of agreement in these languages. In languages that have a strong agreement system (e.g., French, Italian), Agr forces verb movement, but fails to do so in languages with weak agreement (e.g., English).

Building on Pollock (1989) and subsequent work, Belletti (1990) argues on the basis of morphological evidence that the sentence structure actually manifests the reverse hierarchy to that proposed in (18): AgrP dominates NegP, which in turn dominates TP. Belletti (1990) thus argues that the right characterization of clause structures is that represented in (26) (see also Zanuttini 1991; Haegeman 1995a).

(26)   [$_{AgrP}$ [$_{NegP}$ [$_{TP}$ [$_{VP}$...]]]]

Recent research on clause structure suggests the existence of a head that encodes mood specification and projects as the highest functional projection (MoodP) of the inflection system. On the basis of structure (26), we therefore obtain the ordering represented in (27), (see Pollock 1997; Rizzi 1997; Cinque 1999, among others).

(27)   [$_{MoodP}$ [$_{AgrP}$ [$_{NegP}$ [$_{TP}$ [$_{VP}$ ...]]]]]

1.2.1.5.2 The split-C hypothesis: Rizzi (1997)

Pollock's (1989) split-I hypothesis represents a milestone in the field of generative syntax. More recently, this hypothesis was extended to the C-system. Under this approach, the C-system involves a more articulated structure where each of the features traditionally associated with the CP layer is the syntactic head of a maximal projection. In this regard, Rizzi (1997) assumes that each of the force, topic, focus, and finiteness features that manifest the left periphery is the head of a functional projection ForceP, TopP, FocP, and FinP, which projects within the C-system (see Culicover 1992; Shlonsky 1994; Puskás 1995, 1996; Rizzi 1997; Aboh 1998, among many others).

Force represents the highest projection of the C-system: it constitutes an interface between the propositional content expressed by IP and the superordinate structure: the main clause or the discourse. Force encodes whether a sentence is a question, a declarative, or an exclamative, and may be morphologically realized in the language. For example, some languages manifest distinct morphemes for marking questions and declarative sentences. A case in point is the Fongbe question marker *à* that occurs sentence-finally as shown by example (28). See chapter 8 for the discussion.

(28) a.   Kɔjó   tɔ́n
           Kojo   go-Perf out
           'Kojo went out'
      b.   Kɔjó   tɔ́n   à
           Kojo   go-Perf out   QM
           'Did Kojo go out?'

Granting that topic constructions also involve the left periphery, Rizzi (1997) proposes that the C-system includes a functional projection TopP whose head encodes the topic feature and whose specifier hosts topic elements. The topic-comment relation found in sentence (29a) is structurally represented as in (29b), where XP is the topic and YP the comment (Rizzi 1997: 286).

(29) a.   Your book, you should give to Paul (not to Bill)
      b. $[_{TopP}$ XP $[_{Top°}$ $[_{YP}$]]]

This reasoning extends to focus constructions. The focus-presupposition articulation manifested in (30a) is represented as in (30b). ZP is the focused phrase *John* and WP the presupposition that includes the IP domain realized as *came to the party*.

(30) a.   JOHN came to the party
      b. $[_{FocP}$ ZP $[_{Foc°}$ $[_{WP}$]]]

FinP, on the other hand, projects as the lowest functional projection of the C-system. It is relevant with respect to the embedded IP as it "contains a tense specification which matches the one expressed on the lower inflectional system" (Rizzi 1997: 283). Granting that TopP and FocP are projected only when the sentence contains a topic or a focus expression, Rizzi suggests that

> it is reasonable to assume that the topic-focus system is present in a structure only if needed, i.e., when a constituent bears topic or focus features to be sanctioned by a spec-head criterion. If the topic focus field is activated, it will inevitably be sandwiched in between force and finiteness, as the two specifications must terminate the C system upward and downward, in order to meet the different selectional requirements and properly insert the C system in the structure. (1997: 288)

This is represented in (31):

(31)   .... Force ..... (Topic) ..... (Focus) .... Fin... IP

The Italian sentences in (32) further indicate that multiple topics may precede or follow the focused element. These facts led Rizzi (1997) to refine structure (31) as in (33).

(32) a. credo che a Gianni, QUESTO, domani, gli dovremmo dire
                 C   Top   Foc   Top   IP
        'I believe that to Gianni, THIS, tomorrow we should say'
   b. credo che QUESTO, a Gianni, domani, gli dovremmo dire
                 C   Foc   Top   Top   IP
        'I believe that THIS to Gianni, tomorrow we should say'

(33) $[_{ForceP} [_{Force°} [_{TopP*} [_{Top°} [_{FocP} [_{Foc°} [_{TopP*} [_{Top°} [_{FinP} [_{Fin°} [IP\ldots]]]]]]]]]]]]$

Rizzi's split-C hypothesis has led to a new understanding of the C-system. Comparative data play a significant role in the development of this analysis. In chapters 7 and 8, I show that the split-C hypothesis accounts for the distribution and the function of the Gungbe CP-markers in a straightforward manner. In addition, the Gbe data show that the C-system should be expanded to account for both left peripheral and right peripheral makers. See also Puskás (1996, 2000) for an analysis of the Hungarian left periphery in terms of the split-C hypothesis.

1.2.1.6 The noun phrase and the DP hypothesis: Abney (1987)

So far, I have discussed the structures of both the IP and CP layers in the clause. I now look at the structure of noun phrases (NP). Consider example (34):

(34) a. The invasion of Belgium
   b. The Romans' invasion of Belgium

In the early eighties, classical Government and Binding (GB) analysis of the sequences under (34) was to claim that both the article *the* in (34a) and the genitive phrase *the Romans'* in (34b) occupy the specifier position of a noun phrase (NP) headed by the noun *invasion*. The head noun may take a prepositional phrase (PP) complement as shown by example (34b). Accordingly, sentences (34a–b) could be represented as in (35) (Haegeman 1994: 607).

(35)

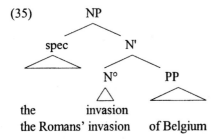

A problem with this analysis is that it amalgamates the determiner and the genitive phrase as potential hosts of [spec NP]. Yet, as extensively discussed by Abney (1987), determiners exhibit several characteristics indicating that they are functional heads. They head a functional projection within the nominal system and occupy a different position than the genitive phrase. The latter is analyzed in (35) as the projection of the lexical head N. Notice further that determiners belong to a closed class: a typical property of functional elements. On the contrary, Ns are lexical elements and form an open class. The French data in (36) lend further support to the hypothesis that determiners are heads. The sentences under (36a–d) show that the determiners *le* and *les* may be incorporated by a preceding preposition. Assuming that incorporation is diagnostic of *headness*, it naturally follows that determiners undergo such development on a par with other heads.

(36) a.   Jean a   parlé   **à la** fille
           John has   talked   to the girl
           'John talked to the girl'
      b.   Jean a parlé (*à le) **au** garçon
           John has talked   to-the boy
           'John talked to the boy'
      c.   Jean a   pris   le livre   **de la** fille
           John has   taken   the book of the girl
           'John took the girl's book'
      d.   Jean a pris le livre (*de le) **du** garçon
           Jean has taken the book   of-the boy
           'John took the boy's book'

Additional evidence that determiners might be functional elements heading a functional projection of the Agr-type is found in many languages. The Hungarian sentences in (37) manifest person/number agreement between the noun *kalap* 'hat' and the possessor bearing nominative case (see Abney 1987: 18).

(37) a.   az en kalap-om
           the I-NOM hat-1sg
           'My hat'
      b.   a te kalap-od
           the you-NOM hat-2sg
           'Your hat'
      c.   a Peter kalap-ja
           the Peter-NOM hat-3sg
           'Peter's hat'

Granting the idea that Agr is responsible for nominative case assignment in the sentence, we can assume that the NPs under (37) also include an agreement projection that assigns nominative case. This analysis is consistent with the agreement facts found in Turkish whereby we see that the genitive case associated with the possessor is

determined by agreement morphology of the possessed noun phrase as in (38)
(Abney 1987: 21).

(38)   sen-in   el-in
       your-GEN   hand-2sg
       'your hand'

Taking seriously the idea that a sentence consists of a VP dominated by the appropriate
functional projections as in (26–27), Abney (1987) suggests that the same reasoning
should extend to the nominal domain. He then reanalyzes NPs in terms of a functional
projection of the Agr-type that selects an NP as complement. Abney proposes that this
functional projection is a determiner phrase (DP) headed by the determiner. Given that
determiners do not always occur with a complement, Abney further concludes that
certain forms of the determiner (e.g., *the*, *a*, in English) require an NP complement
while others can surface in isolation. Representations (39a–b) illustrate these two
situations. In (39c), D is not morphologically realized: it is considered the locus of the
agreement features responsible for the genitive case assigned to the DP *the Romans'*
that occurs in [spec DP].

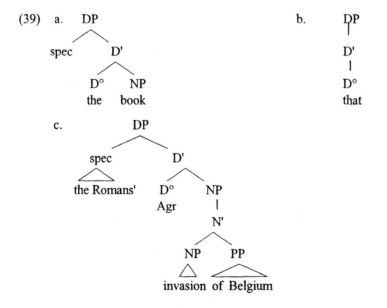

On the basis of the representations (39a–b), the ungrammatical sequence (**the this*
house) is straightforwardly accounted for by saying that the English determiner '*the*'
and the demonstrative '*this*' compete for the same position. They are mutually
exclusive because they are both inserted in D: the head of the determiner phrase.
Extending this reasoning to the English pronominal system, and having observed that
pronouns never select for a complement, Abney proposes that they must be regarded as

intransitive Ds: they realize the D projection only on a par with demonstrative elements like '*that*' represented in (39b).

However, work by Cardinaletti and Starke (1999), among others, shows that Abney's characterization explains only the distribution of clitic pronouns in the sentence. Building on Kayne (1975), they develop an analysis of pronouns in terms of three classes (strong, weak, and clitic), each of which reflects an underlying different structure. Clitic pronouns are Ds in the sense of Abney. Weak pronouns include some (but not all) functional projections associated with the D head. Finally, strong pronouns are full DPs.

Abney's DP hypothesis represents an important step in our understanding of noun phrases. However, it poses a number of problems that are still under study (see Szabolsci 1987; Carstens 1991; Ritter 1991, 1992, 1995; Longobardi 1994). For example, there is strong cross-linguistic evidence against the hypothesis that articles and demonstratives are in complementary distribution because they occupy the D-position. A case in point is Romanian, where the article and the demonstrative co-occur with the noun as shown in (40a). The same is true of the Gungbe example (40b). I return to these facts in chapters 3 and 4, but see also Longobardi 1994, Giusti 1994, 1997, and references cited there.

(40) a. fetele   acestea douà   frumoase
          girls-the   these   two   nice
          'These two nice girls'
      b. mótò vè   éhè   lɔ́   lέ
          car   red   this   Det   Num
          'These red cars'

Notice in passing that the Gungbe example (40b) also includes a morpheme *lέ*, which indicates number. Similar facts in Hebrew led Ritter (1991) to propose the existence of a number phrase (NumP) whose head is the locus of number specifications (singular or plural) that are associated with a noun phrase, as represented in (41).

(41)   [$_{DP}$ [$_{D°}$ [$_{NumP}$ [$_{Num°}$ [$_{NP}$...]]]]]

Granting the split-I and split-C hypotheses discussed above, Ritter's (1991) proposal can be reinterpreted in terms of the split-D hypothesis, which suggests that the DP involves a more articulate structure where each of the specificity, number, and agreement features traditionally treated as n-features is the head of a functional projection that projects within the D-system (see, among others, Szabolcsi 1987; Carstens 1991, 2000; Giusti 1991, 1994, 1997; Siloni 1991, 1997; Brousseau & Lumsden 1992; Longobardi 1994; Ritter 1995; Kinyalolo 1995).

1.2.2 Levels of representation

Under the Principles and Parameters approach, the discussion in previous sections presupposes the existence of four levels of syntactic representation, D-structure (DS), S-structure (SS), logical form (LF), and phonetic form (PF), each of which represents a level of analysis of the sentence.

DS encodes the selectional restrictions of lexical and functional heads: it reflects the basic predicate-argument relations in the clause. In this respect, DS constitutes the level where lexical units are inserted or generated in the structure. For instance, it is commonly assumed that the thematic relations between a verb and its arguments reflect that both the subject and the object are base-generated VP-internally (see Sportiche 1988).

SS is derived from DS by movement operations, that is, the earlier transformations, which are subsumed under 'move-α'. SS reflects the surface ordering as well as the morphological form of the constituents. Pursuing this discussion on verb-argument relations, it is generally assumed that the subject and the object may move from their VP-internal positions to derived surface positions, say Agrs and Agro, to be licensed for nominative and accusative case, respectively. In the literature, this type of NP-movement to an argument position (A-position) is also known as A-movement. Similarly, movement of a maximal projection to a non-argument position, is analyzed as an A'-movement. As I discuss in chapters 7 and 8, Gungbe exhibits a number of constructions (e.g., focus, wh-question, topic) that typically involve such A'-movement.

LF represents semantic relations. It is the interface level where the logico-semantic relations between the constituents of a sentence are interpreted. Postulating LF implies that the surface order does not strictly determine the interpretation of a sentence. A typical case is the multiple wh-question.

(42)   a.   When will John take what?
       b.   *When what will John take?
       c.   John will take [the car] [tomorrow]

In English, only one wh-phrase can occur in sentence-initial position; others must stay in their base positions, or in situ. This is illustrated by the grammatical sentence (42a) as opposed to the ungrammatical sentence (42b). Sentence (42a) questions both the time of action and the theme of action and requires an answer that necessarily pairs time and theme as suggested by example (42c). Omitting either of the bracketed elements will lead to an inappropriate answer to (42a). In order to account for this puzzle, it is proposed that though the wh-phrase *what* remains in its base position at SS, it moves to a specific left-peripheral position at LF where it has scope over the sentence. Extending this reasoning to the relative ordering of quantifiers in a sentence, it is generally assumed that their scope properties are LF specifications (see May 1985).

PF encodes the morpho-phonological rules that give rise to the overt realization of SS. The four levels of representation proposed lead to a model of the grammar as illustrated in (43):

(43)

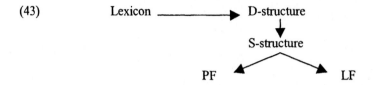

Notice that even though both PF and LF feed from DS and SS, they are totally opaque to each other. There are several constraints on the relation between DS and SS. One such constraint is the Structure Preserving Principle (SPP), which requires that syntactic positions that are created at DS must also be present at SS. Similarly, a given position cannot change its category from DS to SS. This means that a position that qualifies as NP position at DS must remain an NP position at SS. The same holds for head positions. An immediate consequence of this principle is that XP elements must move to corresponding specifier positions, while $X°$ elements move only to corresponding head positions. Finally, any moved category must leave a trace in its base position in order to meet the requirement that positions that are created at DS must also be present at SS. However, the SPP does not exclude that a moved element be attributed a new position that does not exist at DS, provided the new created position respects the X-bar theory and related principles. Adjunction is a typical case where such a new position is created during the derivation.

1.2.3 Minimizing levels of representation

In terms of Chomsky's minimalist program, the four levels of representation discussed are reduced to only two independent levels, including an abstract representation of sounds (PF) and an abstract representation of meaning (LF). The levels of DS and SS are eliminated. In addition to the lexicon, the system postulates the existence of two related and formally simple transformational operations identified as Merge and Move. Merge is defined as an operation that "takes a pair of syntactic objects (SO_i, SO_j) and replaces them by a new combined syntactic object SO_{ij}" (Chomsky 1995: 226, but see Chomsky 1999, 2000, and references cited there for new developments).

On the other hand, the operation Move "selects α and raises it, targeting K, where α and K are categories constructed from one or more lexical items" (Chomsky 1995: 262). These two rules iteratively apply during the course of the derivation. The minimalist program further assumes a non-transformational operation, Spell-out, that may apply at any point in the process and switches to PF, the overt component. After Spell-out, the computational process continues leading to LF, the covert component. Spell-out plays a similar role to SS in the sense that it splits the derivation into two tracks as suggested by the T-model represented in (42). Similarly, Chomsky's theory of trace in terms of copy subsumes certain properties of DS, and expressed in the SPP, that positions that are created at DS are not simply discarded during the derivation. Representation (44) (adapted from Epstein, Tráinsson, & Zwart 1996: 5) illustrates the model of the grammar that the minimalist program assumes.

(44)

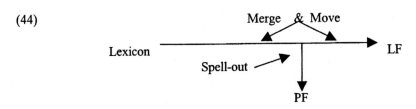

Outline of the Grammar of Gbe

This chapter is a brief summary of the basics of the Gbe languages. It is meant to introduce the reader to the data that will be discussed in the following chapters. I first provide an informal description that points out the morphological, phonological, and syntactic aspects shared by the languages of the Gbe cluster.

The data presented in this study are drawn mainly from Gungbe, my 'father tongue',[1] my native language. Gungbe is a Kwa language of the Gbe cluster. The variety under study here is spoken in Porto-Novo in Benin. As Gungbe is closely related to other Gbe languages, I also present data from Gengbe, my mother tongue; Fongbe of which I have a contact knowledge, as I grew up in Abomey, one of the major cities where this language is spoken; and Ewegbe, of which I have only a limited knowledge.

The Gungbe, Fongbe, and Gengbe data that are analyzed in this study are based on fieldwork with native speakers in Benin and in Geneva. For all transcriptions, I follow the Benin writing system as proposed in DAPR (1984), CENALA (1990). I further adopt the practice of transcribing nasalized vowels with: in - ɛn - un - ɔn - an and the Palatal nasal consonant 'ɲ' into ny. The Ewegbe data are reproduced mainly from various sources cited in the text. For the purpose of this study, the term Gbe refers to these four languages at least.

2.1 ON THE TERM GBE

The term Gbe refers to a cluster, a subgroup of Kwa languages. It comprises all languages or dialects that refer to language by using the lexeme gbe (e.g., Gungbe, Fongbe, Ewegbe, Wacigbe, Tofingbe, Gengbe). Gbe-speaking communities live in West Africa, in the southern part of the Volta region in Ghana, the southern part of Togo, the southern part of Benin, and in different localities of Ogun State and Lagos State in Nigeria. Though different terms, such as Ewe, Eve, Adja, Aja, Adja-Tado, Mono, were often used in the literature to refer to the Gbe cluster, linguists working on the Gbe languages now acknowledge that, such terms are confusing. The name Gbe was thus adopted at the 14th West African Languages Congress, at Cotonou, Benin, 1980. The assembly thus declared that

> it is desirable to depart from the previous and inadequate names used to refer to the whole language unit, because they are confusing. Such names are Ewe, Ewe-Fon, Ajatado, Aja, Foja, Egaf, etc. It was then unanimously agreed upon that much more investigation on the language unit is necessary, and that the name 'Gbe' will be used henceforth to refer to the language unit as a whole. (Capo 1991: 1–2)

However, it is worth mentioning that the name Gbe is not a mere technical term that is used to refer to a group of languages spoken by different communities living in the same geographical area. It is rather the most suitable name that shows the fundamental unity of the cluster with respect to phonetic, phonological, morphological, and syntactic aspects that they share and that indicate their common origin (see Capo 1988, 1991). To the best of my knowledge, no study has clearly established what this origin might be or which of the Gbe languages is the original language. A research program led by the 'Gbe research group' aims at reconstructing a Proto-Gbe that could be seen as mother tongue or at least a language that is almost identical to Gbe mother tongue. Regardless of the outcome of such a study, it should shed more light on the distribution and the classification of the Gbe languages.

2.2 THE GBE CLUSTER

In terms of Capo (1991), the Gbe cluster consists of five major subgroups. The present study focuses on languages of three different subgroups: Vhe (Ewegbe), Fon (Gungbe, Fongbe), and Gen (Gengbe).

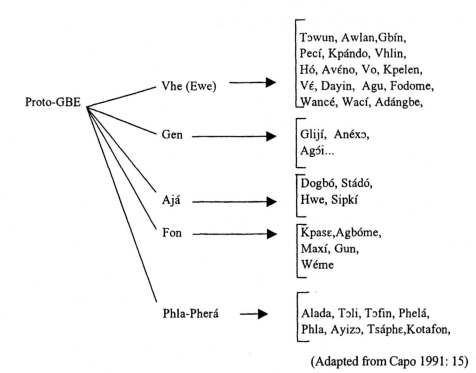

(Adapted from Capo 1991: 15)

Pursuing Capo's hypothesis that the Gbe languages have a common origin, Proto-Gbe, I propose that some general parameters (e.g., the pro-drop parameter) are fixed uniformly for the whole cluster. For instance, the fact that the subject must always be expressed in the Gbe languages is seen as an indication that they are specified as non-pro-drop languages. I further argue that these languages are head-initial: the underlying structure is of the type Spec-head-complement (see Kayne 1994). Since the Gbe languages manifest a number of surface variations, I take these distinctions to result from either a difference in some more limited parameters, such as whether sentential negation is expressed by a specifier or a head (I return to negation later), or from the target of movement: that is, whether movement targets a head and/or a maximal projection. In this regard, the fact that, in sentence (1a), the Gungbe sentential negation marker *má* is preverbal, while the Fongbe sentential negation marker á is postverbal (sentence-final), (1b) does not indicate a fundamental change in structure.

(1) a. Kɔjó   má   ɖù   nú
         Kojo   Neg   eat-Perf   thing
         'Kojo has not eaten'
     b. Kɔjó   ɖù   nú   á
         Kojo   eat-Perf thing   Neg
         'Kojo has not eaten'

That is to say, the contrast between Fongbe and Gungbe is not an indication of a head-final underlying structure for Fongbe (see Lefebvre 1991a, 1992; Avolonto 1992a, b; Kinyalolo 1993, 1993; Ndayiragije 1993; Tossa 1994; Law & Lefebvre 1995) as opposed to a head-initial structure in Gungbe (see Aboh 1993, 1996a, 1998, 1999). If one assumes a more restricted parametric variation, this difference might show that Gungbe negation is realized by a preverbal head, while Fongbe chooses to negate sentences by means of a specifier. As such, Gungbe and Fongbe are just two instantiations of what could be considered the three strategies for marking negation (see Ouhalla 1990, 1993; Haegeman 1995a; Zanuttini 1991, 1997, among others).

A conclusion that could be made at this point is that there is no need to postulate a different underlying structure for Fongbe on the one hand and Gungbe on the other. The variation observed in these two languages results from a change in the value assigned to the parameter responsible for the specification of sentential negation in Gbe, the Neg-parameter. The data presented here show that a hypothesis that assumes a limited parametric variation in Gbe is both elegant and restrictive, as it reduces the number of possible Gbe grammars radically. In fact, such hypothesis postulates only one basic (or underlying) grammar.

In this book, I try to contribute to the discussion by providing a careful analysis of a number of syntactic phenomena (e.g., the SVO vs. SOV orders) that could be accounted for if we adopt a unified analysis for Gbe. But before getting on to that, a brief foreword on the Gbe tone system and its implications in the Gbe syntax seems in order.

2.3 NOTES ON TONES IN THE SYNTAX OF GBE

Like many other West African languages, Gbe languages are tone languages. They require both pitch phonemes (i.e., tonemes) and segmental phonemes in the composition of morphemes. When the realization of tonemes has only a lexical influence, they are called lexical tones. However, they are referred to as syntactic tones when they express or result from a syntactic function. Let's start with lexical tones.

2.3.1 Lexical tones

There is now an extensive literature on tone languages, and a number of proposals have been made to account for the distribution and realization of tonemes in Gbe.[2] However, since their lexical and syntactic implications are still mysterious from various viewpoints, there is no clear agreement among linguists on the number of tonemes involved in Gbe. As pointed out by Capo (1991: 19–20), the difficulty in establishing a precise inventory of the Gbe tonemes might result from the fact that

> there are no clear acoustic or articulatory correlates by which a given pitch may be assigned to a specific tone [...]. The average pitch range referred to as low

tone in one Gbe language may be lower than the average pitch range of the same status in another Gbe language. Finally, segmental, tonal, morphological and syntactic environments may all affect a given tone.

The literature often refers to an eleven level tone system of Gbe that includes five register tones (i.e., High, Low, Mid, Extra-High, Extra-Low) and six contour tones (i.e., High-Low-Falling, High-Mid-Falling, Mid-Low-Falling, Low-High-Rising, Low-Mid-Rising, Mid-High-Rising). No Gbe language has all the five level tones. However, all the Gbe languages have a three level tone system that associates the tonemes High, Mid or Low to every morpheme. These tones are illustrated in the following table. The stroke [´] indicates High tone, while [`] represents Low tone. Mid tone will not be marked.

	Gungbe	Gengbe	Fongbe	Awlangbe	Glosses
High	òtó	etó	tó	tó	'ear'
Mid	ko	ko	ko	ko	'to laugh'
Low	òtà	età	tà	tà	'head'

There are open questions as to the status of Mid tone in the Gbe languages. As discussed by Ansre (1961) and Capo (1991), among others, Mid and Low tones alternate in some specific contexts and function like two realizations, or allotones, of a tone specified as non-High. This suggests that the occurrence of Mid tone is rule-governed, hence predictable. It is realized in specific phonetic or syntactic contexts where it alternates with both High and Low tones depending on the target language. Accordingly, the three level tone system reduces to a two level tone system including High and non-High or High and Low. In those contexts where Mid tone occurs, it stands either for a lowered High tone or for a Low tone that is made higher. This would mean that only the distinction High versus non-High (or Low in our terminology) is marked in the lexicon (see Ansre 1961; Clements 1972, 1975, 1978, 1983; Capo 1991; Bitjaa 1993; and references cited there).

2.3.2 Syntactic tones

Though there is a considerable literature on tones in Gbe, there is, to my knowledge, no clear identification of the function of tones in the clause structure of those languages (but see Clements 1978, Railland 1988; Frechet 1990, Cinque 1993). Even though a non-native speaker could find it somehow easy to identify the two register tones discussed in section 2.3.1, as long as words are kept in isolation, he needs a rather sophisticated machinery once words are put together to form a sentence. Tones can undergo both syntactic and phonetic changes in a sentence formation. Some of the modifications that affect tones have no phonetic explanation, as they always occur in well-known syntactic environments and are therefore predictable. For instance, sentence (2b) illustrates the Gungbe syntactic tone that encodes yes-no questions.

(2)   a.   Àsíbá   tón
           Asiba   go-out-Perf
           'Asiba went out'
      b.   Àsíbá   tôn ?
           Asiba go-out-Perf-QM
           * 'Asiba went out'
           'Did Asiba go out?'
      c.   Àsíbá fón   són   ján   ló   jî ?
           Asiba stand-Perf   from   chair   Det   on-QM
           * 'Asiba got up from the chair'
           'Did Asiba get up from the chair?'
      d.   mì   yró   Àsíbâ ?
           you   call-Perf   Asiba-QM
           * 'You called Asiba'
           'Did you call Asiba ?'

Sentences (2a–b) form a minimal pair: the only thing that opposes them and triggers a difference in meaning is the falling tone that affects the verb in (2b). In the perfective sentence (2a), the verb *tón* 'go out' keeps its original High tone and the sentence is interpreted as declarative. But this is not the case in the yes-no question (2b) where the verb associated with the perfective aspect is affected by a Low tone, that is, the expression of the interrogative force. This process triggers a tone lowering, which gives rise to the High-Low tone assigned to the verb.

As one can see from sentences (2c–d), this lowering process is neither accidental nor limited to verbs. It always occurs on the final vowel or syllable of yes-no questions. More precisely, I argue that Gungbe displays a syntactic Low tone that is necessarily associated to yes-noquestions. This low toneme expresses the interrogative force. Since this syntactic tone occurs sentence-finally, it always affects the last lexical tone involved in the sentence, drawing it to a lower register tone. This process, also known as 'downstep', is specific to syntactic tones. I return to the derivation of the Gungbe yes-no questions in chapter 8.

Under Bitjaa (1993), such syntactic tones could be seen as floating tonemes. They don't have any visible phonological support. They satisfy a grammatical function and can be considered the expressions of the features that are traditionally associated with the C- or I-systems. In this respect, they often correspond to an earlier morpheme that has disappeared as the language has evolved. In the case of the Gbe languages, this would mean that the syntactic tones are the vestiges of some IP or CP markers that were partially deleted. Data from Fongbe clearly underscore this analysis. Consider the following Fongbe yes-no questions:

(3)   a.   Kòjó   yì   à
           Kojo   leave-Perf   QM
           'Did Kojo leave?'

b. Kɔ́jó   klɔ́   mɔ́tɔ   ɔ́   à
    Kojo   wash-Perf   car   Det   QM
    'Did Kojo wash the car?'

As shown by sentences (3a–b), Fongbe displays a sentence-final question marker *à* (i.e., with Low tone). In a similar vein, one could argue that such a morpheme existed in 'Old Gungbe' but disappeared in 'Modern Gungbe' for reasons that are still unclear to us. This also seems to be the case in Adangbe, where the so-called Extra-Low tone always occurs on the last syllable of yes-noquestions. The hypothesis that such syntactic floating tones are the modern counterpart of actual question markers that were realized morphologically in 'Old Gungbe and Old Adangbe' is supported by the fact that not only Fongbe conserves the overt sentence-final question marker. Other Gbe languages (e.g., Ewegbe, Gengbe) also allow for a similar morpheme (see Ansre 1961, 1966; Bole-Richard 1983; Ameka 1991; Avolonto 1992a; Houngues 1997).

2.3.3 Summary

So far I have discussed the term Gbe and shown that it is not a mere term used to refer to a cluster of languages spoken by different communities living in the same locality. Rather, it indicates a fundamental unity of such languages and relates to the fact that they might have a common origin. I further presented the tone system of the Gbe languages and showed that it involves two levels: High versus non-High. From the point of view of the Gbe morphology, both pitch phonemes (i.e., tonemes) and segmental phonemes enter the composition of morphemes. With respect to syntax, I have shown that the Gbe languages manifest syntactic tones. Those tonemes play a grammatical function in the sentence. They are the expressions of grammatical features like force, tense, mood, and aspect and can be considered the vestiges of partially deleted function words.

2.4 WORD ORDER AND CLAUSE STRUCTURE

The aim of this section is to provide a general description of the main syntactic properties found in the Gbe languages. In so doing, I will try to present a fairly exhaustive catalogue of the similarities and/or dissimilarities that characterize these languages.

2.4.1 Word order

One of the most prominent characteristics of the Gbe languages is that they allow for a word order that manifests both head-final and head-initial patterns. In DPs and Postnominal Phrases (*P*Ps), for example, the head D° or *P*° must follow its NP-complement. But in Prepositional Phrases (PPs), the head P° must precede its DP-complement (see chapters 3 and 4 for the discussion). Similarly, the non-imperfective clauses manifest a subject-verb-object order as opposed to the imperfective and related clauses where the object necessarily precedes the verb and the word order is SOV (see chapters 5 and 6). Let us first consider situations where the head is final.

2.4.1.1 Determiner phrases and postnominal phrases

Sentences under (4) show that in the Gbe DPs, the determiner must follow the nominal complement.[3]

(4)	xwé	lɔ́		[Gungbe]
	xwé	ɔ́		[Fongbe]
	àxwé	á		[Gengbe]
	àʄé	a		[Ewegbe]
	house	Det		
	'The house'			

The Gbe languages also manifest *P*Ps where the nominal complement must precede the postnominal morpheme.

(5)	kèkɛ́	lɔ̀	jí	[Gungbe]
	kèkɛ́	ɔ́	jí	[Fongbe]
	kéké	á	jí	[Gengbe]
	gasɔ	a	jí	[Ewegbe]
	bicycle	Det	*P*	
	'On the bicycle'			

In this study, these postnominal morphemes are not analyzed on a par with postpositions found in head-final languages. It will become clear as the discussion follows that the Gbe postnominal morphemes are not involved in case assignment. Actually the Gungbe *P*Ps are simple nominal constituents that appear in case positions. In this perspective, postnominal morphemes are understood as sorts of nominalizers that take a nominal complement (see chapter 3, appendix, for the discussion on PPs and *P*Ps).[4]

Under the data presented in examples (4) and (5), one might conclude that the Gbe languages are head-final: the complement must precede the head. This would be consistent with the traditional analysis of the so-called SOV languages (see Greenberg 1966; Hawkins 1983; and references cited there). But as I show in the following chapters, such a conclusion is not straightforward and cannot account for all the relevant cases in Gbe.

2.4.1.2 Generalized SVO word order

Contrary to the facts illustrated in section 2.4.1.1, the Gbe clauses generally manifest an SVO schema as in (6), except for imperfective and related constructions (see section 2.4.4.2 for the discussion on imperfective clauses).

(6)	dàwé	lɔ́	xɔ̀	kὲké	[Gungbe]
	dáwé	ɔ́	xɔ̀	kὲké	[Fongbe]
	dàwé	á	plè	kéké	[Gengbe]
	ŋútsu	á	ƒlè	gasɔ	[Ewegbe]
	man	Det	buy-Perf	bicycle	
	'The man bought a bicycle'				

2.4.2 Poor agreement

One other major characteristic of the Gbe languages is that they manifest a rather poor inflectional morphology. For instance, nouns are never inflected for number (7).

(7)	xwé	àwè	lɛ́	[Gungbe]
	xwé	wè	lὲ	[Fongbe]
	àxwé	vè	ó	[Gengbe]
	àƒé	ve	ó	[Ewegbe]
	house	two	Num	
	'The two houses'			

There is no subject-verb agreement in Gbe: neither person and number agreement nor gender specification is realized in the language (8).

(8)	é/yé	hɔ̀n	[Gungbe]
	é/yé	hɔ̀n	[Fongbe]
	é/wó	sí	[Gengbe]
	é/wó	sí	[Ewegbe]
	3sg/3pl	flee-Perf	
	'S/he/they fled'		

Similarly, case is not morphologically realized. Consider, for instance, sentences under (6). Those examples represent simple sentences involving two DPs, the subject *'the man'* and the object *'bicycle'*. Following the tradition, I assume that those DPs are assigned nominative case and accusative case, respectively. But as seen in the examples, there is no overt manifestation of case assignment. Unlike languages that show a morphologically rich case system (e.g., Latin, German, Hungarian), the Gbe languages allow for no overt morphological realization of case in full lexical noun phrases. On the other hand, some Gbe languages allow for the realization of case morphology on pronominal DPs. The following table shows that pronouns may appear in different forms depending on whether they are assigned nominative or accusative case (i.e., whether they occur as subject or object of the verb).

Pers-Num	Gungbe		Fongbe		Gengbe		Ewegbe	
	Nom	Acc	Nom	Acc	Nom	Acc	Nom	Acc
1sg	ùn	mì	ùn	mì	ùn	mì	mè	m
2sg	à	wè	à	wè	ò	ò	è (nè)	wò
3sg	é	è	é	è	é	è	é (wò)	è
1pl	mí	mí	mí	mí	mí	mí	míe	mí
2pl	mi	mi	mi	mi	mi	mi	mìe	mì
3pl	yé	yé	yé	yé	ó	ó	wó	wó

In Gungbe, Fongbe, and Gengbe, nominative and accusative are different for the first, second, and third persons singular. For the third person there is a change from High tone into Low tone. On the contrary, plural forms are identical for nominative and accusative cases.

Things are different in Ewegbe, since only the third person plural remains identical for both nominative and accusative cases. All other pronouns are inflected for case. However, the changes triggered by the morphological realization of case are rather minimal, since they involve either partial deletion (e.g., 1sg, 1pl, 2pl) or a tone variation (e.g., 3sg). Only the second person singular seems to involve two genuine forms for nominative and accusative. Notice also that for nominative case, Ewegbe has two other forms *nè* 'you' and *wò* 'he' for second and third person singular, respectively. These forms are used in specific contexts such as certain dependent clauses as well as resultative and causative constructions (see Agbedor 1996 for the discussion on the Ewegbe pronominal system).

The following examples also show that the verb is never inflected for tense/aspect in Gbe (but see section 2.4.4.2 and chapters 5 and 6 for the discussion of imperfective and related constructions).

(9) a.
dàwé	lɔ́	xɔ̀	kèkɛ́	[Gungbe]
dáwé	ɔ́	xɔ̀	kèkɛ́	[Fongbe]
dàwé	á	plè	kéké	[Gengbe]
ŋútsu	á	ƒlè	gasɔ	[Ewegbe]
man	Det	buy-Perf	bicycle	

'The man bought a bicycle'

(9) b.
dàwé lɔ́	ná	xɔ̀	kèkɛ́	[Gungbe]
dáwé ɔ́	ná	xɔ̀	kèkɛ́	[Fongbe]
dàwé á	lá	plè	kéké	[Gengbe]

ŋútsu á	a	ƒlè	gasɔ	[Ewegbe]
man Det	Fut	buy	bicycle	

'The man will buy a bicycle'

The sentences (9a–b) constitute a set of minimal pairs that indicate that the Gbe verb always keeps the same form even though it is specified for perfective aspect (9a) or for the future tense (9b). As I show in chapters 5 and 6, these data clearly suggest that the Gbe languages have a poor inflectional morphology, since the verb always surfaces in its infinitive form. But this need not mean, though, that the Gbe languages manifest a poor inflection system. The Gbe languages display a rich system of tense/aspect markers that encode tense/aspect specifications. I discuss the tense/aspect paradigm next (see also Avolonto 1992a, b, c; Kinyalolo 1992; Sáàh 1993; Tossa 1994; Lefebvre 1995b; Houngues 1997).

2.4.3 Tense licensing

The Gbe languages are characterized by the fact that they allow for a future marker only, as presented in examples (9b), repeated here under (10).[5]

(10)	dàwé	lɔ́	ná	xɔ̀	kὲkέ	[Gungbe]
	dáwé	ɔ́	ná	xɔ̀	kὲkέ	[Fongbe]
	dàwé	á	lá	plè	kéké	[Gengbe]
	ŋútsu	á	a	ƒlè	gasɔ	[Ewegbe]
	man	Det	Fut	buy	bicycle	

'The man will buy a bicycle'

In this study, I propose that the future marker is the morphological realization of the feature [+future]. As no special markers are used in Gbe to specify present or past tenses, I suggest that these temporal specifications are derived from the expression of a null morpheme that encodes the feature [-future]. In some specific contexts, the identification of the [-future] null morpheme is achieved by means of time adverbs like dìn 'now' or dáyí 'before' in Gungbe. This would mean that the expression of the feature [-future] in Gbe does not necessarily result in past reading (see chapters 5 and 6 for the discussion).

2.4.4 Aspect licensing

The Gbe languages are specified for three major aspects: perfective, imperfective, and habitual. By perfective aspect, I refer to an event that is understood as having a definite endpoint in time and is located in the past by default. The imperfective aspect expresses an event that is ongoing in time, while the habitual aspect indicates an event that is repetitive. For the purpose of this study, I assume, in line with Tenny (1987), that aspect is encoded by a syntactic category AspP that projects within the I-system.

2.4.4.1 Perfective aspect

Perfective aspect is not morphologically realized in Gbe, because it is not associated with a particular marker or morpheme that co-occurs with the verb. This is illustrated by the sentences under (9a) repeated here for convenience.

(11)	dàwé	lɔ́	xɔ̀	kὲké	[Gungbe]
	dáwé	ɔ́	xɔ̀	kὲké	[Fongbe]
	dàwé	á	plè	kéké	[Gengbe]
	ŋútsu	á	ʄlè	gasɔ	[Ewegbe]
	man	Det	buy-Perf	bicycle	
	'The man bought a bicycle'				

Contrary to proposals made by Hazoumè (1978) and Avolonto (1992a, b, c, 1995) that Gungbe and Fongbe involve a null morpheme, which is specified as [+perfective] (or [+past] in terms of Houngues (1997)), I argue here that no such morpheme exists in Gbe. Instead, I assume that perfective is the default aspect assigned to the verb when it reaches the topmost aspect head position (i.e., Asp°1) and no other specification is made about time (i.e., in the absence of the future tense marker and time adverbs). I return to the discussion in chapters 5 and 6.

2.4.4.2 Imperfective aspect

The Gbe imperfective constructions involve a bipartite morpheme, one of which occurs in a preverbal position, while the other is realized in postverbal position. In these constructions, the object immediately precedes the verb (12a) and intransitive verbs must reduplicate (12b).

(12)	a.	dàwé	lɔ́	tò	nù	ɖù̃	--	[Gungbe]
		dáwé	ɔ́	ɖò	nù	ɖù	wὲ	[Fongbe]
		dàwé	á	lè	nú	ɖù	ɔ́	[Gengbe]
		ŋútsu	á	lè	nú	ɖù	ḿ	[Ewegbe]
		man	Det	Imperf	thing	eat	NR	
		'The man is eating'						

(12)	b.	dàwé	lɔ́	tò	yìyì̃	--	[Gungbe]
		dáwé	ɔ́	ɖò	yìyì	wὲ	[Fongbe]
		dàwé	á	lè	jójó	ɔ́	[Gengbe]

ŋútsu	á	lè	yìyì		m̀	[Ewegbe]
man	Det	Imperf	RED-leave		NR	

'The man is leaving'

As seen from these examples, Gungbe is the only language where the sentence-final imperfective morpheme is expressed by a syntactic Low tone, represented here by an additional stroke on the verb (see section 2.3.2 for the discussion on syntactic tones). As a consequence, the verb is affected by Low tone and by vowel lengthening. In this study, I consider this process to be the overt manifestation of a *quasi-null* morpheme that is realized by a toneme only. The following table summarizes the bipartite morphemes involved in the Gbe imperfective constructions.

	Preverbal	Postverbal
Gungbe	tò	Ø (quasi-null)
Fongbe	ɖò	wɛ̀
Gengbe	lè	ɔ̀
Ewegbe	lè	m̀

In addition to the fact that they require a bipartite morpheme, the Gbe imperfective constructions represent one of the limited configurations where the object must precede the verb, giving rise to the necessary SOV word order illustrated in sentences under (12a). This is rather surprising, since in all other contexts (except in topic and focus constructions where the object may be moved to the left periphery), the verb always precedes the object. It follows that the Gbe languages manifest a non-imperfective (i.e., future, habitual, and perfective sentences) versus imperfective (and related) constructions asymmetry. The former exhibit an SVO (i.e., head-initial) structure, while the latter display an SOV (i.e., head-final) pattern. The question now arises as to which one of these schemes reflects the Gbe underlying structure.

Anticipating the discussion in section 2.5, I propose that the underlying structure in Gbe is SVO (see Clements 1972; Aboh 1993, 1996a, 1998, 1999; Agbedor 1993; Sáàh 1993; Avolonto 1995; Kinyalolo 1995; Manfredi 1997). This analysis draws on the fact that SVO is the most productive order in the Gbe languages. On the other hand, SOV arises only in limited cases including imperfective and related constructions. To some extent, SOV appears the marked case. It derives from leftward movement of both the verb and the object. Starting from VO order, the object must move leftward far enough to land in a position to the left of the position where the verb surfaces (see chapters 5, 6).

If we were to assume a basic SOV order, then both verb and object movements would be defined upon a negative environment stating just those structures (i.e., imperfective and related constructions) where movement rule does not apply. Similar facts in Ewegbe led Clements (1972: 37) to conclude that

> as far as we know (and we stand open to correction) it has never been shown that a language must have negative-environment syntactic rules in its grammar,

a fact which argues for a general constraint against including such rules in the grammar of any particular language when alternate analyses are available. Thus in this case, the fact that an SOV analysis would entail a negative-environment rule is a good argument against it.

That the Gbe languages manifest various contexts where the complement of a head must precede that head (i.e., examples 3, 4, 5, 12a) can be interpreted as evidence against the SVO hypothesis. In approaches that do not adopt Kayne's (1994) universal base hypothesis and therefore allow for parametric variation in base order, it is commonly assumed that languages in which the noun complement precedes the head (e.g., the determiner or the verb) manifest head-final structures. This is, for example, the case in Oriya where the noun precedes the specificity marker as in *bahitaa* 'book the'. Similarly, Oriya consistently displays subject-object(s)-verb structures that could be taken as evidence of the fact that the language has an underlying SOV (i.e., head-final) structure (Pattanaik 1996).

But the discussion in previous paragraphs suggests that the head-final hypothesis could not be maintained for Gbe. The complement precedes the head in certain limited contexts: DPs, *P*Ps, so-called OV constructions, interrogative and negative constructions (see chapters 5, 6, and 8 for the discussion). In all other contexts, the complement must follow the head. Notice, for example, that PPs[6] (e.g., Locative Phrases, Beneficiary Phrases, Instrument Phrases) exhibit the head-complement ordering.

(13) a.

Kòfí	sà	àgásá	ná	Kòjó	[Gungbe]
Kòfí	sà	àsɔ́n	nú	Kòjó	[Fongbe]
Kòfí	sà	àglán	né	Kòjó	[Gengbe]
Kofi	sell-Perf	crab	Prep	Kojo	

'Kofi sold a crab to Kojo'

(13) b.

Kòfí yi	Kpalime	ku	Kòjó	[Ewegbe]
Kofi go-Perf	Kpalime	Prep	Kojo	

'Kofi went to Kpalime with Kojo'

Under the SVO hypothesis, I propose that sequences where the complement precedes the head (i.e., DPs, *P*Ps, imperfective and related clauses, etc.) must be regarded as instantiations of leftward movement of the complement to a specifier position (see section 2.5 and subsequent chapters for the discussion, also Kayne 1994; Haegeman 1995a; Aboh 1996a, 1999; Zwart 1997a, b).

2.4.4.3 Habitual aspect licensing and the theory of verb movement

Just as they specify imperfective aspect by use of a marker, the Gbe languages use a specific morpheme that encodes habitual aspect (see Avolonto 1992a, b for Fongbe;

Clements 1972, 1975; Ameka 1991; Essegbey 1999 for Ewegbe and Jondoh 1981; Houngues 1997 for Gengbe).

(14)   Kòfí   nɔ̀   sà   àgásá   [Gungbe]
        Kofi   Hab   sell   crab
        'Kofi habitually sells crab(s)'
        Kòfí   nɔ̀   sà   àsɔ́n   [Fongbe]
        Kofi   Hab   sell   crab
        'Kofi habitually sells crab (s)'
        Kòfí   lá   nɔ̀   sà   àglán   [Gengbe]
        Kofi   Fut   Hab   sell   crab
        'Kofi will sell crab(s) habitually'

In these examples, it is the preverbal morpheme *nɔ̀* that is responsible for the habitual aspect assigned to the verb. *Nɔ̀* always occurs between the subject and the verb and triggers the word order S- *nɔ̀* - V O. Notice that the Gengbe situation is more complex as the habitual marker *nɔ̀* is exclusively used when it co-occurs with the future marker *lá*. No such restriction seems to exist in Fongbe and Gungbe.

    Actually, Gengbe and Ewegbe display another strategy to express habitual aspect. Indeed habitual aspect is expressed in Gengbe and Ewegbe by means of the habitual aspect marker *na* that suffixes on to the verb and excludes the future tense marker (15a). Put differently, the Gengbe and Ewegbe postverbal habitual marker always appears in sentences where it does not co-occur with the tense markers, hence the ungrammatical (15b). Ungrammatical sentences under (15c) show that in such habitual constructions, the verb and the postverbal habitual marker form a unit (i.e., a complex head): nothing can intervene between the two.

(15)   a.   Kòfí sà-nà   àglán   [Gengbe]
            Kofi sell-Hab   crab
            'Kofi habitually sells crab(s)'
            Kòfí jrà (n) á   àkɔ̀ɖú   [Ewegbe]
            Kofi sell-Hab   banana
            'Kofi habitually sells banana(s)'

(15)   b.   *Kòfí   sà-nà lá   àglán   [Gengbe]
            Kofi   sell-Hab-Fut   crab
            *Kòfí   jrà-(n)á-á   àkɔ̀ɖú   [Ewegbe]
            Kofi   sell-Hab-Fut   banana

(15)   c.   *Kòfí   sà   té   nà   àglán   [Gengbe]
            Kofi   sell   even   Hab   crab
            *Kòfí   jrà   tété   (n)á   àkɔ̀ɖú   [Ewegbe]
            Kofi sell   at least Hab   banana

These data somehow cloud the issue of the distribution of tense and aspect markers in Gbe in general, but they are not problematic: they are interpreted as evidence of verb movement in these languages. Under Koopman (1984), Pollock (1989), Manfredi (1991, 1997), Déchaine (1993), Tossa (1994), and subsequent work, a natural explanation for the distribution of the verb in the Gengbe and Ewegbe sentences would be to say that the Gbe verb must move to aspect (Asp°) and tense (T°) positions to check its aspect and tense features. Granting this, two major criteria help account for the contrast between examples (14) and (15):

1.   the scope of verb movement and
2.   head- adjunction to T° and/or Asp°.

It appears in example (15) that the Gengbe-type languages allow for the verb to left-adjoin to the aspect marker and then the complex head verb+aspect moves to T° as suggested by the grammatical sentence (15a). However, left adjunction to a morphologically realized T° is impossible hence the ungrammatical sentence (15b). This leads us to the following conclusions with respect to the Gengbe-type languages: (i) verb movement to T° is possible iff the latter is empty (i.e., not morphologically realized); (ii) verb adjunction to morphologically realized Asp° is possible.

On the contrary, the impossibility to have the counterpart of (15a) in the Gungbe-type languages suggests that these languages disallow adjunction to a morphologically realized head. Instead, verb movement to Asp° is possible if and only if the latter is empty (i.e., not morphologically realized). In addition, I propose that verb movement in the Gungbe-type languages does not target T° and that the latter is always occupied by a [±future] tense morpheme that is either overt or null. In Gungbe and Fongbe for example, T° is morphologically realized as *ná* when it is specified for the feature [+future]. But when it is marked as [-future], it is manifested by a null morpheme ∅. I therefore suggest that T° is not accessible for movement in Gungbe and Fongbe. In my discussion of this matter in chapter 5, I demonstrate that this is actually the right situation and show that certain Gungbe adverbial elements like *gbé* 'at least' or *tè* 'even' can intervene between the tense marker *ná* and the verb. Clearly, this will be evidence for the fact that the moved verb doesn't reach T°. As a conclusion, one can say that in the Gungbe-type languages (i) verb movement to T° and (ii) verb adjunction to a morphologically realized Asp° are prohibited.

In other words, verb movement is short in the Gungbe-type languages and long in the Gengbe-type languages. A major consequence of this mechanism is that the Gengbe-type languages allow for the order [verb-habitual marker]. But this order is excluded in the Gungbe-type languages. In these languages, the verb is necessarily stuck in a position lower than the realized aspect head, giving the order [habitual marker-verb]. Put differently, verb movement to Asp° would be possible in such languages only if this position is empty or not morphologically realized. On the other hand, no such restriction holds on Asp° in the Gengbe-type languages where only a morphologically realized T° is inaccessible for movement.

Instances of verb movement in Gbe were originally discussed in Tossa (1994),[7] along the lines of Koopman's (1984) work on the Kru languages.[8] In terms of Tossa (1994), the Gbe clausal structure involves a functional projection (AuxP) whose head Aux° must be filled by verb movement whenever the clause does not contain any auxiliary to be inserted in Aux°. Starting from an underlying SOV order, Tossa further suggested that the SVO order found in the Gbe non-imperfective clauses is derived by means of verb movement to the left of the object. Consequently, verb movement is limited to non-imperfective clauses since these clauses involve no auxiliary. On the other hand, no such movement applies in the imperfective clauses due to the presence of the auxiliary.[9]

At this stage of the discussion, it is worth noticing that a major difference between an analysis along the lines of Tossa (1994) and the verb movement theory advocated in this book is precisely that verb movement to the relevant tense/aspect head is not limited to non-imperfective clauses. In this sense, verb movement in Gbe is never optional: V-to-I movement applies in these languages irrespective of the clausal aspect specifications. In this approach, the surface differences between imperfective and non-imperfective clauses result from the interaction of two movement processes: object shift (i.e., object movement to some licensing spec-position, see chapter 6) and verb movement to some licensing aspect head position. Assuming Kayne's (1994) Universal Base Hypothesis, the directionality parameter thus appears superfluous and theoretically undesirable (Zwart 1997b). If we admit that object shift always applies—say for case reasons (see Chomsky 1993)—then the Gbe SVO versus SOV asymmetry reduces to the 'length' of V-to-I movement:

1.   The verb moves past the object in VO clauses,
2.   The verb is stuck in a position lower than the object in OV clauses.[10]

This need not mean though that there are no language specificities among the Gbe languages. For example, whether adjunction to a morphologically realized head is possible or not is language specific. Recall the contrast between the Gungbe-type and the Gengbe-type languages. On a more general ground, if it is true that the Gbe languages display V-to-I movement, then it cannot be said that the syntax of verb movement is driven by the so-called strong INFL, where the term strong is understood as rich inflectional ending on the verb (see Roberts 1985, 1993; Pollock 1989; Rohrbacher 1994; Vikner 1995, 1997; Haegeman 1995b, 1996c; and references cited there). On the contrary, the study of the Gbe languages clearly indicates that the term 'rich' can also be taken to mean an articulated inflectional system offering room for distinct tense, aspect, and mood markers, each of which heads a functional projection within the clause structure (see Kayne 1992; Aboh 1996a, 1999; Pollock 1997; Rizzi 1997; Cinque 1999).

Since the Gbe verbs are never inflected (see section 2.4.2), I conclude that V-to-I movement applies in these languages because the 'bare' V-stem must be licensed for tense and or aspect. In terms of Chomsky's (1995) checking theory, this amounts to saying that the Gbe functional heads T° and Asp° dominate bundles of abstract features that the verb must check (see chapters 5, 6). In this respect, tense and aspect features are said to be strong in Gbe. When positively set, these features are realized in Gbe by Tense, Mood, and Aspect (TMA) markers. In the Gbe languages where certain TMA are affixes (e.g., the habitual marker in the Gengbe-type languages), verb movement raises the lexical verb and adjoins it to the marker (15a-b). But in the Gbe languages where the TMA markers are non-affixes, adjunction to the morphologically realized head is impossible. Verb-movement therefore raises the lexical verb to a position lower than the TMA marker. As a consequence, the verb surfaces to the right of the aspect marker. This would mean that subsequent verb movement arises only and only if the target head (i.e., the aspect head) is not morphologically realized. This analysis leads us to the following characterization of the Gbe languages.

1. Positively set aspect specifications are morphologically realized as markers. These markers consist of two groups: affixes and non-affixes. Affixes allow for (long) verb movement. The verb adjoins to the marker on its way to T (e.g., the Gengbe-type languages). Non-affixes, on the other hand, block verb movement.

2. Negatively set aspect specifications are not morphologically realized. They are affixes and allow either for V-to-T movement (e.g., the Gengbe-type languages) or V-to-Asp movement (e.g., the Gungbe-type languages).

2.4.5 Summary

In the previous sections, I have shown that the Gbe languages are characterized by the fact that they use distinct tense and aspect markers that appear either in a preverbal position (e.g., future, imperfective, and habitual in Gungbe, Fongbe, Gengbe) or in a postverbal position (e.g., habitual in Gengbe and Ewegbe). In this respect the Asp°-V and V-Asp° order found in the Gbe languages is analyzed as evidence of V-to-I movement in those languages.

With respect to the imperfective markers, I show that they involve a bipartite morpheme. The first component of this morpheme occurs preverbally and precedes the object, the latter preceding the verb. It can be seen as the genuine specification of the imperfective feature in the clause. The second component is realized sentence-finally. It could be considered the counterpart of the English morpheme *ing* that is specific to progressive constructions and gerunds. As it is assumed traditionally (Fabb 1992a, b; Kinyalolo 1992, 1997; Manfredi 1997), the Gbe postverbal imperfective morphemes can be analyzed as nominalizers (see chapter 6).

If it is true that tense and aspect markers are the PF realizations of the features [+future], [+habitual], [+imperfective], which are associated with the heads of tense and aspect phrases (i.e., T° and AsP°, see Tenny 1987), we can conclude that the Gbe I-system involves the following structure.

(16)   [TP [AspP1[±Habitual] [AspP2[±Imperfective]   VP]]]]

The tense and aspect markers do not exclude each other. They can be combined in a
sentence in Fongbe, in Gungbe, and (partially) in Gengbe. The Ewegbe case is slightly
different since future and habitual markers are mutually exclusive (recall the discussion
on verb movement), but future and aspect markers independently co-occur with
ingressive as represented in (17) (see Clements 1972; Ameka 1991; Essegbey 1999).

(17) a.   hàfí   mì   à   nɔ nú   hia   wó   kátaa   wɔ   m̀   a
           before you Fut Ing things Dem Num   all   do   Part Top
           'Before you will be doing all these things'
      b.   mé   nɔ   à   dó   wɔ   m̀
           I   Ing Hab   work do   Part
           'I'm usually working'

These Ewegbe facts are rather obscure, since there is a priori no semantic ban on the
cooccurrence of future and habitual. In Fongbe and Gungbe, the tense and aspect
markers freely co-occur and follow the strict order Future-Habitual-Imperfective.
Representation (18) summarizes the eight possible combinations of tense/aspect
markers in these languages.

(18)

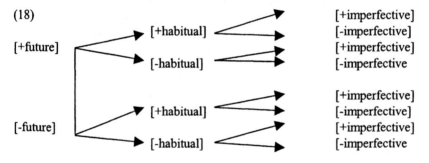

In Gungbe, for example, an implementation of (18) gives the result in (19). For clarity's
sake, each tense/aspect combination is associated with an English translation:

(19)   ná - nɔ - tò...[future-habitual-imperfective] 'John will be eating habitually'
       ná - nɔ - ... [future-habitual]   'John will eat habitually'
       ná - ... tò... [future-imperfective]   'John will be eating'
       ná - ... ... [future]   'John will eat'
       ... - nɔ - tò.. [habitual-imperfective]   'John is eating habitually'
       ... - nɔ - ...[habitual]   'John eats habitually'
       ...- ...- tò...[imperfective]   'John is eating'
       ...- ...- ...[perfective]   'John ate'

2.4.6 Negation in Gbe

As mentioned in section 2.2, the Gbe languages differ among each other with respect to negation. This is shown in the following sections, where it appears that Gbe languages demonstrate three main strategies in expressing sentential negation: preverbal negation (e.g., Gungbe), post-verbal or sentence-final negation (e.g., Fongbe), and bipartite negation (e.g., Gengbe, Ewegbe).

2.4.6.1 Preverbal negation: Evidence from Gungbe

The Gungbe sentential negation is expressed by means of a preverbal marker *má*, which could be considered the equivalent of French *ne* or Italian *non* (Pollock 1989; Zanuttini 1991, 1997; Agbedor 1993; Déchaine 1993; Duffield 1993; Kato 1993; Laka 1993; Ouhalla 1993; Progovac 1993; Sáàh 1993; Haegeman 1995a). *Má* has a fixed position in the sentence and always occurs between the subject and the verb (20a). Though tense and aspect markers, as well as certain adverbial elements like *tè* 'even' can occur between the negation marker and the verb (20b–c), nothing can intervene between the subject and the negation *má* (20d)—except in the case of subject extraction, as shown by subject focusing in sentence (20e). The preverbal negation marker is allowed in main and embedded clauses (20f).

(20) a. Kɔjó   má   ḍù   nú
          Kojo   Neg   eat-Perf thing
          'Kojo has not eaten'

      b. Kɔjó   má   ná   nɔ   ḍù   nú
          Kojo   Neg   Fut   Hab   eat   thing
          'Kojo will not eat (habitually)'

      c. Kɔjó   má   tè   ḍù   nú
          Kojo   Neg   even   eat-Perf thing
          'Kojo didn't even eat'

      d. *Kɔjó   tè   má   ḍù   nú
          Kojo   even   Neg   eat-Perf thing

      e. Kɔjó   wè   má   ḍù   nú
          Kojo   Foc   Neg   eat-Perf thing
          'KOJO did not eat'

      f. yé   sè   dɔ   Kɔjó   má   ḍù   nú
          they hear-Perf   that   Kojo   Neg   eat-Perf thing
          'They heard that Kojo didn't eat'

Following Pollock (1989), Ouhalla (1990), Zanuttini (1991, 1996), Haegeman (1995a), and subsequent work, I regard negation markers as functional elements that belong to the category NegP, a component of the I-system. I thus propose, in line with Aboh (1996a, 1999), that the Gungbe preverbal negation marker *má* is the negative head,

Neg°. I further argue that NegP dominates TP as suggested by the sentences under (20). In all those sentences, the negation marker precedes the tense and aspect markers obligatorily. If it is true that tense and aspect markers are heads, as I assume in this study (chapter 5), this is an argument in favor of the idea that the Gungbe or the Gbe preverbal negation marker is an element of the type X° (i.e., a head). This analysis is consistent with the fact that the Gungbe negation marker (i.e., the preverbal sentential negation) may block head movement. For instance, I show in chapter 7 that the intervention of negation blocks verb focusing, that is, verb movement to the left periphery. In terms of the Neg-criterion (Haegeman & Zanuttini 1991, 1997; Haegeman 1995a), I further conclude that the Gungbe negative sentences involve a null negative operator in [spec NegP] as partially represented in (21).

(21).

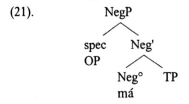

2.4.6.2 Sentence-final negation marker: On the Fongbe ambiguity

In Fongbe, sentential negation is marked by means of both preverbal and sentence-final markers. The preverbal marker is identical to the Gungbe negation marker with respect to morphology and syntax. It has a similar morphological form and syntactic distribution. Observe, for example, that the Fongbe preverbal negation marker *má* always occurs between the subject and the verb. Just as its Gungbe counterpart, the Fongbe *má* can be separated from the verb by tense and aspect markers, but nothing can intervene between the subject and *má* (22a–b). The data discussed in this section are adapted from da Cruz (1993).

(22) a. Kɔkú   má   ná   xɔ   àsɔ́n   lɛ́
          Koku   Neg   Fut   buy   crab   Num
          'Koku will not buy the crabs'
      b. *Kɔkú   tlɛ̀   má   xɔ   àsɔ́n   lɛ́
          Koku   even   Neg   buy-Perf   crab   Num

On the other hand, the negation marker *ǎ* —the equivalent of French *pas*—is always realized in a sentence-final position. It can co-occur with tense and aspect markers (23a–b).

(23) a. Kɔkú   xɔ   àsɔ́n   lɛ́   ǎ
          Koku   buy-Perf   crab   Num   Neg
          'Koku will not buy the crab'

b. Kɔkú   ná   xɔ   àsɔ́n   lɛ́   ǎ
    Koku   Fut   buy   crab   Num   Neg
    'Koku will not buy the crab'

The Fongbe preverbal and sentence-final negation markers never co-occur in main clauses (24).

(24)   *Kɔkú   má   xɔ   àsɔ́n   lɛ́   ǎ
       Koku   Neg   buy   crab   Num   Neg

But the two negation markers do not always exclude each other: they obligatorily co-occur in sentences involving the conditional marker *ní*, the counterpart of English *if*.

(25)   ní   Kɔkú   má   xɔ   àsɔ́n   lɛ́   ǎ,   é   ná   yì
       Cond Koku   Neg   buy-Perf crab   Num   Neg   he   Fut   go
       'If Koku did not buy the crabs, he will leave'

Sentences (24) and (25) lead to contradictory conclusions: the former suggests that the two negation markers are in complementary distribution, while the latter indicates that they are not. Nevertheless, I take sentence (25) to be clear indication that the two negation markers do not compete for the same position. I further assume that double negation in Fongbe is subject to some left peripheral specification (e.g., conditional *ní*). In this respect, I tentatively propose that *má* heads NegP, and *ǎ* —a category of the type X^{max} —realizes a specifier position (Pollock 1989; Ouhalla 1990).[11] Assuming that NegP dominates TP in Gbe, I conclude that in the negative sentences without overt preverbal negation marker *má*, Neg° is not phonetically realized (see Belletti 1990; Zanuttini 1991, 1996, 1997; Haegeman 1995a; Aboh 1996a, 1999, among others). On the other hand, [spec NegP] hosts a negative null operator morpheme that licenses the occurrence of the negative adverbial *ǎ*. Under Zanuttini's (1991) double NegPs hypothesis, we could suggest that the Fongbe adverbial negative element realizes the specifier position of NegP2, which projects below TP, say in the aspectual domain. Alternatively, it could be argued in line with Cinque (1999) that adverbial elements occur in the specifier position of some functional projection within the I-system. This would mean that the negative adverbial realizes the specifier position of a functional projection that dominates the VP. One can therefore account for the fact that the Gbe negative adverbial occurs sentence-finally by proposing that both the object and the verb move leftward to appropriate higher positions than the specifier position occupied by the negative adverbial element *ǎ*.[12]

    I further propose that the negative adverbial *ǎ* must move in [spec NegP1] at LF due to the Neg-criterion. In sentences like (22a) the head Neg° is realized as *má* and may be doubled by the negative adverbial *ǎ*, as suggested by conditional constructions (25). Here again, the specifier position is occupied by an empty operator and must be filled at LF by the negative adverbial. An immediate consequence of this analysis is that the Fongbe or the Gbe sentence-final negation markers like *ǎ* are elements of the type X^{max}. The Fongbe case is illustrated in (26).

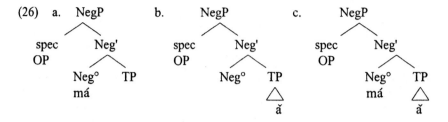

(26) a. NegP   b. NegP   c. NegP

The analysis put forward here is in line with Ouhalla's (1990: 191) proposal that

> sentence negation is expressed in terms of a NegP category which consists of a head element and a specifier. Variation among languages is restricted to whether both or either of the two elements of NegP is realized lexically. In languages like Turkish and Berber the head is realized lexically while the specifier is realized as an empty operator. In languages like German, Swedish and Colloquial French it is the specifier which is realized lexically, while the head is realized as an abstract morpheme. Finally, in languages like Standard French both the head and the specifier are realized lexically.

The third strategy described in Ouhalla (1990) is firmly established in Gengbe and Ewegbe. These languages express sentential negation by use of a bipartite negation marker, hence the simultaneous occurrence of preverbal and postverbal negation markers. Ewegbe and Gengbe thus resemble French with respect to negation (see notes 10–11 and the appendix of chapter 8 for an alternative).

2.4.6.3. Bipartite negation in Gbe: Evidence from Gengbe and Ewegbe

Gengbe and Ewegbe depart radically from Fongbe and Gungbe in the sense that they express sentential negation by means of both a preverbal and a postverbal negation marker. Though they are different with respect to morphology, the Gengbe and Ewegbe preverbal markers have very similar distribution as the Gungbe and Fongbe ones: they occupy a fixed position in the middle field. They always occur between the subject and the verb. They can be separated from the verb by tense and aspect markers as well as certain adverbs. But nothing can intervene between the subject and the preverbal negation markers, except in the case of subject movement to the CP domain. As it is well known for standard French negation, Gengbe and Ewegbe preverbal negation markers must occur simultaneously with the postverbal negation marker. The latter always occurs sentence-finally and cannot be left out in the sentence

(27) Kɔfí   *(mú)   plé   àvɔ́   *(ò)   [Gengbe]
      Kofi   Neg   buy   cloth   Neg
      'Kofi did not buy a cloth'
      Kɔfí   *(me)   ƒle   gasɔ   *(o)   [Ewegbe]
      Kofi   Neg   buy-Perf   bicycle Neg
      'Kofi did not buy a bicycle'

Following Ouhalla (1990), Zanuttini (1991, 1996), and Haegeman (1995a), I propose that Gengbe and Ewegbe cluster with languages that express sentential negation by means of both a preverbal and a postverbal lexical item. The preverbal negation marker is an element of the type $X°$. It is the manifestation of $Neg°$, the head of NegP. On the contrary, the postverbal marker is a negative adverb, the equivalent of French *pas*.[13] It is an element of the type X^{max} that is licensed by a null negative operator occupying [spec NegP]. Accordingly, the negative adverb must move to [spec NegP] at LF in order to satisfy the Neg-criterion. If this is the correct situation, therefore, Ewegbe and Gengbe can be brought back to the Fongbe situation represented in (26c) and repeated here for convenience.

(28)   NegP

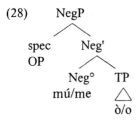

2.4.7 The CP system of Gbe

The data presented in the previous sections deal with the IP domain of the Gbe languages. It appeared in the discussion there that the Gbe languages share a great number of similarities with respect to the manifestation of the components of the I-system: Tense Phrase, Aspect Phrase, and Negation Phrase. In this section I provide an informal description of the Gbe constructions that involve the left periphery, or the CP domain. The set of data discussed here shows that the unity of the Gbe cluster is not limited to the IP domain only. Rather it could be easily extended to the CP domain as all the Gbe languages pattern alike with respect to focus, topic, and interrogative constructions.

2.4.7.1 Focus constructions

Like many other languages (e.g., English, Italian, Hungarian, Arabic), the Gbe languages also allow for focus constructions. But unlike English, Italian, and

Hungarian. (Brody 1990; Ameka 1992; Ndayragije 1992; Ouhalla 1992, 1993; Puskás 1992, 1996; Rizzi 1997; Aboh 1998, 2001a, in press a, c), the Gbe languages exhibit a focalization process that requires leftward movement of the focused element to a position left adjacent to a morphologically realized focus marker written here in bold. In such constructions, the moved phrase always leaves a gap in its base position. In the sentences under (29), the (a) examples represent simple neutral declaratives. The (b) and (c) examples involve object-focusing in the main clauses and the embedded clauses, respectively. Though the Gbe focus constructions may involve different types of clauses (e.g., negative, embedded, subjunctive, injunctive clauses, etc.), the position where focus is assigned is unique. The focused category necessarily appears in a pre-subject position to the left of a focus marker, which itself is located to the right of the complementizer. I return to the discussion of these data in chapter 7, section 7.1.

(29) a.   Kòfí   xɔ   kèké   [Gungbe]
           Kofi   buy-Perf   bicycle
           'Kofi bought a bicycle'
      b.   kèké   wè   Kòfí   xɔ   ec
           bicycle   Foc   Kofi   buy-Perf
           'Kofi bought A BICYCLE'
      c.   ... ɖɔ kèké   wè   Kòfí   xɔ   ec
           that   bicycle   Foc   Kofi   buy-Perf
           '...that Kofi bought A BICYCLE'

(29) a.   Kòfí   gbá   xwé   [Fongbe]
           Kofi   build-Perf   house
           'Kofi built a house'
      b.   xwé   wè   Kòfí   gbá   ec
           house   Foc   Kofi   build-Perf
           'Kofi built A HOUSE'
      c.   ....ɖɔ   xwé   wè   Kòfí   gbá   ec
           that   house   Foc   Kofi   build-Perf
           '...that Kofi built A HOUSE'

(29) a.   Kòfí   tù   àxwé   [Gengbe]
           Kofi   build-Perf   house
           'Kofi built a house'
      b.   àxwé   yé   Kòfí   tù   ec
           house Foc   Kofi   build-Perf
           'Kofi built A HOUSE'
      c.   .. bé   àxwé   yé   Kòfí   tù   ec
           that   house   Foc   Kofi   build-Perf
           '...that Kofi built A HOUSE'

(29) a. Ápàn   fò   Kwésí   [Ewegbe]
          Apan   beat-Perf   Kwesi
          'Apan beat Kwesi'

      b. Kwésí   é   Ápàn   fò   ec
          Kwesi Foc   Apan   beat-Perf
          'Apan beat KWESI'

      c. ... bé Kwésí é   Ápàn   fò   ec
          that   Kwesi   Foc   Apan   beat-Perf
          '...that Apan beat KWESI'

2.4.7.2. Wh-questions

The Gbe languages are also characterized by the fact that wh-questions require the
leftward movement of the wh-phrase to the position immediately to the left of the focus
marker. Here again the moved phrase must leave an empty category in its base position
(30a). The focused elements and moved wh-phrases target the same position. This
hypothesis is supported by the fact that focused elements and wh-phrases cannot co-
occur (30b). Sentences under (30c) show that wh-phrases occur to the right of the
complementizer in embedded clauses. See chapter 7, section 7.2, for the discussion.

(30) a. été   wè   Kòfí   xò   ec ?   [Gungbe]
          what   Foc   Kofi   buy-Perf
          'What did Kofi buy?'

      b. *été   wè   Kòfí   wè   xò ?
          what   Foc   Kofi   Foc   buy-Perf

      c. ...dò   été   wè   Kòfí   xò   ec ?
          that   what   Foc   Kofi   buy-Perf
          '.. that what did Kofi buy ?'

(30) a. été   wè   Kòfí   gbá   ec ?   [Fongbe]
          what   Foc   Kofi   build-Perf
          'What did Kofi build?'

      b. *été   wè   Kòfí   wè   gbá ?
          what   Foc   Kofi   Foc   build-Perf

      c. ...dò   été   wè   Kòfí   gbá   ec ?
          that   what   Foc   Kofi   build-Perf
          '...that what did Kofi build ?'

(30) a. núké   yé   Kòfí   tù   ec   [Gengbe]
          what   Foc   Kofi   build-Perf
          'What did Kofi build?'

      b. *núké   yé   Kòfí   yé   tù ?
          what   Foc   Kofi   Foc   build-Perf

c.   ...bé núkέ   yé   Kòfí   tù   ec ?
     that what   Foc   Kofi   build-Perf
     '..that what did Kofi build?'

(30) a.   ameka   é   Ápàn   fò   ec ?   [Ewegbe]
          who   Foc   Apan   beat-Perf
          'Who did Apan beat?'
     b.   *ameka   é   Ápàn   é   fò   ec ?
          who   Foc   Apan   Foc   beat-Perf
     c.   ... bé ameka é   Ápàn   fò   ec ?
          that who   Foc   Apan   beat-Perf
          '...that who did Apan beat?'

As I have shown in sections 2.4.7.1 and 2.4.7.2, the Gbe focus sentences and wh-questions are two very similar constructions. They both result from a syntactic process that requires the preposing of a phrase to a specific position to the right of the complementizer and immediately to the left of the focus markers wὲ (for Gungbe and Fongbe) and yé, é for Gengbe and Ewegbe, respectively. As movement to that specific position is obligatory, the Gbe languages allow for neither focus in situ nor wh in situ strategies.

In my account for focus constructions and wh-questions in chapter 7, I suggest that focus and wh-phrases occur in the specifier position of a focus projection FocP that projects within the C-system (see Brody 1990; Puskás 1995, 1996; Rizzi 1997). The left periphery of the Gbe phrase structure is understood as involving a more complex and articulated CP domain of which FocP is a component. It is argued that Foc° is endowed with the features [+f, +wh]. I further assume that at PF, Foc° is realized as wὲ, yé, é in the corresponding languages. The motivation for focus- and wh-movements is accounted for in terms of the necessity of the focus- and wh-phrases to check the [focus, wh] features against the focus head. Under the representational theory, such licensing condition can be formulated in terms of focus- or wh-criteria (Rizzi 1996, 1997). See among others Ndayiragije (1993) for an analysis of focus in Fongbe, Ameka (1992) for Focus constructions in Ewegbe and Akan, and Houngues (1997) for wh-questions in Gengbe.

Finally, as focus- and wh-phrases behave in a similar way with respect to their landing site and their relationship with the gap in the IP-internal position, I also assume, as is the case in most of the relevant literature (Cinque 1990; Lasnik & Stowell 1991; Culicover 1992; Puskás 1995, 1996; Rizzi 1997, Aboh 2001a, in press c) that they both involve a quantificational operator that A'-binds a variable in the IP-internal position. This is different from topic constructions, which necessarily contain a resumptive pronoun in the IP-internal position.

2.4.7.3 *Topic constructions*

It has been shown in the literature (Cinque 1990; Culicover 1992; Puskás 1995, 1996; Rizzi 1997) that in addition to focus/wh constructions, languages also manifest another construction that typically involves the left periphery: topicalization. In this study, I adopt Rizzi's (1997) definition that the topic is "a preposed element characteristically set off from the rest of the clause by a 'comma intonation' and normally expressing old information somehow available and salient in previous discourse" (Rizzi 1997: 285). As illustrated in the sentences under (31), the Gbe languages pattern alike with respect to topic constructions. Topic constructions in these languages require leftward movement of the topic phrase to the left periphery. As we saw for focus and wh-constructions, the Gbe topic domain is located to the right of the complementizer. But the topic occurs immediately to the left of a topic marker, leaving a resumptive pronoun in the IP-internal position.

(31) a. ... ɖɔ̀ dàn lɔ́ yà Kòfí wɛ̀ hù - *(ì   [Gungbe]
        that snake Det Top Kofi Foc kill-Perf - it
        '...that the snake, Kofi killed it'

   b. ...ɖɔ̀ dàn ɔ́, Kòfí wɛ̀ hù - *(ì)   [Fongbe]
        that snake Det Kofi Foc kill-Perf - it
        '...that the snake, KOFI killed it'

   c. ...bé àglán á, Kòfí yé kpɔ̀ - *(é)   [Gengbe]
        that crab Det Kofi Foc see-Perf - it
        '...that the crab, KOFI saw it'

   d. ...bé Áma lá Kòfí é a de - *(é)   [Ewegbe]
        that Ama Top Kofi Foc Fut marry her
        '...that Ama, KOFI will marry her'

In my account for topic constructions in chapter 8, I propose an analysis in terms of the topic projection TopP. In Gbe, TopP projects within the C-system where it dominates the focus projection. This is so because topic must precede focus, as illustrated in the examples under (31). Certain Gbe languages express the feature [+topic] by means of topic markers, such as, *yà* and *lá* in Gungbe and Ewegbe, respectively. It is argued here that these morphemes are inserted in Top° where they encode the feature [+topic]. I further assume that movement to [spec TopP] is motivated by the satisfaction of the topic criterion (Rizzi 1997). The relationship between the topic and the IP-internal resumptive element is accounted for on the basic assumption that topic constructions are not quantificational. Accordingly, the topic cannot license an empty category in the base position.

   Notice in passing that the analyses presented to account for focus-, wh-, topic-constructions are grounded on the assumption that the topic-focus system is triggered in a structure only when the clause contains a constituent with a topic-, focus- or wh-feature that must be licensed under spec-head relationship. An immediate consequence of this hypothesis is that TopP and FocP are two independent projections that can be triggered either separately or simultaneously.

2.4.8 Summary

The data I have presented so far clearly indicate that languages of the Gbe cluster are closely related and manifest similar morphosyntactic properties. In this regard, I have shown that these languages involve two types of markers: those that manifest the I-system and those that express the C-system. The former are the expressions of tense, aspect, mood, and negation, and the latter are the realization of the focus, topic, and interrogative features that are traditionally associated with the C-system. I discuss these two classes of markers in chapters 5, 6, 7, and 8.

2.5 MORE ON THE SOV VERSUS SVO ASYMMETRY

A recurring question that arises in the discussion of the Gbe clausal structure is that of word order. I have shown in the previous sections that these languages manifest an ambivalent phrase structure—at least on the surface level—and allow for both head-final and head-initial phrase structures. The complement precedes the head in DPs, *P*Ps, and imperfective (plus related) constructions, but obligatorily follows the head in preposition phrases and non-imperfective sentences. Under the SVO hypothesis, I propose, in section 2.4.4.2 (also chapter 6), that sequences where the complement precedes the head must be interpreted in terms of leftward movement of the complement to some specifier position to the left of the head (Kayne 1994; Haegeman 1995a; Aboh 1996a, 1999; Zwart 1997a, b). In the following sections, I consider other possible accounts for the Gbe word order and show that they cannot be maintained. This can also be taken to support the proposal that the Gbe languages are of the type specifier-head-complement. Finally, I discuss some typological similarities between Kwa and the West Germanic SOV languages and show that the analysis proposed here is extendible to those languages. The parallels that we draw between these typologically different languages (i.e., Kwa and Germanic) strongly favor the head-complement order as a universal.

2.5.1 On possible accounts for word order in Gbe

When we consider the Gbe puzzle, three possible options arise. One could adopt an analysis along the lines of Chomsky's (1995) Bare Phrase Structure and argue that there is no underlying structure; that is, there is no base order. The surface word order is determined at spell-out. This would mean that surface word order variation across languages is a PF phenomenon. A problem with this analysis though is that it simply transfers to PF the GB traditional directionality parameter. Put differently, such analysis would still have to face the problem of what PF condition triggers the head-complement versus complement-head asymmetry cross-linguistically.

Conversely, one could assume Kayne's (1994) Universal Base Hypothesis. In this regard, nothing else should be added: human languages are SVO and specifier-complement-head (i.e., SOV)

> is strictly impossible, in any language, if taken to indicate a phrase marker in which the sister phrase to the head (i.e., the complement position) precedes that head. On the other hand, SOV (and specifier-complement-head) is perfectly allowable if taken to mean a phrase marker in which the complement has raised up to some specifier position to the left of the head. (Kayne 1994: 35)

Finally, one could return to traditional GB analysis and argue for an approach that allows variations in base order, hence the head-initial versus head-final parameter. In this perspective, three possible options arise:

1. the Gbe languages involve mixed (i.e., head-initial and head-final) structures;
2. the Gbe languages are of the type SOV: the complement must precede the head;
3. the Gbe languages are of the type SVO: the complement must follow the head.

The following sections discuss these options and show that the analysis of the Gbe languages in terms of SVO is elegant and superior to possible alternatives. In this respect, the Gbe languages provide both empirical and conceptual evidence for the universal SVO hypothesis. Consider now the first option.

2.5.1.1 Some notes on mixed structures

It has been proposed in the literature that the complement-head and head-complement word orders manifested in these languages reflect their ambivalent structure. For example, Avolonto (1992a, b, c), Kinyalolo (1992, 1993), Lefebvre (1992), Ndayiragije (1993), and subsequent work proposed that Fongbe sentence-internal structure involves head-initial VP and AspPs as opposed to a head-final TP, NegP, and CP. Avolonto (1992a) further argued that Fongbe has no overt tense marker, the morpheme *ná* being an irrealis aspect marker. In this respect, sentence (32a) is attributed the representation (32b).

(32) a. Sìká ná   nɔ̀   ɖà   wɔ̌
          Sika Irr   Hab   cook maize pudding
          'Sika will habitually cook maize pudding'

b.

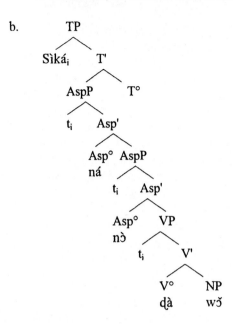

In a similar vein, Kinyalolo (1993) explained the [ɖɔ̀ -wh-phrase] order found in the Fongbe embedded questions (33a) by assuming that that language involves a head-final CP layer whose specifier is to the left and hosts moved wh-phrases. In his framework ɖɔ́ is not analyzed as a complementizer but as a verb selecting a CP-complement. It follows that interrogative sentences like (33) are considered types of serial verb constructions.[14] In this regard, Kinyalolo (1993) proposes that the embedded wh-question in (33a) could be partially represented as in (33b); see Ndayiragije (1993) for a similar proposal.

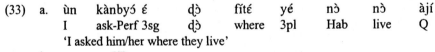

(33) a.   ùn   kànbyɔ́ ɛ́   ɖɔ̀   fíté   yé   nɔ̀   nɔ̀   àjí
          I   ask-Perf 3sg   ɖɔ̀   where   3pl   Hab   live   Q
          'I asked him/her where they live'

      b.   XP

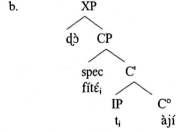

At first sight, the ambivalence hypothesis seems to account for the Fongbe (and possibly the Gbe) data in a straightforward manner. Yet there are a number of complications with respect to other Gbe languages such as Gungbe, which clearly indicate that this hypothesis is hardly tenable.

2.5.1.2 Objecting to the mixed structure hypothesis

As one can infer from examples (32–33), the ambivalence hypothesis strongly suggests that the surface word order found in the Gbe languages essentially matches the underlying structure. But as we know from other languages (French, Italian, English, German, Dutch, West Flemish), this is not obvious as languages may involve movement rules (e.g., wh-movement, scrambling, focus movement, etc.), which derive new surface word orders that do not reflect the underlying structure.

In addition, the proposals made for Fongbe leave unsolved the fact that there seems to be no steady mechanics (or logic rule) in setting the directionality parameter of the Fongbe functional projections. For example, it is not clear from representation (32b) why TP should be head-final as opposed to AspPs and VP, which are head-initial, though they all pertain to the I-system. Furthermore, if we admit that CP is head-final, we still have to accept that the functional projections that belong to the C-system (e.g., TopP and FocP, Rizzi 1997) are head-initial. For instance, the examples (29–31) show that, in wh/focus/topic constructions, the moved wh/focus/topic elements immediately precede a focus marker or a topic marker that in turn precedes tense and aspect makers that occur in the IP domain. Assuming that the focus and topic markers head the focus and topic phrases, respectively (Aboh 1995, 1996a, b, 1998; see also chapters 7, 8), it cannot be reasonably claimed that they involve head-final projections.

Another drawback of the ambivalence hypothesis is that it predicts two different underlying structures with respect to the Gbe nominal system. DPs and *P*Ps are head-final: they manifest a complement-head ordering. On the other hand, PPs are thought of as head-initial as they exhibit a head-complement ordering.

In sum, the ambivalence hypothesis is a pure descriptive device that wrongly suggests that the grammar of Gbe allows for a lot of inconsistency. To admit a grammar with such variance naturally raises the question of how the Gbe learners acquire it.[15]

2.5.1.3 The SOV hypothesis

In his description of Fongbe and Gengbe, Tossa (1994) observed that the two languages pattern alike in that they display a non-imperfective [-imperfective] versus imperfective [+imperfective] asymmetry. Sentences that do not involve the imperfective marker exhibit a strict SVO word order, while sentences that express imperfective aspect manifest an SOV schema, as illustrated in example (43), Tossa's (1994) examples (1) and (2) (pp. 25–27). In his terminology 'Irr' stands for irrealis aspect encoded by *ná* and *lá* in Fongbe and Gengbe, respectively (see Avolonto (1992a, b, c, 1995) for a similar proposal).

(34) a. Kòjó ɖù   làn   [Fongbe]
          Kojo eat-Perf   meat
          'Kojo ate meat'

b. Kɔjó ná   ɖù   làn
    Kojo Irr   eat   meat
    'Kojo will eat meat'

c. Kɔjó ná   ɖɔ̀   làn   ɖù   wὲ
    Kojo Irr   be   meat   eat   Asp
    'Kojo will be eating meat'

(34) a. Kɔjó ɖù   làn   [Gengbe]
         Kojo eat-Perf meat
         'Kojo ate meat'

     b. Kɔjó lá   ɖù   làn
         Kojo Irr   eat   meat
         'Kojo will eat meat'

     c. Kɔjó lá   lè   làn   ɖù   ɔ̀
         Kojo Irr   be   meat   eat   Asp
         'Kojo will be eating meat'

In these Fongbe and Gengbe examples, sentences (34a–b) represent the so-called [-imperfective] sentences, hence their SVO word order. On the other hand, examples (34c) illustrate the [+imperfective] sentences and manifest an SOV word order. Assuming that the imperfective word order as well as the complement-head schema specific to DPs and *P*Ps reflect the Gbe underlying structure, Tossa (1994) concluded that these languages are of the type SOV: the complement must precede its head in every structure. Assuming the traditional T-model grammar of Chomsky (1986), Tossa attributes the deep structure (35) to the Fongbe and the Gengbe sentences under (34c).

(35)

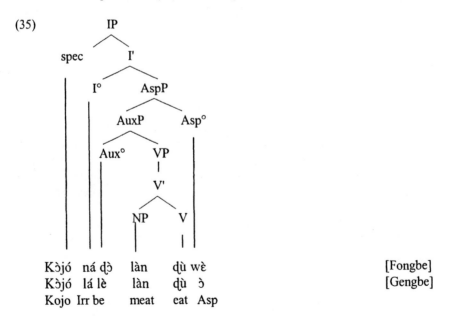

Kɔjó ná ɖɔ̀   làn   ɖù wὲ   [Fongbe]
Kɔjó lá lè   làn   ɖù ɔ̀   [Gengbe]
Kojo Irr be meat   eat Asp

Though not explicit from Tossa's discussion, it is reasonable to conclude from this representation that the DS of imperfective sentences also matches their SS. In such configuration, the particles *wè* and *ɔ́* are considered imperfective markers as they head a head-final aspect phrase (AspP). *Dɔ́* and *lè* are auxiliary verbs, that is, the equivalent of English *be*, and they head a head-initial auxiliary phrase (AuxP). Note here that AspP and AuxP are opposed in directionality, but I will return to this problem later in the discussion.

Granting this representation, Tossa proposes that the SVO surface order manifested in non-imperfective constructions can be accounted for by assuming a movement rule that moves the verb leftward in a position to the left of the object. Put differently, there is V°-to-Aux° movement in Gbe.[16] This is an instantiation of the so-called V°-to-I° movement, which is also found in many other languages like French, and Italian. In the Gbe languages, this movement applies obligatorily whenever Aux° is empty, or not lexically filled. Accordingly, the DS and SS of sentences like (34b) are represented in (36) and (37), respectively.

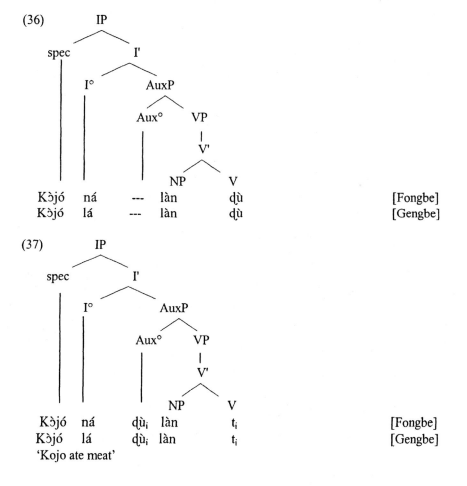

(36)

Kɔ̀jó	ná	---	làn	ɖù	[Fongbe]
Kɔ̀jó	lá	---	làn	ɖù	[Gengbe]

(37)

Kɔ̀jó	ná	ɖùᵢ	làn	tᵢ	[Fongbe]
Kɔ̀jó	lá	ɖùᵢ	làn	tᵢ	[Gengbe]

'Kojo ate meat'

At SS, V°-to-Aux° movement applies and the verb precedes the object. According to Tossa (1994), the motivation for such a movement is the satisfaction of both the theta criterion and the visibility condition. As formulated by Roberts (1985), the visibility condition expresses the fact that a verb cannot assign a theta role if it is not governed. Accordingly, the verb must appear in the configuration (38), where α is a head:

(38)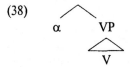

Under representation (38), Aux° is empty and the verb is not governed. This corresponds to scenario (36) where α is not lexically filled. As a consequence, the verb must move in Aux° where it is governed by I° as represented in (37). Since it is now governed, the verb can assign its theta role to its arguments. Tossa further argued that the visibility condition applies at SS in Gbe. However, in imperfective constructions, the verb need not move because Aux is lexically filled by the auxiliary verbs ɖɔ̀ in Fongbe and lè in Gengbe. This also corresponds to scenario (36), but α is lexically realized and the verb is able to assign its theta roles.

2.5.1.4 Some conceptual and empirical problems of the SOV hypothesis

Though it is a considerable breakthrough in the analysis of verb movement in Gbe, Tossa's proposal raises a number of conceptual and empirical problems that I will just mention without discussing. As noted by Avolonto (1995), Tossa's analysis presupposes the existence of an AuxP in every Gbe sentence. In imperfective constructions, for instance, AuxP is the complement of Asp°, the head of an AspP that takes its complement on the left. This suggests that the Fongbe and Gengbe auxiliary verbs ɖɔ̀ and lè manifest Aux° and the sentence-final aspect markers wɛ̀ and ɔ̀, which express Asp° (35).

But the examples I discussed in section 2.4 neatly show that the Gbe languages involve other markers of the I-system that always occur in the middle field. A case in point is the habitual marker that occurs between the subject and the verb in Fongbe and Gungbe (S-Hab-V-O) or immediately to the right of the verb in Gengbe and Ewegbe (S-V-Hab-O). In no circumstances can the habitual marker occur to the right of the direct object (*S-V-O-Hab), as suggested by Tossa's analysis of the Gbe imperfective constructions. The question then arises what position the habitual marker manifests.

Assuming that the Gbe clausal structure involves an iterative AspP, one could answer that nɔ̀ occupies the specifier position of AspP1 (i.e., [spec AspP1]), while the imperfective marker realizes Asp°2, the head of AspP2 (39):

(39)

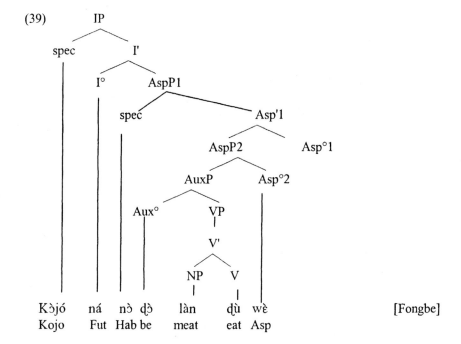

Kòjó	ná	nò	dò	làn	dù	wè	[Fongbe]
Kojo	Fut	Hab	be	meat	eat	Asp	

The problem with such a structure is that it is not clear why the habitual marker should occur in a specifier position and the imperfective marker in a head position, though they are both aspect markers. This representation also raises the problem of directionality of the functional projections that compose the I-system. Tossa's analysis must postulate that certain categories are head-initial and take their complement to the right (e.g., IP, AuxP), while others are head-final and allow for their complement to occur to the left (e.g., AspP, VP). A natural question that arises is what triggers such an ambivalent I-system and how Gbe speakers acquire such structures.

On a more general ground, the underlying SOV hypothesis implies that the object occurs in a case position in imperfective constructions. This has the undesirable effect of forcing us to account for the steady SVO pattern found in the Gbe non-imperfective sentences by postulating a verb movement rule that alternates the underlying OV order except in imperfective constructions (Tossa 1994). But as I show in chapter 6, it is not obvious that the position occupied by the object in OV constructions corresponds to a case position, since it hosts other caseless elements such as reduplicated adverbs. Notice finally that we can straightforwardly account for the OV order found in the imperfective constructions (and related forms) on the basis of general principles of the grammar, if we assume that the underlying order is SVO (see Clements 1972, 1975; Heine 1980; Avolonto 1995; Kinyalolo 1995; Aboh 1996a, 1999; Houngues 1997).

2.5.1.5 *Gbe as SVO: A case of head and complement movements in Gungbe*

I argue that Gungbe (and all the Gbe languages) are underlyingly head-initial. Every structure is of the type specifier-head-complement. Building on this, I propose a unified analysis for the Gungbe D-, I-, and C-systems, assuming that sequences where the complement precedes the head must be regarded as instantiations of leftward movement of the complement to a specifier position (see Kayne 1994; Aboh 1996b, 1999; Manfredi 1997; Zwart 1997; and references cited there).

With respect to the Gbe languages, this is a non-trivial assumption as it implies a complete reanalysis of the Gbe clausal structure that suggests pervasive leftward movement of both heads and complements. Observe, for instance, that in the Gbe DPs and *P*Ps the nominal complement precedes the determiner or the postnominal morpheme, a fact which is compatible with the idea that the nominal complement has moved leftward to the specifier position of the head, that is, the determiner or the postnominal morpheme (see chapter 3). This is informally represented in (40) (see chapter 3; also Koopman 1993, 2000; Kinyalolo 1995; Aboh 1996a, 1999).

(40)

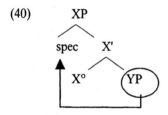

In a similar vein, the SOV order specific to the imperfective constructions is analyzed in terms of object movement to the specifier position of a functional projection to the left of the verb. The idea put forward here is that object movement is not limited to the imperfective constructions. Leftward movement of arguments is independently needed for case reasons, if we assume that case assignment is achieved through specifier-head agreement (Chomsky 1992). As a result, it is reasonable to propose that argument (subject or object) movement to an A-position applies in all the Gbe sentences, independently of whatever principle of the grammar triggers OV order in the imperfective and related constructions.[17]

Assuming that the Gbe verb must move to some aspect position to be licensed for aspect features, I further argue that the OV order manifested in the imperfective constructions results from the fact that the landing site of object-shift is higher in the structure than that of verb movement. The idea here is that verb movement to Asp° is blocked in the imperfective constructions: the verb is stuck in a nominal environment licensed by the Gbe imperfective marker. On the contrary, the VO order found in the non-imperfective clauses could be understood as a consequence of verb movement to a position higher than the landing site of object movement. Representations (41) and (42) illustrate the OV and VO orders, respectively (see chapter 6 for a detailed analysis).

(41)

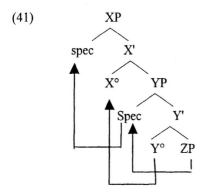

(42)

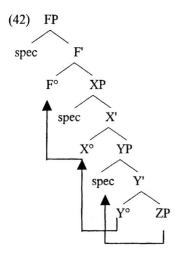

An immediate conclusion here is that both object and verb movements apply in Gbe. The former results from the general principle(s) that trigger(s) A-movement, say case assignment or in some cases the Extended Projection Principle, while the latter follows from the necessity of the verb to get its aspect features checked. The interaction between verb movement and object movement determines the different surface orders found in the Gbe languages. Under this movement theory, I naturally conclude that an analysis of the non-imperfective VO order as derived from the imperfective OV order cannot be taken to mean that the latter is the basic order (see Clements 1972; Aboh 1996a, 1999; Manfredi 1997; Zwart 1997a, b). As I showed in the preceding sections, the SVO hypothesis is empirically motivated. All the Gungbe functional projections of the clausal domain are head-initial as illustrated by the head-complement order found in embedded clauses (43a), wh-questions (43b), negative sentences (43c), subjunctives[18] (43d), and so on.

(43) a. Kòfí ɖɔ̀   ɖɔ̀   Kɔjó   ná   wá   wéxɔ̀mɛ̀
         Kofi say-Perf   that   Kojo   Fut   come   school
         'Kofi said that Kojo will come to school'

  b. Ménú wɛ̀ ɖɔ̀   ɖɔ̀   Kɔjó   ná   wá   wéxɔ̀mɛ̀?
      who Foc   say-Perf that   Kojo   Fut   come   school
      'Who said that Kojo will come to school?'

  c. Kɔjó má   zé   wémà   lɔ́   ná   Kòfí
      Kojo Neg   take-Perf   book   Det   P   Kofi
      'Kojo did not give the book to Kofi'

  d. é jè   ɖɔ̀ Kɔjó   ní   zé   wémà   lɔ́   ná   Kòfí
      it desirable that Kojo Subj   take   book   Det   P   Kofi
      'It is desirable that Kojo give the book to Kofi'

A problem though, with the SVO hypothesis, is that of sentential complements. The contrast in (44a–b) as opposed to the sentences under (44c–e) clearly shows that the sentential complement (CP-complement) and the DP-object do not surface in the same position. The ungrammatical sentence (44b) indicates that the CP-complement cannot remain right-adjacent to the verb. Instead, it must follow the indirect object, as sentence (44a) shows. On the contrary, sentences (44c–d) show that the DP object must precede the indirect object. In a similar vein, the contrast in sentences (44e–f) shows that no adverb can intervene between the verb and the DP-object: the manner adverb *bléún* 'quickly' must occur sentence-finally. But this is not the case in (44f) where the manner adverb necessarily intervenes between the verb and the CP-complement.

(44) a. Kòfí ɖɔ̀ ná   Báyɔ́ [ɖɔ̀   Kɔjó   ná   wá   wéxɔ̀mɛ̀]
         Kofi say-Perf to Bayo that   Kojo   Fut   come   school
         'Kofi told Bayo that Kojo will come to school'

  b. *Kòfí ɖɔ̀   [ɖɔ̀ Kɔjó ná   wá   wéxɔ̀mɛ̀] ná   Báyɔ́
      Kofi say-Perf that Kojo Fut   come   school   P   Bayo

  c. Kɔjó   zé   wémà   lɔ́   ná   Kòfí
      Kojo   take-Perf   book   Det   P   Kofi
      'Kojo gave the book to Kofi'

  d. *Kɔjó   zé   ná   Kòfí   wémà   lɔ́
      Kojo   take-Perf   P   Kofi   book   Det

  e. Kɔjó zé   (*bléún)   wémà   lɔ́   ná Kòfí (bléún)
      Kojo take-Perf quickly   book   Det   P Kofi quickly
      'Kojo quickly gave the book to Kofi'

  f. Kòfí ɖɔ̀   (bléún) [ɖɔ̀   Kɔjó   ná wá wéxɔ̀mɛ̀] (*bléún)
      Kofi tell-Perf quickly that   Kojo   Fut come school   quickly
      'Kofi quickly said that Kojo will come to school'

On his account for similar facts in Fongbe, Kinyalolo (1992) proposes an analysis in terms of the Case Resistance Principle and Adjacency requirement on case assignment. Assuming that the position immediately to the right of the verb is a case position,

Kinyalolo (1992) argues that Fongbe manifests a case adjacency condition that requires that the assignor (i.e., the verb) and the assignee (i.e., the DP-object) be adjacent. In this regard, Fongbe shares with English Stowell's (1981) Case Resistance Principle, which suggests that CP-complements must be extraposed (or right adjoined to VP) because they cannot occur in a case position.

Recent developments of the theory cast some doubt on the application of the adjacency requirement on case assignment in natural languages (see Chomsky 1992 and references cited there). But bearing in mind Kinyalolo's (1992) intuition, one might account for Gungbe sentences in (44a–b) by postulating that the position to the right of the verb is a derived case position, [spec AgroP]. Accordingly, Gungbe DP-objects must surface in [spec AgroP] to be licensed for accusative case. Granting that CP-complements do not need case, they don't qualify for this position and must be realized in some other position different from [spec AgroP].

Assuming Kayne (1994) is right, one cannot propose that the Gungbe CP-complements are right adjoined to VP. I provisionally propose that unlike nominal objects, CP-complements do not have to move to [spec AgroP]. In terms of Zwart (1997a, b),[19] they remain in situ. This analysis is also compatible with a proposal in which the verb undergoes leftward movement to some higher functional head, say Asp°, while the indirect object may move to the specifier position of a functional projection intermediate between AgroP and VP, as partially illustrated in (45).

(45)

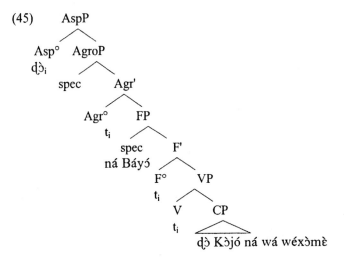

There are a number of complications with the syntax of the Gbe imperfective clauses that cloud the analysis put forth here. It is now a well-known fact that in those constructions, the object must precede the verb, which in turn precedes the indirect object as represented in the Fongbe example (46a). Notice also that nothing can intervene between the imperfective marker and the preposed object, hence the ungrammatical sentence (46b).

(46) a.   yé   ɖò   xó   ɖɔ̀   nú   Sìká   wè
          3pl   Imperf   word   say   to   Sika   Part
          'They are talking to Sika'

      b.   *yé   ɖò   tlé   xó   ɖɔ̀   nú   Sìká   wè
          3pl   Imperf   at least   word   say   to   Sika   Part

CP-complements cannot occur in the preverbal object position. They must appear in a postverbal position, to the right of the imperfective particle. As a consequence, the verb must reduplicate. Consider, for example, the grammatical sentence (47a) and the ungrammatical sentence (47b).

(47) a.   yé   ɖò   ɖìɖɔ̀   nú   Sìká   wè   [ɖɔ̀ Kɔ̀jó tɔ́n]
          3pl   Imperf   RED-say   to   Sika   Part   that   Kojo   leave-Perf
          'They are telling Sika that Kojo has left'

      b.   *yé   ɖò   [ɖɔ̀   Kɔ̀jó   tɔ́n]   ɖɔ̀   nú   Sìká   wè
          3pl   Imperf   that   Kojo   leave-Perf   say   to   Sika   Part

I propose in chapter 6 that the Gbe imperfective constructions could be analyzed in terms of leftward movement of a maximal projection, including the VP, to the specifier position of a functional projection headed by the imperfective particle (i.e., *wè*). If this is the right characterization in Fongbe, and if we assume, as proposed, that CP-complements remain in situ, then we would not expect *ɖɔ̀ Kɔ̀jó tɔ́n* to surface in sentence-final position as in (47a). One option could be to say that CP-complements move to the specifier of a functional projection, say FP_{CL}, immediately dominating the Aspect Projection headed by the imperfective marker *ɖò*. Recall from the ungrammatical example (46b) that there seems to be an adjacency requirement on the imperfective marker *ɖò* and its complement, that is, the functional projection headed by the imperfective particle *wè*, FP_{NOM}, whose specifier normally hosts the preposed maximal projection including the VP (46a). It then follows that the order S-*ɖò*-VV-IO-CP-complement found in (47a) could be explained by postulating that the whole AspP raises leftward to the specifier position of a functional projection dominating FP_{CL} as informally represented in (48).

(48)

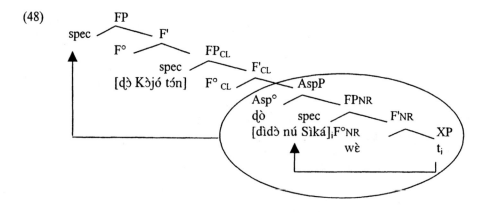

Alternatively, one could still adopt classical GB analysis in terms of extraposition, or rightward movement of the CP-complement, assuming that it is a "PF phenomenon with no syntactic reflex" (Haegeman 1995b). However, I do not follow this line here, because I do believe that the head-initial analysis associated with pervasive leftward movement of both heads and maximal projections is the right characterization in Gbe. This is in line with Manfredi's (1997) analysis of Kwa in terms of head-initial structures.

2.5.2 Some typological similarities between Kwa and Germanic

In sections 2.4 and 2.5, I showed that the Gbe languages manifest a systematic head-complement versus complement-head asymmetry. The NP-complement must precede the head D° or $P°$ in DPs and PPs, but follows the preposition P° in PPs. On the other hand, the object precedes the verb in imperfective and related clauses but follows the verb in non-imperfective clauses (i.e., future, habitual, perfective; see chapters 5, 6). Starting from an underlying head-complement order, the conclusion reached there was that the different surface orders found in the Gbe languages result from the interaction of both object shift (i.e., leftward movement of the complement to some specifier position) and movement of the head.

The issue of the VO versus OV asymmetry is not new in African linguistics. It is now a well-known fact that such asymmetries are found in Kwa, Kru, Gur, and others (see Westermann 1930; Williamson 1965, 1986; Bámgbósé 1971; Clements 1972; Welmers 1973; Awóyalé 1974; Givón 1979; Heine 1980; Koopman 1984; Kinyalolo 1992, 1997; Fabb 1992a, b; Déchaine 1993; Manfredi 1997; Houngues 1997, to cite only a few). In these languages, two major OV constructions are found alongside VO constructions: auxiliated OV (S-Aux-OV) sentences and the controlled OV (S-V-O-V) clauses. As I have already shown for the Gbe languages, additional facts from Nupé and Akyé suggest that the VO versus OV asymmetry is sensitive to tense/aspect specifications (see Manfredi 1997 and references cited there for a careful discussion).

The Nupé sentence (49a) has the SVO order and is interpreted as past. However, the auxiliated (49b) displays the order S Aux OV and has a stative or resultative interpretation. In this regard, Nupé is similar to Akyé (50), which has VO with factative and irrealis verbs (50a), as opposed to auxiliated OV imperfective constructions (50b).[20]

(49) a. Egi   là   tása   [Nupé]
          Child   break   plate
          'The child broke the plate'
      b. Egi   á   tása   là
          Child   Aux   plate   break
          'The child has broken the plate'

(50) a. Apí (ò)   hœ̀n   Yàpí   [Akyé]
          Api 3sg   see   Yapi
          'Api saw Yapi'
      b. Apí wɔ̀   Yàpí   hœ̀n
          Api 3sg-.Anim-Imperf   Yapi   see
          'Api sees Yapi'

In a similar vein, it has been shown that Abɛ̄ has VO in non-control environments. But
control verbs like *begin, want, intend* and *like* take OV constructions (51). The same
situation is found in Yoruba (52) (see Awóyalé 1997; Manfredi 1997; and references
cited there).[21]

(51) a. M   á   dî   sáká   [Abɛ̄]
          1sg Fut   eat   rice
          'I'm going to eat rice'
      b. M   dá   sáká   dí
          1sg begin rice   eat
          'I (have) started to eat rice'

(52) a. ó   kà   ìwé   yen   [Yoruba]
          3sg read   book   that
          'He read that book'
      b. ó   kó   ìwé   é-kà
          3sg learn book   NR -read
          'S/he learned (how) to read'

These data are consistent with the analysis that word order variation (within a single
language or across languages) may be sensitive to temporal and aspectual licensing
(Manfredi 1997). Starting from an original VO order, these data clearly indicate that in
the OV constructions, subsequent verb movement to the higher portion of the I-system
is blocked due to an intervening head (in this case, a non-affixal TMA) or to the fact
that the verb itself is stuck in a sequence that creates an island for extraction. A case in
point is the Gbe imperfective construction where the sequence containing the VP is
nominalized (chapter 6). Assuming this is the right characterization in Kwa, let's now
look at some typologically different languages, which also involve the VO versus OV
asymmetry.

2.5.2.1 Notes on word order in the West Germanic SOV languages

The Kwa sentences under (49–52) obviously remind us of the paradigm of the West
Germanic SOV languages.[22] Let's consider the following Dutch examples taken from
Zwart (1997a). Sentence (53a) shows that the neutral order of the Dutch main clauses

involving a finite verb is SVO. In no circumstance can the object precede the verb in such constructions (53b).

(53) a. Jan   kust   Marie
        John kisses Marie
        'John kisses Mary'
    b. *Jan   Marie   kust
        John Mary   kisses

When the sentence contains an auxiliary bearing tense specifications, the object must precede the past particle (i.e., S-Aux-O-$V_{[Past\ Particle]}$), as illustrated in (54a). The order S-Aux-$V_{[Past\ Particle]}$ -O is ungrammatical (54b).

(54) a. Jan   heeft   Marie   gekust
        John has   Mary   kissed
        'John (has) kissed Mary'
    b. *Jan heeft   gekust Marie
        John has   kissed   Mary

In the main clauses that include a series of verbs (e.g., one finite verb and one or more non-finite verbs), the object must precede the non-finite verbs, yielding the order S-$V_{[Finite]}$-O-$V_{[Non-finite]}$ as shown in (55a–b).

(55) a. Jan   wil   Marie   kussen
        John wants Mary   kiss
        'John wants to kiss Mary'
    b. Jan   heeft   Marie   willen   kussen
        John has   Mary   want   kiss
        'John (has) wanted to kiss Mary'

Contrary to what was found in main clauses including a finite verb (53), the neutral order of the Dutch embedded clauses is SOV. I call the reader's attention to the fact that this order occurs in the embedded clauses irrespective of whether the verb is finite or not (56a–57a). Sentences under (56b–57b) show that SVO is impossible in this context.[23]

(56) a. ..dat Jan   Marie   kust
        that John   Mary   kisses
        '…that John kisses Mary'
    b. *..dat Jan   kust   Marie
        that John   kisses Mary

(57) a.   Piet   ziet   Jan   Mary   kussen
           Pete   sees   John   Mary   kiss
           'Pete sees John kiss Mary'
      b.   *Piet ziet   Jan   kussen   Marie
           Pete   sees   John   kiss   Mary

Finally, as we have seen from the Fongbe example (47), complement clauses cannot occur in the preverbal position but invariably follow the verb (58).

(58) a.   ..dat Piet   zei   [dat   Jan   Marie   kuste]
           that   Pete   said   that   John   Mary   kissed
           '...that Pete said that John kissed Mary'
      b.   *.. dat   Piet   [dat   Jan   Marie   kuste]   zei
           that   Pete   that   John   Mary   kissed   said

2.5.2.2 The traditional analysis

Since Koster's (1975) and den Besten's (1977) seminal work, it is traditionally assumed that Ducth is an SOV language: VP and IP are head-final (see Vikner & Swartz 1991; Vikner 1995; Haegeman 1995b, 1996c). But the position of the complementizer in embedded clauses suggests that CP is head-initial. Accordingly, the Dutch clausal structure could be partially represented as in (59); see Zwart (1997a) and references cited there.

(59)

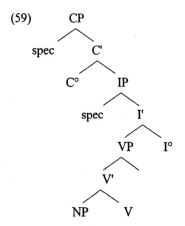

Under representation (59), the SVO versus SOV paradigm is explained in terms of V2: the verb invariably moves to C in finite main clauses. It is generally assumed that the Dutch inflectional morphemes are generated under I and must be combined with the verb in overt syntax.[24] As a result, the verb moves to I and subsequently to C in finite main clauses. This movement has come to be known as I-to-C movement. In subject initial main clauses, [spec CP] is occupied by the subject, or else by any XP[25] that is subject to the focus, topic, or wh-criteria. This situation is illustrated by the structure under (60). (See also chapters 7 and 8 and May 1985; Pollock 1989; Brody 1990; Rizzi 1991, 1996; Puskás 1992, 1996; Vikner 1995, 1997; Aboh 1995, 1998a, 1999 for the discussion.)

(60)

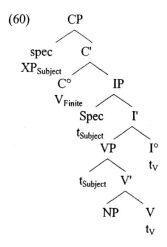

On the other hand, sentences that include a finite auxiliary/verb (labeled here as V_1) and a non-finite verb (labeled as V_2) require movement of the finite V_1 to C. The non-finite V_2 remains in VP-internal position as shown by representation (61).

(61)

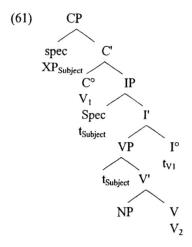

In embedded clauses, the verb raises to I° to collect inflectional morphology. But it cannot move further. I-to-C movement is blocked because C° is occupied by the complementizer (62). The subject remains in [spec IP], but [spec CP] may be filled by topic, focus, or wh-phrases.

(62)

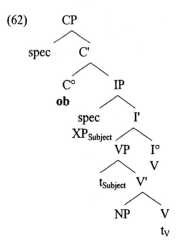

That the complementizer and the finite verb are in complementary distribution underscores this analysis. In sentence (63a), C° is occupied by the complementizer *ob*, the Dutch counterpart of English *if.* In (63b), I-to-C movement applies. The verb *hätte* is moved to C°. It follows from this analysis that sentence (63c) is ungrammatical because the verb and the complementizer are in competition for the same position.[26]

(63)   a.   ..als **ob**   der Himmel   die Erde still   geküßt hätte
            as   if   the   sky   the earth silently kissed   had-Subj
            'As if the sky had silently kissed the earth'
   b.   ..als hätte   der Himmel   die Erde still   geküßt
            as   had-Subj the sky   the earth silently kissed
            'As if the sky had silently kissed the earth'
   c.   ..*als **ob**   der Himmel   hätte   die Erde still geküßt
            as   if   the sky   had-Subj the earth silently kissed
            'As if the sky had silently kissed the earth'

Similar facts are also found in German. Example (64a) involves the complementizer *daß* left adjacent to the subject. In this case, the embedded clause manifests the SOV word order. In sentence (64b) on the other hand, the complementizer *daß* is left out and the embedded clause necessarily has the main clause order, SVO. In terms of V2, we can explain the SVO order in (64b) by proposing that the subject moves to the left periphery, say [spec CP], while the verb moves to C. This clearly explains the ungrammaticality of sentence (64c) where the verb and the complementizer are realized simultaneously.

(64)   a.   Peter behauptet,   daß   Johann Maria   küsse
            Pete   claims   that   John   Mary   kisses-Subj
            'Pete claims that John kisses Mary'

b. Peter behauptet,   Johann küsse   Maria
    Pete   claims   John   kisses-Subj   Mary
    'Peter claims that John kisses Mary'

c. *Peter behauptet,   daß   Johann küsse   Maria
    Pete   claims that   John   kisses-Subj Mary

Finally the fact that sentential complements invariably follow the finite verb is taken to be an indication that the West Germanic SOV languages manifest rightward movement. The complement clause occurs to the right because it is extraposed, where extraposition is understood as rightward adjunction to a maximal projection, VP or IP[27] (see Baltin 1982; Büring & Hartmann 1997; Haegeman 1998a, b, c).

(65)

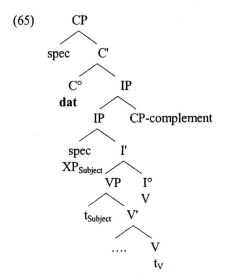

Culicover and Rochemont (1990) argue against the movement analysis of extraposition. They based their argumentation on the fact that extraposition is not subject to the constraints on movement structures. For example, it has been noticed, since Ross (1967), Grosu (1973), Rochemont (1992) and subsequent work, that rightward movement structures create islands: nothing can be extracted from the extraposed sequence. But as shown by Zwart (1997a), the Dutch clausal complements do not trigger any island effect. Consider sentence (66) where the wh-phrase *how* is extracted from the extraposed clause.

(66) Hoe$_i$ heft Piet   gezegd dat Jan zich   t$_i$ gedragen   heeft?
      How has Pete   said   that Jan himself   behaved   has
      'How did Pete say that John behaved himself?'

In terms of Culicover and Rochemont (1990), extraposition results from base-generated structure: the CP-complement is base-adjoined to the right.[28] Alternatively, it has been proposed that DP-arguments and CP-arguments have different base positions. DP-arguments are base-generated to the left of V, while CP-arguments are generated to the right (see Koster 1989). Bayer (1997) couched this analysis in terms of *argument shift* and proposes that CP-extraposition results from the deletion of the object position to the left of the verb. Consequently, a CP that is related to the preverbal argument position, by right-adjunction to VP, is automatically selected by the verb. This structure therefore corresponds to one in which the verb selects its complement to the right.

2.5.2.3. The West Germanic languages as SVO

As the reader may see, an analysis of the West Germanic languages in terms of SOV raises exactly the same problems as those discussed with respect to the Gbe languages in section 2.5.1. Notice, for example, that the SOV hypothesis forces us to the conclusion that the West Germanic languages involve mixed branching structures. DP, PP, and CP are head-initial, while VP and IP are head-final. As I have already mentioned for the Gbe languages, it is not clear how this partition obtains in a language. Furthermore, the traditional treatment of the West Germanic languages in terms of SOV can be fully captured in a framework that assumes an underlying VO order (see Kayne 1994; Zwart 1997a, b, and subsequent work). As correctly mentioned by Zwart (1997a), can it be the case that the Dutch verb moves to some other position than C in subject-initial main clauses?

Following the Universal Base Hypothesis, let's suppose that INFL is located to the left of the verb in the West Germanic languages. This would mean that Dutch is like English, French, or Italian. Granting that verb movement is triggered by the strength of inflection, we can naturally account for the SVO order found in subject-initial main clauses by proposing that the verb moves to some functional head position of the I-system, say Agrs° (see Roberts 1985; Pollock 1989; Haegeman 1995b, 1996c; Vikner 1997; Hoekstra 1997). In terms of Sportiche (1988) and Chomsky (1993), this would mean that the subject raises to [spec AgrsP] where it is licensed for nominative case under spec-head agreement, while the object moves to [spec AgroP] to be licensed for accusative case (see also Holmberg 1986; Kayne 1994; Zwart 1997a, b; Haegeman 1998a, b). This analysis is illustrated by example (67b) as partial representation of sentence (67a).

(67) a. Jan   kust   Marie
          'John kisses Mary'

b.

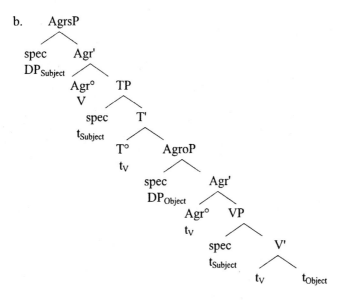

It follows from this analysis that I-to-C movement can only arise in certain limited cases, say in subject-verb inversion constructions. Just as I discussed for the Gbe languages, the analysis of the West Germanic languages in terms of Specifier-Head-Complement automatically suggests that the surface word order differences must be understood as the interaction between two types of movements: (i) verb movement, (ii) object-shift, where object shift is understood as object movement to the spec-position of some functional projection within the I-system (see Kayne 1994; Zwart 1997a, b; Manfredi 1997).

I can now explain the Dutch VO versus OV asymmetry, if I assume that, in embedded clauses but not in main clauses, verb movement is masked by subsequent movement of the object to some position to the left of the verb.[29] As I discuss in chapter 6, this is analogous to the imperfective OV versus non-imperfective VO clauses found in Gungbe.

Granting this, I could a priori account for the fact that clausal complements must follow the finite verb by proposing that they are not subject to leftward movement. In terms of Zwart (1997a), Haider (1997), and subsequent work, the CP-complement remains in its base position to the right of the verb. This analysis also accounts for the fact that the clausal complement does not trigger island effects. Consider again sentence (68) repeated here for convenience.

(68) Hoe$_i$ heft Piet gezegd dat   Jan   zich t$_i$ gedrage heeft?
     How   has Pete said   that   Jan   himself behaved has
     'How did Pete say that John behaved himself?'

However, as I suggested for the Gbe languages in section 2.5.1.5, and as Haider (1997) and Haegeman (1998a) further discussed for the West Germanic languages, this analysis cannot be correct for all the relevant cases. Consider the following West Flemish examples.

(69)   a.   da Valère willen [an Marie zeggen] eet [_CP_da ze dienen boek moet kuopen]
           that Valère want to Mary say had [that she that book must buy]
           '...that Valère has wanted to tell Mary that she should buy that book'

       b.   *da Valère [willen an Marie zeggen [_CP_da ze dienen boek moet kuopen] eet

       c.   Wa peinzje da Valère [willen an Marie zeggen] eet [da ze moet kuopen]?
           What think-you that Valère want to Marie say has that she must buy
           'What do you think that Valère has wanted to tell Marie that she should buy?'

As suggested by Haegeman (1998a), the extraposed CP-complement is separated from the verb *zeggen* in sentence (69a). The verb has moved leftward as part of the extended VP-projection, which includes the PP *an Marie*. On the other hand, the ungrammatical sentence (69b) shows that leftward movement of the VP does not result in a generalized pied-piping of the CP-complement. Accordingly, it cannot be reasonably claimed that the CP-complement is in situ, even though it remains transparent for wh-extraction as shown by (69c). As correctly proposed by Haegeman, a possible solution here could be to argue that the CP-complement occurs to the right edge because it moves to the specifier position of a functional projection dominating VP, say FP$_{CL}$, followed by remnant movement of the whole extended VP-projection to some specifier position to the left of the CP-complement (70) (see Haegeman 1998a, d, and references cited there).[30]

(70)

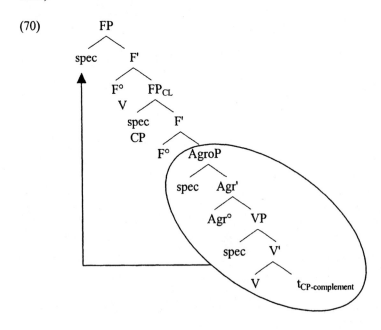

In similar vein, Rochemont and Culicover (1997) argue for an analysis of extraposition in terms of leftward movement. In this framework, the extraposed constituent occurs to the right edge, due to the leftward movement of other elements in the sentence. As suggested by representation (70)—see also structure (48)—this analysis is compatible with situations where the extraposed phrase moves leftward to a specifier position and the phrase that it raises out of subsequently moves to an even higher specifier position.[31]

2.6 CONCLUSION

This chapter shows that the Gbe languages display certain morphosyntactic properties that suggest that they might involve the same underlying structure. Under the SVO hypothesis adopted in this study, I argue that cases where the complement precedes the head in Gbe must be taken to be instances of movement of the complement to some specifier position to the left of the head (e.g., in DPs, *P*Ps). With respect to the clause, I propose that the surface word order variations that occur in these languages result from the interaction of two movement processes: object shift and verb movement. I further show that the West Germanic SOV languages are very similar to the Gbe languages in this regard. In the following chapters, I demonstrate how the system sketched here works in Gbe by providing a detailed analysis of the D-, I-, and C-systems of these languages. From now on, I focus on the Gungbe data. When relevant, I discuss data from Fongbe, Gengbe, Ewegbe, or from typologically different languages either to show some cross-linguistic variations or to cast more light on some puzzling data in Gungbe.

3

The Syntax of Noun Phrases

In Gungbe (and the Gbe languages in general) a nominal expression is interpreted as specific and definite if the noun phrase precedes the specificity marker *lɔ́*. By specific nominal expressions, I mean DPs that necessarily refer to entities that must have been previously established in discourse or context and that the speaker and the hearer necessarily share some knowledge about (Kamp 1981; Heim 1982; Pesetsky 1987; Cinque 1990; Enç 1991; Diesing 1992; Campbell 1996; Ihsane & Puskás 2001; Aboh 2002). When the noun phrase occurs in its bare form (i.e., without any determiner) or with modifiers other than the specificity marker, it is interpreted as indefinite (generic) [1] or definite depending on the context. For instance, the sequence *távò cè* 'my table' in (1a) is interpreted as definite as opposed to *távò lɔ́*, which is specific. In contrast, the bare noun phrase *távò* in (1b) can be interpreted only as indefinite. Example (1c) indicates that the indefinite specific noun phrases must precede the indefinite specificity marker *ɖé*. Note in the ungrammatical sentence (1d) that the indefinite specificity marker and the definite specificity marker exclude each other.

(1)   a.

Kɔ́kú	mɔ̀n	**távò**	**cè**		bɔ̀	ɖɔ̀
Koku	see-Perf	table	1sg-Poss		and	say-Perf
émì		ná	xɔ̀	**távò**	**lɔ́**	
3sg-Log		Fut	buy	table	Spf$_{[+def]}$	

'Koku saw my table and then said he would buy that specific table'
* 'Koku saw my table and then said he would buy a table'

   b.

Kɔ́kú		mɔ̀n		**távò**	**cè**	bɔ̀	ɖɔ̀
Koku		buy-Perf		table	1sg-Poss and		say-Perf

	émì	ná	xɔ̀	**távò**		
	3sg-Log	Fut	buy	table		

'Koku saw my table and then said he would buy a table'

*'Koku saw my table and then said he would buy that specific table'

c. Kɔ́kú mɔ̀n **távò** **cè** bɔ̀ ɖɔ̀
   Koku see-Perf table 1sg-Poss and say-Perf

	émì	ná	xɔ̀	**távò**	**ɖé**
	3sg-Log	Fut	buy	table	Spf[-def]

'Koku saw my table and then said he would buy a specific table'

* 'Koku saw my table and then said he would buy that specific table'

* 'Koku saw my table and then said he would by a table'

d. *Kɔ́kú xɔ̀ távò ɖé lɔ́
   Koku buy-Perf table Spf[-def] Spf[+def]

The facts in (1) suggest that while specificity requires D-linking in terms of Pesetsky (1987), definiteness doesn't. This would mean that the Gungbe definite expressions select an entity only in a class of possible referents, but need not be pre-established in discourse. Put differently, while specific noun phrases might be definite or indefinite, the Gungbe definite expressions need not be specific. This indicates that, while the Gungbe nominal expressions are unmarked with respect to definiteness, they are always unambiguously specific or non-specific.[2] From now on, I adopt the practice of translating the Gungbe specific sequences noun-*lɔ́ / ɖé* into *the, that/a specific N*.

In addition to the specificity markers *lɔ́/ɖé*, Gungbe displays a number marker *lɛ́* that encodes plurality. Like the specificity markers, *lɛ́* occurs to the right of the noun phrase, but it must follow the specificity markers as shown by the examples in (2a–b). The ungrammatical sequence (2c) shows that the order number-specific is prohibited. The examples under (2) are clear evidence that the specificity markers and the number marker target different positions in the D-system.

(2) a. Kɔ́kú xɔ̀ távò lɔ́ lɛ́
      table buy-Perf table Spf[+def] Num
      'Koku bought the specific tables'

   b. Kɔ́kú xɔ̀ távò ɖé lɛ́
      table buy-Perf table Spf[-def] Num
      'Koku bought some specific old tables'

   c. *Kɔ́kú xɔ̀ távò lɛ́ lɔ́
      Koku buy-Perf table Num Spf[+def]

The examples under (3) show that the noun phrase must precede the sequence of modifiers that it occurs with, in a fixed order noun-adjective-numeral-demonstrative-specificity-number.

(3) a. Kɔ́kú xɔ̀   távò   ɖàxó   xóxó   àtɔ̀n   éhè   lɔ́   lέ
         Koku buy-Perf table   big   old   Nral   Dem   Spf[+def]   Num
         'Koku bought these specific three big old tables'
     b. Kɔ́kú xɔ̀   távò   ɖàxó   xóxó   àtɔ̀n   ɖé   lέ
         table buy-Perf table big   old   Nral   Spf[+def]   Num
         'Koku bought some specific three big tables'

Section 3.1 proposes that the Gungbe specificity marker and the number marker encode the features [specific] and [plural] that are associated with the functional heads D° and Num° that compose the D-system (Abney 1987; Szabolcsi 1987, 1994; Ritter 1991, 1992, 1995; Carstens 1991, 2000; Brousseau & Lumsden 1992; Berstein 1993, 1997, 2001a, b; Kinyalolo 1995). Unlike English, in which the demonstrative *this* and the article *the* mutually exclude each other, the Gungbe determiner and the number marker co-occur freely with other nominal modifiers (5). This leads us to the conclusion that the determiner, the number marker, and the DP-internal modifiers are not in competition for the same position. Instead, each of the elements that manifest the D-system expresses either the head position or the specifier position of a functional projection within the nominal system. Building on the parallel that is traditionally made between the nominal sequence and the clause structure, I further argue that D° and Num° consist of the nominal left periphery, while the sequence of the modifiers manifest distinct projections within the nominal inflectional system, which I referred to as ΣP, an extended projection of N. With respect to the nominal left periphery, I develop an analysis in terms of the split-D hypothesis along the lines of Pollock (1989) and Rizzi (1997). In this framework, I show that D° and Num° are the major components of the nominal left periphery, that is, the interface between the nominal predicate and the discourse. I refer to this articulated structure as the D-system. Following Rizzi's (1997) work on the complementizer system, I argue that the D-system expresses two sets of features: those that face the outside and serve as links between the noun phrase and the discourse (e.g., discourse-linked features such as [±specific]) and those that face the inside because they express agreement features that match those present in the nominal inflectional domain ΣP (e.g., number, gender, etc.). D-linked features are encoded by D°, the head of the highest projection within the D-system. On the other hand, Num°, the locus of number features, heads the lowest projection intermediate between the D-system and the nominal inflectional system ΣP. Granting the specifier-head-complement hypothesis (Clements 1972; Kayne 1994; Avolonto 1995; Aboh 1996a, 1999), I derive the noun-determiner order specific to the Gbe languages by raising the nominal complement ΣP to [spec NumP] and [spec DP], respectively. This amounts to saying the Gbe nominal complement is licensed in [spec DP]. Under the representational theory, I suggest that movement to [spec DP] results from the licensing conditions on the Gbe D-system, which requires that a [+specific] noun phrase be in spec-head configuration with a [+specific] head (Sportiche 1992; Koopman 1993, 2000a; Kinyalolo 1995;[3] Rizzi 1996; Aboh 1998a, 2002). Alternatively, one could adopt Chomsky's (1995) checking theory and propose that the nominal inflectional domain moves to [spec NumP] and [spec DP], due to the need of the noun to check the features [±plural] [±specific] under Num° and D°. Since the Gbe languages do not allow for N-raising, the whole inflectional domain is pied-piped to the relevant specifier position. As shown in chapter 8, this analysis is compatible with other Gungbe left peripheral markers, which force movement on to their complement to their specifier position.

Section 3.2 focuses on the architecture of the Gungbe nominal inflectional domain and further proposes that ΣP involves a series of functional projections that dominate the noun phrase NP and whose specifiers host the nominal modifiers such as demonstratives, numerals, and adjectives. In terms of the present analysis, the nominal modifiers are to the noun phrase what adverbs are to the verb phrase. This would mean that the nominal modifiers are maximal projections that are licensed in the specifier positions of distinct projections within the nominal inflectional domain (Valois 1991; Cinque 1994, 1996, 1999; Crisma 1996).

Granting that nominal sequences universally involve the structure Determiner > Number > Demonstrative > Numeral > Adjective > Noun (Hawkins 1983), I further argue, in section 3.3, that the order that the Gungbe modifiers manifest in (3) derives from a second movement type, prior to ΣP-raising to [spec DP]. Said differently, the Gungbe nominal system displays another movement that is internal to the inflectional domain ΣP. This movement, referred to as snowballing movement, consists of successive XP movement of the noun phrase and the modifiers (i.e., the demonstrative, the numeral, the adjective). Snowballing movement raises the NP to the left of the adjective. The sequence noun-adjective moves to the left of the numeral. Subsequently, the sequence noun-adjective-numeral moves to the left of the demonstrative. I further propose that snowballing movement is the Gbe analogue of the Romance N-raising because it is determined by the licensing conditions of the noun head. In this regard, snowballing movement appears to be a disguised head movement that results from the impossibility of the Gbe noun to be extracted. As a consequence, the whole NP is pied-piped, triggering successive XP movement. Finally, ΣP raises cyclically to [spec NumP] and [spec DP] where it is licensed for the features [±plural] and [±specific]. Section 3.4 concludes the chapter.

3.1 THE GUNGBE D-SYSTEM AND THE SPLIT-D HYPOTHESIS

It is generally assumed in the literature that the category D° is an 'Infl-like' or 'Comp-like' element of the nominal system, in the sense that it is the anchorage of certain nominal features that are licensed through spec-head relationship or checking mechanism in Chomsky's (1995) terminology (Abney 1987; Szabolcsi 1987, 1994; Grimshaw 1991; Carstens 1991, 2000; Ritter 1991, 1995; Siloni 1991, 1996, 1997; Bernstein 1991, 1993, 1997, 2001a, b; Koopman 1993, 2000a; Cardinaletti 1994; Giusti 1994; Cinque 1994, 1996; Longobardi 1994, 2001; Zribi-Hertz & Hanne 1995; Kinyalolo 1991, 1995; Brugè 1996; Campbell 1996; Cardinaletti & Starke 1999; Panagiotidis 2000; Aboh 2002). The following section provides empirical evidence in support of the split-D hypothesis. In this framework, the specificity marker and the number marker (D°, Num°) manifest the components of the nominal left periphery upward and downward, respectively.

3.1.1 Evidence for an articulated nominal left periphery

As I already mentioned in the introduction, the Gungbe noun phrases may be marked for specificity and number. When that is the case, the noun phrase and its modifiers (that is, the inflectional domain) precede the specificity and number markers, the latter being somehow set off to the right edge. In example (4a) the sequence noun-modifier precedes the specificity and number markers. In sentence (4b), however, the relative clause *ɖě mí mɔ̀n* 'that we saw' is sandwiched between the noun phrase and the specificity and number markers (Aboh 2002). That nothing can intervene between the specificity marker and the number marker (4c) is additional evidence that they belong to the same system.

(4) a. Kɔ́kú xɔ̀   távò   xóxó   lɔ́   lɛ́
         Koku buy-Perf table   old   Spf$_{[+def]}$ Num
         'Koku bought the specific old tables'
     b. Kɔ́kú xɔ̀   távò   xóxó   ɖě   mí   mɔ̀n   lɔ́   lɛ́
         Koku buy-Perf table   old   that   1pl   see-Perf Spf$_{[+def]}$ Num
         'Koku bought the specific old tables that we saw'
     c. *Kɔ́kú xɔ̀   távò   lɔ́   xóxó ɖě mí   mɔ̀n   lɛ́
         Koku buy-Perf table   Spf$_{[+def]}$ old   that 1pl   see-Perf Num

That the specificity and number markers encode two aspects of the D-system is further illustrated by the examples in (5). In sentence (5a), the noun phrase *távò* precedes the numeral *àwè* 'two' and is interpreted as indefinite. In this context, the customer wants to buy two tables and is not particularly interested in any particular type or set. In (5b), however, the sequence *távò àwè lɛ́* including the number marker singles out a particular set of two tables, which the customer wants to buy. Put differently, the usage of the number marker in a context such as (5b) presupposes the existence of a set of two tables, hence the definite reading assigned to the noun phrase. Finally, example (5c) illustrates a situation where the seller and the customer had previously discussed the set of two tables and then the customer wants to buy that specific set.

(5) a. mì   sà   távò   àwè   ná   mì
         2pl-NOM   sell-Perf   table   two   to   1sg-ACC
         'Sell me two tables, please'
     b. mì   sà   távò   àwè   lɛ́   ná   mì
         2pl-NOM   sell-Perf table   two   Num   to   1sg-ACC
         'Sell me the two tables, please'
         '*Sell me two tables, please'

c. mì   sà   távò àwè   lɔ́   lέ   ná   mì
2pl-NOM sell-Perf table two   Spf[+def] Num   to   1sg-ACC
'Sell me the two specific tables, please'

What the data in (5) suggest is that, in addition to encoding plurality, the number marker may also express definiteness. This correctly explains the contrast between (5a) and (5b), on the one hand, and between (5b) and (5c), on the other. Granting this, the specificity marker and the number marker, are manifestations of the category Determiner in Gbe. Under the split-D hypothesis, this implies that the specificity marker and the number marker are the expressions of distinct projections, DP and NumP, respectively (Abney 1987; Ritter 1991, 1992, 1995; Carstens 1991, 1997, 2000; Siloni 1991, 1996, 1997; Giusti 1994; Cinque 1994, 1996; Aboh 1996a, 1999, 2002; Panagiotidis 2000). In this framework, the specificity marker under D° links the noun phrase (or the nominal predicate) to previous discourse, while the number marker under Num° encodes plurality and definiteness. As the interface between the nominal left periphery and the inflectional domain, Num° encodes features that agree with those expressed in the nominal inflectional system.[4] This correctly predicts the concord effects (and possibly determiner spreading) discussed in the literature (see Alexiadou & Wilder 1998; Carstens 2000; and references cited there).

In this regard, the data in (6) indicate that even though the specificity marker and the number marker can occur independently as in (6a–b), the complex noun-numeral modifier *távò àwè* 'table two' cannot occur with the specificity marker alone (contrast (5b) to the ungrammatical (6c)). It appears that in such contexts, the number marker is required so as to establish a concord between the plurality expressed in the nominal inflectional domain and the nominal left periphery (6d).

(6) a. mì   sà   távò   lέ   ná   mì
          2pl-NOM   sell-Perf   table Num   to   1sg-ACC
          'Sell me the tables, please'

     b. mì   sà   távò   lɔ́   ná   mì
          2pl-NOM   sell-Perf   table Spf[+def] to   1sg-ACC
          'Sell me the specific table'

     c. *mì   sà   távò   àwè   lɔ́   ná   mì
          2pl-NOM   sell-Perf table two   Spf[+def] to   1sg-ACC
          'Sell me the two specific tables, please'

     d. mì   sà   távò àwè   lɔ́   lέ   ná   mì
          2pl-NOM sell-Perf table two   Spf[+def] Num   to   1sg-ACC
          'Sell me the two specific tables'

Additional empirical evidence that Num° might bear some agreement features is that the Gbe plural marker might have derived from the third person plural pronoun. This is quite transparent in Gengbe and Ewegbe where the plural marker and the weak third person plural pronouns have the same form *wó*. For instance, in a sentence like *Ama kpɔ ɖevi-a-wo, e be wo yi suku*, meaning 'Ama saw the children, he said they went to school', the first instance of *wó* in the sequence *ɖevi-a-wo* [child-Spf$_{[+def]}$-Num] expresses plural specifications on the DP *ɖevi-a* 'the (specific) child', while the second *wó* in the conjunct *e be wo yi suku* [3sg said 3pl go school] represents the third person plural '*they*' taking the noun phrase '*children*' as antecedent.[5] That the plural marker has some pronominal origin makes it a suitable candidate (or target) for related agreement/finiteness positions, as it is often argued for clitics (or agreement morphemes) cross-linguistically (Bresnan & Mchombo 1987; Belletti 1990, 1993, 2001; Cardinaletti 1994; Veenstra 1996; Friedemann & Siloni 1997; Zribi-Hertz 1998). Building on this, I conclude that Num° delimits the nominal left periphery downward as the interface between the nominal left periphery and the inflectional domain and may as such encode both nominal agreement (and finiteness) features that match those of the nominal inflectional domain.

The facts that I have discussed so far clearly establish the Gungbe specificity marker and number marker as components of the D-system. In what follows, I provide additional evidence that this system corresponds to what I refer to as the nominal left periphery under the split-D hypothesis (see also Campbell 1996; Knittel 1998; Ihsane & Puskás 2000; Aboh 2002).

A first piece of evidence comes from the fact that, when the noun phrase is wh-questioned as in (7a), the noun (including its modifiers) precedes a question marker *té*, which appears to target D°. For instance in (7b–c), the nominal question marker and the specificity markers are mutually exclusive. This is expected though, assuming that both the nominal question marker and the specificity marker encode 'nominal clause type' (see the appendix and chapter 6 for the analysis of the Gbe nominalizers as nominal left peripheral elements).

(7) a.

		Távò	xóxó	té	wè	Kòfí	xɔ ?
		table	old	Inter	Foc	Kofi	buy-Perf
		'Which old table did Kofi buy?'					
	b.	*Távò	xóxó	lɔ́	té	wè	Kòfí	xɔ ?
		table	old	Spf$_{[+def]}$	Inter	Foc	Kofi	buy-Perf
	c.	*Távò	xóxó	ɖé	té	wè	Kòfí	xɔ
		table	old	Spf$_{[-def]}$	Inter	Foc	Kofi	buy-Perf

Under the split-D hypothesis, and granting that the nominal question marker *té* realizes D°, that is, the head of the topmost projection within the nominal left periphery, I predict that it should be compatible with the number marker, which realizes the head of the lowest projection of the nominal left periphery. This predication is borne out as illustrated by the example (8a). Example (8b) simply shows that the order Inter-Number cannot be alternated.

(8) a.

		Távò	xóxó	té	lé	wè	Kòfí	xɔ ?
		table	old	Inter	Num	Foc	Kofi	buy-Perf
		'Which old tables did Kofi buy?'						

b.	*Távò	xóxó	lέ	té	wὲ	Kòfí	xɔ ?
	table	old	Num	Inter	Foc	Kofi	buy-Perf

Granting the specifier-head-complement hypothesis adopted in this book, I further propose that the surface order [noun+modifiers]-[specificity marker]-[number marker] derives from cyclical leftward movement of the nominal inflectional domain as a whole (i.e., ΣP) to [spec NumP] and [spec DP], respectively, as illustrated in (9).

(9)
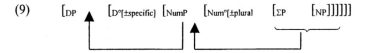

$$[_{DP} \quad [_{D°[\pm specific]} \; [_{NumP} \quad [_{Num°[\pm plural]} \quad [_{\Sigma P} \quad [_{NP}]]]]]]$$

I come back to the analysis of (9) in section 3.1.2. For the sake of the discussion, let us assume that the motivation for such movement is the need for the noun to check its number and specificity specifications against Num° and D° (Kynialolo 1995, Aboh 1996a, 1998a; Ihsane & Puskás 2001; Bernstein 1997, 2001a, b). Given that the notion of specificity as discussed here is very similar to that of topic constructions in the clause (Cinque 1977, 1990; Rizzi 1997; see also chapters 7 and 8), this would mean that cyclical movement to [spec DP], via [spec NumP] is the nominal counterpart of topic (and focus) A'-movements, which are known to be typical of the left periphery. That the Gungbe C-system displays movement operations that parallel the situation sketched in (9) further confirms the close link between the articulated D-system argued for here and the clausal left periphery (Campbell 1996; Aboh 1999, 2002).

In the focus construction under (10a), the focused constituent occurs to the left of the Gungbe focus marker wὲ, in a position to the right of the complementizer ɖɔ. In example (10b), however, the propositional content (i.e., the embedded IP in terms of Rizzi 1997) surfaces to the left of the focus marker, which occurs in sentence-final position. In this case the whole prepositional content is focused.

(10)	a.	ùn	sὲ	ɖɔ	[távò	lɔ́]	wὲ	Kòfí	xɔ
		1sg	hear-Perf	that	table	Spf[+def]	Foc	Kofi	buy-Perf

'I heard that Kofi bought THE SPECIFIC TABLE'

	b.	ùn	sὲ	ɖɔ	[[Kòfí	xɔ	távò	lɔ́]	wὲ
		1sg	hear-Perf	that	Kofi	buy-Perf	table	Spf[+def]	Foc

'I heard that KOFI BOUGHT THE SPECIFIC TABLE '

The Gbe languages manifest distinct clause typing markers, which occur to the right edge. A case in point is the Gungbe yes-no question marking toneme. As the sentence (11a) shows, the yes-no question marking toneme surfaces in sentence-final position where it affects the last syllable of the final word, hence the additional stroke [`] on lέsì 'rice'. Similarly, the sentence (11b) involves the sentence-final clause typing marker lá, which encodes insistence (Aboh 1996b, 1999; Ndayiragije 2000; Haddican 2001). See also chapters 7 and 8 for a detailed discussion on the Gungbe left peripheral constructions and the markers they require.

(11) a. Kòfí ɖù   lésî
          Kofi eat-Perf rice-Inter
          'Did Kofi eat rice?'
      b. Kòfí ɖù   lésì   lá
          Kofi eat-Perf rice   Insistence
          'Kofi did eat rice!'

If true, as I assume in chapters 7 and 8, that the Gbe markers expressing clause type (i.e., interrogative force, insistence, focus, topic, etc.) are all properties of the clausal left periphery (i.e., the C-system) where they head distinct projections, then we can further conclude that such markers occur to the right edge as a result of movement of their complement to the left. More precisely, I suggest that the Gbe left peripheral markers are licensed under a spec-head requirement that forces leftward movement of their complement to their specifier position or else to some higher relevant specifier position within C (Aboh 1995, 1996b, 1998b, 1999; Rizzi 1997). This would mean that the sentences (10b), (11a), and (11b) derive by movement of the embedded IP to the specifier position of the functional projection headed by the respective clause typing markers. The situation is schematized in (12). Here again movement is motivated by the need to check the features under some left peripheral head.

(12)   … [CP [C° ɖò [FP [IP Kòfí xò távò lɔ́] [F° wɛ̀/lá [IP t-IP]]]]]

3.1.2 The analysis

Granting the parallels we establish between the clausal domain and the nominal domain, we can now conclude that the Gbe specificity marker and number marker occur to the right edge because they represent the nominal left periphery. Like clausal left peripheral markers, they are licensed under a spec-head relation that forces movement of the complement to the specifier position of the head (9). In this framework, ΣP-movement to [spec NumP] and [spec DP] is determined by the need to check the features [± plural], [±specific] under Num° and D°.[6] This analysis is compatible with Campbell's (1996) proposal that in languages that do not manifest NP-raising (e.g., English) specificity is checked thanks to a null operator in [spec DP]. Under the assumption that common noun phrases are predicates and therefore involve a small clause that is embedded in DP, the author proposes that the English noun phrase 'the thief' is interpreted as specific if [spec DP] hosts a null operator that binds the subject position within the embedded small clause.

(13)   [DP Op$_i$ [D° the [SC [e]$_i$ thief]]]

A similar reasoning is found in Panagiotidis (2000), who proposes that the Greek constructions involving a prenominal demonstrative followed by the definite article (14a) force deictic reading because the demonstrative raises from some NP-internal position to [spec DP] to check the [deictic] features under D° (14b). Notice, however, that the notion of deixis invoked by the author could be reasonably interpreted as a left peripheral feature as I propose for specificity in Gbe.

(14) a.
Afti	i	nei	katiki	ti	polis
these	the	new	inhabitants	the-GEN	city-GEN

'These new inhabitants of the city'

b. [$_{DP}$ afti [$_{D°}$ i [$_{NumP}$ [$_{AP}$ nei] [$_{Num°}$ [$_{NP}$ t$_{afti}$ [$_{N°}$ katiki [$_{DP}$ tis polis]]]]]]]

(Adapted from Panagiotidis 2000: 732–733)

Similarly, Bernstein (1997, 2001a, b) proposes that we can account for the contrast between the Germanic demonstrative reinforcement construction (15) and the Romance example (16) if we assume that, unlike Germanic, the Romance construction involves phrase movement to the left of the demonstrative reinforcer.

(15) a. This here guy   [non-standard English]
     b   den här mannen   [Swedish]
         the there man-the
         'This man'

(16) a. Ce   livre-ci   [French]
         this book here
         'This book'
     b. Questo   libro   qui   [Italian]
         this   book   here
         'this book'   (Adapted from Bernstein 2001a: 552)

In her framework, the reinforcer is dependent on the demonstrative (Berstein 1997: 91). Accordingly, the demonstrative is merged as the specifier of a projection headed by the reinforcer. That projection, FP, intervenes between the determiner phrase and the extended projection of N represented by XP in (17).

(17) [$_{DP}$ [$_{FP}$ Demonstrative [$_{F°}$ Reinforcer [$_{XP}$ ... Noun ...]]]]

Under (17) the Germanic sequence demonstrative-reinforcer-[modifier]-noun is accounted for by assuming movement of the demonstrative to [spec DP] to check the deictic features under D°. Everything else remains in situ as shown by (18a). With regard to Romance, Berstein (1997: 100–101) proposes that demonstrative movement to [spec DP] is followed by XP-movement to adjoin to FP as in (18b).

(18)

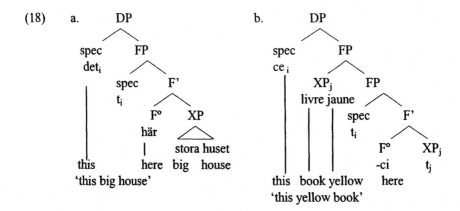

a. 'this big house'

b. 'this yellow book'

A drawback of this analysis, though, is that it expresses the demonstrative-reinforcer dependency in terms of spec-head relation: the demonstrative being merged as the specifier of the reinforcer. But this need not be the case if we assume the split-D hypothesis. Alternatively, we could assume that the reinforcer is merged under Num° as a left peripheral specification (or else in some intermediate topic/focus position between D° and Num°, see Knittel 1998; Ihsane & Puskás 2001). Recall from the Gungbe data in (5) that Num° may host other features (e.g., definite) in addition to number.[7] Following Giusti (1991, 1994, 1997), Brugè (1996), and subsequent work, let us further assume that the demonstrative is merged in the specifier position of a functional projection within the nominal inflectional domain (i.e., XP), but raises to [spec DP] to check the deictic feature (Sportiche 1992; Longobardi 1994; Kinyalolo 1995; Aboh 1996a, 1998a, 1999, 2002). Granting this, the difference between Germanic and Romance reduces to subsequent XP-movement to [spec NumP] or else to [spec FocP] in a theory that allows FocP to project within the nominal left periphery in Romance but not in Germanic. The Romance situation is represented in (19).[8]

(19)

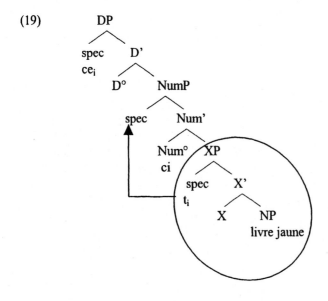

With respect to Germanic, we assume that the demonstrative moves to [spec DP] as in Romance, the reinforcer is merged in Num° and no XP-raising arises (20).

(20)

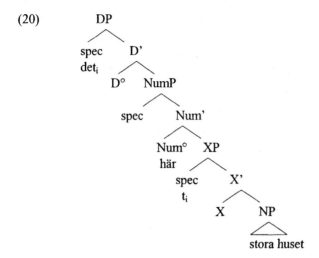

If true that definite articles are not first merged under D° as suggested by the Gungbe facts in (5–6), but in some lower position within the D-system, say Num°,[9] and granting that they may subsequently move to D°, then the split-D hypothesis predicts that certain languages will allow for co-occurring pronominal demonstratives and definite articles. This prediction is borne out as correctly shown by the Greek examples in (14a), repeated here as (21a) and represented in (21b). My analysis differs minimally from that of Panagiotidis (2000) in that the definite article starts out from Num°.

(21) a. Afti i   nei   katiki   ti   polis
         these the   new   inhabitants   the-GEN city-GEN
         'These new inhabitants of the city'

     b. [DP afti [D° ik [NumP [AP nei] [Num° tk [NP tafti [N° katiki [DP tis polis]]]]]]]

Granting the split-D hypothesis, we can conclude that the dependency between the demonstrative and the reinforcer, as discussed in Bernstein (1997, 2001a, b) results from the structural dependency between D° and Num°, the head of the projections that delimit the D-system upward and downward.[10] On analogy, D° and Num° could be regarded as the counterparts of Force° and Fin° in the nominal domain (Rizzi 1997; Aboh 2002). In this respect, the fact that the demonstrative and the reinforcer must be realized simultaneously in both Germanic and Romance reminds us of Puskás' (1996: 129) discussion on the Hungarian topic/focus articulation where it is shown that "a Topic can occur only if a Focus is present in the sentence, in the structural focus position." In terms of the split-D hypothesis, the demonstrative-reinforcer sequence in Germanic and Romance could be described along the same line. Suppose the deictic feature under D° encodes topic-like properties (e.g., relating the nominal expression to the context), which need to be checked by the raised demonstrative. Let's further assume that the reinforcer under Num° expresses some focus properties (Bernstein 1997, 2001a, b). Granting this characterization, the dependency patterns observed in Germanic and Romance parallel with the Hungarian topic-focus facts discussed by Puskás (1996). It appears that in Romance and Germanic, a topic can be present (i.e., the demonstrative can raise to [spec DP]) if and only if there is a focus within the nominal left periphery, hence the presence of the reinforcers. For the time being, I have no formal explanation for why such a link should hold and I leave the matter for further research. But I draw the reader's attention to the fact that it cannot be true for all languages that the structural dependency between D° and Num° necessarily results in simultaneous overt realization of both heads. Recall from the previous discussion that the specificity marker and the number marker need not be realized simultaneously (22).

(22) a. Kɔ́kú ná   xɔ̀   **távò**   lɔ́   tò   àxìmè
          Koku Fut   buy   table   Spf$_{[+def]}$ at   market
          'Koku will buy the specific table at the market'
      b. Kɔ́kú ná   xɔ̀   **távò**   tò   àxìmè
          Koku Fut   buy   table   at   market
          'Koku will buy a table at the market' or
          'Koku will buy tables at the market' [generic]
      c. Kɔ́kú ná   xɔ̀   **távò**   lέ   tò   àxìmè
          Koku Fut   buy   table   Num   at   market
          'Koku will buy the tables at the market'

Yet a piece of evidence that even the Gbe languages require splitting D (i.e., both D° and Num° are syntactically active) is that non-specific (i.e., bare) nouns and specific nouns, as well as singular and plural nouns, appear to have the same distribution. They can occur in various positions, such as subject (23a), direct object (23b), prepositional object (23c), complement of the postnominal nominalizer (23d), focus (23e), etc.

(23) a. ògán (lɔ́)   (lέ)   má   jà   égbè
          chief Spf$_{[+def]}$ Num   Neg   come   today
          'The (specific) chief(s) is/are not coming today'
      b. yé   mɔ̀   ògán   (lɔ́)   (lέ)
          3pl   see-Perf chief   Spf$_{[+def]}$ Num
          'They saw the (specific) chief(s)'
      c. yé   ɖɔ̀   xó   ná   ògán   (lɔ́)   (lέ)
          3pl   say-Perf word   to   chief   Spf$_{[+def]}$ Num
          'They spoke to the (specific) chief(s)'
      d. yé   zé   Kòfí   yì   ògán   (lɔ́)   (lέ)   dè
          3pl   take-Perf Kofi   go   chief   Spf$_{[+def]}$ Num   at
          'They took Kofi to the (specific) chief(s)'

e. ògán   (lɔ́)   (lɛ́)   wɛ̀   yé   mɔ̀
    chief   Spf[+def] Num   Foc   they   see-Perf
    'They saw THE (specific) CHIEF(S)'

Granting that the D-system turns noun predicates into arguments (Longobardi 1994,
2001), the distributional facts in (22) clearly suggest that both non-specific and specific
nouns, as well as singular and plural nouns, require splitting D in Gungbe. In other
words, I propose that D° is always occupied by an overt or a null morpheme. When D°
manifests the feature [+specific], it is realized as *lɔ́*. On the contrary, a D° marked as [-
specific] is occupied by a null morpheme ∅. Similarly, the plural marker *lɛ́* encodes
the feature [+plural] on Num°. However, when Num° is specified as [-plural] (i.e.,
singular), it is occupied by a null morpheme ∅. The combination of these four
morphemes gives rise to the different possibilities described in (23). Building on the
representation in (9), we now conclude that cyclical movement to [spec DP] via [spec
NumP] always holds irrespective of whether the heads of the left periphery (i.e., D° and
Num°) are overtly realized or not. The derivation is represented in (24) where ΣP is an
extended NP.

(24)   DP

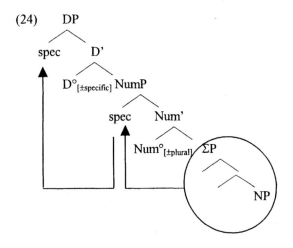

In this analysis, the motivation for movement is determined by the need of the noun to
check the strong features [±specific] and [±plural] under D° and Num° (Chomsky
1995, Carstens 2000). As I will show in section 3.3, the fact that Gungbe allows for XP
movement, contrary to N-raising (e.g., in the Romance languages) can be explained by
arguing that the Gbe languages lack inflectional morphology. As a result, the noun is
stuck in a complex phrase that derives from snowballing movement, a successive XP-
adjunction movement that seems determined by the licensing conditions on the head
noun. Alternatively, one could assume that movement to [spec DP] (via [spec NumP])
is dictated by the satisfaction of some licensing criterion, similar to focus/wh-criterion,
which requires that at the appropriate level (of representation), an element of the type
X^{max} that is endowed with a feature [f] must be in a spec-head configuration with an

element of the type X° bearing the same feature and vice versa. Put differently, a [+specific] D° must be in a spec-head relation with a [+specific] NP, and a [+specific] NP must be in spec-head relation with a [+specific] D° (May 1985; Brody 1990; Rizzi 1991, 1996; Haegeman & Zanuttini 1991; Kinyalolo 1991, 1995; Sportiche 1992; Puskás 1992, 1996; Haegeman 1995a, 1996a; Zribi-Hertz & Hanne 1995; Campbell 1996; Aboh 1998a, b).

3.2 THE NOMINAL INFLECTIONAL DOMAIN

This section discusses noun-modifier sequences in Gungbe. It shows that, while word variations in Romance and Germanic can be accounted for in terms of presence versus absence of N-raising, the Gbe languages seem not to fall in that generalization. Instead, these languages provide evidence for NP-raising structures where the noun phrase successively adjoins to the modifiers to its left.

As I briefly discussed in the introductory section to this chapter, the Gungbe noun always precedes its modifiers. Note in the example (3a), repeated here as (25a), that the noun precedes the modifiers in the fixed order: noun-adjective-numeral-demonstrative-[specific]-[plural]. The example (25b) illustrates a possessive construction. Here again, possessor precedes the possessive marker *sín*, which in turn precedes the possessee. [11]

(25) a. Kókú xɔ̀   [távò ɖàxó xóxó àtɔ̀n   éhè   lɔ́   lɛ́]
          Koku buy-Perf table big   old   Nral   Dem   Spf$_{[+def]}$ Num
          'Koku bought these specific three big old tables'
      b. Kókú xɔ̀   [àgásá sín fɛ̀n   ɖàxó àtɔ̀n   éhé   lɔ́   lɛ́]
          crab buy-Perf crab Poss pincers big Nral   Dem   Spf$_{[+def]}$ Num
          'Koku bought these specific three crab's pincers'

In terms of the split-D analysis proposed in section 3.1, I argue that the Gungbe left peripheral elements D and Num end to the right edge as a result of the movement of the complement (i.e., the extended NP labeled here as ΣP) to [spec NumP] and [spec DP] where it checks the features [±plural] and [±specific], respectively. This would mean that the bracketed sequence in (25a) is derived as in (26). [12]

(26) [$_{DP}$ [$_{ΣP}$ távò ɖàxó xóxó àtɔ̀n éhè]$_{l}$ [$_{D°}$ lɔ́   [$_{NumP}$ t'$_{i}$...[$_{Num°}$ lɛ́.....[$_{ΣP}$ t$_{i}$]]]]]

Yet this cannot be the end of the story, since the sequence of modifiers that occurs to the right of the Gungbe noun manifests the mirror image of what Hawkins (1983) suggests might be the universal order. In addition, under Kayne's (1994) spec-head-complement universal hypothesis, we don't expect to find the modifiers to the right of the noun head. The question then arises what structure the nominal complement manifests.

THE SYNTAX OF NOUN PHRASES

3.2.1 On the relative order of certain noun modifiers

It has been long observed that languages tend to use modifying expressions "either consistently before or consistently after modified elements or heads" (Hawkins 1983: 2).[13] In other words, in a language where the direct object immediately precedes the verb (i.e., OV order), the genitive, the adjective, and the relative clause also precede the modified noun. This is shown by the Japanese examples in (27a–c). Such languages also manifest postpositions. A case in point is the Japanese example (27d) where the nominal complement occurs before the head (Hawkins 1983: 2 examples (6–9)).

(27) a. Taroo no ie
Taroo 's house
b. kono omosiroi hon
'This interesting book'
c. Taroo ga issyoni benkyoosita hito
Taroo together studied person
'The person with whom Taroo studied'
d. Taroo ga zidoosya de Hanako to Tokyo kara ryokoosita
Taroo car by Hanako with Tokyo from traveled
'Taroo travelled from Tokyo with Hanako by car'

On the other hand, it is often the case that, in a language where the object follows the verb (i.e., VO order), the modifying genitive, the adjective, and the relative clause occur to the right of the modified noun. In this case the language is prepositional, as shown by the Samoan examples in (28a–d) (Hawkins 1983: 2 examples (11–14)).

(28) a. o le paopao o Tavita
'The canoe of David'
b. o le teine puta
the girl fat
'The fat girl'
c. le teine o le sa moe i Iona fale
the girl who was sleep in her house
'The girl who was asleep in her house'
d. i le potu
'In the room'

Similar observations made over 350 typologically different languages led Hawkins (1983) to conclude that four major patterns characterize languages with respect to the sequencing of modifiers (e.g., numeral, adjective, demonstrative) in noun phrases:

(29) **A: 3 modifiers on the left / 0 on the right,**
Dem - Nral - Adj - N (e.g., Mandarin, English, Finnish, Hungarian).
B: 2 modifiers on the left / 1 on the right,

(i)   Dem - Nral - N - Adj (e.g., French, Italian),
(ii)   *Dem - Adj - N - Num (no examples),
(iii)   *Nral - Adj - N - Dem (no examples),

C: 1 modifier on the left / 2 on the right
(i)   Dem - N - Adj - Nral (e.g., Kabardian, Warao),
(ii)   Nral - N - Adj - Dem (e.g., Basque, Maori, Welsh, Vietnamese, etc.),
(ii)   *Adj - N - Nral - Dem (no examples).

D: 0 modifier on the left / 3 on the right,
           N - Adj - Nral - Dem (e.g., Selepet, Yoruba)

The starred word orders are unattested sequences, which (in other respects) are ruled out by Hawkins' (1983) Universals (V') and (VI') based on the following empirical observation:

V.   If a language has noun before demonstrative, then it has noun before adjective; i.e., N Dem $\supset$ N A (equivalently: A N $\supset$ Dem N),

VI.   If a language has noun before numeral, then it has noun before adjective; i.e., N Nral $\supset$ N A (equivalently: A N $\supset$ Nral N)

Building on these observations, Hawkins reformulated Greenberg's (1966: 87) universal hypothesis with respect to word sequencing in Noun Phrases as follows:

When any or all of the modifiers (demonstrative, numeral, and descriptive adjective) precede the noun, they (i.e., those that do precede) are always found in that order. For those that follow, no predictions are made, though the most frequent order is the mirror image of the order for preceding modifiers. In no case does the adjective precede the head when the demonstrative or numeral follow. (1983: 120–121)

This would mean that two major patterns are found in languages. The sequence in (A) corresponds to languages where modifiers precede the noun and the relative order adopted is demonstrative-numeral-adjective-noun. Sequence (D), on the other hand, represents the preferred order in languages where the modifiers follow. Observe that in the latter case, the order, noun-adjective-numeral-demonstrative, mirrors that in sequence A, where the modifiers precede.

As we can see from the Gungbe example (30), the situation D perfectly describes the facts in the Kwa languages. In these languages, the noun must precede the adjective, which precedes the numeral, which, in turn, precedes the demonstrative.

(30)   àgásá   ɖàxó   àtɔ̀n   éhè   lɔ́   lɛ́
       crabs   big   Nral   Dem   Spf$_{[+def]}$ Num
       'These specific three big crabs'

If one assumes Kayne's (1994) universal hypothesis that all languages are of the type specifier-head-complement, an immediate consequence is that only one basic order, (A) here, exists: all the other sequences or situations (i.e., B–D) are obtained through N or NP movement to the left of the nominal modifiers, to the specifier or head positions of an intermediate projection between D° and NP. Accordingly, it is reasonable to propose a universal base order as represented in (31). (See Hawkins 1983; Abney 1987; Szabolcsi 1987, 1994; Carstens 1991, 2000; Cardinaletti 1994; Kinyalolo 1991, 1995; Ritter 1991, 1992, 1995; Siloni 1991, 1996, 1997; Brousseau & Lumsden 1992; Kayne 1994; Cinque 1994, 1996; Brugè 1996; Giusti 1994, 1997, among others.) [14]

(31)

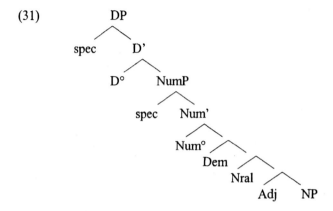

Granting representation (31), it is now clear that we cannot account for the Gungbe sequence in (30) by arguing that the extended NP-complement simply raises cyclically to [spec DP] via [spec NumP] to check the features [±plural] and [±specific] under Num° and D°. Similarly, we cannot say that the NP raises left of the adjective, the numeral, the demonstrative, and finally to [spec NumP] and [spec DP]. Observe from representation (26), repeated here as (32), that such derivation has nothing to offer as to the mirror image manifested by the noun modifiers.

(32)   [$_{DP}$ [$_{\Sigma P}$ távò dàxó xóxó àtòn éhè]$_I$ [$_{D°}$ ló [$_{NumP}$ t'$_i$...[$_{Num°}$ lé.....[$_{\Sigma P}$ t$_i$]]]]]

In this respect, I suggest that the movement of the extended NP (Grimshaw 1991) to [spec NumP] and [spec DP] is preceded by another movement internal to the nominal inflectional domain. Put differently, the order noun-adjective-numeral-demonstrative-determiner-number results from two movement-types. The first movement consists of successive movement of bigger chunks (i.e., snowballing movement) within the nominal inflectional system, due to formal licensing conditions of the noun head. The second movement, on the other hand, allows for cyclic movement of nominal inflectional domain, that is, the extended NP labeled here as ΣP, to [spec NumP] and [spec DP] (see section 3.1). Under snowballing movement, the NP-complement moves to the left of the adjective. The phrase noun-adjective further moves to the left of the numeral. The phrase noun-adjective-numeral moves to the left of the demonstrative to form ΣP or the phrase noun-adjective-numeral-demonstrative. In a second step, the whole ΣP moves cyclically to [spec NumP] and [spec DP], giving rise to the word order noun-adjective-numeral-demonstrative-determiner-number manifested in (30) and represented as (33).

(33)

[DP [D° lɔ́ [NumP [Num° lέ [ΣP ...demonstrative [...numeral [...adjective [NP]]]]]]]

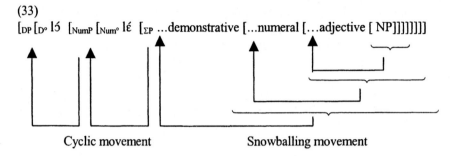

Cyclic movement   Snowballing movement

If true that cyclical movement of the extended NP to [spec DP], via [spec NumP], is dictated by some left peripheral conditions, that is, the need to check the [±specific] and [±plural] features, then it must be the case that snowballing movement arises from other licensing conditions operating on the nominal inflectional domain. I will come back to the discussion on snowballing movement and its possible motivations in section 3.3. But before getting on to that, a question that needs to be answered here is that of the categorial status of the Gungbe nominal modifiers. Let's first consider the demonstratives and the numerals.

3.2.2 Head versus maximal projection

One way to account for the facts presented would be to propose that each of the modifiers that precede the noun in the underlying structure (33) (e.g., demonstrative, numeral) is an element of the type X° (i.e., a functional head) that projects between Num° and NP. This would imply that demonstratives and numerals head distinct projections, say DemP and NralP within the nominal inflectional system. Building on this, the sequence in (34a) could be assigned the representation in (34b), where the NP àgásá 'crab' moves to [spec NralP]; then NralP àgásá àtɔ̀n 'crab three' moves to [spec DemP] to form àgásá àtɔ̀n éhè 'crab three this'. Finally, DemP moves cyclically to [spec NumP] and [spec DP], giving the sequence àgásá àtɔ̀n éhè lɔ́ lέ 'crab three these'.

(34)   a.   àgásá àtɔ̀n   éhè   lɔ́   lέ
            crabs   Nral   Dem   Spf[+def]   Num
            'These specific three crabs'

       b.   [DP [D° lɔ́ [NumP [Num° lέ [DemP ... [Dem° éhè [NralP ... [Nral° àtɔ̀n [NP àgásá]]]]]]]]]

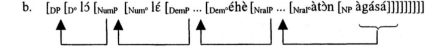

An alternative would be to propose that the modifiers of the nominal system are maximal projections that occupy the specifier position of a projection within the nominal inflectional system (Valois 1991, Bernstein 1993, 1997, 2001a, b; Cardinaletti 1994; Giusti 1994, 1997; Longobardi 1994, 2001; Brugè 1996; Carstens 2000).[15] In this respect, Cinque (1994) suggests that the fact that adjectives are postnominal in Romance and prenominal in German does not follow from a head versus maximal projection asymmetry. Under the Head Movement Constraint, it cannot be claimed that the Germanic adjectives are heads and block N-movement, while their Romance counterparts, being maximal projections, do not have such effect on the noun movement.

Instead, it can be assumed that the Germanic and the Romance adjectives are elements of the type X^{max} occupying a specifier position. As a result, the different surface position of adjectives in Romance as opposed to Germanic is attributable to N-movement in Romance (but not in Germanic) to a head position intermediate between N and D. This is also the line adopted by Giusti (1994, 1997), who proposed that demonstratives as well as certain numerals are maximal projections that occupy the specifier position of a functional projection, say an agreement projection. This analysis is grounded on the observation that demonstratives and articles do not compete for the same position. Unlike in English, there are many languages where elements that are commonly referred to as determiners (e.g., demonstratives, possessives, quantifiers, articles, etc.) may co-occur. Recall, for instance, that Gungbe allows for both the 'D-element' *lɔ́* and the demonstrative *éhè* 'this' to co-occur (35a), unlike in the English example (35b), where the article and the demonstrative exclude each other.

(35) a. àgásá éhè   lɔ́
          crab Dem   Spf$_{[+def]}$
          'This specific crab'
      b. *the this crab

The distribution of demonstratives is also comparable to that of other modifiers (e.g., adjectives) that may precede or follow articles across languages. Note, for instance, the following word sequencings: demonstrative > article > noun (36a); demonstrative > noun > article (36b); article > noun > demonstrative (36c); and finally noun > article > demonstrative (36d).

(36) a. autòs ó aner̄   'This the boy'   **Greek**
          ika n̄í anak   'This the boy'   **Javanese**
          ez a haz   'This the house'   **Hungarian**
      b. toj čovek-ot   'This man-the'   **Macedonian**
      c. ƀan wig jainan   'The way this'   **Gothic**
      d. omul acesta   'man-the this   **Romanian**

In this regard, it has been shown that noun modifying elements such as demonstratives do not trigger minimality effects with respect to N-raising (Grosu 1988; Dobrovie-

Sorin 1994; Giusti 1994, 1997; Cinque 1994; Longobardi 1994, 2001; Brugè 1996; Bernstein 1997, 2001a, b). Data from Romanian provide evidence for this analysis. In this language, the noun may occur in its bare form (i.e., without the article) as in (37a) or in combination with the article as in (37b).

(37) a.   acest/ acel   băiat
           this/ that   boy
      b.   băiat*ul*   acest*a* / acel*a*
           boy-the   this-a/ that-a

In sentence (37b), the demonstrative is postnominal and bears a morpheme *a*, which is also found in pronominal demonstratives. In her account for the postnominal demonstrative and the article in (37b), Giusti (1994) suggests that the noun head raises to D°, where it adjoins to the enclitic. This implies that the enclitic is first merged under D°. As she observes, movement of the head noun to the left of the demonstrative *acest* is clearly indicated by the fact that the position of *acest* is fixed with respect to other modifiers.

There seems to be no leftward movement of the demonstrative to some higher position in the structure. For instance, the examples in (38) show that the demonstrative does not move from its base position, since *aceste* is always left adjacent to the numeral *două*, whether the latter occurs prenominally as in (38a) or postnominally as in (38b). A change in the order Dem-Num leads to ungrammaticality as shown by (38c–d).

(38) a.   aceste   două   frumoase   fete
           these   two   nice   girls
      b.   fetele   acestea   două   frumoase
           girls-the   these   two   nice
           'These two nice girls'
      c.   *fetele   două   acestea   frumoase
           girls-the   two   these   nice
      d.   *fetele   două   frumoase   acestea
           girls-the   two   nice   these

Giusti (1994) further concluded that the constructions involving postnominal demonstrative are instantiations of N-to-D° movement. For instance, the ungrammatical sentence (39a) suggests that the demonstrative blocks movement of the adjective. However, prenominal adjectives are possible without the demonstrative (39b).

(39) a.   *importantele acestea (recente) măsuri
      b.   importantele recente măsuri
           important-the (*the) (recent) measures
           'Important recent measures'

Under Relativized Minimality, we can account for the data in (38–39) by proposing that the demonstrative is an X^{max} element that occurs in the specifier position of a functional category. It can be crossed over by the head noun on its way to $D°$ (40b), but not by maximal projections (e.g., numerals (38c) and adjectives (38d–39a)). In this respect, the morpheme *a*, which surfaces in postnominal demonstrative constructions, is regarded as a spec-head agreement marker that indicates the presence of an intermediate trace in $Agr°$, subsequent to N-to-$D°$ movement. In other words, the nominal inflectional system (i.e., ΣP in my terms) involves a series of AgrPs that project between DP and NP (Rizzi 1990; Cinque 1994, 1996). This is represented in (40b) derived from (40a).

(40)   a.   fetele acestea frumoase
            girls-the these nice
            'These nice girls'

       b.

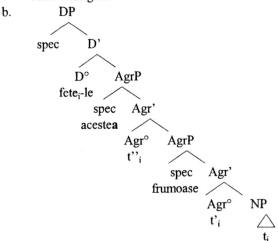

Assuming this to be the correct characterization in Romanian, we now have evidence against an analysis of Gungbe nominal modifiers in terms of head elements. To maintain such analysis would force us to postulate a language parametric variation in order to capture the distribution of nominal modifiers in natural languages (e.g., Germanic, Romance, Gbe, etc.). But, as far as I can see, there is no strong evidence showing that the Gungbe and Romanian nominal modifiers differ in nature. Recall that in both languages modifying elements co-occur with the determiner. For instance, it appeared in example (20a) that the Gungbe specificity marker *ló* and the number marker *lέ* co-occur freely with the demonstratives and the numerals. I take this to be a salient indication that demonstratives, numerals, and the left peripheral markers $D°$ and $Num°$ do not compete for one and the same position.

       I therefore argue that the Gungbe demonstratives and their Romanian counterparts are X^{max} elements. They occupy the specifier position of a functional projection that projects between NumP and NP. I extend this analysis to the numerals and propose that they are maximal projections. Like the demonstratives, they realize the specifier position of a functional projection that occurs between NumP and NP. In this study, I remain vague with respect to the categorial label of those functional projections. I simply suggest, in line with Cinque (1994, 1996) and Giusti (1994, 1997), that there are intermediate projections, say DemP and NralP, between the Num° and NP.[16] The labels DemP and NralP are used to indicate that the specifier positions of these functional projections host the demonstratives and the numerals, respectively.[17] In other words, the Gungbe D-system consists of an articulated structure that involves several functional projections DP, NumP, DemP, NralP. Under the assumption that the nominal environment and the clausal domain manifest the same architecture, we suggest that the Gungbe DP and NumP form the nominal left periphery. On the other hand, DemP, NralP, and NP are expressions of the nominal inflectional system, ΣP. In terms of Cardinaletti (1993), Giusti (1994), and Cinque (1994), for instance, DemP and NralP are considered agreement projections. (See also Abney 1987; Szabolcsi 1987, 1994; Carstens 1991, 1997; Ritter 1991, 1992, 1995; Siloni 1991, 1996, 1997; Brousseau & Lumsden 1992; Koopman 1993, 2000a; Berstein 1993, 2001; Longobardi 1994, 2001; Giusti & Leko 1995; Kinyalolo 1995; Brugè 1996, among others.)

3.2.3 NP licensing and relativized minimality

Within the system outlined here, sequence (34a) repeated in (41a) can be derived if, everything being held constant, we assume that the NP first moves leftward to [spec YP], a position preceding the numeral. Afterward YP as a whole moves to [spec ΣP] to the left of the demonstrative. Finally, the functional projection ΣP moves cyclically into [spec NumP] and [spec DP] where it checks the features [±plural] and [±specific]. The derivation is illustrated in (41b).[18]

(41) a.   àgásá   àtɔ̀n   éhè   lɔ́   lέ
            crabs   Nral   Dem   Spf[+def] Num
            'These [specific] three crabs'

      b. [DP [D° lɔ́ [NumP [Num° lέ [ΣP [Σ° [DemP éhè [YP [Y°[NralP àtɔ̀n [NP àgása]]]]]]]]]]]

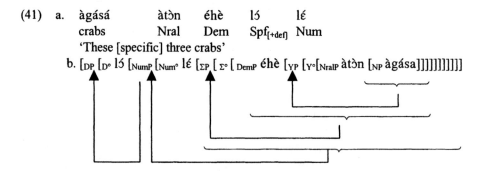

An objection to this analysis could be to say that NP-movement to [spec YP], as well as movement of the whole YP to [spec ΣP], should yield relativized minimality effect, due to the intervening numeral and demonstrative, respectively. But let's assume, as already proposed in the literature, that nominal modifiers, (i.e., numerals and demonstratives) realize an agreement position, that is, an A-position (see Giusti 1994 and references cited there). Suppose that [spec YP] and [spec ΣP] are A-bar (or adjoined) positions.

An immediate consequence is that no relativized minimality effect should arise, since movement to [spec YP] and [spec ΣP] creates an A-bar chain that cannot be blocked by intervening A-positions in terms of Rizzi (1990).

In this perspective, one could propose, along the lines of Rizzi (2001), that specifier positions are licensed if and only if they share certain features with the corresponding heads. This suggests that the "typology of positions reduces to the clustering of features into natural classes" (Rizzi 2001: 101). An immediate consequence of this analysis is that we can reduce relativized minimality to the interaction of the features of the same class. Therefore, minimality effects arise only within classes of features but not across them. Building on this, let us further assume that the nominal modifiers (i.e., demonstratives, numerals, adjectives) occupy the specifier position of heads bearing certain 'modifier features', say [+modifier].[19] Let's further assume, as I suggest in section 3.3, that snowballing movement is triggered by the strong n-features of Σ. If true, then the target positions, that is, [spec YP] and [spec ΣP], are licensed by Y° and Σ° that also share those n-features. If true that relativized minimality only holds within classes of features, then we do not expect the intervening [+modifier] specifier positions, [spec NralP], [spec DemP], to trigger minimality effect (see also Roberts 2001; Ura 2001).

3.2.4 On other possible intervening positions

Setting aside the positions where demonstratives and numerals are realized, we are forced to assume that there are at least two other positions, labeled here as AP and ZP, that may host other modifiers. This idea is supported by the fact that modified nouns must precede adjectives as in (42a). When the noun is modified by a series of adjectives, the latter always follow as illustrated in (42b). In constructions where the adjective is combined with other noun modifiers, the order manifested is noun-adjective-numeral-demonstrative-determiner-number (42c).

(42) a. távò xóxó
          table old
          'Old table'
      b. àvǔn yù   ɖàgbèɖàgbè   lɔ́   lέ
          dog black nice   Spf[+def]   Num
          'The specific nice black dogs'
      c. àvǔn ɖàxó àtɔ̀n   éhè   lɔ́   lέ
          dog big   Nral   Dem   Spf[+def]   Num
          'These specific three big dogs'

Assuming the underlying structure adopted in (41b), I propose that adjectives are like demonstratives or numerals: they occupy the specifier position of a functional projection (Giusti 1994, 1997; Cinque 1994, 1996). The order noun-adjective-numeral-demonstrative-specific-number in (42c) can therefore be seen as evidence that there must be a position to the left of the adjective, where the NP can move. Then the phrase noun-adjective, represented here by ZP, can move to the specifier position of the maximal projection YP, which in turn moves to [spec ΣP]. Finally, ΣP moves successively in [spec NumP] and [spec DP] to be licensed (43).

(43)

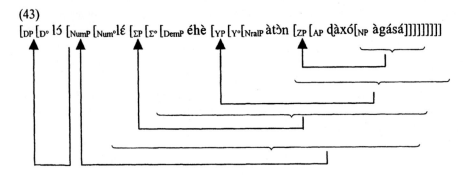

$[_{DP} [_{D°} l\acute{\jmath} [_{NumP} [_{Num°}l\acute{\epsilon} [_{\Sigma P} [_{\Sigma°} [_{DemP} \acute{e}h\grave{e} [_{YP} [_{Y°}[_{NralP} \grave{a}t\grave{\jmath}n [_{ZP} [_{AP} \d{d}\grave{a}x\acute{o}[_{NP} \grave{a}g\acute{a}s\acute{a}]]]]]]]]]]]$

Alternatively, it could be proposed that the Gungbe adjectives are elements of the type X°. As such, they must target a head position within the nominal inflectional domain. The word order obtained in (42c) would therefore be derived by NP movement to [spec AP], that is, the specifier position of the functional projection headed by the adjective. Then, AP moves leftward to [spec YP], which in turn moves to [spec ΣP]. Finally, ΣP as a whole moves cyclically to [spec NumP] and [spec DP]. This analysis has the advantage to dispense with ZP, the functional projection whose specifier receives the sequence noun-adjective in structure (43). But it also has several drawbacks. First, it loses the generalization I am trying to reach here that certain nominal modifiers (e.g., demonstratives, numerals, and adjectives) are elements of the type XP, which occupy the specifier position of a functional projection (Cinque 1994, 1996; Giusti 1994, 1995, 1997; Brugè 1996, Bernstein 1997, 2001a, b). Second, if true that the Gungbe adjectives manifest a head position within the D-system, they should not be expandable. But the examples (44a–b) clearly show that modified adjectives are possible in Gungbe. This is also true of the complex numeral *kò-nùkú-àtɔn* 'twenty-three' in (44c).

(44) a. ùn   mɔ̀n   àvūn   [yù   tàùún]   àtɔn   éhè   lɔ́   lέ
          1sg   see-Perf   dog   black   Int   Nral   Dem   Spf[+def]   Num
          'I saw these specific three really black dogs'

     b. Asíbá xɔ̀   [àvɔ̀   àmàmú   màtàn-màtàn]   dέ
          Asiba buy-Perf   cloth   green   odd   Spf[-def]
          'Asiba bought a specific ugly green cloth'

     c. Asíbá xɔ̀   kòklò   [kò-nùkú-àtɔn]   éhè   lɔ́   lέ
          Asiba buy-Perf   chicken   twenty-seeds-three Dem   Spf[+def]   Num
          'Asiba bought these specific twenty-three chickens'

Granting representation (43), I take these facts to be strong evidence that the Gungbe adjectives are maximal projections[20] that occupy the specifier position of a functional projection, which projects within the nominal inflectional domain, that is, the extended projection ΣP.[21] The Gungbe data discussed here further show that the potential heads of the nominal inflectional system (i.e., Dem°, Nral°, etc.) superficially differ from D° and Num°, which realize the left periphery in that the former have no overt manifestation, unlike the latter, which host the specificity and the number markers. The two sets of elements also differ formally in that the inflectional heads allow only for their specifiers to be realized, while the left peripheral heads (at least D°) allow for both the specifier and the head to be simultaneously realized.

3.3 DP LICENSING AND SNOWBALLING MOVEMENT

It has been proposed in the literature that movements that proceed by pied-piping of bigger chunks (i.e., snowballing movements) are typical of languages that are traditionally treated as SOV (Kayne 1994; Cinque 1996). Assuming that SVO is the universal base order, the generalization seems to be that the licensing conditions that trigger head movement in some languages (e.g., the Italian N-to-D movement under Longobardi 1994, 2001) are responsible for snowballing movement of the maximal projection including the head in other languages. In order to see how the system works, let's go back to Hawkins' (1983) observation (29) summarized under (45).

(45)   **A: 3 modifiers on the left / 0 on the right,**
            Dem - Nral - Adj - N (e.g., Mandarin, English, Finnish, Hungarian).

    B: 2 modifiers on the left / 1 on the right,
    (i)   Dem - Nral - N - Adj (e.g., French, Italian),

    C: 1 modifier on the left / 2 on the right
    (i)   Dem - N - Adj - Nral (e.g., Kabardian, Warao),
    (ii)   Nral - N - Adj - Dem (e.g., Basque, Maori, Welsh, Vietnamese, etc.),

    D: 0 modifier on the left / 3 on the right,
    (i)   N - Ad j - Nral - Dem (Gungbe, Yoruba, etc...)
    (ii)   N- Dem - Nral - Adj (Kikuyu...)
    (iii)   N - Adj - Dem - Nral (Aghem...)
    (iv)   N - Dem - Adj - Nral (Noni ...)[22]

Under Hawkins' assumption that the sequence in A expresses the universal base order of the nominal modifiers, we can derive all the sequences in B, C, and D by N-raising, NP-movement, or a combination of both (Grosu 1988; Dobrovie-Sorin 1987; 1994; Carstens 1991; Berstein 1993; Giusti 1994, 1997; Cinque 1994; Longobardi 1994, 2001; Kynialolo 1995; Siloni 1997; Aboh 1998a; Jun 1999; Aljovic 2000). Under N-raising, for example, the situations in B (i) and D (ii) can be derived by N-movement to D. In B (i) this movement is thought to be partial. The noun head moves to a position immediately to the left of the adjective, between the numeral and the adjective. In D (ii), however, cyclical N-to-D movement applies and the noun head occurs to the left edge, where it may adjoin to D. Notice that in both cases there is no alternation with respect to the hierarchy of the nominal modifiers: the demonstrative precedes the numeral, which in turn precedes the adjective. For instance, it is argued in Grosu (1988), Dobrovie-Sorin (1994), Giusti (1994, 1997) and subsequent work that Romanian involves both scenarios. In this respect, the contrast between the sequence *un frumos băiat român* 'a nice boy Romanian' and the sequence *băiatul frumos (cel român)* 'boy-the nice (the Romanian)' is accounted for by assuming that in the first case the noun undergoes partial N-movement to an intermediate head position, to the left of the adjective *român*. Here cyclical N-movement is blocked by the non-affix indefinite determiner *un*. But this is not the case in the second sequence where the noun moves cyclically and adjoins to the clitic determiner *ul*. The two situations are schematized in (46a-b).

(46)   a.

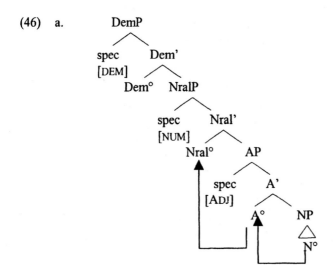

b.

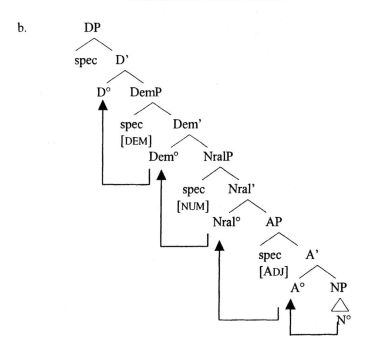

The existence of N-to-D movement helps account for word order variations within the nominal sequence across languages. For instance, the fact that the noun surfaces to the left of the adjective in Italian is taken to be an indication of N-to-D movement. On the other hand, no such movement arises in English, where the noun occurs to the right of the adjective. This would mean that English (and more generally the Germanic languages) manifests the underlying universal base order described in situation A and extensively discussed in section 3.2. In terms of Longobardi (1994: 620), the motivation for N-to-D movement is grounded on the licensing condition on nominal expressions that "A 'nominal expression' is an argument only if it is introduced by a category D."

In this framework, an overtly realized D turns the nominal expression into an argument. It therefore follows that in cases where there is no determiner to insert in D°, N-to-D movement allows for the bare NP to function as an argument.[23] In a similar vein, argumenthood forces N-to-D movement in languages like Romanian where the determiner (or article) is an enclitic (see also section 3.2.). In languages where the determiner is not an affix though, N-to-D movement may be short (34a) or postponed to LF. This would mean that in the Germanic languages where the nominal sequence matches the underlying structure in (A), N-to-D movement occurs at LF. Longobardi (1994) further proposes that N-raising to D is not optional. It is a well-formedness condition that holds universally at LF. In terms of Chomsky (1995), this implies that D has n-features that must be checked for convergence (where checking involves N-to-D movement). In languages where the n-features of D are strong, they must be eliminated by checking. On the other hand, N-to-D movement occurs in covert syntax, at LF, in languages where the n-features are weak. Accordingly two language-types arise:

1.   languages where N-to-D occurs in overt syntax (e.g., Italian, French, Kikuyu, etc.),
2.   languages where N-to-D occurs at LF (e.g., English, German, etc.).

As the reader may see, a theory that assumes such parametric variation fails to account for the orders described in situations under C (i, ii) and D (i, iii, iv). Possible derivations of these word sequences follow.

In situation C (i), the phrase N-Adj is inserted between the demonstrative and the numeral, suggesting that the whole NP first moves to the left of the adjective. The phrase noun-adjective then moves to the left of the functional projection whose specifier hosts the numeral, as shown by representation (47a). This analysis is also compatible with a theory that assumes successive movement of the head noun to Z°, followed by movement of the whole ZP to [spec YP]. For the sake of the discussion, I take representation (47a) to be the right characterization.[24]

(47)   a. DP

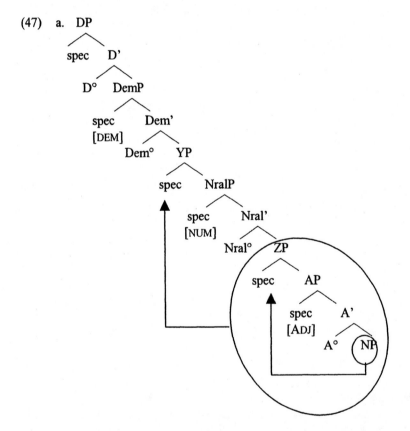

Situation C (ii), however, is compatible with an analysis where the noun head moves successively to A° and Nral°, the functional head positions whose specifiers host the adjective and the numeral, respectively. Then, after, the whole phrase numeral-noun-adjective raises to some specifier position to the left of the demonstrative, say [spec DP], as in (47b).

(47)   b.   DP

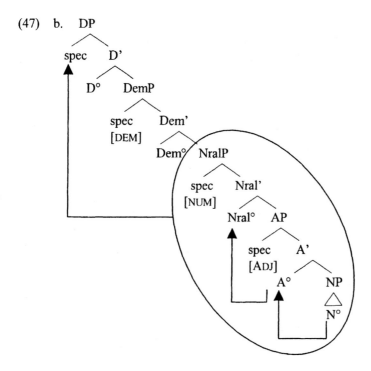

As I discussed in previous sections, the sequence D (i) matches the Gungbe word order. It is the mirror image of the underlying universal order described by Hawkins' (1983) generalization A. Under snowballing movement, the sequence D (i) derives through movement of the whole NP to the left of the adjective. Then the phrase noun adjective moves to the left of the numeral. Subsequently, the phrase noun-adjective-numeral moves to the left of the demonstrative, that is, [spec DP] as represented in (35c). By analogy to the representations (46a–b), the situations C (i) and D (i) can be referred to as short versus long snowballing movement. This is not trivial since it will become clear as I proceed that snowballing movement is the perfect replica of head movement (47c).

(47)   c.   DP

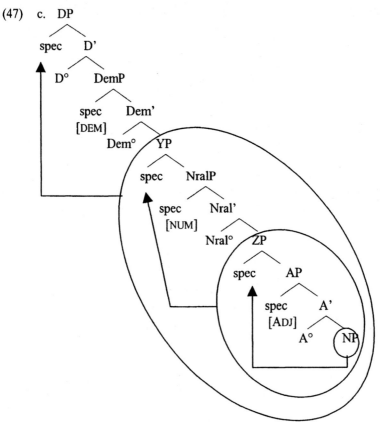

On the other hand, the sequence D (iii) is an extension of representation (47a). The surface word order derives through movement of the whole NP to an intermediate specifier position between the numeral and the adjective, that is, [spec ZP]. Then the whole ZP moves cyclically to the left of the numeral, [spec YP] and finally to the left of the demonstrative, [spec DP] as represented in (47d).

(47)   d.   DP

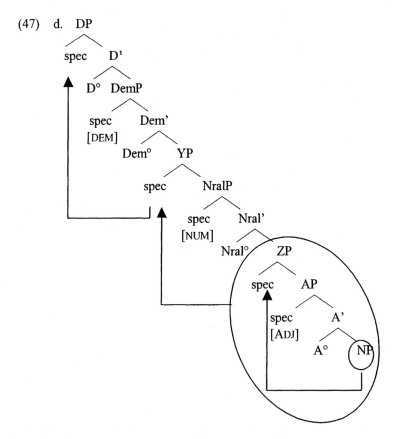

The situation D (iv) is also an extension of representation (47a). The only difference here is that movement of ZP to [spec YP] is followed by subsequent movement of the head noun to Dem° and D°. At this stage of the discussion, it is worth mentioning that the representation under (47e) is to some extent consistent with the analysis of clitic-movement. It is traditionally assumed in the literature that clitics are heads and must surface in a derived position. Assuming that the clitic is generated VP-internally as DP, clitic-movement involves movement of the DP to some specifier position, say [spec AgroP], followed by movement of the head D° to some licensing head position within the I-system (Belletti 1993, 2001; Rizzi 1993; Chomsky 1995; Friedemann & Siloni 1997; and references cited there). Anticipating the discussion, the analogy between clitic-movement and snowballing movement (whether short or long) already hints at the fact that snowballing movement might be linked to head movement.

(47) e.

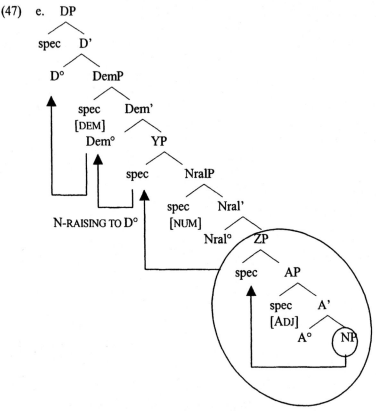

Under Hawkins' (1983) universal base hypothesis, the cross-linguistic analysis of the nominal expressions obviously shows that none of the sequences under C (i, ii) and D (i, iii, iv) is consistent with Longobardi's (1994) parametric proposal. In other words, the licensing condition on nominal expressions does not simply result in a parametric variation between languages that perform N-to-D movement in overt syntax versus languages where N-to-D movement applies in covert syntax, that is, at LF. We therefore need to refine the theory in order to include languages that display the sequences under C (i, ii) and D (i, iii, iv).

In this respect, let's assume, in line with Longobardi (1994, 2001), that argumenthood or else the licensing condition on nominal expressions requires some sort of α-raising cross-linguistically. In my terms, α may define as XP or as X°. If true, then the correct characterization seems to be that certain languages systematically resort to a generalized pied-piping where X°-raising is impossible. In other words, where the head is inaccessible for movement, N-to-D movement necessarily results either in XP-raising or in a combination of XP-raising and X°-raising, as shown by the representations (47b) and (47e). Observe, for example, that all the cases of XP-raising described here involve either residual or cyclical snowballing movements as illustrated by the representations (47a, 47d, 47e) and (47c), respectively. The term residual refers to situations where snowballing movement is preceded or followed by N-movement.

On the other hand, by cyclical snowballing movement, I mean those situations where there is successive snowballing movement to the highest appropriate specifier position. Building on this, the difference between Kikuyu and Romanian, which manifest the order N-Dem-Num-Adj on the one hand and Gungbe, which displays N-Adj-Num-Dem on the other, would be that the Kikuyu-type languages involve cyclical N-to-D movement, while the Gungbe-type languages involve snowballing movement. Granting that these two movement types are contingent on the licensing conditions on a head, I conclude that there must be a third strategy to Longobardi's parametric proposal:

1.   languages where N-to-D $\begin{cases} \text{occurs in overt syntax (e.g., Italian,} \\ \text{French, Kikuyu, etc.),} \\ \\ \text{occurs in covert syntax, LF (e.g., English,} \\ \text{German, etc.),} \end{cases}$

2.   languages where N-to-D results in snowballing movement (e.g., Gungbe, Yoruba, etc.).

While this theory underscores the analysis of the nominal modifiers as XPs occupying distinct specifier positions in an articulated D-structure, it also indicates that snowballing movement is a disguised head movement. It is a last resort phenomenon that arises when the target of movement, the head, is inaccessible for movement. Put differently, snowballing movement seeks to raise only the head. When the head cannot be extracted from the projection it heads, the whole projection is pied-piped to the shortest specifier position and so on. In this respect, snowballing movement should be distinguished from successive cyclic movement of a maximal projection to a specifier position. The former proceeds by pied-piping: the moved phrase substitutes for the intermediate target specifier positions and movement necessarily involves successive bigger chunks (47c). This amounts to saying that even though snowballing movement involves successive steps, it is similar to an adjunction rule: a two property typical of head movement. However, in a simple cyclic spec-to-spec movement, the intermediate specifier positions only serve as escape hatches or successive 'check points' for movement. With respect to the Gungbe data discussed in previous sections, partial snowballing movement raises bigger chunks to [spec ΣP], the specifier position of the phrase right-adjacent to NumP. Subsequently, ΣP as a whole moves cyclically to [spec NumP] and [spec DP].

A question that one may ask here is why snowballing movement does not proceed through [spec NumP] and [spec DP] but must stop in [spec ΣP]. There are two possible answers to this question. As a first attempt, one could argue along the following lines. If true that snowballing movement is a disguised head movement, then it should obey the same locality constraints on head movement. For example, no intervening position can be skipped. Starting from an original sequence A-B-C-D, movement of D-to-A necessarily creates the mirror image D-C-B-A due to the head movement constraint (Travis 1984; Rizzi 1990, and references cited there).

As I suggested in chapter 2, one language-specific constraint on head movement in Gungbe is that adjunction to an overtly realized head is prohibited. The conclusion reached there (see also chapters 5, and 6) is that the moved verb necessarily stops immediately to the right of the tense or aspect marker. It can move further only if the preceding positions are not morphologically realized. Suppose snowballing movement of the nominal expression mimics this constraint. If true, this could be an explanation for why movement of the nominal expression targets only the specifier position immediately to the right of the morphologically realized head.

I will not follow this analysis here. Alternatively, I suggest that snowballing movement is triggered by the strong n-features of the nominal inflectional head $\Sigma°$. I further argue that the Gbe languages allow for snowballing movement because the noun head is not extractable. Recall from the discussion in previous sections that the Gungbe noun is never inflected (e.g., for number or gender), a sign that may be interpreted as the absence of N-raising in Gbe. In this respect, snowballing movement to [spec ΣP] is therefore considered a means of satisfying the licensing requirements on the static head noun. On the other hand, subsequent movement of ΣP to [spec NumP] and [spec DP] is triggered by the licensing conditions of the nominal left periphery: the need to check the features [±plural] [±specific] under Num° and D°.

Going back to the parallel between the nominal sequence and the clause, I suggest that snowballing movement is the counterpart of V-to-I movement (assuming V is not extractable). On the other hand, subsequent movement of ΣP to [spec NumP], [spec DP] reduces to complement-to-specifier movement that seems to be required by certain Gbe left peripheral markers. In this respect, ΣP-movement is similar to V-focusing in imperfective clauses where the impossibility of verb-movement leads to a generalized pied-piping of the verb and its argument to the relevant licensing specifier position in the left periphery. In a similar vein, the Gungbe yes-no question formation necessitates that the whole FinP be moved to the C-system; see chapters 7 and 8 for the discussion. At this stage of the discussion, it suffices to observe that only the licensing conditions of a head—be it of the C- or I-type—may trigger snowballing movement or pied-piping. Observe that in certain languages, snowballing movement may also involve the nominal left periphery. A case in point is Korean, where it has been proposed that snowballing movement proceeds through the number marker up to D (Jun 1999). That snowballing is short in Gungbe and long in Korean leads to no contradiction. To my view, the difference between these languages reminds us of the distinction between the Romance languages and the Germanic languages with respect to verb movement. Why is it that verb-movement is a priori limited to the I-system in the former but involves the C-system in the latter? The right characterization seems to be that language variations with respect to the length of movement may arise from language specificity. In this respect, they should not necessarily be linked to the licensing conditions that trigger movement. This leads me to conclude that snowballing movement is triggered in Gungbe and Korean due to the licensing conditions on the noun head. Under the analysis developed here, the following data on adverb placement in Malagasy clearly underscore the analogy between V in the clause and N in the nominal sequence.

3.3.1 Snowballing movement and adverb placement

Cinque (1999) shows that the so-called middle field adverbs fall into different classes that display a rigid hierarchy in the clause. Sentence (48a) indicates the habitual adverbs like *solitamente* 'usually' precede the negative adverb *mica*. In example (48b) we see that the negative adverb *mica* precedes *già* 'already', which in turn precedes *più* 'any longer' (48c). *Più* then precedes adverbs like *sempre* 'always' (48d), the latter preceding adverbs such as *completamente* 'completely' (48e). Finally, adverbs like *completamente* 'completely' or *parzialmente* 'partially' necessarily precede manner adverbs like *bene* 'well' (48f).

(48) a. Alle due, Gianni non ha [solitamente mica] mangiato, ancora
'At two, Gianni has usually not eaten yet'
b. Non hanno [mica già] chiamato, che io sappia
'They have not already telephoned, that I know'
c. All'epoca non possedeva [già più] nulla
'At the time s/he did not possess already any longer anything'
d. Da allora, non ha [più sempre]
'Since then, he has no longer always won'
e. Gianni ha [sempre completamente] perso la testa per lei
'Gianni has always completely lost his mind for her'
f. Ha rifatto [parzialmente tutto bene] Gianni
'Has done again partially everything well Gianni'

By transition, the adverb sequencing found in (48) suggests the rigid hierarchy in (49), where each type of adverb corresponds to a class. Each of these classes targets a specific position in the middle field which Cinque (1999: 6) defines as "the space delimited on the left by the leftmost position an (active) past participle can come to occupy, and on the right by a complement (or the subject) of the past participle." In other words, the middle field adverbs all follow the Italian finite verb.[25]

(49) 1   2   3   4   5   6   8   9
solidamente > mica > già > più > sempre > completamente > tutto > bene
usually > not > already > any longer > always > completely > all > well

Cinque's seminal comparative work suggests that the hierarchy under (49) is supported by cross-linguistic data from French, Dutch, and various languages. But as Pearson (1998, 2000) shows, there are language variations with respect to (49). In Malagasy, for example, these adverbs fall in two groups: preverbal and postverbal adverbs. Preverbal adverbs fall into classes 1 to 3, while postverbal adverbs include classes 4 to 9. But as one can see from the examples under (50), the postverbal adverbs manifest exactly the mirror image of Cinque's hierarchy described in (49).

(50) a. Manasa   lamba   [tsara   tanteraka]   Rakoto
          wash   clothes well   completely   Rakoto
          'Rakoto completely washes clothes well'
      b. Manasa   lamba   [tanteraka   foana]   Rakoto
          wash   clothes completely   always   Rakoto
          'Rakoto always washes clothes completely'
      c. Tsy manasa   lamba   [foana   intsony] Rakoto
          Neg wash   clothes always   anymore   Rakoto
          'Rakoto doesn't always wash clothes anymore'

By transitivity, I arrive at the following hierarchy in Malagasy (adapted from Pearson 1998).

(51)   1   3   9   6   4   3
        matetika > efa   > VERB > tsara > tanteraka > foana > intsony
        generally   already   well   completely always   anymore

In terms of Cinque (1999), adverbs are maximal projections. Each class of adverb targets the specifier position of a distinct functional projection, say the specifier position of an Aspect Projection, or a Mood Projection, that projects above the VP. With respect to the Italian data, the finite verb precedes the adverbs because it moves cyclically to some head position to the left of the relevant adverb. But this analysis cannot be maintained for Malagasy. As we can see from the data under (50), the verb does not move past the adverb in this language. This need not mean, though, that the hierarchy in (49) should be modified. Instead, that the postverbal adverbs manifest the mirror image of Cinque's hierarchy is taken to be an indication of snowballing movement. The whole VP moves to the left of the adverb of class 9. Then the phrase verb-adverb$_{[class\ 9]}$ moves to the left of the adverb of class 6. The phrase verb-adverb$_{[class\ 9]}$-adverb$_{[class\ 6]}$ further moves to the left of the adverb class 4 and the phrase verb-adverb$_{[class\ 9]}$-adverb$_{[class\ 6]}$ -adverb$_{[class\ 4]}$ subsequently moves to the left of the adverb of class 3, forming the phrase verb-adverb$_{[class\ 9]}$ -adverb$_{[class\ 6]}$ -adverb$_{[class\ 4]}$ -adverb$_{[class\ 3]}$. The derivation is represented in (52). Observe that the fact that the adverbs of all the classes are not realized simultaneously in Malagasy does not preclude this analysis. Instead, such incompatibility might result from semantic or language-specific constraints on the combination of adverbs.

(52)

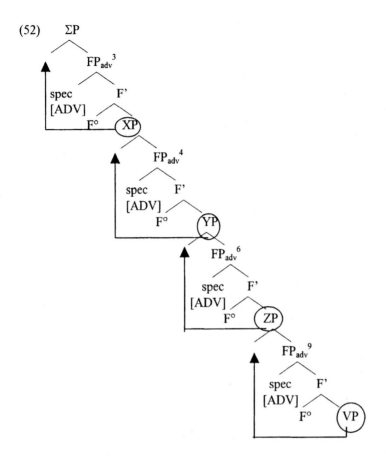

Notice that even a theory that assumes partial VP movement to the left of the adverb, followed by subsequent leftward movement of the verb, cannot account for the adverb sequencing that the data in (50) suggest. Here again, I argue that the necessity of snowballing movement results from the impossibility of verb-movement. V is not extractable, and the whole VP is pied-piped to the relevant licensing specifier position.

3.3.2 Summary

This section shows that the Gungbe nominal system involves two movement-types: snowballing movement and cyclical movement. Snowballing movement—the XP-replica of head movement—is triggered by the strong n-features of $\Sigma°$. In this respect, snowballing movement is seen as a disguised head movement, that is, the Gbe counterpart of N-raising in the Romance languages. Like head movement, snowballing movement proceeds by successive adjunction. The NP moves to the left of the adjective. Then the phrase noun-adjective moves to the left of the numeral leading to the phrase noun-adjective-numeral. This phrase moves to the left of the demonstrative, creating as such the phrase noun-adjective-numeral-demonstrative. On the other hand, cyclic movement targets the whole cluster noun-adjective-numeral-demonstrative, ΣP, which raises cyclically to [spec NumP] and [spec DP] to check the [±plural] and [±specific] features under Num° and D° (53)

(53) $[_{DP}.[_{D°} l\acute{o}[_{NumP}..[_{Num°} l\acute{\epsilon}[_{\Sigma P}..[_{\Sigma°}[_{Demonstrative} [_{YP}..[_{Numeral} [_{ZP}..[_{Adjective} [_{NP} ..]]]]]]]]]$

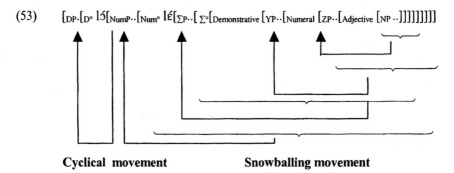

Cyclical movement   **Snowballing movement**

The analysis I propose here naturally raises the question of whether snowballing movement is a third type of movement, in addition to spec-to-spec movement and head movement. The answer to this question is no, since I have demonstrated that even though snowballing movement targets specifier positions, it is contingent to head movement. It occurs only and only if the head is not extractable. This leads me to conclude that, unlike cyclical spec-to-spec movement, which uniquely involves maximal projections, head movement may involve both lexical heads and phrases. To some extent, the proposal that snowballing movement is a disguised head movement suggests that head movement is not a uniform phenomenon, a fact that motivates Chomsky's (1999) analysis of head movement as a PF phenomenon. Whether this is true is subject to further research, but we already have enough evidence from Gungbe and the Gbe languages that head movement is not a uniform phenomenon (i.e., X°-to-Y° movement), as it is generally assumed in the literature.

3.4 CONCLUSION

This chapter further supports the idea, already developed in the literature (Abney 1987; Szabolcsi 1987, 1994; Ritter 1991, 1995; Longobardi 1994) that noun phrases involve a structure similar to that of the clause consisting of a left periphery and an inflectional domain. Under the split-D hypothesis, I propose that the nominal left periphery consists of an articulated structure that encodes two types of features: those that face the outside and serve as links between the noun phrase and the discourse (e.g., discourse linked features such as [±specific]) and those that face the inside because they express agreement features that match those present in the nominal inflectional domain ΣP (e.g., number, gender etc.). D-linked features are encoded by D°, the head of the highest projection within the D-system. On the other hand, Num°, the locus of number features, heads the lowest functional projection intermediate between the D-system and the nominal inflectional system ΣP. Building on this, I propose that the Gbe languages manifest the order noun-specific-number because the nominal inflectional domain ΣP must raise to [spec NumP] and [spec DP] to check the features [±plural], [±specific], respectively (Sportiche 1992; Koopman 1993, 2000a; Kinyalolo 1995; Chomsky 1995; Rizzi 1996; Aboh 1998a, 2002; Carstens 2000; Panagiotidis 2000). As I show, in chapter 8, other Gungbe left peripheral markers (e.g., yes-no question marker, clausal determiner) seem to trigger a similar movement on to their complement.

With respect to the nominal inflectional domain ΣP, the discussion shows that it involves a series of functional projections that dominate the noun phrase NP and whose specifiers host the nominal modifiers such as demonstratives, numerals, and adjectives. In this framework, I suggest that the nominal modifiers are like adverbs in the sense that they are maximal projections that are licensed in the specifier positions of distinct projections within the nominal inflectional domain (Cinque 1994, 1999). Granting Hawkins' (1983) universal order, I propose that the Gungbe nominal system displays snowballing movement. This movement consists of successive XP movement that raises the NP to the left of the adjective. The sequence noun-adjective moves to the left of the numeral. Subsequently, the sequence noun-adjective-numeral moves to the left of the demonstrative. I further propose that snowballing movement is the Gbe analogue of the Romance N-raising because it is determined by the licensing conditions of the noun head. In this regard, snowballing movement appears to be a disguised head movement that results from the impossibility of the Gbe noun to be extracted.

APPENDIX: ON THE GUNGBE 'FAKE POSTPOSITIONS'

In chapter 2, I showed that Kwa languages (e.g., Gbe) manifest certain constructions where the nominal complement precedes a number of elements such as *jí* 'on', *gló* 'under', *mè* 'inside', *dé* 'at', *kpá* 'beside', which, at first sight, function as locational postpositions.

(1) távò   ló   jí / gló
     table   Spf[+def] Post
     'On/under the old table' (literally the table's on/under)

It has been proposed in the literature that "location is expressed in Gbe languages not by prepositions but by nouns referring to location which are possessed by the things they locate" (Fabb 1992a: 13). Though the intuition underlying Fabb's proposal seems correct, an analysis of the Gungbe (or possibly all Gbe) postnominal morpheme in terms of nouns is not tenable. For instance, sequences (2a–b) show that unlike lexical nouns, none of these elements can occur in isolation with the specificity marker or be modified. In addition, the Gungbe locational morphemes constitute a closed class, a typical property of functional elements in Abney's (1987) approach. In the present · study, the Gungbe locational morphemes are understood as functional categories that express a kind of possessive relation, as shown by the literal interpretation (table's on) assigned to example (1). This need not mean, though, that such items may not derive from nouns.

(2)   a.   *jí / glɔ́   lɔ́
              On/under   Spf[+def]
       b.   *jí / glɔ́   xóxó
              On/under   old

In light of the discussion on the Gungbe D-system, we can a priori account for the surface word order manifested in (1) by hypothesizing a licensing condition that universally postulates that, at the appropriate level of representation, the complement of a category P must be in spec-head relation with the head P. This exactly expresses the kind of possessive relation that exists between the nominal complement and the postnominal morpheme. Notice that if we were to formulate this relation in terms of (some variant of) case assignment, the licensing condition would be consistent with Chomsky's (1992) proposal that all case assignment is licensed through as spec-head agreement relation.

        Assuming that languages may vary with respect to the level of application of the licensing condition (i.e., overt vs. covert syntax), the DP-P order found in Gungbe can be regarded as a consequence of DP complement movement to the specifier position of the head P. To some extent, this amounts to saying that the Gungbe elements such as (*jí* 'on'; *glɔ́* 'under'; *mè* 'inside'; *dé* 'at', *kpá* 'beside', etc.) are types of prepositions. But Gungbe differs from other prepositional languages such as French and English because it requires that the head preposition and its complement be in a spec-head configuration in overt syntax. Instead, English and French seem to adopt an LF strategy and thus display the order Preposition-DP complement. On the basis of the present analysis, the Gungbe example (1) could be assigned the two structures in (3). The representation under (3a) represents the underlying structure and (3b) illustrates the surface structure.

(3)   a.   PP

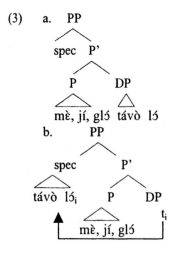

This analysis leads to two possible predictions:

1. Gungbe is prepositional but exclusively manifests contexts where DP complements precede the preposition (due to DP-movement);

2. Gungbe displays contexts where the DP complements precede or follow the preposition. But these two contexts are in complementary distribution and there shouldn't be any case where the DP complement would surface between two preposition-like elements, one preceding and the other following.

As I will show, neither of these predictions holds, suggesting that the Gungbe case is more complex than it might have appeared in previous discussion. Starting from the first prediction, it is certainly not the case that Gungbe exclusively manifests DP-P word order. Sentence (4a) clearly shows that the language also exhibits constructions where the DP complement immediately follows a prepositional element. As indicated by ungrammatical (4b), nothing can intervene between the prepositional element and the DP complement, a piece of evidence that they might belong to the same syntactic category, or else share a close syntactic relation, for instance, the type of relation that establishes between a head and its complement (Rizzi 1990). Unlike postnominal morphemes, the Gungbe prepositions generally encode a direction, an addressee, a recipient, and so on.

(4)   a.   Kòfí zé   kwé   xlán   Àsíbá
           Kofi take-Perf   money   Prep   Asiba
           'Kofi sent money to Asiba'

      b. *Kòfí zé   kwé   xlán   sò   Àsíbá
           Kofi take-Perf   money Prep   yesterday   Asiba
           'Kofi sent money to Asiba yesterday'

The second prediction is also wrong, since Gungbe has the peculiarity of exhibiting constructions where the DP complement appears in between two elements that can qualify as prepositions if one were to adopt the prior analysis. In example (5a) for instance, the noun *távò* 'table' immediately follows the preposition *dó* and immediately precedes the morpheme *jí*. Notice also that no element can intervene between the preposition and the noun (5b). The same holds true of (5c), where the intervening element between the nominal complement and the postnominal morpheme leads to ungrammaticality.

(5)   a   Àsíbá zé   kwé   dó   távò   ló   jí
          Asiba take-Perf   money Prep   table $Spf_{[+def]}$ Post
          'Asiba put the money on the specific table'

      b *Àsíbá zé   kwé   dó   sò   távò ló   jí
          Asiba take-Perf money Prep   yesterday table $Spf_{[+def]}$ Post

      c *Àsíbá zé   kwé   dó   távò   ló   sò   jí
          Asiba take-Perf money Prep   table $Spf_{[+def]}$ yesterday   Post

The existence of constructions like (5a) in Gungbe leads to the natural question of the function of prepositions and postnominal morphemes in the language. Are we confronted with a type of serial construction, or do prepositions and postnominal morphemes constitute two different elements playing two distinct syntactic roles?

Having observed that prepositional elements like *xlán, dó, ná* precede a nominal complement (6a) and occur in a surface position corresponding to that of the second verb in a serial verb construction, a number of linguists working on Kwa languages propose that these morphemes are 'verbal elements' that could be qualified as function words or verbids (Westermann 1930; Ansre 1966a, b). Compare, for example, the serial verb construction (6b) and sentence (4a), repeated here as (6c) for convenience.

(6) a. Àsíbá   tón   són   *(cócì)
         Asiba   get-Perf   Prep   church
         'Asiba went out from church'
     b. Àsíbá   kùn   mótò   yì   Kútònù
         Asiba   drive-Perf   car   go   Cotonou
         'Asiba drove the car to Cotonou'
     c. Kòfí zé   kwé   xlán   Àsíbá
         Kofi take-Perf   money   Prep   Asiba
         'Kofi sent money to Asiba'

The analysis of prepositions in terms of function words, or verbids, was grounded on the hypothesis that West African languages lack a prepositional category and use serial verb constructions[26] as a means of circumvention of such deficiency. Though so-called verbids were considered close to verbs, it was admitted that they constitute a different lexical class, because they also display other non-verbal properties (e.g., they cannot co-occur with tense or aspect markers; see Westermann 1930; Ansre 1966a; Lefebvre 1990; and references cited there for the discussion).

One major drawback of this analysis is that the so-called verbids never occur as main predicates of a clause, contrary to the second verb of a serial verb construction. This is illustrated by the contrast between the grammatical (7a) as opposed to the ungrammatical (7b).

(7) a. Àsíbá   yì   Kútònù
         Asiba   go-Perf   Cotonou
         'Asiba went to Cotonou'
     b. *Kòfí   xlán   Àsíbá
         Kofi   Prep   Asiba

Notice further that certain verbs select a closed class of verbs with which they can enter into serial verb constructions. For example, the verb *hèn* 'hold' can be combined with *yì* 'go', *wá* 'come', *gò* 'return' as exemplified in (8a) but not with *hòn* 'flee' as in

(8b). Yet sentences (8c–d) show that *hὲn* can freely occur with prepositions like *sɔ́n* 'from', *ná* 'for'.

(8) a. Ján   hὲn   kwɛ́   yì /   wá /   gɔ̀
         John   hold-Perf   money go   come   return
         'John went/ came back/ returned with some money'

     b. *Ján   hὲn   kwɛ́   hɔ̀n
         John   hold-Perf   money flee
         'John fled with the money'

     c. Ján   hὲn   kwɛ́   ná   mi
         John   hold-Perf   money Prep 1sg
         'John kept some money for me'

     d. Ján   hὲn   kwɛ́   sɔ̀n   yòvótòmὲ
         John   hold-Perf   money Prep   Europe
         'John brought money from Europe'

If it is true that such prepositional elements are verbids, then we would be forced to assume that verbs like *hὲn* 'hold' also select a special class of verbids with which they can form series (see da Cruz 1993 for the discussion). Such a distinction seems rather superfluous, since it tells us nothing about why the so-called verbids invariably occur in a fixed position to the right of the verb they are combined with.

Instead of pursuing this analysis, I will assume that the Gungbe prepositions and postnominal morphemes are instantiations of two different syntactic categories. The former are involved in case assignment, just like French or English prepositions, while the latter are nominalizing heads that take DPs as complement.

For example, the following focus constructions show that in case of movement, the Gungbe postnominal morphemes (i.e., *mὲ, jí, glɔ́*, etc.) must move together with their DP complement to the left of the focus marker *wὲ* (9a).[27] On the other hand, the Gungbe prepositions (i.e., *ɖó, ná, xlán*, etc.) never undergo such a movement: they must stay in situ (9b). In other words, the postnominal morphemes behave like determiners because they cannot be separated from their complements (9a'). Conversely, the Gungbe prepositions must be stranded when movement arises (9b'). When a preposition and a postnominal morpheme co-occur, only the latter can be affected by movement of the DP complement, as illustrated in (9c).

(9) a.   távò lɔ́   jí   wὲ   Àsíbá   xɛ́   —
          table $Spf_{[+def]}$ Post   Foc   Asiba   climb-Perf
          'Asiba climbed ON THE SPECIFIC TABLE'

     a'. *távò   lɔ́   wὲ   Àsíbá   xɛ́   —   jí
          table $Spf_{[+def]}$ Foc   Asiba   climb-Perf   Post

     b.   Àsíbá   wὲ   Kòfí   zé   kwɛ́   xlán   —
          Asiba   Foc   Kofi   take-Perf   money Prep
          'Kofi sent money to ASIBA'

b'. *xlán   Àsíba   wè   Kòfí   zé   kwέ
    Prep   Asiba   Foc   Kofi   take-Perf   money

c. távò lɔ́   jí   wè   Àsíba   zé   kwέ   ɖó   —
    table Spf[+def] Post Foc   Asiba   take-Perf money Prep
    'Asiba put the money ON THE SPECIFIC TABLE'

In sentence (10a), the verb fɔ́n 'stand-up' immediately precedes the prepositional phrase sɔ́n zàn lɔ́ jí 'from the bed'. As shown by (10b–c), it is always possible to insert an adverb (10b) or a direct object (10c) between the verb and the prepositional phrase when the latter is headed by a preposition. However, such strategy is not possible when the internal argument is headed by a postnominal morpheme. Ungrammatical (10d–e) strongly suggest that there exists an adjacency constraint that holds on the verb and the phrase headed by the postnominal morpheme,[28] since no element can intervene between them.

(10) a. mì   fɔ́n   sɔ́n   zàn   lɔ́   jí
          2pl   stand-up-Inj   Prep   bed   Spf[+def] Post
          'Get out from the specific bed'

      b. mì   fɔ́n   hàɖòkpólɔ́   sɔ́n   zàn   lɔ́   jí
          2pl   stand-up-Inj immediately Prep   bed   Spf[+def] Post
          'Get out immediately from the specific bed'

      c. mì   fɔ́n   vì   lὲ   sɔ́n   zàn   lɔ́   jí
          2pl   stand-up-Inj kids Num   Prep   bed   Spf[+def] Post
          'Get the kids out from the specific bed'

      d. *Kòfí   bíɔ́   dὲdὲ   mótò   mὲ
          Kofi   enter-Perf   slowly   car   Post
          'Kofi entered the car slowly'

      e. *Kòfí   zé   ɖó   távò   jí   yòvózὲ lέ
          Kofi   take-Perf Prep   table   Post   orange Num
          'Kofi put the oranges on the table'

The adjacency facts illustrated in (10) seem to indicate that postnominal phrases (PPs) occur in a governed position, in the sense that they are exclusively licensed in argument or case positions. The fact that PPs may occur in subject positions further supports this analysis (11).

(11) tó   mὲ   nɔ̀   klú   mi
      ear   Post   Hab scratch   me
      'My ear makes me itch'

As a consequence, I propose that the Gungbe postnominal morphemes are 'light Ps' in the sense that they fail to assign case. Instead, they function as (nominalizer) heads and force the DP they select to appear in case or governed positions. Consequently, they are in complementary distribution with normal DPs, as shown by sentences under (12). In sentences (12a–b), the verb selects a DP-complement and a PP-complement, respectively. The ungrammatical sentence (12c) indicates that the two complements cannot be realized simultaneously, unless we insert a preposition as shown by the grammatical sentence (12d).

(12) a.   Kòfí   kpón   wémà   lɔ́
           Kofi   look-Perf   book   Spf$_{[+def]}$
           'Kofi looked at the specific book'
      b.   Kòfí   kpón   távò   lɔ́   jí
           Kofi   look-Perf   table   Spf$_{[+def]}$ Post
           'Kofi looked on the specific table'
      c.   *Kòfí kpón   wémà   lɔ́   távò   lɔ́   jí
           Kofi look-Perf   book   Spf$_{[+def]}$ table   Spf$_{[+def]}$ Post
      d.   Kòfí kpón   wémà   lɔ́   tò   távò   lɔ́   jí
           Kofi look-Perf   book   Spf$_{[+def]}$ Prep   table   Spf$_{[+def]}$ Post
           'Kofi looked at the specific book on the specific table'

Both object DPs and *P*Ps can precede the verb in imperfective constructions. Sentences (13a–b) are instances of perfective constructions involving an object DP and an object *P*P, respectively. As exemplified by their imperfective counterparts (13'–b'), the DP and *P*P objects must follow the imperfective marker *tò* and immediately precede the verb.

(13) a.   Kòfí nù   sìn   lɔ́
           Kofi drink-Perf   water   Spf$_{[+def]}$
           'Kofi drunk the specific water'
      a'. Kòfí tò   sìn   lɔ́   nù
           Kofi Imperf   water   Spf$_{[+def]}$ drink
           'Kofi is drinking the specific water'
      b.   Kòfí xé   távò   lɔ́   jí
           Kofi climb-Perf   table   Spf$_{[+def]}$ Post
           'Kofi climbed on the specific table'
      b'. Kòfí   tò   távò   lɔ́   jí   xê
           Kofi   Imperf   table   Spf$_{[+def]}$ Post   climb- NR
           'Kofi is climbing on the specific table'

As I discussed in chapter 6, section 6.2, suppose the position immediately to the right of the imperfective marker and to the left of the verb corresponds to an argument position, [spec AspP3]. Once again, we are led to the conclusion that the Gungbe *P*Ps have the same distribution as DPs, unlike the Gungbe Prepositional Phrases (PPs). In this respect, Collins (p.c.) suggested that the *P*Ps that can move to the preverbal position are nominal phrases. They are arguments of the verb and they have a case feature to check. In the case of prenominal PPs, they never move to the preverbal position, precisely because they do not have any nominal characteristics. A fairly correct generalization here is that *P*Ps that move to the preverbal position are the ones where case is assigned in the same direction as in DPs, that is, to the left of D or *P*. Even though I don't want to claim that movement to the preverbal position in imperfectives is case-driven, we can explain the distribution of *P*Ps by saying that 'light Ps' (*P*) are nominal heads that specify the nominal complement for the values *jí* 'on', *glɔ́* 'under', *mè* 'inside', *kpá* 'beside', and so on. Granting that the nominal heads are similar to determiners, I further propose that the head *P°* requires a spec-head configuration. As a result, the DP complement must move in syntax to [spec *P*P] to be licensed. The Gungbe *P*Ps can be represented as in (14a).

(14)   a.   *P*P

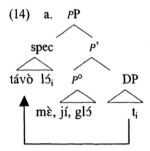

In order to account for the Gungbe prepositions, I propose that they constitute the Gungbe syntactic category Preposition. They are involved in case assignment and can take a nominal complement (DP or *P*P) to which a specific thematic role is assigned. For example *xlán* is addressee, *ɖó* locative, *ná* beneficiary (see Lord 1973; Lefebvre 1990, 1995a; da Cruz 1993; Tossa 1994).

The co-occurrence of 'light Ps' and prepositions is straightforwardly accounted for in this framework, since *P*Ps are similar to ordinary DPs. They can survive only in case positions, and therefore belong to the class of typical categories that are selected as complement of a preposition. I thus propose that the Gungbe PPs can be represented as in (14b).

(14)   b.   PP

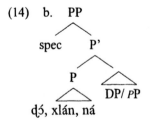

Recapitulation

The data presented in this appendix clearly indicate that Gungbe is not a postpositional language in the traditional sense. It is rather a language that manifests postnominal heads, which take DPs as their complements. Accordingly, the DP-*P* order found in such sequences is analyzed in terms of movement of the DP-complement to [spec *P*P] in overt syntax, in order to check the nominal features such as [under], [inside], [beside]. On the other hand, Gungbe manifests genuine prepositions, which are involved in case assignment. These prepositions can take both DPs and *P*Ps as complement.

4

The Syntax of Pronouns

Assuming Abney's (1987) analysis that pronouns are determiners, the question arises how to extend the analysis proposed in chapter 3 to the Gungbe pronominal system. In this chapter, I show that the split-D hypothesis—as it is formulated here—helps to account for the Gungbe pronouns. As convincingly argued by Ritter (1992, 1995), a split-D hypothesis (i.e., the existence of D° and Num° in languages such as Gungbe, Fongbe, Hebrew, Haitian Creole, etc.) presupposes "the existence of at least two classes of pronouns, those of the category D°, and those that involve the category Num°" (Ritter 1992: 1).

In this respect, section 4.1 discusses current theoretical analysis of the pronominal system cross-linguistically (Kayne 1975, 1991; Abney 1987; Ritter 1991, 1992, 1995; Cardinaletti 1994; Agbedor 1996; Cardinaletti & Starke 1999; Zribi-Hertz & Mbolatianavalona 1997, 1999, Koopman 2000a). Extending this analysis to the Gungbe data, section 4.2 demonstrates that the Gungbe pronominal system can be characterized in terms of a tripartition that postulates the existence of strong, weak, and clitic pronouns. Strong pronouns are like lexical DPs and project a similar internal structure. Weak pronouns have a deficient internal structure because they lack some of the categories that are normally present in lexical DPs. They project the functional projections to which number and person specifications are associated. As for clitic pronouns, they are considered intransitive Ds in the sense of Abney (1987). Contrary to weak pronouns, they are not endowed with the category that is responsible for number specification, which is why they are specified only for person. Section 4.3 concludes the chapter.

4.1 THEORETICAL BACKGROUND

Natural languages exhibit a contrast between the so-called strong and deficient personal pronouns. For instance, these two classes display different lexical forms and syntactic properties. Since Kayne's (1975) analysis of French personal pronouns, it has generally been assumed that strong pronouns pattern like lexical DPs, while deficient pronouns must appear in a derived position, in overt syntax. As Kayne (1975) proposed for the description of the French pronominal system, there are four major properties that help distinguish between strong and deficient (or clitic pronouns). First, strong pronouns may be cleft, while clitic pronouns cannot (1a–b), (see Cardinaletti 1994; Ritter 1995; Agbebor 1996; Zribi-Hertz & Mbolatianavalona 1997, 1999; Cardinaletti & Starke 1999).

(1) a. c'est lui   qui   parle
         it is 3sg   who   talk-Pres-3sg
         'It is he who is talking'
     b. *c'est   il   qui   parle
         it is   3sg-CL   who   talk-Pres-3sg

Second, coordination is possible with strong pronouns, but not with clitic pronouns.

(2) a. lui   et   Mari   parlent
         3sg   and   Marie   talk-Pres-3pl
         'He and Marie are talking'
     b. *il   et   Marie   parlent
         3sg-CL   and   Marie   talk-Pres-3pl

Third, strong pronouns can be modified, while clitic pronouns resist modification.

(3) a. lui   aussi/seul   parle
         3sg   too/alone   talk-Pres-3sg
         'He too/alone is talking'
     b. *il   aussi/seul   parle
         3sg-CL   too/alone   talk-Pres-3sg

Fourth, strong pronouns can bear contrastive stress, but clitic pronouns cannot.

(4) a. LUI   parle
         3sg   talk-Pres-3sg
         'He is talking'
     b. *IL   parle
         3sg-CL   talk-Pres-3sg

More recently, Cardinaletti (1994) and Cardinaletti and Starke (1999), among others, pointed out that Kayne's (1975) generalization expresses the fact that pronouns fall into two distinct classes. They first showed that there is a systematic correlation between the first property and the feature [+human]. For example, pronouns diverge radically with respect to coordination and reference, when considered from the perspective of the feature [+human]. Consider the Italian third person plural nominative pronouns in (5).

(5)   a.   Loro   (e quelle accanto)   sono   troppo   alte
       b.   Esse   (*e quelle accanto)   sono   troppo   alte
             3pl-NOM   (and those besides)   are   too   tall

In sentence (5a) the pronoun *loro* is coordinated, but its referent must be specified [+human]. Conversely, example (5b) shows that *esse* resists coordination. *Esse* is not sensitive to the features [±human] and may refer to both non-human and human entities. According to the authors, these facts suggest the existence of two distinct classes of pronouns: class (A) includes those pronouns that may be coordinated but can have only a [+human] referent; class (B) includes pronouns that resist conjunction but refer to [±human] entities. Many languages exhibit similar subtle distinction with respect to certain pronouns. A case in point is the French third person plural feminine nominative pronoun *elles*:

(6)   a.   Elles   sont   trop   grandes
       b.   Elles et celles d'à côté   sont   trop   grandes
             3pl-NOM and those besides   are   too   tall

In sentence (6a), the pronoun *elles* 'they' can have a [±human] referent, but in (6b) where coordination applies, the non-human reading is discarded and only a [+human] referent can qualify as possible antecedent. This particular behavior of personal pronouns could be understood if one assumes the existence, at a more abstract level, of a two class-system. Cardinaletti and Starke (1999) elaborate on Kayne's (1975) analysis and propose that elements of class (A) represent strong pronouns, while class (B) includes deficient pronouns. The labels 'strong' and 'deficient' are interpreted in terms of internal structure and morphological richness: strong pronouns are regarded as involving more internal syntactic structure and a richer morphology than deficient pronouns.

Cross-linguistic data confirm the distinction between strong and deficient pronouns. The Italian sentences under (7) show that strong pronouns display the same distribution as lexical DPs. They can occur in normal DP positions: they are always realized in postverbal position (7a). Instead, deficient pronouns surface in a preverbal position (7b).

(7)   a.   Conosco   lui/*lo
             I know   him

    b.   *Lui/lo   conosco --

Strong pronoun can be topic, or left dislocated, unlike deficient pronouns. Consider the following French examples.

(8)   a.   Lui,   Marie   l'épousera
           3Msg   Marie   him-marry-Fut-3sg
      b.   *il,   Marie   l'épousera
           3Msg   Marie   him-marry-Fut-3sg

In addition, strong pronouns can appear in isolation, unlike deficient pronouns. In the following Gungbe sentences, the first person strong pronoun *nyé* in (9b) can be used in isolation as an answer to question (9a). But the first person deficient pronoun *ún* never surfaces in such context, hence the ungrammatical (9b').

(9)   a.   Ménú   wè   tɔ́n ?
          who   Foc   go-out-Perf
          'Who went out?'
      b.   Nyé   b'.   *ún
          1S-sg   1W-sg
          'Me'   'I'

In light of Kayne (1975), Cardinaletti and Starke (1999), and subsequent work, the Italian, French, and Gungbe data presented in (1–9) seem to indicate that the distribution of strong versus deficient pronouns cannot be reduced to typological differences or language specificity. Instead, the distributive properties of pronouns express the fact that strong pronouns are licensed in canonical DP positions, while deficient pronouns must occur in derived positions.

     Strong pronouns are like lexical DPs in that they have a semantic content similar to that of nouns and must be referential. They cannot be used either as expletives or as non-referential elements (Cardinaletti & Starke 1999). They must have a referent (recall they are specified as [+human]), and they can be coordinated, focused, or topicalized. No such property is available for deficient pronouns. They cannot be coordinated, focused, or topicalized. In addition, they have no independent referent and therefore pick [±human] entities and must be discourse-anaphoric. Under Kayne's (1975) generalization, DP-like pronominal elements are referred to as strong pronouns. On the contrary, the deficient elements form the class of weak and clitic pronouns.

     A closer look at the class of deficient pronouns led Cardinaletti and Starke (1999) to the conclusion that this class could be further subdivided into two groups: weak pronouns and clitic pronouns. This gives rise to a tripartition in terms of strong, weak, and clitic pronouns. The tripartition is based on facts like those in French examples (10), where it appears that the strong pronoun *lui* 'he' and its deficient counterpart *il* 'he' share similar properties but also differ from certain perspectives. On the one hand, they both occur in subject position and can be deleted under ellipsis (10a–b).

(10)   a.   Lui aime les choux mais -- ne les mange que cuit ?
       b.   Il aime les choux mais -- ne les mange que cuit ?
            'He likes cauliflower but -- not them eat other than cooked'

On the other hand, sentences (11a–b) neatly show that these pronouns are also opposed to each other, since *lui* 'he' allows coordination while *il* 'he' disallows it.

(11)   a.   Lui et son frère ont accepté ?
       b.   *il et son frère ont accepté ?
            'He and his brother have agreed?'

French exhibits two weak pronouns *il* 'he': one being weaker or more deficient than the other. Put differently, French involves both weak and clitic pronouns *il* 'he'. A fact that supports this idea is that the weak form, *il*, used in (10b), resists subject inversion, while its homophonous clitic counterpart doesn't (12a–c).

(12)   a.   *Aime-t-il les choux mais ne les mange que cuit ?
            like-he cauliflower but not them eat other than cooked
       b.   *Ont-il et son frère accepté ?
            have-he and his brother accepted
       c.   A-t-il accepté le marché ?
            have-he accepted the deal
            'Did he accept the deal ?'

As argued by Cardinaletti and Starke, weak pronouns are intermediate between strong and clitic pronouns in the sense that they share some distributional properties with the first, while displaying deficiency characteristics of the second, such as the lack of coordination. The authors thus propose that there is a ranking: clitic pronouns are deficient compared to weak pronouns, which in turn are deficient compared to strong pronouns:

(13)   clitic   <   weak   <   strong

Assuming that deficiency implies lack of a functional category, natural language pronominal systems can be represented as in (14), adapted from Cardinaletti and Starke (1999). In this representation, L stands for lexical category, (see also Ritter 1991, 1992, 1995; Zribi-Hertz & Mbolatianavalona 1997, 1999).

(14)   a. $[_{CPL} [_{C°L} [_{\Sigma PL} [_{\Sigma°L} [_{IPL} [_{I°L} [_{LP}]]]]]]]$ [Strong Pronouns]
       b. $[_{\Sigma PL} [_{\Sigma°L} [_{IPL} [_{I°L} [_{LP}]]]]]$ [Weak Pronouns]
       c. $[_{IPL} [_{I°L} [_{LP}]]]$ [Clitic Pronouns]

Pronouns are represented as including a CP projection whose head C° is responsible for case and referentiality (Giusti 1992; Cardinaletti 1994), a Polarity/Force projection ΣP whose head Σ° hosts support morphemes[1] (Laka 1990; Cardinaletti 1994) and an inflectional (or agreement) projection IP (Cinque 1994, 1996).

Strong pronouns have the CP projection and display distributional properties of lexical DPs with respect to Kayne's (1975) generalization. Weak pronouns, on the other hand, lack the CP layer and must therefore surface in special derived positions. Clitic pronouns are the weakest of all, since they lack the superior layer of weak elements, that is, ΣP. They too must move in syntax to be licensed. Though their distribution across languages remains rather puzzling, it is traditionally assumed that clitics occur in a head position (Rizzi 1986; Sportiche 1993; Starke 1993; Friedemann & Siloni 1997).

4.2 THE GUNGBE PERSONAL PRONOUNS

The following table is an inventory of the Gungbe personal pronouns. Column 2 includes the so-called strong pronouns, while columns 3 and 4 represent nominative and accusative deficient pronouns, respectively. Column 5 displays the Gungbe possessive pronouns.

Gungbe personal pronouns				
Pers/Numb	Strong forms	Weak forms		Possessives
		Nominative	Accusative	
1sg	nyè	(ù)n	mi	cé
2sg	jè	à	wè	tòwè
3sg	éɔ̀ (úɔ̀)	é	e (ɛ - i)	étɔ̀n
1pl	mílɛ́	mí	mí	mítɔ̀n
2pl	mìlɛ́	mì	mì	mìtɔ̀n
3pl	yélɛ́	yé	yé	yétɔ̀n

4.2.1 Morphology

A first observation that could be made with respect to the Gungbe personal pronouns is that the possessive pronouns display only two genuine forms: first and second person singular cé and tòwè, respectively. All other forms are derived by a combination of weak pronouns and the Gungbe second possessive marker tɔ̀n. I do not discuss possessives in this study, but see Brousseau and Lumsden (1992), Kinyalolo (1995), and Aboh (2002) for the discussion on genitive constructions in Gbe.

The Gungbe strong forms have only one set of realizations. They keep the same shape whether they occur in an A-bar left dislocated position (15a), or as

complement of a preposition, that is, in a case position (15b). See also section
4.2.2.3 on the distribution of strong pronouns.

(15) a. nyè   yà,   ùn   ná   yì
          1S-sg   Top   1W-sg   Fut   leave
          'As for me, I will leave'
      b. Dótù   ɖɔ   xó   ná   nyè
          Dotu   speak-Perf   word   to   1S-sg
          'Dotu spoke to me'

Instead, weak pronouns (i.e., first, second, and third person singular) manifest two
different sets of forms with respect to nominative and accusative. Note, however,
that the plural forms remain identical. Furthermore, the weak third person singular
accusative has different allophones, as it cliticizes on to the preceding verb or
preposition, leading to an alternation into [i], [ɛ], or their respective nasalized
counterparts (16).[2]

(16) a. yé   gbà   e   yé   gbɛ̀
          3W-pl break-Perf   3W-sg   ⟹   3W-pl break-Perf-3W-sg
          'They broke it'
      b. yé   hù   e   yé   hù-ì
          3W-pl kill-Perf   3W-sg   ⟹   3W-pl kill-Perf-3W-sg
          'They killed it'
      c. yé   hì   e   yé   hì-ì
          3W-pl smoke-Perf   3W-sg   ⟹   3W-pl smoke-Perf-3W-sg
          'They smoked it'
      d. yé   xɔ   e   yé   xɔ-ɛ̀
          3W-sg buy-Perf   3W-sg   ⟹   3W-pl buy-Perf-3W-sg
          'They bought it'
      e. yé   zɛ̀   e   yé   zɛ̀-ɛ̀
          3W-pl cleave-Perf   3W-sg   ⟹   3W-pl cleave-Perf-3W-sg
          'They cleft it'

When the final vowel of the verb is [o] or [e], no change arises, as shown by (16f):

(16) f. yé   xɔ/zé   è
          3W-pl   beat/take-Perf   3W-sg
          'They beat/took it'

In discussing the Gbe vowel harmony process specific to clitics, certain authors (da
Cruz & Avolonto 1993; Agbedor 1996) have proposed that these languages involve
phonetic clitics. They thus argued that the Gbe clitics are not subject to movement
operations like the Romance clitics. Instead, the Gbe clitics are licensed in the
internal argument position, immediately to the right of the verb. Such a static

analysis of clitics also presupposes that the Gbe languages do not involve verb movement. I demonstrate, in section 4.2.2.7 (see also chapter 6), that this analysis is not tenable. I therefore propose a more dynamic analysis that assumes both verb movement and clitic movement in the Gbe languages.

The Gungbe strong pronouns manifest a morphologically richer form than the weak pronouns. For example, the plural forms of the strong pronouns are a combination of the weak forms plus the plural marker as in *mílɛ́* 'we', *mìlɛ́* 'you', *yélɛ́* 'they'. A possible conclusion here is that strong pronouns are similar to lexical DPs, in that they involve a full D-system (i.e., DP > NumP > ΣP; see Ritter 1991, 1995; Cardinaletti 1994; Cardinaletti & Starke 1999; Aboh 2001d). This would mean that the morpheme *yé* is merged in N°, where the pronoun *yélɛ́* derives by ΣP-internal snowballing movement, followed by subsequent cyclical ΣP-movement to [spec NumP] and [spec DP] to check number and person specifications respectively.

On the other hand, I suggest that the Gungbe weak pronouns lack ΣP. They are directly inserted in Num° where they encode the feature [±plural] and subsequently move to D° to check person specifications. This naturally accounts for the fact that these pronouns are incompatible with the number marker *lɛ́* and the specificity marker *lɔ́*, unlike the strong pronouns. The weak pronouns and the nominal left peripheral markers compete for the same position. Note that the plural nominative/accusative forms *mí* 'we', *mì* 'you', *yé* 'they' do not involve the plural marker. Granting this, the Gungbe pronominal system exhibits the two classes that I identified as strong and deficient in section 4.2.1. Under the split-D hypothesis proposed in chapter 3, the distinction between strong pronouns and weak pronouns reduces to whether ΣP projects or not. Put differently, deficient pronouns involve only the nominal left periphery, that is, the locus of discourse-linked specifications. This correctly explains why the deficient pronouns must be discourse-anaphoric. In the following sections, I further discuss the distribution of the Gungbe pronouns and show that the deficient pronouns do not form a homogeneous class. In this regard, I propose an analysis in terms of a three-type pronominal system including strong, weak, and clitic pronouns (Cardinaletti & Starke 1999, Aboh 2001d). As a first step toward this analysis, let's see some distributional differences between strong and weak pronouns.

4.2.2 Some distributional differences

In this section, I will essentially rely on Kayne's (1975) generalization, as well as Cardinaletti and Starke's (1999) analysis of pronouns (see also Agbedor 1996 for the discussion on the Ewegbe pronouns). The distribution of the Gungbe strong and weak pronouns will be discussed on the basis of their structural relation with a verb; their ability to be modified, focused, or topicalized; their capacity to appear in isolation and to enter coordinate structures; and finally their distribution in imperfective/prospective constructions. In so doing, I will show how the split-D hypothesis helps account for the Gungbe pronominal system.

4.2.2.1 Structural relation with the verb

The Gungbe weak personal pronouns can occur in subject or object positions. Accordingly, they are in complementary distribution with other subject and object DPs as illustrated in (17a–b) and (17c–d), respectively.

(17) a. ùn / à / é / mí / mì / yé   ná   yì
         1W-sg/2W-sg/3W-sg/1W-pl/2W-pl/3W-pl   Fut   leave
         'I, you, he (s)he, we, you, they will leave'
     b. Kòfí (*é)   ná   yì
         Kofi 3W-sg Fut   leave
         'Kofi he will leave'
     c. Dótù dín   mi / wè / i / mí / mì / yé
         Dotu look-Perf   1W-sg/2W-sg/3W-sg/1W-pl/2W-pl/3W-pl
         'Dotu looked for me, you, him, us, you, them'
     d. Dótù   dín   Kòfí   (*i)
         Dotu   look-Perf   Kofi   3W-sg
         'Dotu looked for Kofi-(him)'

Strong forms are excluded from ordinary subject and object positions (18), except when they bear contrastive stress, as illustrated by the grammatical (18c). The ungrammatical sentence (18d) suggests that when stressed, the strong pronouns compete with lexical DPs for the same position.[3] Conversely, the ungrammatical example (18e) indicates that the Gungbe weak pronouns cannot be stressed.

(18) a. *nyè / jè / éɔ̀ / mílé / mìlé / yélé   ná   yì
         1S-sg/ 2S-sg/3S-sg/1S-pl/2S-pl/3S-pl   Fut   leave
     b. *Dótù   dín   nyè / jè / éɔ̀ / mílé / mìlé / yélé
         Dotu   look-Perf   1S-sg/2S-sg/3S-sg/1S-pl/2S-pl/3S-pl
     c. nyè   ná   yì
         1S-sg Fut   leave
         'I (not you) will leave'
     d. *Kòfí   éɔ̀   ná   yì
         Kofi   3S-sg Fut   leave
     e. *ùn   ná   yì
         1W-sg   Fut   leave

Observe also that the Gungbe strong pronouns occur in genitive constructions involving the genitive case marker sín. As one can see from the phrases under (19), this genitive marker selects only for strong pronouns or lexical DPs (19a–b). The ungrammatical example (19c) indicates that *sín* never co-occurs with weak pronouns.

(19) a. Dótù   sín   àkwé
          Dotu   Poss   money
          'Dotu's money'
      b. éɔ̀   sín   àkwé
          1S-sg   Poss   money
          'His money'
      c. *é   sín   àkwé
          1W-sg   Poss   money
          'His money'

4.2.2.2 Ability to be modified

Just as lexical DPs, the Gungbe strong pronouns can be modified by noun phrase internal modifiers, that is, adjectives, and demonstratives (20a), as well as quantifiers that can modify the whole noun phrase (20b).

(20) a. jè   xóxó   éhè   ná   yì
          2S-sg   old   Dem   Fut   leave
          'You old   this   will   leave'
      b. nyè   có   ná   yì
          1S-sg   alone   Fut   leave
          'I alone will leave'

It is interesting to note that, in some contexts, strong pronouns can co-occur with the specificity marker *lɔ́* (21a) on a par with common nouns or proper names (21b–c). Similarly, strong pronouns can be relativized as illustrated by the examples (21d–e); see Longobardi (1994, 2001) for the discussion on proper names.

(21) a. jè   éhè   lɔ́,   àdɔ̀   wè   ná   hù   wè
          2S-sg Dem Spf$_{[+def]}$ greediness Foc Fut   kill   2W-sg
          'YOU [specific] THIS, you will die from greediness'
      b. òví   lɔ́   wè   ùn   tò   díndîn
          child   Spf$_{[+def]}$ Foc 1W-sg Imperf search-search
          'I'm looking for THE SPECIFIC CHILD'
      c. Kòfí   lɔ́   wè   ùn   tò   díndîn
          Kofi   Spf$_{[+def]}$ Foc 1W-sg Imperf search-search
          'I'm looking for THAT KOFI'
          [e.g., Kofi did something wrong and I badly want to see him]
      d. Kòfí ɖě   tà   tò   ɖùɖù   lɔ́   nίὲ   yằ?
          Kofi that$_{[Rel]}$ head Prog   RED-eat Spf$_{[+def]}$ there Top-QM
          'Is that that Kofi who has headache?'

e. Jὲ   dĕ   tà   tò   dùdũ   lɔ   nîὲ   yã̀?
    2S-sg that[Rel]   head   Prog   RED-eat   Spf[+def] there Top-QM
    'Is that you who have headache?'[4]

The Gungbe weak subject and object pronouns are never modified, or realized with
the specificity marker, as exemplified by the ungrammatical examples under
(22a–c). In addition, they cannot be relativized (22d).

(22) a. *à   xóxó   éhè   ná   yì
          2W-sg   old   Dem   Fut   leave
          'You old   this   will   leave'
      b. *Dótù   ná   yrɔ́   mi   có
          Dotu   Fut   call   1W-sg   alone
          'Dotu will call me alone'
      c. *à   éhè   lɔ,   à   ná   yì
          2W-sg   Dem   Spf[+def] 2W-sg Fut   leave
          'You [specific] this you will leave'
      d. *à   dĕ   tà   tò   dùdũ   lɔ   nîὲ   yã̀?
          2W-sg that[Rel] head   Prog   red-eat Spf[+def] there Top-QM
          'Is that you who have headache?

4.2.2.3 Strong versus weak pronouns: Evidence for the split-D hypothesis

Building on the Gungbe DP-internal structure I proposed in chapter 3, I can account
for the Gungbe pronominal system by postulating that strong pronouns consist of an
articulated DP structure. This structure involves all the projections of the nominal
left periphery and inflectional system. The internal structure of the Gungbe strong
pronouns includes D° and Num°, the locus of the specificity marker and the number
marker, respectively. Recall from the discussion that all plural strong forms take the
plural marker *lέ*. The strong pronouns also involve all the functional projections
whose specifiers host the nominal modifiers (i.e., demonstratives, numerals,
adjectives, etc.). This amounts to saying that pronominal DPs corresponding to the
Gungbe strong pronouns have an articulated structure similar to that of lexical DPs
(see chapter 3).

In addition, the fact that the demonstrative *éhè* intervenes between the
strong pronoun and the specificity marker *lɔ* in (21a) strongly suggests that there is
no N-to-D movement in the Gungbe pronominal DPs.[5] If that were the case, the
pronoun should be left adjacent to the specificity marker, yielding as such
ungrammatical *jὲ lɔ éhè* 'you [specific] this'. I thus propose that, like lexical
nouns, the Gungbe strong pronouns are generated under N°. The NP then moves to
the left of the projection hosting the numeral. Afterward, the phrase pronoun-
numeral moves to the left of the demonstrative before the whole phrase pronoun-

numeral-demonstrative moves cyclically to [spec NumP], where it is specified for number, that is, [±plural], and then to [spec DP] where it is specified for person.

(23)   a.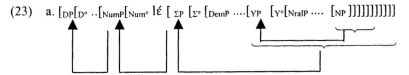

In the Gungbe strong pronouns, D° is marked for person, while Num° contains number specifications (Ritter 1992, 1995). When the pronoun is marked as [+plural], the head Num° is phonetically realized as *lέ*, as in first, second, and third person plural. But when the pronoun is specified as [-plural], Num° is occupied by a null morpheme. As for D°, the locus of person specification, it is always realized by a null morpheme (except in some limited cases where the pronoun co-occurs with the specificity marker *lɔ́*, which is inserted in D° (21a)). I then conclude that the underlying structure of the Gungbe strong pronouns can be represented as follows:

(23)   b.

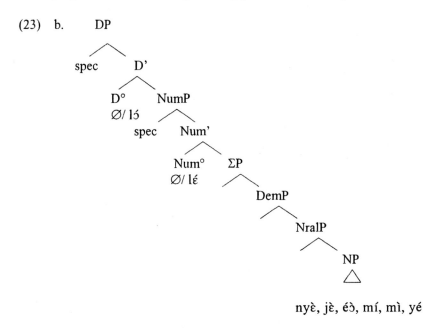

nyὲ, jὲ, éɔ̀, mí, mì, yé

An indirect argument in favor of representation (23b) is that, in Gengbe and Ewegbe, the strong plural forms appear to be a combination of a weak pronoun plus the specificity and plural markers. In his account for the Ewegbe pronouns, Agbedor (1996: 21) writes: "For the first person plural strong pronoun, we have the form *mi+la+wo* from which we derive *mi-a-wo*." The same analysis could be extended to the Gengbe first person plural strong form, which is realized as *míáwó*, literally 'we + specificity marker + plural marker'. The Gengbe case is even more telling since neither the specificity marker *á* nor the plural marker *ó* undergoes any morphological change (assuming [w] is a support morpheme).

The difference between Gungbe and these languages is that D° is not always realized in the Gungbe strong plural forms, hence the ungrammatical *mílɔ́lɛ́* 'we + specificity marker + plural marker' as opposed to the grammatical *mílɛ́* 'we + plural marker'. Yet this does not mean that D° is absent in such configurations, since it can co-occur with modified strong pronouns as in (21a), repeated here for convenience.

(21) a. jɛ̀   éhɛ̀ lɔ́,   àdɔ̀   wɛ̀ ná   hù   wɛ̀
          2S-sg Dem Spf[+def]   greediness Foc Fut   kill   2W-sg
          'You [specific] this, you will die from greediness'

In addition, the pronoun can be separated from the plural marker by intervening material such as the demonstrative, the adjective, and the specificity marker, as illustrated in (24a).

(24) a. mì   xóxó   àtɔ̀n   éhɛ̀   lɔ́   lɛ́
          2S-pl old   three Dem   Spf[+def] Num
          'These old three of you'

     b.   DP

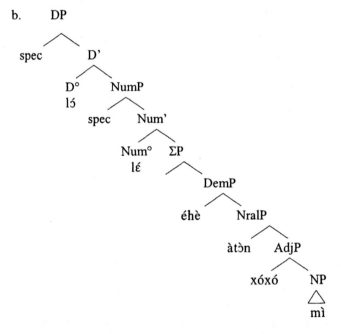

Granting the structure in (24b), the example (24a) appears as strong evidence that there is no N-to-D° movement in the Gungbe D-system. Instead, snowballing movement raises the NP pronoun to the left of the adjective, followed by the movement of the phrase pronoun-adjective to the left of the numeral. The phrase pronoun-adjective-numeral moves to [spec ΣP] to the left of the demonstrative. Subsequently the whole ΣP, that is, the phrase pronoun-adjective-numeral-demonstrative, moves cyclically through the specifier of NumP, thus finally surfacing in [spec DP], as represented in (25).

(25)

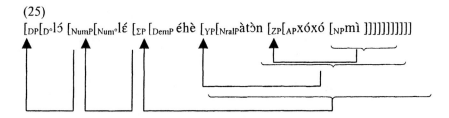

Notice in passing that an analysis in terms of N-to-D° movement would wrongly predict that the pronoun precedes the plural marker and the determiner, while adjectives, demonstratives, and numerals should remain in their base position, as exemplified by the ungrammatical example (26).

(26)	*mì	lɛ́	lɔ́	éhè	àtɔ̀n	xóxó
	2S-pl	Num	Spf$_{[+def]}$	Dem	Nral	Adj

Granting the analysis proposed here for strong pronouns, I conclude that the Gungbe weak pronouns cannot be modified because they involve a reduced internal structure. Their structural make-up lacks the projections whose specifier positions host adjectives, demonstratives, and other modifying elements. To some extent, this corresponds to Cardinaletti and Starke's (1999) analysis of deficiency in terms of 'missing structure'. A major difference though is that structural deficiency, in my term, doesn't lead to peeling off the topmost projection in the structure. Instead, deficiency is interpreted here from the perspective of less articulated structure.

In a similar vein, the impossibility of having a weak pronoun with the specificity or plural markers can be considered a consequence of the head status of weak pronouns. Let us assume that weak pronouns are 'D-elements' in the sense that they realize only the projections DP and NumP. Suppose further that weak pronouns are of the category Number where they are generated and specified for number, or [±plural]. Assuming this is the correct characterization, we can argue that the head pronoun must undergo head-to-head movement, or Num°-to-D° movement in order to check person features. The analysis proposed here straightforwardly accounts for the incompatibility of weak pronouns and modifiers, as well as the specificity and plural markers. In addition, it helps explain the nature of deficiency that characterizes weak pronouns. The Gungbe weak pronouns can therefore be attributed the underlying structure represented in (27). Observe that in a theory that allows empty nouns, we can further suggest that weak pronouns do involve an NP complement whose head is null (Carstens 1997; Panagiotidis 2000, 2001).

(27)

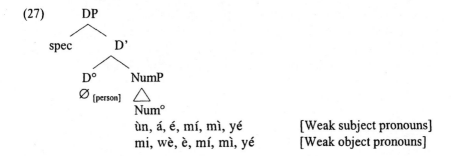

	[Weak subject pronouns]
ùn, á, é, mí, mì, yé	
mi, wè, è, mí, mì, yé	[Weak object pronouns]

4.2.2.4 The Gungbe pronouns in focus and topic constructions

Additional evidence that strong pronouns have an articulated structure like lexical DPs, while weak pronouns involve a reduced internal structure, is that the former allow for focus and topic constructions (i.e., on a par with nouns), while the latter don't. Recall from chapter 2 that focus constructions require that the focused category be fronted in a position immediately to the left of the focus marker *wè* (28a). Example (28b) shows that strong pronouns occur in this position, unlike weak pronouns (28c).

(28) a. Kòkú   wè   Dótù   ná   yró —
          Koku   Foc   Dotu   Fut   call
          'Dotu will call KOKU'
      b. nyè   wè   Dótù   ná   yró —
          1S-sg   Foc   Dotu   Fut   call
      c. *mi   wè   Dótù   ná   yró —
          1W-sg   Foc   Dotu   Fut   call
          'Dotu will call ME'

Similarly, topic constructions require movement of the topic to the left of the topic marker *yà*. The topic leaves a resumptive pronoun in IP-internal position (29a). Note, from example (29b), that strong pronouns can be topics, as opposed to weak pronouns, which resist such constructions (29c).

(29) a. Kòkú   yà,   Dótù   ná   yró - è
          Koku   Top   Dotu   Fut   call-3sg
          'As for Koku, Dotu will call him'
      b. nyè   yà   Dótù   ná   yró - mi
          1S-sg   Top   Dotu   Fut   call-1W-sg
      c. *mi   yà   Dótù   ná   yró - mi
          1W-sg   Top   Dotu   Fut   call -1W-sg
          'As for me, Dotu will call me'

The focus/topic contrast exhibited by strong and weak pronouns is confirmed by the fact that only strong pronouns can be used in isolation as an answer to questions (30a–b).

(30) a. ménú   wɛ̀   Dótù   ná   yrɔ́ --
      who   Foc   Dotu Fut   call
      'Who will Dotu call?'
  b. nyɛ̀ (*mi) wɛ̀
      1S-sg 1W-sg Foc

In addition, Gungbe manifests a question morpheme *lò* that occurs postnominally (31a). The contrast in (31b–c) indicates that only strong pronouns can precede the question marker. See Agbedor (1996) for a description and discussion of similar facts in Ewegbe.

(31) a. Kɔkú   lò ?
      Koku   QM
      'How about Koku?' or 'Where is Koku?'
  b. éɔ̀   lò ?
      3S-sg   QM
  c. *é   lò ?
      3W-sg   QM
      'How about him/her?'

The data presented so far clearly indicate that the Gungbe pronominal system involves two sets of elements. On the one hand, we have strong pronouns: *nyɛ̀ - jɛ̀ - éɔ̀ - mílɛ́ - mìlɛ́ - yélɛ́*. They are like lexical DPs, in the sense that they project a similar articulated internal structure including the D-system and the inflectional system expressed by ΣP. This correctly predicts that strong pronouns can co-occur with distinct modifiers (e.g., demonstratives, numerals, adjectives) as suggested by the representations (23b–24b). On the other hand, we have weak subject and object pronouns. They are in complementary distribution with strong pronouns: where a weak pronoun is allowed, a strong pronoun is always excluded (unless it is emphatic) and vice versa. Furthermore, weak pronouns never co-occur with demonstratives or adjectives. This leads me to the conclusion that their 'weakness' results from structural deficiency. They lack some of the categories that are normally present in strong pronouns. For example, they are deprived of the projections that host demonstratives, numerals, and adjectives. This strongly suggests that the weak pronouns do not involve the nominal inflexional system. They only project the left periphery, that is, the nominal complementizer system, which in this case, among other things, expresses case, person, number, and gender features (27). But for the purpose of the discussion, I assume that Num° encodes number, while D° expresses person and presumably case.

4.2.2.5 A refined characterization of weak pronouns

If it is conceivable that the Gungbe strong pronouns form a homogeneous class, things are not so clear-cut with regard to weak pronouns. Their differences with respect to strong pronouns cannot always be accounted for by means of the simple bipartition in terms of strong versus weak elements. Actually, there is at least one context where the Gungbe weak pronouns do share the properties of strong pronouns. For example, sentences under (32) show that both strong and weak pronouns can be deleted under ellipsis.

(32) a. Dótù   dù   nú   bò   nù   sìn
        Dotu   eat-Perf thing   Coord   drink-Perf water
        'Dotu ate and drank some water'

    b. éwɔ̀ wɛ̀   dù   nú   bò   nù   sìn
        3S-sg Foc   eat-Perf thing   Coord   drink-Perf water
        'HE ate and drank some water'

    c. é   dù   nú   bò   nù   sìn
        3W-sg   eat-Perf thing   Coord   drink-Perf water
        'He ate and drank some water'

Moreover, a look at the Gungbe coordinate structures indicates that weak elements do not form a homogeneous class. In coordinate structures, a lexical noun-phrase can be conjoined with any strong pronoun, as shown by (33a).

(33) a. Dótù   ná   yrɔ́   Kɔ̀kú   kpó..
        Dotu   Fut   call   Koku   and
        ...nyɛ̀/ jɛ̀/ éɔ̀ / mílé / mìlé / yélé   kpó
        1S-sg/2S-sg/3S-sg/1S-pl/2S-pl/3S-pl   and
        'Dotu will call Koku and me/you/him(her)/us/you/them'

With respect to weak pronouns, first and second person singular pronouns are excluded from such constructions, as illustrated by (33b).

(33) b. Dótù   ná   yrɔ́   Koku   kpó ...
        Dotu   Fut   call   Koku   and
        ...*mi/*wé/é /mí / mì/ yé   kpó
        1W-sg/2W-sg/3W-sg/1W-pl/2W-pl/3W-pl   and
        'Dotu will call Koku and him (her) /us /you/them'

Notice further that it is possible to coordinate two strong pronouns or a strong pronoun and a weak pronoun (i.e., 3sg, 1pl, 2pl, 3pl), as illustrated in (33c–d). However, it is not possible to coordinate first and second person singular weak pronouns. Observe, for instance, the contrast between (33e) and (33f). Notice also that sentence (33f) would still be ungrammatical even if the order of the conjuncts is reversed.

(33)	c.	Dótù ná	yrɔ́	nyɛ̀	kpó	yélɛ́	kpó	
		Dotu Fut	call	1S-sg	and	3S-pl	and	
		'Dotu will call me and them'						
	d.	Dótù ná	yrɔ́	ɛ̀	kpó	nyɛ̀	kpó	
		Dotu Fut	call	3W-sg	and	1S-sg	and	
		'Dotu will call him/her and me'						
	e.	Dótù ná	yrɔ́	mì	kpó	é	kpó	
		Dotu Fut	call	1W-sg	and	3W-sg	and	
		'Dotu will call me and him/her'						
	f.	*Dótù	ná	yrɔ́	mì	kpó	wè	kpó
		Dotu	Fut	call	1W-sg	and	2W-sg	and
		'Dotu will call me and you'						

The distribution of weak pronouns with respect to coordination calls for a more refined distinction within the class of the deficient Gungbe pronouns. In fact the data presented in (33) suggest that the Gungbe weak pronouns fall into two different subgroups. The first deficient group includes the Gungbe weak pronouns that pattern like strong pronouns with respect to coordination: they can be conjoined with lexical noun phrases as well as with other strong or weak pronouns. This group includes third person singular and all the plural forms (i.e., 3sg, 1pl, 2pl, 3pl). The second group consists of first and second person singular (1sg and 2sg). They cannot be coordinated, as illustrated by the contrast in (33e–f), and they resist coordination with lexical nouns (33b). In line with Cardinaletti and Starke's (1999) analysis, pronouns of group one are considered 'weak pronouns', while those of group two will be regarded as 'clitics'.[6]

We now have enough evidence to abandon the two-way system proposed in (23b–27). I therefore suggest a finer characterization by postulating a three-way system that perfectly captures the Gungbe facts in terms of strong, weak, and clitic pronouns. A context where these three pronominal types neatly appear is that of imperfective constructions.

Recall from chapter 2 that the Gungbe imperfective construction requires the occurrence of the imperfective marker *tò* followed by the object, which in turn precedes the verb, as illustrated in (34a). Sentence (34b) shows that intransitive verbs must reduplicate when associated with the imperfective marker. As seen from sentence (34c), the imperfective marker somehow licenses the parasitic prospective marker *nà*. In prospective constructions, the fronted object occurs to the right of the imperfective marker but precedes the prospective marker *nà* (34c). Observe in example (34d) that the intervening prospective blocks verb reduplication. Notice also that imperfective constructions involve a floating low tone that occurs sentence-finally and is represented here by an additional stroke [`].

(34) a. Dótù tò   Kòkú   yrɔ́
          Dotu   Imperf Koku   call- NR
          'Dotu is calling Koku'
      b. Dótù   tò   yìyǐ
          Dotu   Imperf   leave-leave- NR
          'Dotu is leaving'
      c. Dótù   tò   Kòkú nà   yrɔ́
          Dotu   Imperf Koku Prosp   call- NR
          'Dotu is about to call Koku'
      d. Dótù   tò   nà   (*yì) yǐ
          Dotu   Imperf Prosp leave- NR
          'Dotu is about to leave'

Given that the object precedes the verb or the prospective marker in imperfective or
prospective constructions involving transitive verbs (34a–34c), a natural question
that arises here is that of the position occupied by pronominal objects in such
structures: can we pronominalize the noun object *Kòkú* in examples (34a–34c)
leading as such to the word order Subject- *tò*-Pronoun- (*nà*) -Verb (XP)- NR?

It appears that the three-way system explains better the distribution of the
Gungbe pronouns in the imperfective, prospective, and related constructions.
Example (35a) shows that strong pronouns are normally excluded from the
preverbal object position, unless they are read as emphatic. Sentence (35b)
illustrates the fact that weak first, second, and third person plural are allowed in this
position while first, second, and third person singular are excluded (35c). Sentence
(35d) indicates that first, second, and third person singular must remain in a
postverbal position, and the verb must reduplicate. In prospective constructions,
however, verb reduplication is blocked even though weak pronouns must follow, as
shown in (35e).

(35) a. Dótù   tò   nyè   yrɔ́
          Dotu   Imperf 1S-sg   call- NR
          '*Dotu is calling me'
          'Dotu is calling me (specifically as opposed to somebody else)'
      b. Dótù   tò   mí   /mì   /yé   yrɔ́
          Dotu   Imperf 1W-pl 2W-pl 3W-pl call- NR
          'Dotu is calling us, you, them'
      c. Dótù   tò   *mi/*wè/*é   yrɔ́
          Dotu   Imperf 1/2/3W-sg   call- NR
          'Dotu is calling me, you, him'
      d. Dótù   tò   yíyrɔ́   mì   /weˇ / ɛ̀
          Dotu   Imperf call-call 1W-sg/2W-sg/3W-sg- NR
          'Dotu is calling me, you, him/her'

e. Dótù   tò   nà   yrɔ́   mì̀   /weˋ / ɛ̀
   Dotu   Imperf Prosp call   1W-sg/2W-sg/3W-sg- NR
   'Dotu is about to call me, you, he/she'

Suppose that the position occupied by the shifted object corresponds to an argument position, that is, the specifier position of the aspect projection, say AspP3, that hosts the prospective marker (see chapter 6). Assume further that object movement to [spec AspP3] results from the fact that the Gungbe imperfective/prospective sentences involve a small (or reduced clause) whose subject position (i.e., [spec AspP3]) must be filled in overt syntax to satisfy the EPP. Granting this, it is reasonable to think of [spec AspP3] as a position that can host object noun phrases and possibly pronouns that qualify as lexical DPs (e.g., emphatic strong pronouns). Since nothing in principle prevents weak object pronouns from targeting this position, we should expect [spec AspP3] to host all the pronouns that are normally found in object positions, as illustrated in (36):

(36)   Dótù yrɔ́   mi / wè / ɛ̀   /   mí / mì / yé
        Dotu call-Perf   1W-sg/2W-sg/3W-sg   1W-pl/2W-pl/ 3W-pl
        'Dotu call me /you /him /we /you /them'

Yet the contrast in (35a–c) indicates that this prediction is not borne out: only strong pronouns and weak plural pronouns are allowed in the preverbal position. The three types of pronouns that we found in coordinate structures also emerge here: strong pronouns are like lexical DPs; they occasionally occur in [spec AspP3] when they are read as emphatic. Though they share a number of properties with deficient elements with respect to focus, topic, question, modifiers, and so on, weak pronouns (i.e., first, second, and third person plural) appear to be less deficient since they too can occur in [spec AspP3] and be coordinated (just as strong pronouns). Finally, the clitic pronouns, first and second person singular, are the weakest of all. They are banned from [spec AspP3] and cannot be coordinated, focused, topicalized, or modified. See chapter 6 for the discussion on clitic placement in the Gungbe imperfective and prospective constructions.

As for third person singular, it should be regarded as a 'mutant form' in the sense that it belongs neither to weak pronouns nor to clitic pronouns. Rather, it shares properties of both classes. In the preceding paragraphs, it appeared that third person singular é was involved in coordinate structures and therefore could be classified as a weak pronoun. This was exemplified by (33d) repeated here for convenience.

(33) d. Dótù   ná   yrɔ́   ɛ̀   kpó   nyɛ̀   kpó
          Dotu   Fut   call   3W-sg and   1S-sg and
          'Dotu will call he and me'

But as seen from example (35c), this pronoun is excluded from the preverbal object position, [spec AspP3], and must occur postverbally together with first and second person singular, which I consider clitic pronouns.

A fact that supports the analysis of the Gungbe third person singular object pronoun as a mutant form is that there is now a development in the language, where the third person singular *é* can occur in the preverbal object position being cliticized on to the imperfective marker *tò*, which is changed into *do* (37a). No such strategy is available for the first and second person singular (37b).

(37) a. %Dótù   do-é   yrɔ́
          Dotu   Imperf-3W-sg   call- NR
          'Dotu is calling him/her'
      b. *Dótù   do-mi /wè   yrɔ́
          Dotu   Imperf-1W-sg/2W-sg   call- NR
          'Dotu is calling me/you'

In addition, the third person singular pronoun sharply contrasts with genuine weak pronouns (i.e., the plural forms of object pronouns) when it comes to prospective, a construction that is parasitic on imperfectives. As seen from examples (34c–d), a prospective sentence necessarily bears an imperfective feature that is realized by the imperfective marker *tò*, immediately followed by a DP-object, a strong pronoun or marginally a weak pronoun, which in turn precedes immediately the prospective marker *nà* (38a–c). However, the third person singular pronoun is totally excluded from such constructions, on a par with the first and second person singular pronouns. This explains the degradation of sentence (38d), as opposed to (38c) and also (37a).

(38) a. Dótù   tò   Kòfí   nà   yrɔ́
          Dotu   Imperf   Kofi   Prosp   call- NR
          'Dotu is about to call Kofi'
      b. Dótù   tò   éɔ̀   nà   yrɔ́
          Dotu   Imperf   3S-sg   Prosp   call- NR
          'Dotu is about to call him/her'
      c. ?Dótù   tò   mì   nà   yrɔ́
          Dotu   Imperf   2W-pl   Prosp   call- NR
          'Dotu is about to call you'
      d. *Dótù   do-é   nà   yrɔ́
          Dotu   Imperf-3W-sg   Prosp   call- NR
          'Dotu is about to call him/her'

For the purpose of this study, I will continue to consider the Gungbe third person object pronoun a mutant form, that is, a pronoun that is halfway in its mutation from weak pronoun to clitic. Consequently, it displays properties that intersect with those of both weak and clitic elements. Just as all members of the deficient class, it cannot be focused, topicalized, or modified. Like weak elements, it enters coordinate structures contrary to clitic elements, which resist such constructions. Finally, in imperfective sentences, it shares the same distribution as clitic pronouns, or first and second object pronouns.

The facts that I discuss here are consistent with Benveniste's (1966) observation that the so-called third person does not form a natural class with the first and second person pronouns. In his terms, the third person better qualifies as a 'non-person' pronoun. Though I do not strictly follow this line here, it is interesting to note, in the following table, that both Benveniste's distinction and the distributive asymmetries discussed here seem to reflect in the morphological shape of the Gungbe possessive pronouns. Observe, for example, that the Gungbe third person patterns like first, second, and third person plurals in selecting for the Gungbe possessive marker *tɔ̀n*. The first person and second person singular, on the other hand, manifest two distinct forms that exclude the possessive marker.[7]

Possessives pronouns	
1st-sg	cé/*tɔ̀n
2nd-sg	tòwè/*tɔ̀n
3rd-sg	étɔ̀n
1st-pl	mítɔ̀n
2nd-pl	mìtɔ̀n
3rd-pl	yétɔ̀n

4.2.2.6 Recapitulation

The Gungbe pronominal system can be characterized as involving three subgroups: strong pronouns, weak subject/object pronouns, and clitic object pronouns. As proposed earlier, strong pronouns are like lexical DPs: they project a more articulated internal structure involving different functional projections such as DP, NumP, whose heads D° and Num° are the locus of person and number specifications, as well as functional projections (e.g., Nral, DemP, AP) whose specifiers host modifying elements as demonstratives, numerals, and adjectives (23). I further propose that the Gungbe strong pronouns involve both cyclical and snowballing movements. The NP-complement raises to the left of the adjective, then the phrase Pronoun-Adjective moves to the left of the numeral, giving rise to the phrase Pronoun-Adjective-Numeral. The phrase Pronoun-Adjective-Numeral in turn moves to the left of the demonstrative and then the phrase Pronoun-Adjective-Numeral-Demonstrative moves cyclically to [spec NumP] and [spec DP] to be specified for number and person. This DP-internal movement leads to the word order Pronoun-Adjective-Numeral-Demonstrative-Det-Num observed in (24a) and repeated here, for convenience.

(24) a.   mì   xóxó   àtɔn   éhè   lɔ̌   lɛ́
           2S-pl old   three   Dem   Spf[+def] Num
           'These specific old three of you'

As for subject and object weak pronouns, they are weaker than strong pronouns because they include less articulated structure. They involve only the projections DP and NumP and thus qualify as elements of the category Num. Accordingly, it is argued here that weak pronouns are generated under Num° where they are specified for number. As D° is the locus of person specification, Num°-to-D° movement applies in order for the pronoun to be specified for person (27). Notice in passing that the head status of weak pronouns helps account for the degradation of (38c), assuming that adjunction to a phonetically realized aspect head, here Asp°3, is banned in Gungbe (see chapter 2).

Object clitic pronouns are the weakest of all. As seen from example (35), they basically include first and second person singular *mi* and *wè*: two elements that inherently lack number (or plural) specification. Following Ritter's (1992, 1995) analysis of Hebrew pronominal system, I propose that the Gungbe object clitics are DPs, which contain only the head D°, which is only specified for person. In other words, the Gungbe object clitics lack the projection NumP; they are intransitive Ds in the sense of Abney (1987). Accordingly, they can be represented as in (39).

(39)   DP
                  △
              D°[person]
              mi / wè

We can now characterize the Gungbe pronominal system as follows.

Gungbe personal pronouns				
Pers/Numb	Strong forms	Weak forms		Clitics
		Nominative	Accusative	Object
1sg	nyɛ̀	(ù)n	–	mi
2sg	jɛ̀	à	–	wè
3sg	éɔ̀ (úɔ̀)	é	e (ɛ - i)	e (ɛ - i)
1pl	mílɛ́	mí	mí	–
2pl	mìlɛ́	mì	mí	–
3pl	yélɛ́	yé	yé	–

4.2.2.7 Why the Gungbe clitics are not phonetic clitics

An alternative to the analysis of the Gungbe clitics in terms of structurally deficient elements could be to assume, in line with da Cruz and Avolonto (1993) and Agbedor (1996), that the Gbe languages involve the so-called phonetic clitics. This would mean that the Gungbe personal pronouns involve two classes: strong versus weak (or deficient) pronouns. According to Agbedor (1996), deficient pronouns are of the D-type (in terms of Abney 1987; Cardinaletti 1993). Strong pronouns, on the other hand, are like full lexical DPs.

This analysis is partly based on the facts, briefly discussed in section 4.2.1, that the Gbe third person singular enters a vowel harmony process with the element immediately to its left. The sentences under (40) are illustrations of this process in Gungbe.

(40) a. yé   gbà   e   ⟹   yé   gbὲ
          3W-pl break-Perf   3W-sg   3W-pl   break-Perf-3W-sg
          'They broke it'

      b. yé   hù   e   ⟹   yé   hù-ì
          3W-pl kill-Perf   3W-sg   3W-pl   kill-Perf-3W-sg
          'They killed it'

As one can also see from the Gungbe and Ewegbe sentences in (41) and (42), respectively, no element can intervene between the verb and the pronoun.

(41) a. yé   gbὲ   égbè   [Gungbe]
          3W-pl break-Perf-3W-sg   today
          'They broke it today'

      b. *yé   gbà   égbè   ὲ
          3W-pl break-Perf   today   3W-sg

(42) a. Kòfì   kpɔ - e   [Ewegbe]
          Kofi   see-3sg(CL)
          'Kofi   saw him/her/it' (Kofi l'a vu)

      b. *Kòfì kpɔ   egbea   e
          Kofi   voir-Perf   aujourd'hui   3sg
          'Kofi l'a vu aujourd'hui'   (Adapted from Agbedor 1996: 43)

Under Stowell (1981) and Kinyalolo (1992), the adjacency facts described in the sentences (41–42) could be interpreted as an indication that the verb and the clitic object are in their base positions. Building on this, Agbedor (1996) further argued that if true that clitics head the DP (Abney 1987), then one could propose that the Ewegbe object clitic (and possibly the Gbe clitics) is embedded in a DP projection, which is licensed in the object base position, where it is assigned case and thematic roles. It therefore follows that clitic movement, as proposed by Kayne (1975) and subsequent work, does not hold in Gbe. This static analysis assumes that even though the Gbe clitics are deficient elements, they are not subject to movement rules like their Romance or Germanic counterparts. Instead, cliticization in Gbe seems to be a mere PF phenomenon that has no syntactic trigger. Even though this analysis might look attractive, it raises a number of questions that find no answer in such a static approach to clitic licensing in Gbe.

First, if true that the Gbe clitics are phonetic clitics that sit in their base position, why do they have different distributive properties than other weak pronouns as I have shown in section 4.2.2.5? Recall, for example, from the sentences under (35)—repeated here—that the Gungbe strong and weak pronouns precede the verb in imperfective and related constructions. On the other hand, the object clitics must follow.

(35) a.   Dótù tò   nyè   yrɔ́
           Dotu Imperf 1S-sg call- NR
           '*Dotu is calling me'
           'Dotu is calling me [i.e., specifically as opposed to somebody else]'
      b.   Dótù tò   mí   /mì   /yé   yrɔ́
           Dotu Imperf 1W-pl 2W-pl 3W-pl call- NR
           'Dotu is calling us, you, them'
      c.   Dótù tò   *mi/*wè/*é   yrɔ́
           Dotu Imperf 1/2/3W-sg   call- NR
           'Dotu is calling me, you, him'

Second, if true that the Gbe clitics belong to the class of the deficient pronouns (like their Romance and Germanic counterparts), why is it that they are not subject to Kayne's (1975) movement rule? Actually, a static approach to clitic placement in Gbe forces us to an analysis in term of parametric variation:

(43)   a.   Phonetic clitics are licensed in the argument base position.
       b.   Syntactic clitics are licensed in a derived position: they must move out of their base position in overt syntax.

The distributive variations found cross-linguistically could therefore be accounted for by saying that clitics of the Romance and Germanic type are syntactic clitics as opposed to those of the Gbe type, which are phonetic clitics. At the present stage, there is no independent and clear data that show that languages may vary along these lines. On the contrary, cross-linguistic studies on clitic placement (Kayne 1975; Belletti 1993; Haegeman 1993; Roberts 1993; Cardinaletti 1994; Cardinaletti & Starke 1999; Ritter 1995; Zribi-Hertz & Mbolatianavalona 1997, 1999; Friedemann & Siloni 1997) favor a more dynamic approach to clitic placement that assumes that clitics are licensed in a derived position.

Third, the analysis of the Gbe clitics in terms of phonetic clitics is grounded on the fact that the clitics are adjacent to the licensing verb. But, as the discussion here shows, the verb and the clitic are licensed in derived positions. The verb must move to some aspect head, due to aspectual licensing. The clitic, on the other hand, must move to Agr° to be licensed for case. The Verb-CL order found in the Gbe languages indicates that the clitic first moves to Agr°. The verb then adjoins to the clitic, and the complex unit verb-clitic subsequently moves to the nearest aspect head. Observe that the analysis put forward here makes the parametric proposal in (43) superfluous and theoretically undesirable.

Fourth, if true that the Gbe clitics are phonetic, they should therefore stay in situ in double object constructions where the second object is pronominalized. The sentences (44a–b) show that both theme-goal and goal-theme orders occur in the Gungbe double object constructions.[8] But, when pronominalization arises, the clitic pronoun (whether theme or goal) necessarily remains right adjacent to the verb. Note, from the example (45b), that the counterpart of (44a) with the goal *Kɔkú* being pronominalized in situ is ungrammatical. The contrast in (45c–d) shows that the sentence is ungrammatical because the theme *hàn* 'song' has been prono-minalized to the right of the goal *Kɔkú.*

(44) a. Dótú   kplɔ́n   hàn   Kɔ́kú
         Dotu   teach-Perf   song   Koku
     b. Dótú   kplɔ́n   Kɔ́kú   hàn
         Dotu   teach-Perf   Koku   song
         'Dotu taught Koku a song'

(45) a. Dótú   kplɔ́n-mi/wè/ɛ̀   hàn
         Dotu   teach-Perf-1W-sg/2W-sg/3W-sg   song
         'Dotu taught me /you /her/him a song'
     b. *Dótú   kplɔ́n   hàn- mi/wè/ɛ̀
         Dotu   teach-Perf   song-1W-sg/2W-sg/3W-sg
     c. Dótú   kplɔ́n- ɛ̀   Kɔ́kú
         Dotu   teach-Perf-3W-sg   Koku
         'Dotu taught it to Koku'
     d. *Dótú   kplɔ́n   Kɔ́kú   - ɛ̀
         Dotu   teach-Perf   Koku   -3W-sg

The static approach to clitic placement offers no solution for these data. Suppose, on the other hand, that the Gbe clitics are licensed in a derived position, say Agr° (Friedemann & Siloni 1997 and references cited there). Let us further assume, in line with Sáàh and Ezè (1997), that the Gbe double object constructions involve the following structure, where the theme and the goal occur either as the specifier or as the complement of the head X.[9]

(46)   AgroP

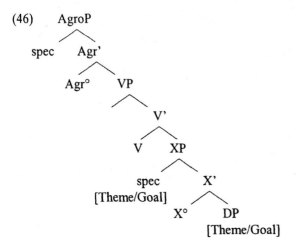

Assuming this to be the right characterization, we can account for the data under (45) by proposing that cliticization involves either the specifier or the complement of X°. In the first case, the clitic starts out as a phrase in [spec XP], but moves to Agr°. See, for instance, chapter 6 (also Rizzi 1993; Belletti 1993; Haegeman 1993; Chomsky 1995; Friedemann & Siloni 1997) for the analysis of clitic movement as involving two steps: DP-movement out of the VP, followed by subsequent movement of D°. Then the verb adjoins to the clitics on its way to the nearest aspect head, as illustrated in (47a). This structure does not involve intermediary clitic movement as a phrase.

(47)   a.   AgroP

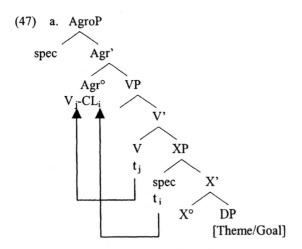

In the second case, the clitic originates as the complement of X° and moves to Agr° to be licensed. Subsequently, the verb adjoins to it on its way to the aspect head, as shown by (47b).

(47)   b.   AgroP

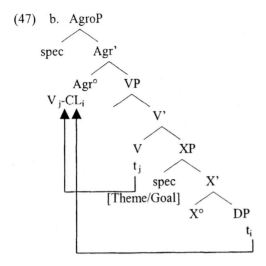

Under clitic movement, the analysis I propose here meets the predictions suggested by the sentences under (45a) and (45c): the verb always occurs to the left adjacent position to the clitic object. This analysis also excludes the sentences (45b) and (45d) naturally: the object-clitic cannot resort to clitic in situ strategy.

4.3 CONCLUSION

This chapter extends the split-D hypothesis to the Gungbe pronominal system. Under Kayne (1975), Cardinaletti and Starke (1999), Zribi-Hertz & Mbolatianavalona (1999), I suggest that the Gungbe noun system involves three types of pronouns. Strong pronouns involve a similar articulated structure to that of lexical DPs. An argument that favors this hypothesis is that strong pronouns can co-occur with the Gungbe nominal modifiers: adjectives, numerals, and demonstratives. In addition, the morphology of first, second, and third person plural forms of the strong pronouns clearly indicates that they too involve NumP whose head Num° hosts the number marker, as exemplified by *mílé, mìlé, yélé*, literally '1/2/3 person +number marker'. A natural explanation that derives from these facts is that, in the Gungbe DP structure, number specifications are properties of the head Num°, while person specifications are attributed to D° (Ritter 1992, 1995). Assuming this is the right characterization, I further suggest that like the Gungbe lexical DPs, strong pronouns involve ΣP-internal snowballing movement followed by subsequent cyclical ΣP-movement to [spec NumP] and [spec DP], respectively.

Weak pronouns are members of the deficient class. They lack some of the categories that are present in strong pronouns, that is, ΣP. For example, the impossibility of having a weak pronoun plus a demonstrative or an adjective suggests that the structural make-up of the weak pronouns does not include the nominal i-system (i.e., the categories DemP and NralP). On the other hand, the fact that these pronouns never co-occur with the specificity or number markers is interpreted as a reflex of their head status. I therefore conclude that the Gungbe weak pronouns are 'D-elements'. They project only the categories DP and NumP, that is, the left periphery. The weak pronoun is inserted in Num° where it is specified for number and moves to D° to check person specification. This would mean that these pronouns manifest Num°-to-D° movement, as opposed to strong pronouns and lexical DPs, which display no such movement.

Object clitic pronouns are the weakest of all. They are analyzed as intransitive Ds in the precise sense that they manifest a DP, which contains only the head D°, the anchorage of person specifications. That is to say, the Gungbe object clitics lack the projection NumP as well as all the projections that are normally present in lexical DPs. Contrary to Cardinaletti and Starke (1999), the tripartition theory developed here is not grounded on the hypothesis that structural deficiency automatically leads to peeling off the topmost projection in the structure. Instead, deficiency or weakness is interpreted from the perspective of less articulated or missing internal structure, regardless of the level of such lack (Aboh 2001d).

5

Tense, Aspect, and Mood: The Preverbal Markers

The aim of this chapter is to discuss some aspects of the Gungbe clause structure in terms of the split-I and split-C hypotheses. It is argued here, in line with Pollock (1989), that each of so-called 'I-features' is the head of a maximal projection that projects within the I-system. Evidence from Gungbe shows that these functional heads are morphologically realized by tense and aspect markers that occur in a position between the subject and the verb. On the other hand, certain manifestations of the Gungbe left periphery support Rizzi's (1997) proposal that the split-I hypothesis should be extended to the C-system. Accordingly, each of the force, topic, focus, and finiteness features traditionally associated with the C-system is a syntactic head that projects between the complementizer and the propositional content expressed by IP.

Section 5.1 provides a general overview of the Gungbe preverbal markers. It is shown there that the Gungbe preverbal markers are of two types: negation, tense, and aspect markers, which encode I-features (i.e., IP-markers), and the markers that manifest the left periphery and express C-features (i.e., CP-markers). Section 5.2 discusses the distribution and the syntactic function of the IP-markers in the Gungbe sentences. The structure developed there is grounded in the Pollockian tradition. Each of the IP-markers is a syntactic head (e.g., Neg°, T°, Asp°) that projects as a component of the I-system (i.e., NegP, TP, AspP). For instance, I propose that the Gungbe negative sentences involve a negative phrase, NegP, whose head Neg° hosts the Gungbe negative marker *má*, the counterpart of French *ne* or Italian *non*. The same reasoning extends to the Gungbe tense and aspect markers (Tenny 1987; Pollock 1989; Haegeman & Zanuttini 1991; Zanuttini 1991, 1997; Avolonto 1992a, b, c, 1995; Agbedor 1993; Haegeman 1995a; Cinque 1999). [1]

Section 5.3 discusses the Gungbe mood markers. It is an extension of Pollock's split-I hypothesis to the Gungbe C-system. It is argued that the C-system involves a more articulated structure (Culicover 1992; Muller & Sternefeld 1993; Puskàs 1995, 1996; Haegeman 1996a, b; Rizzi 1997, among others). The assumption made there is that each of the force, finiteness, topic and focus features that are inherent to the left periphery, is the realization of a head that projects within the C-system. In this respect, conditional *ní*, the Gungbe counterpart of English *if* or French *si*, appears to manifest Force°, which heads the topmost functional projection of the C-system. On the other hand, subjunctive/injunctive *ní* is argued to encode tense and mood specifications that are associated with Fin°, the head of the lowest functional projection FinP in the C-system. Section 5.4 concludes the chapter.

5.1 SETTING THE STAGE

Two outstanding properties characterize Gungbe. Like all Gbe languages, it manifests a rather 'poor' inflectional morphology.[2] Yet the language displays several preverbal markers that occur between the subject and the verb and encode inflection specifications (i.e., tense, aspect, negation, etc.).

5.1.1 On poor inflectional morphology

Unlike languages with "rich inflection"[3] (e.g., Italian, Spanish), Gungbe is a non-pro-drop language. The subject must always be realized in the clause (1).[4] There is no subject-verb agreement in the language, because person and number agreement are never overtly realized on the verb (1–2). In addition, Gungbe displays no gender specification on pronouns, determiners, and adjectives. This is illustrated in sentence (2b), in which the third person singular pronoun refers to both feminine and masculine referents.

(1)   *(ùn)   hɔn
         1sg   flee-Perf
         'I ran away'

(2)   a.   yé   hɔn
              3pl   flee-Perf
              'They ran away'
         b.   é   hɔn
              3pl   flee-Perf
              'S/he ran away'

Case is not morphologically realized on the Gungbe lexical DPs. As illustrated by the sentences in (3a–b), the DP *dàwé lɔ́* 'the man' keeps the same form irrespective of whether it functions as subject or object. Assuming that subject and object DPs bear abstract case, I conclude that Gungbe lexical DPs don't display case morphology (Chomsky 1981, 1995; Sportiche 1988; Pollock 1989; Belletti 1990, 2001; Koopman 1992, 2000b).

(3)   a.   dáwè   lɔ́   xɔ̀   kèké
           man   Spf[+def] buy-Perf   bicycle
           'The specific man bought a bicycle'
      b.   Kɔ̀kú yrɔ́   dáwè   lɔ́
           Koku call-Perf   man   Spf[+def]
           'Koku called the specific man'

Notice, however, that, unlike lexical DPs, weak pronouns show nominative versus accusative case morphology (see chapter 4 for the discussion on pronouns).

(3)   c.   é   xɔ̀   ɛ̀
           3sg   buy-Perf   3sg
           'S/he bought it'
      d.   *ɛ̀   xɔ̀   é
           3sg   buy-Perf   3sg

Unlike French, Italian, or English, where the verb may bear tense, aspect, or mood morphology, the Gungbe verb has no affix on it to reflect tense, aspect, or mood specifications. As shown by the sentences in (4), the Gungbe verb always keeps the same shape irrespective of the tense/aspect marker(s) with which it occurs. These sentences also suggest that Gungbe displays only one basic verb form in both non-finite and finite clauses. For instance, the verb xɔ̀ 'to buy' keeps its basic form in the finite sentences (4a–c) as well as in the non-finite clause (4d). [5]

(4)   a.   dáwè   lɔ́   xɔ̀   kèké
           man   Spf[+def] buy-Perf   bicycle
           'The specific man bought a bicycle'
      b.   dáwè   lɔ́   ná   xɔ̀   kèké
           man   Spf[+def] Fut   buy   bicycle
           'The specific man will buy a bicycle'
      c.   dáwè   lɔ́   nɔ̀   xɔ̀   kèké
           man   Spf[+def] Hab   buy   bicycle
           'The specific man habitually buys a bicycle'
      d.   dáwè   lɔ́   jró   ná [6]   xɔ̀   kèké
           man   Spf[+def] want   for   buy   bicycle
           'The specific man wants to buy a bicycle'

The sentences under (1–4) clearly indicate that Gungbe (and Gbe in general) manifests a poor inflectional or agreement morphology. Recall, for instance, that the verbs always surface in the infinitive form and never reflect the finiteness specifications of the clause. In addition, the language has no participle and therefore lacks passive constructions (Aboh 2001c).

5.1.2 The Gungbe preverbal and periphrastic markers

Though Gungbe seems to involve no inflectional morphology, it displays a rich system of preverbal and periphrastic markers that encode inflectional specifications. This is exemplified in sentences under (5), where it appears that Gungbe exhibits a number of markers (here in boldface), which indicate conditional as in (5a), subjunctive or injunctive as in sentences (5b–c), future as exemplified in (5d), habitual as shown in (5e), imperfective as in sentence (5f), and prospective as illustrated in (5g).

(5) a. **ní** Kɔ̀jó zé wémà lɔ́ Kòfí ná gblé xòmὲ
         Cond Kojo take book Spf$_{[+def]}$ Kofi Fut damage stomach
         'If Kojo take the specific book, Kofi will get angry'

     b. é jὲ ɖɔ̀ Kɔ̀jó **ní** zé wémà lɔ́ ná Kòfí
         it desirable that Kojo Subj take book Spf$_{[+def]}$ Prep Kofi
         'It is desirable that Kojo gives the specific book to Kofi'

     c. Kɔ̀jó **ní** zé wémà lɔ́ ná Kòfí
         Kojo Inj take book Spf$_{[+def]}$ Prep Kofi
         'Kojo should give the specific book to Kofi'

     d. dáwè lɔ́ **ná** xɔ̀ kὲkέ
         man Spf$_{[+def]}$ Fut buy bicycle
         'The specific man will buy a bicycle'

     e. dáwè lɔ́ **nɔ̀** xɔ̀ kὲkέ
         man Spf$_{[+def]}$ Hab buy bicycle
         'The specific man habitually buys a bicycle (e.g., every year)'

     f. dáwè lɔ́ **tò** kὲkέ xɔ̀
         man Spf$_{[+def]}$ Imperf bicycle buy- NR
         'The specific man is buying a bicycle'

     g. dáwè lɔ́ **tò** kὲkέ **nà** xɔ̀
         man Spf$_{[+def]}$ Imperf bicycle Prosp buy- NR
         'The specific man is about to buy a bicycle'

Recall from chapters 2 and 4 that the Gungbe imperfective and prospective constructions necessarily involve a sentence-final low tone (i.e., a nominalizer toneme) that is represented here by an additional stroke on the verb xɔ̀ 'buy'. I also draw the reader's attention to the fact that prospective is parasitic on the imperfective aspect in Gungbe, hence the simultaneous occurrence of the markers tò – nà in example (5g).

As the sentences under (6) show, the Gungbe aspect markers co-occur in a fixed order [Habitual-Imperfective-Prospective] with the future marker (6a), the conditional marker (6b), and the subjunctive/injunctive marker (6c).

(6) a. Kòfí **ná** **nɔ̀** **tò** gbɔ́ lɔ́ **nà** sà̀
         Kofi Fut Hab Imperf goat Spf$_{[+def]}$ Prosp sell- NR
         'Kofi will often be about to sell the specific goat [e.g., before we get there]'

b. **ní** Kòjó **ná nò tò**   gbó   ló   **nà**   sá`   bé ...
     Cond Kojo Fut Hab Imperf goat Spf$_{[+def]}$ Prosp sell- NR then
     'If it is the case that Kojo will often be about to sell the specific goat, then..'

c. Kòfí **ní**   **nò**   **tò**   gbó ló   **nà**   sá`
     Kofi Inj   Hab   Imperf goat Spf$_{[+def]}$ Prosp sell- NR
     'Kofi should often be about to sell the specific goat [e.g., before we get there]'

On the other hand, future and subjunctive/injunctive makers are mutually exclusive as shown in (7). I return to this incompatibility in sections 5.2.1.4 and 5.3.3.2.

(7) ***Kòfí**   **ní**   **ná**   sà   gbàdó mímè
     Kofi   Inj   Fut   sell maize roasted

With the exception of conditional *ní* illustrated in (5a) and (6b), all the preverbal markers presented in sentences (5b) to (6c) necessarily appear in a position between the subject and the verb. Yet it will become clear in the course of the discussion that these markers are of two types. The first type includes preverbal markers that necessarily follow the Gungbe negation marker *má* (8a), and the second type involves those preverbal markers that must precede negation (8b). Needless to say, conditional *ní* falls in the second group, as it always occurs in sentence-initial position as in (8c).

(8) a. Kòfí [má] **ná nò tò**   gbàdó mímè **nà**   sá`
       Kofi Neg   Fut Hab Imperf maize roasted Prosp sell- NR
       'Kofi will not often be about to sell roasted maize'

    b. Kòfí **ní**   [má] sà   gbàdó mímè bló
       Kofi Inj   Neg sell maize roasted anymore
       'Kofi should not sell roasted maize anymore'

    c. **ní**   Kòjó [má] sà   gbàdó mímè,
       Cond Kojo Neg sell maize roasted
       é   [má] **ná** dó   kwé
       3sg Neg Fut possess money
       'If Kojo does not sell roasted maize, he will not become rich'

As we could see from the sentences in (8), the first group of markers (*ná, nò, tò, nà*) includes preverbal markers that are commonly assumed to be manifestation of the I-system (Koopman 1984; Tenny 1987; Pollock 1989, 1997; Cinque 1999). More precisely, they are considered the morphological realization of certain 'I-features' that express tense/aspect specifications, that is, future, habitual, imperfective and prospective. I refer to these markers as IP-markers. The second group includes two Gungbe periphrastic markers, 'conditional' *ní* and 'subjunctive/injunctive' *ní*, which appear to encode features Force and Finiteness that are associated with the C-system (Rizzi 1997). They are thus argued to be CP-markers on a par with topic and focus markers, which I discuss in chapters 7 and 8. The following table is an inventory of the Gungbe periphrastic and IP-markers.[7]

Gungbe periphrastic and IP-internal markers	
CP-Markers	IP-markers
ní: Conditional	*ná*: Future
yà: Topic	*nɔ̀*: Habitual
wɛ̀ :Focus	*tò*...[`]: Imperfective
ní: Subjunctive/Injunctive	*nà*...[`]: Prospective

I discuss the future marker in section 5.2.1, the habitual marker in section 5.2.2, the imperfective and prospective markers in section 5.2.3 (see also chapter 6), and the conditional, injunctive, and subjunctive constructions in section 5.3.

5.2 THE GUNGBE IP-MARKERS

A close look at the Gungbe IP-markers presented in the sentences under (5) and this table suggests that the I-system involves a complex structure that allows for the combination of a future tense marker realized as *ná* with several aspect markers represented by the habitual *nɔ̀*, the imperfective *tò*, and the prospective *nà*. In order to understand how this system works, let us first concentrate on the future marker.

5.2.1 *Ná:* Tense or aspect?

In my description of the Gungbe IP-markers, I suggested without discussion that the language allows for only one morphologically realized tense marker *ná*. The latter necessarily occurs between the subject and the verb, in a fixed position right adjacent to the negation marker *má*, where it triggers future specification. Consider, for instance, the grammatical sentence (9a) as opposed to the ungrammatical example (9b).

(9)   a.   Àsíbá   má   ná   xɔ̀   wémà   lɔ́
           Asiba   Neg   Fut   buy   book   Spf[+def]
           'Asiba will not buy the specific book'
      b.   *Àsíbá   ná   má   xɔ̀   wémà   lɔ́
           Asiba   Fut   Neg   buy   book   Spf[+def]

Now, if we consider the distribution of the Gungbe habitual and imperfective aspect markers, nothing, a priori, distinguishes them from the future marker, since they too occur between the subject and the verb in a position to the right of the negation marker, as illustrated in examples (10a–b):

(10) a.   Kòfí [má]   nò   tò   gbàdó   mímè   sà`
           Kofi Neg   Hab   Imperf   maize   roasted sell- NR
           'Kofi is not selling roasted maize habitually'
      b.   *Kòfí   nò   tò   [má]   gbàdó   mímè   sà`
            Kofi   Hab   Imperf   Neg   maize   roasted sell- NR

If this is the right characterization, then a conclusion we might draw here is that *ná* is
an irrealis marker and that there is actually no overt specification of the category tense
(i.e., T°) in the language. That is to say, Gungbe is a pure aspect language whose
inflectional system involves several aspect markers: irrealis *ná*, habitual *nò*,
imperfective *tò*, and prospective *nà*. It can therefore be assumed that the Gungbe tense
is derived either from the context, or the interpretation of individual aspect markers,
and the semantics of the combinations they give rise to, when they are simultaneously
realized in the sentence (see Avolonto 1992a, b, c, 1995; da Cruz 1993; Tossa 1994;
Lefebvre 1998; Ndayiragije 2000 for the discussion on the Fongbe morpheme *ná* and
Essegbey 1999 for the Ewegbe *a*). Yet, as I will show in the next section, Gungbe
provides strong evidence that an analysis of the IP-marker *ná* in terms of irrealis aspect
marker is not empirically correct.

5.2.1.1 Some objections against ná as irrealis aspect marker

One piece of evidence that the future marker *ná* and the habitual/imperfective markers
nò and *tò* manifest two distinct categories in Gungbe comes from the fact that they
display a different distribution with respect to certain middle field adverbs, which
typically occur between the subject and the verb. We see, for example, in sentences
under (11) that the future marker precedes the adverb *sɔ́* 'again' (11a) but habitual and
imperfective aspect markers must follow it (11b–c).

(11) a.   Àsíbá   ná   sɔ́   xɔ̀   wémà
           Asiba   Fut   again   buy   book
           'Asiba will buy a book again'
      b.   Àsíbá   sɔ́   nò   xɔ̀   wémà
           Asiba   again   Hab   buy   book
           'Asiba buys book(s) again (habitually)'
      c.   Àsíbá   sɔ́   tò   wémà   xɔ̀
           Asiba   again   Imperf book   buy- NR
           'Asiba is buying a book again'

Another significant fact that underscores the difference between the future marker as
opposed to habitual and imperfective markers is that the former never serves as main
predicate of a clause, while the latter do. Consider the following examples:

(12) a. Àsíbá   nɔ̀   Kútɔ̀nù
          Asiba   stay-Perf   Cotonou
          'Asiba stayed in Cotonou'
      a'. Àsíbá   tò   xwé   gbè
          Asiba   be   home   at
          'Asiba is at home'
      b. Àsíbá   [má   ná   tè]   nɔ̀   Kútɔ̀nù
          Asiba   Neg   Fut   even   stay-Perf   Cotonou
          'Asiba will not even stay in Cotonou'
      b' Àsíbá   [má   ná   tè]   tò   xwé   gbè
          Asiba   Neg   Fut   even   be   home   at
          'Asiba will not even be at home'
      c. *Àsíbá   nɔ̀   ná   xwè   àtɔ̀n   Kútɔ̀nù
          Asiba   stay-Perf   for   year   three   Cotonou
      c'. *Àsíbá   tò   tègbè   xwé   gbè
          Asiba be   always   home   at

As seen in the sentences under (12), Gungbe allows for the usage of the habitual marker *nɔ̀* and the imperfective marker *tò* in certain 'verbless sentences'. When used as main predicate, the aspect markers *nɔ̀* and *tò* surface in a position corresponding to that of a lexical verb in a finite clause (12a–a'). Accordingly, they can be separated from the subject by intervening adverbs, the negation marker or the future marker (12b–b'). But nothing can be inserted between *nɔ̀* or *tò* and its complement, hence the ungrammaticality of sentences (12c–c'). Recall from chapter 2, section 2.5.1.5, that similar adjacency facts are found in sentences involving the Gungbe lexical verbs.[8] This need not mean, though, that the Gungbe aspect markers form a natural class with the Gungbe lexical verbs. I come back to this discussion in section 5.2.2. At this stage of the discussion, it suffices to say that contrary to habitual *nɔ̀* and imperfective *tò*, which may serve as predicate in a verbless sentence, the future marker *ná* cannot occur in isolation: it must co-occur with a lexical verb or a predicative aspect marker.

Finally, the future marker also differs from both the habitual and the imperfective markers because it is incompatible with the Gungbe subjunctive/injunctive marker *ní*. Compare, for example, the ungrammatical injunctive and subjunctive sentences (13a) and (13b), respectively, with the grammatical sentences (13c–d). It appears that, unlike the future marker *ná*, the habitual and the imperfective markers *nɔ̀* and *tò* are perfectly combinable with *ní* in the fixed order subjunctive/injunctive-habitual-imperfective.

(13) a. *Kòfí   ní   ná   sà   gbàdó   mímè
          Kofi   Inj   Fut   sell   maize   roasted
          'Kofi should sell roasted maize'   [Future-Injunctive]
      b. *ùn   jrɔ́   ɖɔ̀   Kòfí ní ná   sà   gbàdó   mímè
          1sg   want   that   Kofi Inj Fut   sell   maize   roasted
          'I wish Kofi should sell roasted maize'   [Future-Subjunctive]

d. Kòfí **ní**   **nɔ̀**   **tò**   gbàdó   mímɛ̀   sã̀
    Kofi Inj   Hab   Imperf maize   roasted sell- NR
    'Kofi should be selling roasted maize habitually'

c. ùn   jrɔ́   dɔ̀   Kòfí **nɔ̀ ní tò**   gbàdó mímɛ̀ sã̀
    1sg   want that Kofi Hab Inj Imperf maize roasted sell- NR
    'I wish Kofi should be selling roasted maize'

If we analyze *ná* as an aspect marker like *nɔ̀* and *tò* (Avolonto 1992a, b, c; Ndayiragije 2000), we would not be able to account for the contrast in (13) because nothing, in principle, excludes the combination of injunctive mood with an adverbial specification that implies future reading, as shown by the example (14).

(14) Kòfí   **ní**   yì   wéxɔ̀mɛ̀   **sɛ̀**   **gódó**
      Kofi   Inj   go   school   week   after
      'Kofi should go to school next week'

Anticipating the analysis in section 5.2.1.4 and in section 5.3.3.2, I propose that the Gungbe future marker *ná* is the morphological realization of T°, the head of a tense projection TP. I will then explain the ungrammaticality of sentence (13a) by assuming that injunctive constructions are like imperatives and subjunctives, in that they lack the TP projection. This amounts to saying that the incompatibility of the Gungbe injunctive marker and the future tense marker results from the fact that there is no insertion point for the future marker in injunctive/subjunctive constructions (Zanuttini 1991, 1996, 1997, and references cited there).

In summary, I propose that the Gungbe tense marker and aspect markers encode distinct sets of features (e.g., future, habitual, imperfective, prospective, etc.) that are specific to the Gungbe tense and aspect projections TP and AspPs, respectively. The analysis I develop here does not simply oppose the fact that the Gbe languages may derive future tense reading from a morphologically realized T° to the view that these languages are aspectually prominent (i.e., they lack a grammatical category Tense) because they derive tense reading from the context. Note in sentences (1–4) that, even in my terms, a verb that is associated with the null tense necessarily obtains its tense value from something other than morphological content, and that necessarily implicates context. Instead, the fact I want to establish here is that context is not the only way for a Gungbe sentence to achieve temporal reference. A case in point is the future tense marker that blocks default (contextual or past) reading by specifying future in the position of T°.

5.2.1.2 Ná and Ø as realizations of tense phrase in Gungbe

Pursuing the discussion, I therefore conclude that the Gungbe tense marker manifests a tense projection TP within the I-system. Following the Pollockian tradition, I further propose that *ná* is the morphological expression of the feature [+future] on T°. On the other hand, there is, in the language, no tense marker that encodes the features specifications [±present] or [±past] on T°.

As I suggest in the previous section, the interpretation of the Gungbe past or present tenses derives from tense or aspect adverbs that occur in the sentence or else from the context (i.e., the discourse). In a sense, one could argue that present and past specifications are necessarily controlled in Gungbe (15).

(15) a. Àsíbá   tɔ́n   **dìn**
          Asiba   get-out-Perf now
          'Asiba has just gone out'

      b. Àsíbá   sè   jámá   gbé   gànjí   **dìn**
          Asiba   hear-Perf German language   well   now
          'At the moment we are speaking now, Asiba can speak German quite well'

      c. Àsíbá   gɔ̀   sɔ̀-zámè
          Asiba   return-Perf [-1day night]
          'Asiba returned yesterday night'

These data suggest that present and past tense interpretations are a manifestation of the feature [-future]. I further propose that the relevant interpretation is encoded either by tense adverbs or by means of the Gungbe default perfective aspect, which is normally associated with sentences involving no preverbal aspect marker (15d).

(15) d. Àsíbá   gɔ̀
          Asiba   return-Perf
          'Asiba has returned'

Notice that, everything being held constant, the default perfective aspect is systematically assigned to the so-called dynamic verbs as in (15e), as opposed to the state verbs, which are read as bearing present tense (15f). [9]

(15) e. tò   gǎn   mí   tɔ̀n   xɔ̀   àgà   hún
          State chief 1pl   Poss   buy-Perf   sky   engine
          'Our President bought an aircraft'

      f. tò   gǎn   mí   tɔ̀n   nyɔ́n   Jak Cirak
          State chief 1pl   Poss   know-Pres   Jacques Chirac
          'Our President knows Jacques Chirac'

The sentences under (15) suggest that T° is specified only for the features [±future] in Gungbe. A strong piece of evidence in support of this hypothesis is that the Gungbe time adjunct sɔ̀, which literally means '[± 1 day] from the speech time', is assigned the interpretative values [yesterday], [- 1 day], or [tomorrow], [+ 1 day], depending on whether T° is phonetically null, that is, specified for the feature [-future], or phonetically realized as ná, that is, marked as [+future]. In sentence (16a) the verb is specified as perfective and there is no tense specification on T°. As a consequence, the time adjunct sɔ̀ is interpreted as [-1 day], that is, *yesterday* (or the day before speech time). In sentence (16b), however, T° is realized as *ná*, which encodes the feature [+future]. Accordingly, the time adjunct sɔ̀ is assigned the value [+ 1 day] and interpreted as *tomorrow* (or the day after speech time).

(16) a. Àsíbágɔ̀   sɔ̀   (ɖé wá yì)
          Asiba   return-Perf   day that passed
          'Asiba returned yesterday'

      b. Àsíbáná   gɔ̀   sɔ̀   (ɖé jà)
          Asiba   Fut   return   jour that coming
          'Asiba will return tomorrow'

      c. *Àsíbá   gɔ̀   sɔ̀   ɖé   jà
          Asiba return-Perf   [+ 1day] that   coming

      d. *Àsíbá   ná   gɔ̀   sɔ̀   ɖé wá yì
          Asiba   Fut   return   [- 1day]   that passed

The ungrammatical sentences (16c–d) further confirm this analysis. They show that the presence of *ná* triggers future interpretation, while its absence generally corresponds either to past or perfective reading for dynamic verbs and present reading for state verbs. This leads me to conclude that there is no situation in Gungbe that could support an analysis in terms of a transparent or inactive T° in those cases where the sentence involves no overt tense specification. More precisely, it cannot be reasonably assumed that a phonetically null T° is vacuous or inert, as opposed to a phonetically realized active T°, which hosts the future marker *ná*. Instead, I propose that, when present, T° is always marked for one of the features [±future]. When the feature [-future] is triggered, T° is realized by a null morpheme ∅ that is controlled by an adverbial time specification or else by the default perfective aspect assigned to sentences involving no aspect marker. On the other hand, when the feature [+future] is activated, it is phonetically realized by *ná*, the future marker.[10]

      Based on the fixed order *má-ná*-Adverb-*nɔ̀-tò*, found in the Gungbe sentence (17a), I further conclude that the future marker *ná* manifests a higher position intermediate between the negation marker *má*, on the one hand, and the aspect markers *nɔ̀* and *tò*, on the other hand. Ungrammatical (17b) shows that no element can intervene between the Gungbe negation marker and the future marker.

(17) a. Kòfí má   ná   [sɔ́]   nɔ̀ tò   gbàdó mímè sã̀
          Kofi Neg   Fut   again   Hab Imperf maize roasted sell- NR
          'Kofi will not be selling roasted maize again'

      b. *Àsíbá má   sɔ́   ná   xɔ̀   kèké
          Asiba Neg   again   Fut   buy   bicycle

Granting that the Gungbe subject precedes negation, which in turn precedes tense, I assume that the subject is base generated in [spec VP], but moves to the specifier position of an AgrsP, where it enters in agreement relationship with the nominal features (i.e., person and number) associated with the category Agr. In this framework, AgrP dominates the Negative Phrase (NegP) headed by the negative marker *má* (Ouhalla 1990),[11] which in turn dominates the Tense Phrase (TP), whose head hosts the future marker *ná*. In this respect, sentence (17a) is attributed the representation in (18) (Sportiche 1988; Belletti 1990; Zanuttini 1991; Chomsky 1992, 1995; Haegeman 1995a, b; Pollock 1989, 1997; Cinque 1999).

(18)

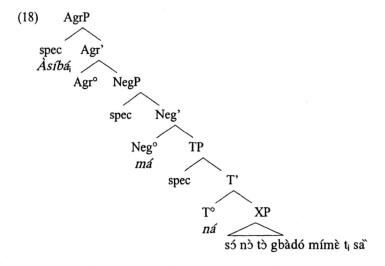

5.2.1.3 Why T° cannot assign nominative case in Gungbe

The structure (18) accounts for the surface word order observed in sentence (17a) in a straightforward manner. In addition, it strongly suggests that T° does not qualify as nominative case assignor in Gungbe. In fact, if this were the case, sentence (17a) would be ruled out as a violation of the case-assigning condition that requires that case be licensed through a spec-head agreement relation (Belletti 1990, 2001; Chomsky 1992). Said differently, example (17a) should be ungrammatical because T° is not in a spec-head relation with the subject *Àsíbá*, due to the intervening negation marker *má*. Consequently, the grammaticality of (17a) suggests that Agr° is responsible for nominative case in Gungbe.

A possible objection to this claim might be that the subject is assigned nominative case in [spec TP] before it moves higher in the clause, say, [spec NegP] when the negative functional projection is projected. This proposal may look attractive as it apparently has the advantage of accounting for the Gungbe data without necessarily postulating the existence of the category Agr. But this immediately raises the problem of whether AgrP is universally present in natural languages or not (see Chomsky 1995 for more details).

On the other hand, the question arises how to explain how case is assigned to first and second person plural subject pronouns in Gungbe imperatives and how the DP subject is licensed for case in the injunctive and subjunctive constructions in (19a–b).

(19) a. *(mì)   hɔ̀n
          2pl   flee
          'Run away!'
      b. yé ɖɔ̀   *(mì) ní   hɔ̀n
          3pl say-Perf 2pl Inj   flee
          'They said you should run away'

Let's assume that the Gungbe true imperatives and subjunctive/injunctive structures "do not have a projection TP, neither lexically realized nor abstract" (Zanuttini 1991: 73); the question arises how the subject is licensed in such constructions. Suppose $T°$ is responsible for nominative case in Gungbe, we must then postulate an exception rule or else some additional mechanism that allows the subject to be licensed otherwise (i.e., possibly in some other position) in the Gungbe imperative and subjunctive/injunctive sentences. In this regard, I therefore suggest that $Agr°$ is responsible for nominative case in Gungbe.[12] Granting that the Gungbe subject is base generated in [spec VP], then it follows that it must move to [spec AgrP] where it is licensed for case, but it may move on in some higher specifier position when necessary (see section 5.3.3.2 for the discussion).

5.2.1.4 The structural relation between NegP and TP

The analysis proposed here implies that NegP dominates TP in Gungbe or Gbe languages and possibly in every natural language. This is consistent with the observation recently made in the literature that there is a correlation between NegP and TP in the sense that whenever NegP is excluded from a structure, TP is also banned from that structure, but not vice versa (Belletti 1990; Zanuttini 1991, 1996, 1997; Haegeman 1995a, b; Pollock 1997).

Taking into account the fact that Italian true imperatives cannot be negated (e.g., *non finiscilo 'don't finish it'), Zanuttini (1991, 1996) proposed that the reason of such incompatibility is precisely that TP is neither lexically nor abstractly realized in true imperatives. This hypothesis is consistent with Beukema and Coopmans' (1989) proposal that imperatives and subjunctives are marked as [-tense]. Assuming the impossibility of negating Italian true imperatives is a strong evidence of the structural correlation between TP and NegP, Zanuttini thus concluded that NegP is necessarily licensed by the tense projection TP: if NegP, then TP.[13]

At first sight, this analysis matches the Gungbe situation. As seen in sentences under (20), certain 'tenseless' constructions (i.e., imperatives) realize neither the tense marker ná (20a–a') nor the negative marker má (20b).

(20) a. mì   ɖù
          2pl   eat-Imp
          'Eat!'
      a'. *mì   ná   ɖù
          2pl   Fut   eat-Imp
      b. *mì   má   ɖù
          2pl   Neg   eat-Imp

In order to negate imperative sentences like (20a), Gungbe makes use of the injunctive constructions, which require the realization of a mood marker with injunctive force *ní.* This injunctive marker has a fixed position in the structure: it must precede negation (21a). For the sake of discussion, I provisionally assume, in line with Avolonto (1992c), that the injunctive sentences involve an Injunctive Phrase (InjP) headed by *ní.* The latter dominates NegP, as suggested by the order *ní– má* in (21b). But see section 5.3.3.2 for a refinement of this proposal.

(21) a. mì   ní   má   ɖù   nú   blô
          2pl   Inj   Neg   eat   thing   anymore
          'Don't you [2pl] eat!'
      b. InjP

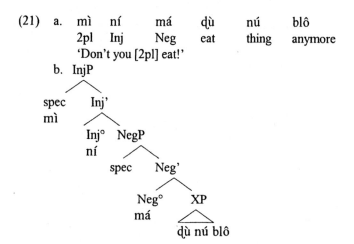

If we transpose Beukema and Coopmans' (1989) and Zanuttini's (1991, 1996, 1997) proposal to these facts, we could hypothesize that NegP, headed by the negative marker *má,* is licensed by InjP in injunctive constructions (21a). Put another way, InjP plays the same role as TP in tensed constructions (see Kayne 1992 and Pollock 1997 for an alternative). A distinction with regard to these two functional projections is that the Injunctive Projection InjP appears to dominate NegP (21b), while NegP dominates TP, as the negation marker always precedes the tense marker in Gungbe.

       A natural way to capture this contrast might be to suggest that InjP actually manifests the C-system, where it encodes tense and mood features, or [± injunctive], that match those expressed by the I-system.[14] Instead, TP is a component of the I-system where it indicates tense features [±future]. The intuition underlying this analysis is that NegP is not structurally dependent on TP, but rather on the feature [±tense] that is normally associated with every sentence. Granting that [±tense] features are expressed by different functional categories belonging to both C- and I-systems, I propose that NegP can be licensed by the functional head to which some tense (or mood) specifications are associated. We can therefore reinterpret Zanuttini's proposal by postulating that NegP can project as long as the C-system or the I-system, or both, manifests the feature [+tense]. This is consistent with the Gungbe imperative, injunctive, and subjunctive data, which suggest that the I-system lacks the feature tense associated with TP because finiteness is encoded by some functional head of the C-system. In Gbe, Inj° is such a head: it allows for NegP to project. Assuming that injunctive constructions involve a structure lacking (active) TP projection, it follows that the injunctive marker and the tense marker *ná* do not co-occur. *Ní* and *ná* are never realized simultaneously in the sentence, as illustrated by the ungrammatical example (22).

(22) *mì   ní   má   ná   ɖù   nú   blô
       2pl   Inj   Neg   FUT   eat   thing   anymore

Last but not least, the analysis advocated here strongly underscores the idea that the Gungbe future marker *ná* is not an aspect marker, in contrast to what is often proposed in the Gbe (and Kwa) literature with respect to similar markers (Avolonto 1992a, b, c, 1995; da Cruz 1993; Tossa 1994; Lefebvre 1998; Ndayiragije 2000). Instead, if we assume, as I do here, that *ná* realizes T° while *nɔ̀*, *tò* encode the Gungbe habitual and imperfective aspects, respectively, the contrast between the ungrammatical sentence (22) and the grammatical example (23) follows in a straightforward manner.

(23) yé   ní   nɔ̀   tò   gbàdó   mímè   sã̀
       3pl   Inj   Hab   Imperf   maize   roasted sell- NR
       'They should be selling roasted maize habitually'

5.2.1.5 Summary

The theory developed in this section assumes that Gungbe and the Gbe languages in general involve a tense marker that is inserted in T°, the head of a Tense Phrase TP that projects between NegP and the functional projections that host aspect markers (18). This marker (*ná* in Gungbe and Fongbe, *lá* in Gengbe, and *á* in Ewegbe) encodes the feature [+future] that is associated with T°. On the other hand, past and present tenses are analyzed as resulting from the identification of the feature [-future] associated with T° and realized by a null morpheme ∅. In other words, [±future] T° is always manifested in Gbe either by the future marker, which expresses feature [+future], or by the null morpheme, which stands for feature [-future]. That verb movement to T° is not possible in Gungbe and Fongbe also follows because T° is permanently filled in these two languages (see chapter 2, section 2.4.4.3).

5.2.2 The Gungbe aspect markers

I showed in chapter 2 that the Gbe languages display certain constructions that are assigned perfective, habitual, imperfective, or prospective aspect. The Gungbe sentences in (24) suggest that these clauses require the occurrence of the relevant aspect marker: habitual *nɔ̀* (24a), imperfective *tò* (24b), and prospective *nà* (24c). Example (24d) indicates that the Gungbe perfective sentences involve no aspect marker.

(24) a.   Kòfí   nɔ̀   yrɔ́   vǐ   lɔ́

             Kofi   Hab   call-Perf   child   Spf$_{[+def]}$

             'Kofi habitually calls the specific child'

    b.   Kòfí   tò   hìhɔ̀n[15]

             Kofi   Imperf   flee-flee- NR

             'Kofi is running away'

    c.   Kòfí   *(tò)   nà   hɔ̀n

             Kofi   Imperf Prosp   flee- NR

             'Kofi is about to run away'

    d.   Kòfí   yrɔ́   vǐ   lɔ́

             Kofi   call-Perf   child   Spf$_{[+def]}$

             'Kofi called the specific child'

5.2.2.1 Why the Gungbe aspect markers are not lexical verbs

As briefly discussed in section 5.2.1.1, the Gungbe aspect markers *nɔ̀* and *tò* may also occur in a verbless sentence, where they function as predicate and seem to compete with the Gungbe lexical verbs for the same position. Consider, for instance, the grammatical sentences (12b–b') repeated here as (25a–b) as opposed to the examples (25c–d). In the latter case, the sentences are ungrammatical because the markers *nɔ̀* and *tò* —interpreted as 'stay' and 'be', respectively—are in competition with the lexical verbs *yì* 'go' and 'come'.

(25) a.   Àsíbá   [má   ná   tɛ̀]   nɔ̀   Kútɔ̀nù

             Asiba   Neg   Fut   even   stay-Perf   Cotonou

             'Asiba have not even stayed in Cotonou'

    b.   Àsíbá   [má   ná   tɛ̀]   tò   xwé   gbè

             Asiba   Neg   Fut   even   be   home   at

             'Asiba will not even be at home'

    c.   *Àsíbá   [má   ná   tɛ̀]   nɔ̀   yì   Kútɔ̀nù

             Asiba   Neg   Fut   even   stay-Perf go   Cotonou

    d.   *Àsíbá   [má   ná   tɛ̀]   tò   wá   xwé   gbè

             Asiba   Neg   Fut   even   be   come   home   at

Yet one cannot conclude on the basis of examples (25c–d) that the Gungbe aspect markers form a natural class with lexical verbs. The Gungbe markers actually lack some of the typical properties that are associated with lexical verbs. For example, though *tò* can co-occur with the habitual marker (26a), it cannot be conjugated with the imperfective marker (26b). This is unexpected since the lexical verb combines with the aspect markers freely.

(26) a. àhàn   nɔ̀   tò   távò   jí   hwèlɛ́pkónù
          drink   Hab   be   table   on   always
          'There is always a drink on the table'

     b. *àhàn   tò   távò   jí   tò   hwèlɛ́pkónù
          drink   Imperf   table   on   be   always

In addition, the ungrammatical examples (27a–b) show that *tò* cannot be focused, unlike the verbs (c–d), see chapter 7 for the discussion on verb focusing.

(27) a. *tò   àhàn   tò   távò   jí   hwèlɛ́pkónù
          be   drink   be   table   on   always
          'There IS always a drink on the table'

     b. nù   yé   nù   àhàn   lɔ́
          drink   3pl   drink-Perf   drink   Spf$_{[+def]}$
          'They DRANK the specific drink'

Sentence (27c), on the other hand, shows that when it is used as predicate, the imperfective marker *tò* cannot enter serialization.

(27) c. *Kɔ̀jó   yì   xwégbè   tò
          Kojo   go   home   be
          'Kojo left and he is (now) at home'

Finally, unlike most Gungbe lexical verbs, *tò* does not reduplicate to derive a noun (28).

(28) a. sɛ̀n   ➔   sìsɛ̀n   b.   tò   ➔   * tìtò
          'To adore'   'Adoration'   'To be'   'Being'

With respect to the habitual marker *nɔ̀*, it is more like a verb than *tò*. It can be conjugated with both the habitual marker (29a) and marginally with the imperfective markers (29b).

(29) a. Kɔ̀jó   nɔ̀   nɔ̀   bàbà   étɔ̀   dè
          Kojo   Hab   stay   father   his   at
          'Kojo habitually stays with his father'

b. ? Kɔjó   tò   bàbà   étɔ   dè   nɔ
    Kojo   Imperf father his   at   stay
    'Kojo is staying with his father'

In addition, it can be focused and reduplicated as shown in (30a–b), respectively.

(30) a. nɔ   é   nɔ   yòvótòmè   káká....
         stay 3sg   stay   Europe   long
         'He STAYED in Europe for a long time [i.e., before coming back]
     b. mὲ   dè   nìnɔ   má   fá
         Someone   at   staying   Neg   cool
         'It is not easy to stay with someone'

But one characteristic that clearly distinguishes the habitual marker from the Gungbe
lexical verbs is that it cannot enter serial verb construction (31); see Tossa (1993,
1994), Collins (1997), da Cruz (1993, 1997) for the discussion on serial verb
constructions in Gbe.

(31) *yé   kplán   Kɔjò   nɔ   bàbà   étɔ   dè
     3pl   take-Perf Kojo   stay   father his   at

The facts I discuss here strongly indicate that the Gungbe aspect markers do not belong
to the class of lexical verbs. They are best thought of as the morphological expressions
of the features [habitual] and [imperfective] that are associated with the I-system.

5.2.2.2 Nɔ̀, tò, nà, and the functional projection AspP

The data in (32) indicate that the Gungbe tense and aspect markers are not mutually
exclusive. They are realized in a fixed order Future-Habitual-Imperfective-Prospective.
Any alternation in this sequencing leads to ungrammaticality as shown by the
ungrammatical sentence (32e).[16]

(32) a. Àsíbá ná   nɔ   tò   lέsì   nà   ɖù
         Asiba Fut   Hab   Imperf rice   Prosp   eat- NR
         'Asiba will always be about to eat rice' [e.g., whenever we meet him]
     b. Àsíbá   nɔ   tò   lέsì   ɖù̀
         Asiba   Hab   Imperf rice   eat- NR
         'Asiba is always eating rice'
     c. Àsíbá   ná   nɔ   ɖù̀   lέsì
         Asiba   Fut   Hab   eat   rice
         'Asiba will habitually eat rice'

d.	Àsíbá	**ná**	**tò**	lésì	ɖù
	Asiba	Fut	Imperf	rice	eat- NR
	'Asiba will be eating rice'				
e.	*Àsíbá	**tò**	**nɔ̀**	**ná**	ɖù	lésì
	Asiba	Imperf	Hab	Fut	eat	rice

Pursuing this analysis with respect to tense specification in Gungbe, one could naturally account for these examples by proposing that aspect markers belong to a separate category Asp°. More precisely, I assume, in line with Tenny (1987), that the Gungbe aspect markers are the morphological realization of each of the features, [+habitual], [+imperfective], [+prospective], that are associated with the heads of the Aspect Phrases (AspPs) intermediate between TP and VP (see also Pollock 1989, 1997; Avolonto 1992a, b, c, 1995; Tossa 1994).

A further piece of evidence in support of the analysis that *ná* realizes the category T°, while *nɔ̀* and *tò* encode the category Asp°, is that the future marker can be separated from the aspect markers by intervening adverbs, as shown in (33a) (see also sections 5.2.1.1 and 5.2.1.2). In addition, the contrast observed between sentences (33b–c) and (33d) clearly suggests that the aspect markers *nɔ̀* and *tò* manifest two distinct aspect heads having their own specificities. Similarly, that they may co-occur (32a–b) cannot be treated as a simple iteration of AspP. For instance, even though an adverb can marginally intervene between the habitual aspect marker and the verb or the imperfective marker (33b–c), it is impossible to insert any material between the imperfective marker and its complement (33d).

(33)	a.	Àsíbá	ná	gbé		nɔ̀	ɖù	lésì
		Asiba	Fut	at least		Hab	eat	rice
		'Asiba will eat some rice at least'					
	b.	?Àsíbá	nɔ̀	gbé	ɖù	lésì
		Asiba	Hab	at least	eat	rice
	c.	?Àsíbá	nɔ̀	gbé	tò	lèsì	ɖù̃
		Asiba	Hab	at least	Imperf	rice	eat- NR
	d.	*Àsíbá	tò	gbé		lèsì	ɖù̃
		Asiba	Imperf	at least		rice	eat- NR

That each aspect marker manifests a distinct aspect head in the Gungbe syntax is also confirmed by prospective constructions where we see that the two aspect markers *tò* (imperfective) and *nà* (prospective) can be separated by the intervening object (34a). Yet nothing can be inserted between the imperfective marker and the object, on the one hand, and the prospective marker and the verb, on the other (34b).

(34)	a.	Àsíbá	tò	lésì	nà	ɖù̃
		Asiba	Imperf	rice	Prosp	eat- NR
		'Asiba is about to eat some rice'				

b. Àsíbá   tò   (*gbé) lέsì   (*gbé) nà   d̀u
    Asiba   Imperf at least rice   at least Prosp eat- NR

If it were the case that the Gungbe structure involves a simple iterative AspP strategy, then no natural explanation could account for the intervening object between the imperfective marker and the prospective marker (see also Cinque 1999 for the discussion on the position of AspPs in natural languages). Accordingly, I consider all the examples given so far to be clear indications of the fact that the aspect markers (i.e., nɔ̀, tò, nà) are the expressions of Asp°1, Asp°2, and Asp°3, which head the projections AspP1, AspP2, AspP3. These projections express the features [+habitual], [+imperfective], [+prospective] and occur between TP and VP as the components of the I-system that are associated with Asp°1, Asp°2, and Asp°3, respectively.[17] The Gungbe tense/aspect articulation is partially represented as in (35).

(35)

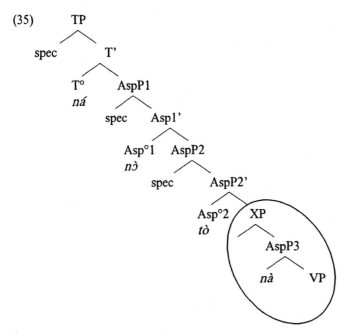

Structure (35) raises two questions:

1. What type of relationship holds between AspP1/AspP2 and AspP2/AspP3?

For example, recall from the data discussed so far that the prospective marker is parasitic on the imperfective marker, contrary to the habitual marker, which can be realized independently. In this respect, sentences under (33–34) show that the object can intervene between AspP2 and AspP3, a possibility that is not available with respect to AspP1, which hosts the habitual marker, and AspP2, the locus of the imperfective marker.

2.   What is the nature of the projection XP?

As a first attempt to these two questions, I propose that the contrast observed in (33b–d) is also an indication that AspP1 and AspP2 are 'adjacent' in the sense that they provide no room for intervening material (e.g., adverbs that occur in the middle field). This need not mean, though, that they enter a selection requirement or a government relation in terms of GB. Observe that they can surface individually in the sentence, as illustrated in examples (5e–f) repeated here for convenience.

(5)   e.   dáwè   lɔ́   **nɔ̀**   xɔ̀   kɛ̀kɛ́
            man   Spf[+def] Hab   buy   bicycle
            'The man habitually buys a bicycle [e.g., every year]'
      f.   dáwè   lɔ́   **tò**   kɛ̀kɛ́   xɔ̀
            man   Spf[+def] Imperf   bicycle buy- NR
            'The man is buying a bicycle'

In addition, the fact that the prospective marker *nà* is parasitic on the imperfective marker *tò*, from which it can be separated by the object, suggests that the Gungbe I-system even involves more structure. In order to express the relationship between Asp°2, the host of the imperfective *tò*, and Asp°3, the insertion point of the prospective *nà*, I propose that Asp°3 is included in a nominalized 'small clause' (labelled here XP) that is selected by the imperfective marker (or else by some aspectual verb). I regard the sentence-final low tone as an indication that those sentences involve a nominalizer toneme that expresses the left periphery of the embedded small clause (see chapter 6 for the discussion). In other words, the Gungbe 'imperfective/prospective constructions can be regarded as 'biclausal'.[18] They involve a main clause containing the imperfective marker, which selects a small clause. On the other hand, the Gungbe non-imperfective clauses are monoclausal and involve a less articulated structure than their imperfective counterpart.

Anticipating the discussion in chapter 6, I conclude that the fact that the Gungbe imperfective and related constructions typically manifest an OV order, as opposed to the non-imperfective clauses, which display a VO order, is reducible to the biclausal versus monoclausal asymmetry. In this respect, I propose, as commonly assumed in the literature, that the Gungbe object must raise to [spec AgroP] to be licensed for case (Johnson 1991; Chomsky 1992, 1993; Friedemann & Siloni 1997; Zwart 1997a, b; Manfredi 1997). When needed, the object may subsequently move leftward in some higher specifier position. I further suggest that the Gungbe verb must move (if possible) to some aspect head (i.e., Asp°) in order to be licensed for aspect (Aboh 1996a, 1999).

Granting this, the VO versus OV asymmetry therefore results from the fact that in the non-imperfective constructions, the verb subsequently moves to some head position, say Asp°1, to the left of the object licensing position, [spec AgroP]. But in the imperfective and related clauses, the verb cannot move that high because it is stuck in the nominalized 'small clause' labeled here as XP. Recall from example (34a) (repeated here) that the object *lέsì* 'rice' is sandwiched between the imperfective marker and the prospective marker, both preceding the verb. I return to this discussion in chapter 6.

(34) a. Àsíbá[tò   lέsì   nà]   dù̃
          Asiba Imperf rice   Prosp   eat- NR
          'Asiba is about to eat some rice'

5.2.2.3 Some remarks on kò

It is worth mentioning that Gungbe also displays a number of other markers that occur in the middle field, that is, the position immediately to the right of the future marker and to the left of the verb, and whose categorical status remains ambiguous. A case in point is *kó*, which indicates anteriority (36).

(36) Kòfí   ná   kó   sà   hwévì
      Kofi   Fut   Ant   sell   fish
      'Kofi will have already sold some fish'

Following Hazoumè (1978), I (1993) proposed that *kó* is better qualified as anteriority aspect marker. In that framework, the element *kó* constitutes a natural class with the other aspect markers (i.e., habitual, imperfective, prospective) that manifest the Gungbe I-system. Yet, as the reader can see from the data, *kó* displays certain peculiar distributive properties that suggest that it might have a different categorial status.

The sentences under (37) indicate that *kó* does not occur in a fixed position. Unlike the habitual and imperfective markers, it may target different positions in the clause. The examples (37a–b) indicate that it can precede or follow the habitual marker, as schematized in example (37c).

(37) a. Kòfí kó   nò   sà   hwévì
          Kofi Ant   Hab   sell   fish
          'Kofi would have already sold fish'
      b. %Kòfí   nò   kó   sà   hwévì
          Kofi   Hab   Ant   sell   fish
          'Kofi would have already sold fish'
      c. …. Future - (*kó*) - Habitual - (*kó*) - Imperfective - Prospective

The diacritic in sentence (37b) shows that not all the Gungbe speakers accept these constructions. Similar distributive facts in Fongbe led Avolonto (1992a) to conclude that *kó* is an adverbial element. It is base-generated in distinct positions in the structure and takes scope over the structure immediately to its right.[19] Building on representation (35), this would mean that in a sequence where *kó* realizes the position to the left of the habitual marker *nɔ̀* (37a), it takes scope over AspP1, and when it occurs to the right of the aspect marker it has scope over the AspP2 (38a).

(38)   a. $[_{FP}$ kó $[_{AspP1}$ nɔ̀ $[_{FP}$ kó $[_{AspP2}$ tɔ̀...$[_{VP}]]]]]$

The idea that there exists an intermediate position between the habitual marker and the imperfective marker that might host the adverb is further supported by sentence (33b) repeated here as (38b). Recall from the discussion there that certain middle field adverbs may marginally occur to the left of the habitual marker.

(38)   b.   ?Àsíbá   nɔ̀   gbɛ́   dù   lɛ́sì
               Asiba   Hab   at least   eat   rice
               'Asiba habitually eat rice at least'

Alternatively, one could adopt Cinque's (1999) analysis of adverb placement and propose that the adverbial phrase (AdvP) *kó* occupies the specifier position of a specific projection within the Gungbe I-system. This suggests movement operations might relate the two positions represented in (37c). The adverbial phrase including *kó* moves from its base position—presumably to the right of the habitual marker *nɔ̀*—to some specifier position, intermediate between the future marker and the habitual marker. In terms of Cinque (1999), adverbs can be grouped into different classes (see also chapter 3). Each class of adverbs enters into a specifier-head relationship with a specific head, that is, Mood Phrase, Tense Phrase, Aspect Phrase, and vice versa. Cinque further argues that the projection whose head hosts the habitual aspect marker underlyingly precedes that which hosts the anterior marker. The latter precedes the projection that hosts the progressive marker. Under the spec-head hypothesis this suggests that *kó* is generated in [spec FP$_{Ant}$] and may subsequently move to [spec AspP1] as represented in (39).

(39) $[_{AspP1}$ kó $[_{Asp°1}$ nɔ̀ $[_{FPAnt}$ kó $[_{F°Ant}$ $[_{AspP2}$ tɔ̀...$[_{VP}]]]]]]$

Further research is in need to choose between these two competing analyses. But it is worth noting that the conclusion reached in terms of both Avolonto (1992a) and Cinque (1999) is that *kó* is best thought of as an adverb, that is, an element of the type XP that targets the specifier position of a functional projection within the I-system. It is clear from this analysis that *kó* does not naturally fall in the class of the Gungbe habitual and imperfective aspect markers that I have considered as elements of the type X°. I further argue that the aspect markers are first merged under Asp°1 and Asp°2, where they encode the features [+habitual] and [+imperfective] that are associated with I-system. Having discussed the Gungbe tense and aspect markers, let's now look at mood markers that signify conditional, subjunctive/injunctive statement, or the Gungbe CP-markers.

5.3 THE CP-MARKERS: CONJUNCTION *Ní* AND INJUNCTIVE *Ní*

In this section, I focus on two particular constructions involving the morpheme *ní*. When it is used as a conjunction, *ní* behaves like English *if* or French *si* and always occurs sentence-initially. On the other hand, when found in the middle field, between the subject and the negation marker, *ní* appears as a mood morpheme expressing injunctive or subjunctive force. In my account for conjunction *ní* and mood *ní*, I propose that they manifest the Gungbe left periphery, that is, two different functional heads included in the C-system. This complex system involves several projections whose heads are the realization of the sets of Force, Finiteness, mood, features that are normally understood as 'C-features' (see Rizzi 1997 and chapters 7 and 8 for the discussion on the Gungbe focus and topic markers).

5.3.1 Distribution and characteristics of conjunction *ní*

As mentioned earlier, the conjunction *ní* always occurs sentence-initially in Gungbe as exemplified in (40):

(40) a. **ní**   gbɔ́   lέ   bíɔ́   glè   lɔ́   mὲ,
        Conj   sheep   Num   enter   farm   Spf$_{[+def]}$ in
        mì   nyà   yé
        2pl   chase 3pl
        'If the sheep enter the specific farm, chase them'

     b. *gbɔ́ lέ   **ní**   bíɔ́   glè   lɔ́   mὲ,
        sheep Num   Conj   enter   farm   Spf$_{[+def]}$ in
        mì   nyà   yé
        2pl   chase 3pl

Ní freely occurs with the Gungbe tense and aspect markers as shown in example (41).

(41) a. **ní**   yɔkpɔ́ lέ   **ná**   **nɔ̀**   bíɔ́   fĭ   hwὲlέkpónù,
        Conj   child   Num   Fut   Hab   enter   here   anytime,
        bé   nyὲ   má   ná   wá   bà
        then   1sg   Neg   Fut   come anymore
        'If the children keep entering here, then I will not come anymore'

     b. **ní**   pɔ́npì lɔ́   tò   kùnkùn lê,
        Conj   tap   Spf$_{[+def]}$ Imperf run-run this way- NR,
        mí   má   sìgǎn wà   àzɔ́n   lɔ́
        2pl   Neg   can   do   job   Spf$_{[+def]}$
        'If the specific tap keeps running this way, you cannot do the job'

     c. **ní**   ún   ɖó   kwέ,   ún   ná   xɔ   mótò
        Conj   1sg   have   money, 1sg   Fut   buy   car
        'If I had some money, I would buy a car'

In focus or topic constructions, that is, sentences where focus or topic markers are realized (42a–b), *ní* always precedes the topic and the focus markers, suggesting that it occupies a position higher than the topic and the focus positions, respectively.

(42) a. **ní**   Kòfí   wè   yé   yró,
          Conj   Kofi   Foc   3pl   call,
          bé   Àsíbá   má   ná   wà
          then   Asiba   Neg   Fut   come
          'If they invite KOFI, then Asiba will not come'

      b. **ní**   hwěnènú   yà,   Kòfí wè   yé   yró,
          Conj   at that time   Top   Kofi Foc   3pl   call,
          bé   Àsíbá   má   ná   wà
          then   Asiba   Neg   Fut   come
          'If at that time they invited KOFI, then Asiba would not have come'

      c. *hwěnènú   yà,   Kòfí   **ní**   wè   yé   yró,
          at that time   Top Kofi   Conj   Foc   3pl   call,
          bé   Àsíbá   má   ná   wà
          then   Asiba   Neg   Fut   come

A natural explanation for the data presented in examples (40–42) is to say that the morpheme *ní* always occurs sentence-initially because it is generated in the highest head position of the CP domain. In sentences (42a–b), for example, we clearly see that *ní* necessarily precedes the topic and the focus markers. Example (42b) is particularly telling in the sense that it strongly suggests that *ní* cannot be accounted for in terms of adjunction to the focus head. In other words, it cannot be assumed that *ní* has raised from a lower head position in the structure and left-adjoins to the focus marker. If this were the case, *ní* would occur in an intermediate position between the focused constituent and the focus marker, leaving ungrammatical (42c) unexplained. In a similar vein, it cannot be assumed that conjunction *ní* raises to some higher position in the structure, since the intervention of the topic marker *yà* should normally block such movement due to the head movement constraint (Travis 1984; Chomsky 1986). The same reasoning can be extended to the focus marker *wè*. I return to the focus marker in chapter 7.

I take the grammatical sentence (42b) to show that the conjunction *ní*, as well as the topic and focus markers, do not compete for the same head position. More precisely, I argue that the precedence requirement that leads to the fixed order Conjunction-Topic-Focus in Gungbe (42b, 43a–b) is a manifestation of the fact that each of these morphemes is the morphological realization of a separate head that is a component of the left periphery, or the C- system. It is now a common observation that topic/focus constructions are expressions of the CP domain in natural languages (Culicover 1992; Puskás 1995; Rizzi 1997; Aboh 1995, 1996b, 1998b, 1999, in press a, c). Accordingly, we may conclude that conjunction *ní* is realized as $X°$, the head of a projection above the topic/focus articulation. Note in example (43a) that the projection that hosts *ní* dominates the topic projection whose specifier hosts the topic and whose head, Top°, is realized as *yà*. TopP in turn dominates the focus projection FocP whose specifier is occupied by the focus and whose head, Foc°, is expressed as *wè*. The ungrammatical example (43c) shows that the topic marker and the focus marker must occur in a fixed order Top-Foc, when they surface in the left periphery (see also chapters 7 and 8 on the Gungbe CP domain).

(43) a. Kòfí yà   Àsíbá wè   ná   ɖɔ̀   xó   ní- è
          Kofi Top   Asiba   Foc   Fut   talk   word   Prep-3sg
          'As for Kofi, ASIBA will talk to him'
      b. *Àsíbá   wè   Kófí   yà, ná ɖɔ̀   xó   ní- è
          Asiba   Foc   Kofi   Top, Fut talk   word   Prep-3sg
      c.

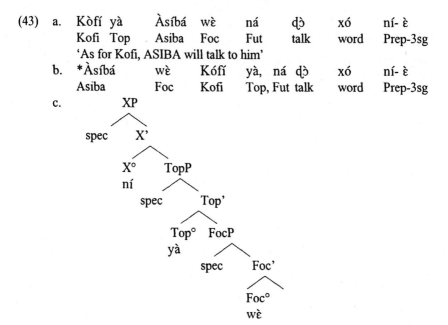

Assuming the correctness of representation (43c), the questions then arises: what category is X°?

5.3.2. The conjunction *ní* and the Force Projection (ForceP)

I assume, in line with Rizzi (1997), that *ní* manifests Force°, the head of the topmost projection of the C-system: ForceP. In his account for the left periphery, Rizzi (1997: 283) proposed that the complementizer system should be seen as

> the interface between a propositional content (expressed by the IP) and the superordinate structure (a higher clause or, possibly, the articulation of discourse, if we consider a root clause). As such, we expect the C-system to express at least two kinds of information, one facing the outside and the other facing the inside.
>
> Consider first the information looking at the higher structure. Complementizers express the fact that a sentence is a question, a declarative, an exclamative, a relative, a comparative, an adverbial of a certain kind, etc., and

can be selected as such by a higher selector. This information is sometimes called . . . the specification of Force (Chomsky 1995). . . . Force is expressed sometimes by overt morphological encoding on the head (special C morphology for declaratives, questions, relatives, etc.) sometimes by simply providing the structure to host an operator of the required kind, sometimes by both means. . . .

The second kind of information expressed by the C system faces the inside, the content of the IP embedded under it. It is a traditional observation that the choice of the complementizer reflects certain properties of the verbal system of the clause, an observation formalised e.g., by 'agreement' rules between C and I, responsible for the cooccurrence of *that* and a tensed verb, or *for* and an infinitive in English (Chomsky & Lasnik 1977), etc. A straightforward manner to account for these dependencies would be to assume that C contains a tense specification, which matches the one expressed on the lower inflectional system.

Assuming these two types of information are the expressions of two separate heads Force° and Fin°, which project their own X-bar schema within the C-system, Rizzi further proposes that when the topic/focus domain is triggered, it necessarily projects between ForceP and FinP, which manifest the outside and inside frontiers of the CP layer. In other words, the C-system involves a more articulated structure, as illustrated in (44).

(44)   .... Force...(Topic)....(Focus)...Finiteness   (Adapted from Rizzi 1997: 288)

If it is true that the C-system involves such "rich" structure, and if we consider that the Gungbe *ní* is a head, just as its English counterpart *if*, the data presented so far lead us to the conclusion that conjunction *ní* occupies the topmost head position in the structure, that is, Force° as represented in (45). Accordingly, *ní* is a complementizer in Gungbe.

(45)

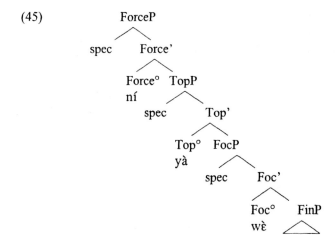

One prediction that is made by the analysis of the conjunction *ní* as a complementizer inserted in Force° (45) is that it must be in complementary distribution with other Gungbe elements that also qualify as complementizer. This prediction is borne out since the conjunction *ní* never co-occurs with *ɖɔ̀*, the Gungbe counterpart of the English *that*, which is commonly assumed to realize Force°. Consider, for example, the sentences under (46).

(46) a.   ún   kánbíɔ́   (*ɖɔ̀)   ní   [wémà lɔ́   wὲ Kòfí xɔ̀]
           1sg   ask-Perf that   Conj   book Spf[+def] Foc Kofi buy-Perf
           'I asked if Kofi bought THE SPECIFIC BOOK'

      b.   ún   kánbíɔ́   *(ɖɔ̀)   [wémà lɔ́   wὲ Kòfí xɔ̀]   yà
           1sg   ask-Perf that   book Spf[+def] Foc Kofi buy-Perf Top-QM
           'I asked did Kofi buy THE SPECIFIC BOOK'

Sentences (46a–b) are instances of embedded yes/no questions in Gungbe. Leaving aside some complications related to the pragmatics of these sentences, as well as the presence of the morpheme *yà* in sentence-final position in (46b), it is rather interesting to note that in sentence (46a) the conjunction *ní* and the complementizer *ɖɔ̀* are mutually exclusive. Suppose, as I demonstrate in chapter 8, that example (46b) involves leftward movement of the complement of Top° *yà* in [spec TopP] and subsequently to [spec InterP] the specifier of the interrogative projection whose head Inter° hosts the Gungbe yes-no question marker (i.e., the sentence-final low tone). Then the impossibility of having the complex *ɖɔ̀-ní* 'that-if' in (46a) can be accounted for in a straightforward manner. The complementizer *ɖɔ̀* and the conjunction *ní* compete for the same position in the structure. Similarly, the availability of (46b) becomes explainable as the complementizer *ɖɔ̀*, the topic marker *yà*, and the yes-no question marker manifest distinct positions in the structure: Force°, Inter°, and Top°, respectively. Let's now focus on the Gungbe constructions involving injunctive/subjunctive *ní*.

5.3.3 The injunctive *ní* and the subjunctive *ní* as expressions of Mood

In the previous paragraphs, I showed that Gungbe displays certain constructions where the morpheme *ní* is inserted in sentence-initial position and behaves like its English or French counterparts *if* and *si*, respectively. But, as I mentioned in section 5.1.2, Gungbe also manifests certain constructions where the morpheme *ní* appears in an intermediate position between the subject and the verb and triggers an injunctive (or subjunctive) reading.[20] Consider, for example, the following minimal pair:

(47) a.   Kòfí jì   hàn
           Kofi sing-Perf   song
           'Kofi sang a song'

b. Kòfí   ní   jì   hàn
    Kofi   Inj   sing   song
    'Kofi should sing a song'

As the reader may notice, the only difference between these examples is the intervention of the morpheme *ní* in (47b). The interpretation assigned to these two sentences differs radically in the sense that the declarative perfective sentence (47a) is changed into an order in (47b).[21] But when it is selected by a 'volition-verb' like *jró* 'to want' or a 'wish expression', *ní* expresses subjunctive mood, as illustrated in sentences under (48). Sentences (48a–b) express a wish, while example (48c) indicates an invocation.

(48) a. ún   jró   ɖɔ̀   yé   ní   sà   xwé   lɔ́
          1sg   want   that   3pl   ni   sell   house   Spf$_{[+def]}$
          'I want them to sell the specific house'
      b. é   jὲ   ɖɔ̀   jíkùn   ní   jà
          3sg   suit   that   rain   ni   fall
          'It would be nice if it could rain'
      c. ún   ɖɔ̀   yé   ní   jàlé
          1sg   say   3pl   ni   pardon
          'I beg their pardon'

The data in (47–48) suggest that the morpheme *ní* encodes mood or injunctive/subjunctive force. For clarity's sake, I thus refer to this instantiation of the morpheme *ní* as mood *ní*. In this framework, *ní* is just like the other Gungbe (tense or aspect) markers described in the previous sections. Notice that it occurs in an intermediate position between the subject and the verb and encodes feature injunctive.

5.3.3.1 The mood ní and the finiteness projection (FinP)

Even though it occurs in the middle field, mood *ní* exhibits different properties that differentiate it from ordinary Gungbe tense and aspect markers and that suggest that the mood marker better qualifies as a left peripheral element.

As exemplified in sentences under (49), mood *ní* immediately follows the subject and precedes the negation marker *má*.

(49) a. Kòfí   (*tὲ)   ní   tὲ   jì   hàn
          Kofi   even   Inj   even   sing   song
          'Kofi should even sing a song'
      b. Àsíbá   ní   má   wá   blô
          Asiba   Inj   Neg   come   anymore
          'Asiba should not come'

b.'	*Àsíbá	má	ní	wá	blô
	Asiba	Neg	Inj	come	anymore

The fact that mood *ní* is right adjacent to the subject[22] and must precede the negation marker is a clear indication that mood specification in Gungbe is not associated with TP but rather to some higher projection in the structure. Recall, for example, from the discussion in section 5.1 and subsequent sections that negation precedes the future marker in Gungbe, as illustrated in (50).

(50)	Àsíbá	má	ná	tón	égbè
	Asiba	Neg	Fut	go out	today

'Asiba will not go out today'

In other words, mood is realized in some intermediate position between the subject and the negation as illustrated in (51). See also Pollock (1997) and Cinque (1999).

(51)   subject .... Mood .... Negation .... Tense ....

Similarly, mood *ní* can be combined with other Gungbe aspect markers.

(52)	a.	ún	ɖɔ	ɖɔ́	Àsíbá	ní	nɔ	jì	hàn	xέ	yé
		1sg	say-Perf	that	Asiba	Inj	Hab	sing	song	with	3pl

'I said that Asiba should sing a song with them'

	b.	mì	ní	tò	títɔ́n	bléblê
		2pl	Inj	Imperf	get-get out	quickly- NR

'You should start getting out quickly'

In no circumstance can mood *ní* be combined with the future marker *ná* as suggested by the ungrammatical sentence (53).

(53)	*ún	ɖɔ́	Àsíbá	ní	ná	jì	hàn	xέ	yé
	1sg	say	Asiba	Inj	Fut	sing	song	with	3pl

In order to account for these data, I propose that, like indicative, subjunctive, or imperative clauses, the Gungbe injunctive sentences are specified for mood. In other words, these constructions involve in their C-system the feature [+injunctive], which can be analyzed on a par with imperative or subjunctive as a mood specification.[23] The only difference between injunctive and other Gungbe mood specifications of the C-type (e.g., imperative, indicative) is that the former is morphologically realized in the language by *ní*, while the latter could be assimilated to a null morpheme (Kayne 1992).[24] If the analysis put forth here is correct and if Rizzi (1997) is right in proposing that the head responsible for tense/mood specifications in the C-system is Fin°, then I can further assume that, in the Gungbe C-system, Fin° hosts the injunctive marker *ní* when specified as [+injunctive]. This hypothesis is corroborated by evidence from subordinate clauses.

(54) a. ún   ɖɔ̀   ɖɔ̀   Àsíbá   ní   ɖà   làn
         1sg   say-Perf that   Asiba   Inj   cook   meat
         'I said that Asiba should cook some meat'

      b. ún   ɖɔ̀   ɖɔ̀   làn   lɔ́   yà
         1sg   say-Perf that   meat   Spf$_{[+def]}$ Top
         Àsíbá   wè   ní   ɖà - è̀
         Asiba   Foc   Inj   cook- 3sg
         'As for the specific meat, I said that Asiba should cook it'

The sentences under (54) show that the subject *Àsíbá* follows the complementizer *ɖɔ̀* and necessarily precedes mood *ní* in subordinate clauses (54a). In addition, the Gungbe embedded topic/focus constructions involving mood *ní* display the order Comp-Topic-Focus-mood (54b). This order clearly matches Rizzi's characterization that the C-system reflects the hierarchy Force-(Topic)-(Focus)-Finiteness as expressed in (44) and represented in (45).

Building on representation (45), I propose that *ní* encodes the mood specifications that are associated with Fin°. In this study, FinP constitutes a kind of frontier projection between the I-system and the C-system. Note in the example (54) that the Gungbe mood specification cannot be accounted for in terms of adjunction to some head position of the C-system. This is so because *ní* is neither adjacent to Force° nor to the focus/topic domain manifested by the topic and focus markers, respectively. Observe further that the occurrence of *ní* in a position to the right of the subject cannot be seen as a manifestation of a TopP, which is dominated by the focus projection FocP. This is so because the order Foc°-Top° is systematically excluded in Gungbe, hence the ungrammaticality of (55), but see Rizzi (1997) on recursive TopP in Italian.

(55) *dàn   lɔ́   wè   Kòfí   yà,   é   hù-i
       snake   Spf$_{[+def]}$ Foc   Kofi   Top   3sg   kill-Perf- 3sg

Alternatively, one could adopt Cinque's (1999) universal hierarchy of the functional heads and propose that *ní* heads a Mood Phrase that projects within the upper portion of the I-system, say above the AgrsP (see also Pollock 1997; Durrleman 1999; Mboua 1999; and references cited there).

Further study is needed to determine whether the functional head responsible for injunctive/subjunctive specifications belongs to C or I. However, cross-linguistic evidence seems to favor the idea that the injunctive/subjunctive marker occurs in Fin°, or on the borderline between C and I. A case in point is the Romanian subjunctive marker *să*, which necessarily precedes the verb and appears to have similar distributional properties as the Gungbe Injunctive/subjunctive marker. The sentences under (56) illustrate some of those properties (see Motapanyane 1995 for a detailed discussion).

Just as I showed for Gungbe, the Romanian subjunctive marker co-occurs with the complementizer *ca* 'that' in the fixed order Comp-Subject- *să*. The ungrammatical sentence (56b) shows that the subjunctive marker cannot substitute for the complementizer.

(56) a. …vreau   [ca   Ion   *să*   plece]
          want-1sg   that   John   Subj   leave-3sg
          'I want John to leave'

      b. *vreau   [*să*   Ion   pleace]
          want-1sg   Subj   John   leave-3sg

Observe in sentence (56a) that the verb is inflected for subject agreement. This clearly suggests that the verb has moved up to Agrs°. The fact that *să* intervenes between the subject and the verb (just as the Gungbe *ní*) indicates that the subjunctive marker (both in Romanian and Gungbe) occurs in a position higher than Agrs°, assuming the subject has moved subsequently to its left. Another parallelism between Gungbe and Romanian is that the subjunctive marker can co-occur with other C-type elements, such as wh-phrases.

(56) c. Spune-mi   [cu   cine   [*să*   vorbesc]]
          tell-2sg-Imp me with   whom   Subj   talk-1sg
          'Tell me to whom I should talk'

In a theory that adopts the unitary C hypothesis, one could account for the sentences under (56) by saying that *să* can occur freely with elements of the C-system because mood specification is a property of the I-system. In this respect, *să* could be understood as the expression of MoodP that projects above AgrsP (Motapanyane 1995). The problem here is that we now have enough evidence that C does not consist of a single position and that there are intermediary head positions (Top, Foc, Fin) between the complementizer Force° and the subject (i.e., [spec AgrsP]). In terms of the split-C hypothesis, however, the natural locus for the Romanian subjunctive marker is Fin°.

5.3.3.2 Subject licensing and the lack of tense in the injunctive and subjunctive sentences

Assuming that Fin° is the locus of the Gungbe and Romanian injunctive/subjunctive marker, we now face two questions, that is, why the subject always precedes mood specification in Gungbe and why *ní* is incompatible with the future marker (53).

In order to answer the first question, I propose that the order subject-Fin° manifested in injunctive constructions results from the satisfaction of the EPP in the sense that when Fin° is projected in the sentence, it functions as the topmost projection that delimits the frontiers of both the I- and C-systems. If true, [spec FinP] will inevitably become the highest subject position of the clause, with Fin° being associated with tense and mood specifications that match those exhibited by the lower inflectional system (Rizzi 1997). Since injunctive constructions lack tense projection, Fin° appears as the only valid locus of tense/mood specifications in the clause. This amounts to saying that injunctive constructions possess a 'rich' finiteness node whose specifier position must satisfy the EPP.[25] This is possible in Gungbe by allowing for elements that qualify as subject to move to [spec FinP] as illustrated in (57).[26]

(57) a.   ForceP

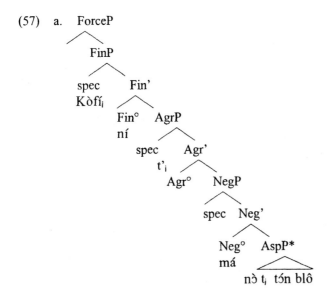

It appears from this analysis that [spec FinP] cannot be taken to be the position responsible for case assignment. Instead, it is proposed that elements that need case move cyclically through [spec AgrP] to check case features and to [spec FinP], where they satisfy the EPP. An immediate prediction here is that not only case assigned elements move to [spec FinP]. This prediction is borne out, since [spec FinP] may host heterogeneous elements such as subject DPs (57), certain adverbs (58a), 'locative phrases' (i.e., *P*s) (58b), or in some contexts, elements that qualify as theme (see the contrast in 58c–d).[27]

(58) a.   dédé   ní   kpé   mì
           slowly   Inj   impregnate   2pl
           'Be prudent'

      b.   xɔ   mὲ   ní   fá   ná   mì
           belly in   Inj   fresh   for   2pl
           'Be cool'

      c.   yé   gbà   gò   lɔ́
           3pl   break bottle   Spf[+def]
           'They broke the specific bottle'

	d.	mì	má	dìké	gò	lɔ́	ní	gbà	blɔ́
		2pl	Neg	allow	bottle	Spf[+def]	Inj	break	anymore

'Don't you let the specific bottle broke'

An alternative to this analysis would be to adopt a version of Cardinaletti and Roberts' (1991) and Cardinaletti's (1997) split AgrsP hypothesis that there are two available 'subject' positions in the clause, as illustrated in (59):

(59)   [Agr1P ....Agr°1... [Agr2P ..... Agr°2 ....]]

In adapting this proposal to the Gungbe facts, it can be assumed that Agr°1 is actually Fin°, the head of a projection FinP, which is the joint between the CP domain and the embedded IP. As proposed earlier, Fin° is the locus of tense/mood specifications as well as other 'rudimentary' features that match with those of the required inflectional domain. On the other hand, Agr2P is AgrsP, the agreement phrase whose head Agr° is responsible for nominative case assignment (or case checking in terms of the minimalism framework) through spec-head configuration (Chomsky 1993, 1995).

Sentences under (58) clearly suggest that movement to [spec FinP] cannot be motivated by case reasons. But we see from the data presented so far that the element occurring in [spec FinP] qualifies as the "subject of the predication that occurs in the clause"(Cardinaletti 1997: 55). Consequently, it is reasonable to assume that, among other features that are specific to Fin°, there must be a 'subject-of-predication' feature that requires a spec-head configuration. That requirement is satisfied by heterogeneous elements such as subject DPs, certain adverbs, locative phrases and so on. In this respect, Cardinaletti (1997: 55) further proposes that

> what seems to put together DPs and fronted phrased is a semantic property: their being subjects of predication. . . . If so, Agr1 must contain a 'subject-of-predication' feature. Agr1P would thus be subjP, meaning that the specifier of this projection defines the subject of predication.

In terms of the theory developed here, Fin° bears tense/mood specifications as well as the feature [subject-of-predication] that must be sanctioned by a spec-head configuration, hence the movement of the subject in [spec FinP]. This analysis extends to the Romanian facts in a straightforward manner. See also Aboh (2001a) for extending this analysis to Saramaccan quasi-modal *fu* and Damonte (2002) for the discussion of Salentino *ku*.

With respect to the second question, let's return to example (53) repeated here for convenience:

(60)	*ún	ɖɔ̀	Àsíbá	ní	ná	jì	hàn	xɛ́	yé
	1sg	say	Asiba	Inj	Fut	sing	song	together	3pl

The ungrammaticality of sentence (60), that is, the impossibility of inserting the future marker *ná* in an injunctive sentence, is evidence that injunctive constructions lack tense projection (Zanuttini 1991, 1996, 1997). In this respect, injunctive sentences are very similar to both imperative and subordinate subjunctive clauses, which also disallow the occurrence of the future marker, as shown in examples (61a–b).

(61) a. mì   (*ná) ɖù
          2pl   Fut   eat
          'Eat'

     b. ún   jró   ɖɔ̀ yé ní   (*ná) sà   xwé   lɔ́
          1sg   want   that 3pl Subj Fut   sell   house Spf[+def]
          'I want them to sell the specific house'

It has been proposed, in the literature, that imperative and subjunctive forms display similar properties with respect to tense (Beukema & Coopman 1989; Zanuttini 1991, 1996, 1997; among others). From this perspective, the Gungbe data clearly show that injunctive and subjunctive clauses are related constructions, since they involve a single mood morpheme *ní* (42–61b), which systematically excludes the future tense marker as exemplified by sentences (53–61b). It then appears that the mood force expressed by *ní* varies from [+injunctive] to [+subjunctive] depending on whether it is selected by the verb of the main clause. As seen in examples (48a–c), such verb can be *jró* 'to want', *jè* 'to suit'. This leads me to the conclusion that the similarities found in the Gungbe injunctive, subjunctive, and imperative clauses are not accidental. Consequently, it is reasonable to propose a unified analysis for these constructions.

As many linguists proposed for imperative and subjunctive, (Picallo 1984; Beukema & Coopmans 1989; Cowper 1991; Zanuttini 1991, 1996, 1997; among others), we can assume that the Gungbe, injunctive/subjunctive, and imperative clauses are specified [-tense] as "they lack the functional projection TP, not only in the sense that they don't have any morphology corresponding to tense, but also in the sense that they don't have an abstract tense projection in their structural make-up" (Zanuttini 1991: 70).[28]

With respect to Gungbe, this signifies that the features [±future] encoded by the marker *ná* and the null morpheme Ø under T° cannot be realized in injunctive/subjunctive and imperative sentences. Consequently, the injunctive/subjunctive and imperative forms correspond to a reduced or deficient structure that does not contain the TP projection normally found in the Gungbe tensed constructions, hence ungrammatical (53).

A problem with this analysis, however, is that if we were to maintain the idea that NegP is present in a clause if and only if TP is projected, then we cannot account for the occurrence of the Gungbe negative markers in injunctive and subjunctive clauses (62).

(62) a.   ún   ɖɔ̀ ɖɔ̀ yé   ní   má   sà   xwé lɔ́   bló
           1sg   say that 3pl   Inj   Neg   sell house Spf[+def] anymore
           'I say that they shouldn't sell the specific house (anymore)'

      b.   ún jró   ɖɔ̀   yé ní   má   sà   xwé   lɔ́   bló
           1sg want that 3pl Subj Neg sell house Spf[+def] anymore
           'I wish they will not sell the specific house'

In addition, if neither feature [+future] nor [-future] can be associated with injunctive/subjunctive sentences, then it is not clear how to account for the future or past readings that are sometimes assigned to these structures in case of adverbial specifications.

(63) yé   ní   sà   xwé   lɔ́   sɔ̀
      3pl   Inj   sell   house Spf[+def] tomorrow
      'I want them to sell the specific house tomorrow'

Granting the discussion in section 5.2.1.4, a natural explanation for these facts is to interpret the feature [-tense] specific to injunctive/subjunctive and imperative constructions as a syntactic operation that results in promoting tense features to Fin°, which encodes tense/mood specifications and is realized as *ní* in the language. Here Fin° appears to be a complex head that can license AgrP, which dominates NegP, which in turn dominates AspP1 and AspP2 (64). I leave open the question of whether there is an abstract or transparent TP projection in the structural make-up of such constructions. Notice, however, that the answer to this question does not significantly affect the theory put forth here. I thus propose that the Gungbe injunctive/subjunctive sentences involve the partial structure represented in (64).

(64) [$_{ForceP}$ ɖɔ̀   [$_{FinP}$ ní [$_{AgrP}$ ...[$_{NegP}$ má [$_{(TP)}$ [$_{AspP1}$ nɔ̀ [$_{AspP2}$ tò]]]]]]]

If this is the correct characterization, then we can conclude that there are two kinds of mood *ní* in Gungbe. The first type is responsible for injunctive constructions and need not be selected by the verb. But the second unifies with the complementizer selected by the higher verb, that is, the verb of the main clause. As we can see in representation (65), the verb *jró* 'to want' selects a complementizer *ɖɔ̀* endowed with a subjunctive Force. Yet, as suggested by the intervention of the subject (but also topic and focus elements) between *ɖɔ̀* and *ní*, it cannot be assumed that the subjunctive marker *ní* raises from Fin° and adjoins to the complementizer *ɖɔ̀*. In other words, there is no Fin°-to-Force° movement in subjunctives. Accordingly, I propose that the specification [+subjunctive] that is attributed to Force° percolates down on to Fin°, where it is morphologically realized as *ní* in subordinate subjunctive sentences.

(65) ún   jró [$_{ForceP}$ ɖɔ̀ [$_{FinP}$ yé [$_{Fin°}$ ní   [sà   xwé   lɔ́]]]]
      1sg   want   that   3pl   Subj   sell   house   Spf$_{[+def]}$
      'I wish they could sell the specific house'

On the basis of this analysis, I thus conclude this section saying that Gungbe essentially manifests two different types of *ní*, that is, conjunction *ní* and mood *ní*. The former realizes Force° while the second is inserted in Fin° and encodes injunctive/subjunctive features, depending on whether it is selected by a volition, a wish, or an invocatory verb. This is illustrated by the configuration in (66).

(66) [$_{ForceP}$ [$_{Force°}$ ní (conjunction) [$_{FinP}$ [$_{Fin°}$ ní (mood) [$_{AgrP}$]]]]]

5.4 CONCLUSION

In this chapter, I propose a general description as well as an analysis of the Gungbe IP-markers by assuming Pollock's (1989) split-I hypothesis that each tense and aspect feature, say future, habitual, imperfective, and prospective normally attributed to I°, constitutes the realization of a functional head that projects within the I-system. I further suggested that the Gungbe IP-markers are the morphological realizations of tense and aspect features that are associated with the functional projections TP and AspPs that constitute the I-system. This leads me to the conclusion that the future marker *ná* is inserted in T° in Gungbe, where it encodes the feature [+future]. When specified as [-future], T° hosts the null morpheme $\emptyset$. This amounts to saying that T° is never accessible for verb movement in Gungbe, because it is always filled either by the future marker *ná* or by the [-future] null morpheme, and it necessarily precedes the Gungbe middle field adverbs, which in turn precede the verb. In a similar vein, the Gungbe aspect markers are considered the morphological realizations of the different aspect heads Asp°1, Asp°2, and Asp°3 that form the Gungbe aspect system. It is therefore proposed that Asp°1 and Asp°2 host *nɔ̀* [+habitual], and *tò* [+imperfective], which encode habitual and imperfective aspects, respectively. Since the Gungbe imperfective sentences involve a nominalization process and allow for the occurrence of prospective aspect, I suggest that Asp°2 can select a nominalized small clause labeled here as XP. This small clause includes AspP3, whose head Asp°3 hosts the Gungbe prospective marker. This analysis leads us to the conclusion that a difference between the Gungbe imperfective and related constructions and the non-imperfective constructions is that the former are biclausal while the latter are monoclausal. Extending Pollock's split-I hypothesis to the CP domain, I accounted for the sentence-initial and preverbal markers *ní* by assuming, in line with Rizzi (1997), that the C-system involves a more articulated structure that reflects, among other things, the feature 'force' (e.g., a declarative, relative, interrogative, etc.) and 'finiteness' (e.g., mood or tense specifications) that are associated with the left periphery. I further conclude that the two types of *ní* we find in Gungbe are the expressions of conjunction *ní*, which behaves like English *if* and occurs in Force° and mood *ní*, which appears to be an expression of Fin°. That this marker is realized in the middle field, in a position immediately to the right of the subject, is interpreted in terms of movement of the subject to [spec FinP]. In terms of the analysis I present in this chapter, the Gungbe clause structure can be represented as in (67).

(67)

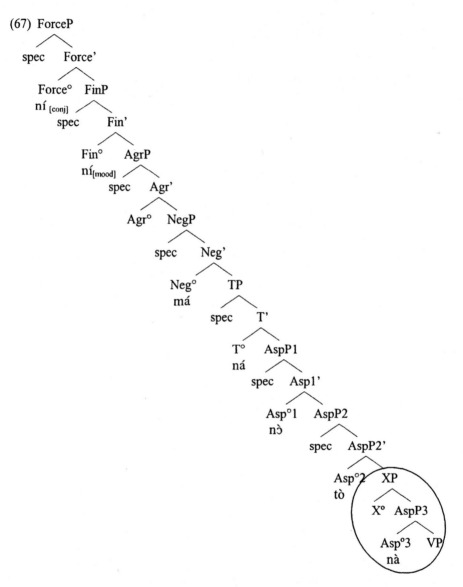

An immediate question that arises with respect to representation (67) is that of the structure of XP and its role in regard to the OV versus VO orders specific to imperfective and non-imperfective clauses, respectively. I discuss this question in the next chapter.

6

Object Shift and Verb Movement

I have shown in the preceding chapters that Gungbe (like all the Gbe languages) manifests the SVO versus SOV asymmetry. The observation made there was that the object must precede the verb in the imperfective and related constructions. In the non-imperfective constructions, however, the object necessarily follows the verb. Consider, for example, the imperfective and purpose sentences under (1a) and (1b), as opposed to the perfective clause in (1c).

(1)   a.   Kɔ̀jó tò   [$_{DP}$ àmì lɔ́]   zân
            Kojo Imperf   oil Spf$_{[+def]}$ use-NR
            'Kojo is using the specific oil'
      b.   Kɔ̀jó yì   [$_{DP}$ àmì lɔ́]   sà   gbé
            Kojo go-Perf   oil Spf$_{[+def]}$ sell   purpose
            'Kofi left in order to sell the specific oil'
      c.   Kɔ̀jó zán   [$_{DP}$ àmì lɔ́]
            Kojo use-Perf   oil   Spf$_{[+def]}$
            'Kojo used the specific oil'

Starting from an original SVO order, I argued that instances of OV orders must be analyzed as leftward movement of the object to some licensing specifier position higher than the target of the verb (2a). In this framework this movement is referred to as 'object shift'. On the other hand, cases of VO orders result from subsequent movement of the verb to the left of the object (2b) (Kayne 1994; Aboh 1996a, 1999; Manfredi 1997; Zwart 1997b).

(2)   a.   YP   b.   ΣP

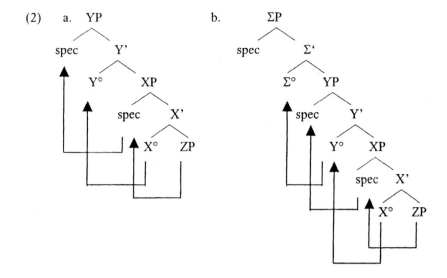

Assuming that object shift and verb movement are never optional in Gungbe, we can conclude that the VO versus OV asymmetry results from the interaction of these two movement-types. Granting the situations described in (2a–b), a question that arises immediately is what blocks subsequent verb movement in (2a) and allows for the OV order. In this respect, section 6.1 discusses certain structural properties of the Gungbe imperfective and related clauses, which suggest that these constructions involve a more articulated structure than it might appear a priori. I further argue that the Gungbe imperfective clauses are more articulated than the non-imperfective constructions (i.e., sentences that do not involve the imperfective marker). Granting that object shift and verb movement are never optional, this analysis accounts for the VO versus OV asymmetry in Gbe in terms of the interaction between verb movement and object movement (Johnson 1991; Chomsky 1992, 1993; Friedemann & Siloni 1997; Zwart 1997a, b; Manfredi 1997).

Building on this, section 6.2 brings out certain shortcomings of mine (1995) and proposes a reanalysis of the conclusions reached there. I therefore propose that the Gungbe imperfective constructions involve a nominalized small clause that is selected by the imperfective marker. The small clause consists of a left periphery and an inflectional system. The Nominalizer Phrase (NomP) expresses the left periphery and its head represents the locus of the sentence-final low tone. On the other hand, the inflectional system lacks some of the projections (e.g., TP and NegP) that are traditionally associated to the I-system. Instead, it involves an Aspect Phrase (AspP3), which dominates an Agreement Phrase (AgroP), which in turn dominates the VP. Asp°3 is the locus of the prospective marker. When negatively set, it is available for verb movement via Agr°. Under this analysis, [spec AspP3] represents the subject position of the small clause. Under the EPP, this position must be filled in overt syntax. This requirement is met, in the imperfective clauses, by movement of the object to [spec AspP3], via [spec AgroP], the accusative case assigning position. I further argue that the low tone occurs sentence-finally due to movement of AspP3 as a whole to [spec NomP], for nominalization. It therefore follows that subsequent movement of the verb out of the small clause is blocked due to nominalization. This analysis is extended to the Gungbe purpose clauses, which also manifest an OV order.

Section 6.3 further shows that a major distinction between the Gungbe imperfective and related clauses and the so-called non-imperfective clauses is that the latter involve a reduced (or less articulated) structure. They do not include NomP and AspP3, since they exclude the prospective marker and never allow for nominalization. As a consequence, the object moves to [spec AgroP] for case reasons and the verb moves further to the left due to aspectual licensing. This would mean that, in non-imperfective constructions, subsequent verb movement to a higher aspect head position masks object shift (Manfredi 1997; Aboh 1999).

6.1 THE OV ORDER IN IMPERFECTIVE AND RELATED CONSTRUCTIONS

I showed in the preceding chapters that the Gungbe imperfective construction requires the occurrence of the imperfective marker *tò* together with a floating low tone that is realized sentence-finally and affects the last syllable of the sentence-final word. Actually, the Gungbe imperfectives involve two strategies. The first requires object shift: the 'internal argument' of the verb moves to a preverbal position immediately to the right of the imperfective marker. The surface word order is S-*tò*-OV-NR (3a).

(3)   a.   Àsíbá   tò   wémà lɔ́   dìn
             Asiba   Imperf book   Spf[+def] search-NR
             S   tò   O   V
             'Asiba is looking for the specific book'

For clarity's sake, I call the reader's attention to the fact that the term 'internal argument' labeled here as 'O' is used in a broad sense to refer to elements that normally occur in the position immediately to the right of the verb in non-imperfective clauses, as exemplified in (3b).[1]

(3)   b.   Àsíbá   dín   (*tɛ̀)   wémà lɔ́
             Asiba   search-Perf   even   book   Spf[+def]
             'Asiba even looked for the specific book'

Elements that can surface in the preverbal position in imperfective constructions are DPs, including headed relatives (3a, 4a), *P*Ps (4b), and certain reduplicated adverbs (4c). Observe also from examples (4d–e) that in those cases where the sentence involves an object and a reduplicated adverb, only the object is preposed. This is a clear indication that the reduplicated adverbs and the preposed object compete for the same position. As I show in section 6.2.1, the examples (4d–e) strongly favor the hypothesis that object movement to the preverbal position is not motivated by case reasons. This argument must be maintained even though the reduplicated adverbs appear to form a very limited class that may share certain features with the class of the Gungbe nouns.

(4) a. Àsíbá   tò   [dáwè ɖě mí mɔ̀n   lɔ́] **ɗìn**
         Asiba   Imperf man   that 1pl see-Perf Spf$_{[+def]}$ search-NR
         'Asiba is looking for the specific man that we saw'
     b. Àsíbá   tò   àxì   mɛ̀   yì
         Asiba   Imperf market   Post   go-NR
         'Asiba is going to market'
     c. Àsíbá   tò   dédɛ́   zɔ̀n
         Asiba   Imperf slowly   walk-NR
         'Asiba is walking slowly'
     d. Kòfí **tò** lésì   ɖù   dédɛ̂
         Kofi Imperf rice   eat   slowly-NR
         'Kofi is eating rice slowly'
     e. *Kòfí   **tò** dédɛ́   ɖu   lésì
         Kofi   Imperf slowly eat   rice-NR

The second strategy is generally found with intransitive verbs. It consists of a verb reduplication process that creates the word order S- *tò* -VV.[2] The Gungbe low floating tone specific to imperfective constructions is also found with intransitive verbs (see Fabb 1992a, b for the discussion on the Fongbe and Ewegbe data). Here, it occurs sentence-finally and is assigned to the last syllable of the doubled verb. The situation is exemplified in (5b) derived from (5a), a Gungbe perfective sentence involving the intransitive verb *sà* 'pour'. The ungrammatical sentence (5c) shows that reduplication is obligatory in imperfective constructions involving intransitive verbs.

(5) a. sìn lɔ́   sà
         water Spf$_{[+def]}$ pour-Perf
         'The specific water poured out'
     b. sìn lɔ́   **tò**   sìsà
         water Spf$_{[+def]}$ Imperf pour-pour-NR
         'The water is pouring out'
     c. *sìn lɔ́   **tò**   sà
         water Spf$_{[+def]}$ Imperf pour-NR

The reduplication process is blocked when the intransitive verb is immediately preceded by the prospective marker *nà* (6).

(6) sìn   lɔ́   **tò**   nà   (*sì)sã̀
     water   Spf[+def] Imperf   Prosp   pour-NR
     'The specific water is about to pour out'

An observation that needs to be made here is that reduplication is not limited to intransitive verbs. In fact, a more precise generalization with respect to verb reduplication is that, in imperfective constructions, the verb must double when it is not immediately preceded by the internal argument. This is, for example, the typical situation that we find with imperfective constructions involving a clitic object pronoun that necessarily follows the verb (7a). The same situation arises when the object has been extracted by wh-movement or focus-movement, as shown by the sentences (7b–c), respectively.

(7) a. Àsíbá   tò   **díndín**   wè
         Asiba   Imperf   search-search   2sg-NR
         'Asiba is looking for you'
     b. ménù   wè   Àsíbá   tò   **díndîn** ?
         who   Foc   Asiba   Imperf   search-search-NR
         'Who is Asiba looking for?'
     c. Kɔ̀jó   wè   Àsíbá   tò   **díndîn**
         Kojo   Foc   Asiba   Imperf   search-search-NR
         'Asiba is looking for KOJO'

As seen from sentences (7d–e), reduplication is once again blocked in these contexts by the intervening prospective marker *nà*.

(7) d. Àsíbá   tò   nà   **dín**   wè
         Asiba   Imperf   Prosp   search   2sg-NR
         'Asiba is about to look for you'
     e. ménù   wè   Àsíbá   tò   nà   **dîn** ?
         who   Foc   Asiba   Imperf   Prosp   search-NR
         'Who is Asiba about to look for?'

In addition to these facts, some Gungbe speakers exhibit a 'parasitic construction' on the format S-*tò*-VV-CL-NR found in (7a) and optionally allow for transitive verbs to reduplicate, providing the internal argument occurs postverbally as in (8a). Here again, reduplication cannot apply when the prospective marker intervenes (8b). Example (8c) represents the unmarked case in prospective constructions.

(8) a. Àsíbá   tò   **díndín**   wémà   lɔ́ [3]
         Asiba   Imperf   search-search   book   Spf[+def] -NR
         S   tò   V-V   O
         'Asiba is looking for the specific book'

b. Àsíbá   tò   nà   **dín**   wémà   ló
    Asiba   Imperf Prosp   search   book   Spf$_{[+def]}$-NR
    S   **tò** **nà** **V**   **O**- NR
    'Asiba is about to look for the specific book'

c. Àsíbá   tò   wémà   ló   nà   **dîn**
    Asiba   Imperf book   Spf$_{[+def]}$ Prosp   search
    S   **tò** **O**   **nà** **V**-NR
    'Asiba is about to look for the specific book'

First, the sentences under (5–8) suggest that reduplication is not related to the verb argument structure, or whether it is transitive or intransitive. "Instead it appears to depend on the surface constituent string" (Fabb 1992a: 15). That is to say, reduplication is triggered whenever the verb is immediately right adjacent to the imperfective marker *tò*.

Second, the generalization is therefore that the Gungbe imperfective constructions involve either movement of the internal argument to a preverbal position (7), or verb reduplication, provided no other element (e.g., the prospective marker or the preposed internal argument) intervenes between the imperfective marker and the verb. I discuss reduplication and the nature of the preverbal position in section 6.2.1.

Third, it appears in the examples presented that the Gungbe prospective constructions are obligatorily parasitic on the imperfective sentences, with which they share the occurrence of the imperfective marker *tò*, word order alternation, as well as the sentence-final floating low tone. In these contexts, the preposed internal argument precedes the prospective marker, which in turn immediately precedes the verb. On the other hand, clitic pronouns necessarily follow the verb. The different scenarios described there give rise to the five word orders S-*tò*-O-(*nà*)-V- NR; O-S-*tò*-VV- NR; O-S-*tò*-*nà*-V- NR; S-*tò*-*nà*-V-CL- NR; S-*tò*-VV-CL- NR, illustrated by the sentences under (7–8). Observe, for instance, that the intervening prospective marker always blocks verb reduplication (7d–e, 8b–c). Moreover, nothing can intervene between the prospective marker and the verb, as illustrated by the ungrammatical example (9).

(9)   *Àsíbá   tò   wémà   ló   nà   bléún   dîn
        Asiba   Imperf book   Spf$_{[+def]}$ Prosp   quickly   search-NR

Fourth, the various word orders observed in sentences (7–8) suggest that the complex [(O)-*nà*-V-(CL)-NR] involves an articulated structure that contains an aspect head Asp°3—the host of the prospective marker *nà*—and provides enough room for the verb and its internal argument(s) as well as the nominalizer element (i.e., the sentence-final low tone).

If we assume that *nà* heads a prospective aspect projection AspP3, which dominates AgroP, whose specifier hosts objects, we can further interpret the leftward movement of the internal argument to a position preceding the prospective marker as an evidence that the landing site is not [spec AgroP]. Recall that even though they are specified for case, clitics immediately follow the verb. This would mean that object shift targets some higher position, say [spec AspP3]. The question then arises as to what forces movement of the internal argument to that position. I will come back to this question in section 6.2.1. To start with, let's first look at other Gungbe constructions that share the same properties as imperfective and prospective sentences.

6.1.1 *Gbé*-clauses

One other context where Gungbe also displays an OV sequence similar to imperfective and prospective sentences (i.e., subject -marker-[Internal Argument]-Verb-[clitic]-nominalizing morpheme), including verb reduplication, is that of the *gbé*-clauses. These Gbe specific constructions can be regarded as types of serial verb constructions. Unlike the Gungbe imperfective/prospective constructions, which require the combination of an aspect marker and the verb, the *gbé*-clauses involve two different verbs (V1, V2). V1 is similar to the imperfective marker *tò* with which it shares the same position in the clause, between the subject and the preposed object. V2, on the other hand, behaves on a par with the lexical verb in the imperfective/prospective sentences.

Only three verbs—*yí* 'to go', *wá* 'to come', and *jà* 'about to come'—can occur as V1. These verbs can be combined to form two complex verbs: *wá-yì* 'to pass' and *jé-yí* 'on the purpose to go', which can also occur as V1. On the other hand, any other Gungbe verb can realize V2 (see Fabb 1992a and Kinyalolo 1992 for the discussion on Ewegbe and Fongbe, respectively).[4]

(10) a. Àsíbá   yì   hwèví   **jrá**   *(gbé)
          Asiba   go-Perf fish   sell   Purpose
          'Asiba went to sell fish'
      b. Àsíbá   **wá**   hwéví **jrá**   *(gbé)
          Asiba   come-Perf   fish   sell   Purpose
          'Asiba came to sell fish'
      c. Àsíbá **jà**   hwéví   **jrá**   *(gbé)
          Asiba coming   fish   sell   Purpose
          'Asiba is coming to sell fish'
      d. Àsíba   **wá-yì**   hwéví **jrá**   *(gbé)
          Asiba   pass-Perf   fish   sell   Purpose
          'Asiba passed by to sell fish'
      e. Àsíbá   **jé-yí**   hwéví **jrá**   *(gbé)
          Asiba   going   fish   sell   Purpose
          'Asiba is on her way to sell fish'

As seen from sentences (10a–e), a *gbé*-clause obligatorily requires that the internal argument, here *hwéví* 'fish', be moved to a preverbal position preceding V2, here *jrá* 'to sell'. The surface position of the preposed internal argument is similar to that of the object in the Gungbe imperfective/prospective constructions. Put differently, just as the imperfective/prospective constructions require that the internal argument surface between the imperfective marker *tò* and the verb (or the prospective marker), the *gbé*-clauses necessitate that the internal argument be "sandwiched" between V1 and V2, leading to the word order SV1-O-V2-*gbé*. In addition, these constructions necessarily include the sentence-final morpheme *gbé* that literally means 'purpose or goal'. In no circumstance can the sentence-final morpheme *gbé* be left out in these constructions. It is possible, though, to have *gbé* as postposition of a nominal expression. Compare the sentences under (10f–g) below.

(10) f. yé   tón   Kòfí   gbé
         3pl   get-out-Perf   Kofi   Purpose
         'They came to visit Kofi'

     g. [Kòfí   gbé]   wè   yé   tón
         Kofi   Purpose Foc   3pl   get-out-Perf
         'They came to visit KOFI'

When the purpose clause involves an intransitive verb, V2 undergoes reduplication, and the word order is SV1-V2V2-*gbé* as shown by sentence (11).

(11) xè   ló   yì   kúkú   *(gbé)
     bird   Spf$_{[+def]}$ go-Perf die-die Purpose
     'The bird went [somewhere] to die'

Along with the imperfective/prospective data presented earlier, the *gbé*-clauses exhibit verb reduplication whenever the internal argument is pronominalized, wh-, or focus-extracted, as illustrated by the examples (12a–b).

(12) a. Àsíbá   yì   díndín   mi   gbé
         Asiba   go-Perf search-search   1sg   Purpose
         'Asiba went out to look for me'

     b. ménù wè   Àsíbá yì   díndín   gbé ?
         who Foc   Asiba go-Perf search-search   Purpose
         'Who did Asiba go out to look for?'

When a *gbé*-clause involves the prospective marker (13a), nothing can intervene between the verb and the prospective marker (13b). In addition, verb reduplication is blocked as shown by the ungrammatical sentence (13c).

(13) a.

Àsíbá	wá	hwéví	nà	xɔ̀	gbé
Asiba	come-Perf	fish	Prosp	buy	Purpose

'Asiba came and she is now just about to buy'

    b.

*Àsíbá	wá	hwéví	nà	sɔ́	xɔ̀	gbé
Asiba	come-Perf	fish	Prosp	again	buy	Purpose

    c.

*été	wè	Àsíbá	wá	nà	xìxɔ̀	gbé ?
who	Foc	Asiba	come-Perf	Prosp	buy-buy	Purpose

Notice, finally, that contrary to the situation in the imperfective sentence (8a), a lexical DP object cannot occur postverbally in the *gbé*-clauses (14), (but see section 6.1.2 for the discussion of clausal complements).

(14)

*Àsíbá	wá	nà	xɔ̀	hwéví	gbé
Asiba	come-Perf	Prosp	buy	fish	Purpose

In addition to the properties they share with respect to word alternation and verb reduplication, the *gbé*-clauses and the imperfective /prospective sentences appear to exhibit other similarities. The next section focuses on the parallels that can be drawn between these constructions.

6.1.2 Some parallels between imperfective-, prospective- and *gbé*-clauses

First, it appears that the sentence-final low tone involved in the imperfective/prospective sentences is absent in the *gbé*-clause. Instead, the latter includes a sentence-final morpheme *gbé* that seems to have the same syntactic role and position as its tone counterpart exhibited in the imperfective/prospective sentences. Recall from examples (10f–g) that the morpheme *gbé* occurs freely as postposition of a nominal expression (see chapter 3, appendix, for the discussion on *P*Ps in Gbe). This observation underscores the hypothesis, already developed in chapter 2, section 2.4.4.2, that the floating low tone is a quasi-null morpheme (i.e., a toneme) that has survived the disappearance of a full imperfective morpheme existing in 'Old Gungbe'.[5] Building on this, I conclude that an analysis that accounts for the Gungbe imperfective/prospective constructions should also accommodate the *gbé*-clauses. I return to these facts in the discussion and show that data from Fongbe, Gengbe, and Ewegbe are also consistent with this approach (section 6.2.1).

Second, the imperfective/prospective constructions and the *gbé*-clauses behave alike with respect to sentential complement. Recall from chapter 2 that, unlike nominal complements, a CP-complement never occurs in the position immediately to the right of the verb. The examples (15a–b) indicate that when the sentence involves a direct object and an indirect object, the former necessarily precedes the latter. But when the object is a clausal complement, it necessarily follows the indirect object. This gives rise to the word order S-V-IO-CP-complement in (15c). On no circumstance can the CP-complement precede the indirect object (15c).

(15) a. Kòfí   ɖɔ̀   [DP xó]   ná   Báyɔ́
     Kofi   say-Perf   word   to   Bayo
     'Kofi talked to Bayo'

    b. *Kòfí   ɖɔ̀   ná   Báyɔ́   [DP xó]
     Kofi   say-Perf   to   Bayo   word

    c. Kòfí ɖɔ̀   ná Báyɔ́ [CP ɖɔ̀ Kɔjó   ná   wá   wéxɔmè]
     Kofi say-Perf to Bayo that Kojo Fut   come   school
     'Kofi told Bayo that Kojo would come to school'

    d. *Kòfí ɖɔ̀   [ɖɔ̀ Kɔjó ná wá   wéxɔmè] ná   Báyɔ́
     Kofi say-Perf   that Kojo Fut come   school   to   Bayo

With respect to the Gungbe imperfective/prospective and *gbé*-clauses, we observe that CP-complements are also excluded from the position normally filled by the preposed internal argument, that is, the position between the imperfective marker *tò* and the prospective *nà* in the imperfective/prospective constructions (16b, 16e) and the position between V1 and V2 in the *gbé*-clauses (16h). Notice also from the ungrammatical sentences (16c, 16f, 16i) that a CP-complement is even excluded from the position immediately to the right of the reduplicated verb. This is contrary to the situation described earlier in (8a), where some speakers allow for lexical DPs to occur immediately to the right of the reduplicated verb, on a par with the Gungbe clitic pronouns (7a, 7d).

Imperfective

(16) a. Àsíbá tò   ɖìɖɔ̀   ná Kòfî [CP ɖɔ̀ Báyɔ́ xɔ̀   mótò]
     Asiba Imperf say-say to Kofi-NR that Bayo buy-Perf car
     'Asiba is telling Kofi that Bayo bought a car'

    b. *Àsíbá tò   [CP ɖɔ̀ Báyɔ́   xɔ̀   mótò] ɖɔ̀   ná   Kòfí
     Asiba Imperf   that Bayo buy-Perf car   say   to   Kofi

    c. *Àsíbá tò   ɖìɖɔ̀   [CP ɖɔ̀ Báyɔ́   xɔ̀   mótò] ná   Kòfí
     Asiba Imperf say-say that   Bayo buy-Perf car   to   Kofi

Prospective

(16) d. Àsíbá tò   nà   ɖɔ̀ ná   Kòfî [CP ɖɔ̀ Báyɔ́ xɔ̀   mótò]
     Asiba Imperf Prosp say to   Kofi-NR   that Bayo buy-Perf car
     'Asiba is about to tell Kofi that Bayo bought a car'

    e. *Àsíbá tò [CP ɖɔ̀ Báyɔ́ xɔ̀   mótò] nà   ɖɔ̀   ná Kòfî
     Asiba   Imperf that Bayo buy-Perf car   Prosp say   to   Kofi-NR

    f. *Àsíbá tò   nà   ɖɔ̀ [CP ɖɔ̀ Báyɔ́ xɔ̀   mótò] ná Kòfî
     Asiba Imperf Prosp say   that Bayo buy-Perf car   to Kofi-NR

Gbé-clauses

(16) g. Àsíbá wá   dìdɔ̀   ná   Kòfí   gbé
          Asiba come-Perf   say-say to   Kofi   Purpose
          [CP dɔ̀   Báyɔ́   xɔ̀   mótò]
                that   Bayo   buy-Perf car
          'Asiba came (on the purpose to) tell Kofi that Bayo bought a car'

     h.   *Àsíbá   wá   [CP dɔ̀ Báyɔ́ xɔ̀   mótò]
          Asiba   come-Perf that Bayo   buy-Perf car
          dɔ̀   ná   Kòfí   gbé
          say   to   Kofi   Purpose

     i.   *Àsíbá wá   dìdɔ̀   [CP dɔ̀ Báyɔ́ xɔ̀   mótò]
          Asiba   come-Perf   say-say that Bayo   buy-Perf car
          ná   Kòfí   gbé
          to   Kofi   Purpose

In accounting for these facts, I first assume that the VO order found in the so-called non-imperfective constructions results from the interaction between object shift and verb movement. The verb moves cyclically to some higher head position, say Asp°1, due to aspectual licensing. On the other hand, the object raises to [spec AgroP] for case reasons (see section 6.2.1, and Johnson 1991). I further propose that in the imperfective/prospective constructions and the *gbé*-clauses, the preposed internal argument is moved leftward in a derived position immediately to the right of the imperfective marker or V1 and to the left of the prospective marker. In section 6.2.1, I argue that this position is [spec AspP3], the subject position of the small clause selected by the imperfective marker *tò* or the aspect verbs of the type V1 that are involved in the *gbé*-clauses. [Spec AspP3] must be filled in overt syntax in order to satisfy the Extended Projection Principle (EPP), which necessitates that sentences must have a subject. Alternatively, it could be proposed that Asp°3 has a strong EPP feature that must be checked in overt syntax (Chomsky 1995, 1999, 2000, 2001).

Granting this analysis, we can capture the data in (16) by postulating that the imperfective/prospective and *gbé*-clauses share the same properties as all the Gungbe sentences. They don't allow for CP-complements to move in an argument position: neither [spec AgroP] nor [spec AspP3]. Instead, CP-complements must be realized in some different position, either to the right of the purpose morpheme *gbé* (16e) or to the right of the quasi-null morpheme (i.e., floating low tone) found in imperfective and prospective sentences (16a and 16c). In terms of Kayne (1994), it cannot be argued that CP-complements surface in this position as a result of rightward movement (see also Johnson 1991 and references cited there for a discussion on English data that preclude a rightward movement analysis). I therefore assume that the contrast between CP-complements and other elements that occur as complement of the verb in Gungbe follows from the fact that CP-complements must target non-argument positions. They cannot be licensed in argument or case-related positions. I thus propose, as in chapter 2, section 2.5.1.5, that CP-complements surface sentence-finally in Gungbe due to leftward movement of other elements in the clause (i.e., internal argument, adjuncts, etc.) to a position higher than that targeted by the clausal complement. The reader is also referred to Kinyalolo (1992) for the discussion of similar facts in Fongbe; Stowell (1981), Johnson (1991), Haegeman (1995a, 1996c, 1998a, c), Zwart (1997a, b) for Germanic; Mahajan (1997) and references cited there for Hindi.

Third, it appears from the imperfective/prospective constructions and the *gbé*-clauses that elements that qualify as theme can be moved in the preverbal position. Gungbe allows for both the orders theme-goal and goal-theme in double object constructions (17a–b). But only the order theme-goal is attested in the imperfective/prospective sentences and the *gbé*-clauses (17c–e). In these constructions, the verb is never allowed to follow both complements. See also Kinyalolo (1992) for Fongbe data.

(17) a. Àsíbá   kplɔ́n   hàn   Kòfí
         Asiba   teach-Perf   song   Kofi
         'Asiba taught Kofi a song'

     b. Àsíbá   kplɔ́n   Kòfí   hàn
         Asiba   teach-Perf   Kofi   song
         'Asiba taught Kofi a song'

     c. Àsíbá   tò   hàn   kplɔ́n   Kòfî
         Asiba   Imperf song   teach   Kofi-NR
         'Asiba is teaching Kofi a song'

     d. Àsíbá   tò   hàn   ná   kplɔ́n   Kòfî
         Asiba   Imperf song   Prosp teach   Kofi-NR
         'Asiba is about to teach Kofi a song'

     e. Àsíbá   wá   hàn   kplɔ́n   Kòfí   gbé
         Asiba   come-Perf song   teach   Kofi   Purpose
         'Asiba came (on purpose) to teach Kofi a song'

Yet it cannot be concluded that only elements that qualify as "theme" can appear in the preverbal position in the imperfective/prospective sentences and the *gbé*-clauses. For instance when the theme is wh-extracted, the goal is allowed to precede the verb, as shown in (17'a–b), the counterparts of (17d–e) where the theme *hàn* is focused.

(17') a. hàn   wè   Àsíbá   tò   Kòfí   ná   kplɔ́n
          song   Foc   Asiba   Imperf Kofi   Prosp   teach-NR
          'Asiba is about to teach Kofi A SONG'

      e. hàn   wè   Àsíbá   wá   Kòfí   kplɔ́n   gbé
          song   Foc   Asiba   come-Perf   Kofi   teach   Purpose
          'Asiba came (on purpose) to teach Kofi A SONG'

Also recall from sentence (4c), repeated here in (18a), that the preverbal position may also host manner adverbs such as *dɛ́dɛ́* 'slowly', *gidigidi* 'brutally', and *gɔ̀jɔ̀gɔ̀jɔ̀* 'awkwardly'. As examples (18b) shows, these adverbs also occur preverbally in the *gbé*-clauses.

(18) a. Àsíbá tò   dédé /gidigidi/gɔ̀jɔ̀gɔ̀jɔ̀   (nà)   zɔ̃n
         Asiba Imperf slowly/ brutally/awkwardly   Prosp   walk-NR
         'Asiba is walking slowly/brutally/awkwardly'
         Asiba is about to walk slowly/brutally/awkwardly'
     b. Àsíbá jà   dédé/gidigidi/ gɔ̀jɔ̀gɔ̀jɔ̀   (nà)   zɔ̀n gbé
         Asiba come-Perf slowly/ brutally/ awkwardly   Prosp   walk Purpose
         'Asiba was on the verge to walk slowly/brutally/awkwardly purposely'

The presence of these adverbs in the preverbal position in the imperfective/ prospective and *gbé*-clauses favors the idea, briefly mentioned in the preceding paragraphs, that movement to this position cannot be motivated by case reasons. More precisely, the preverbal position occupied by the preposed internal argument cannot be considered [spec AgroP], the position where accusative case is assigned (or checked).

There is no agreement among linguists working on the Gbe languages with regard to the status of elements like *dédé / gidigidi / gɔ̀jɔ̀gɔ̀jɔ̀* in (18). Given that Gungbe and, more generally, the Gbe languages use reduplication as a nominalization device, one may think that the reduplicated form of these adverbs actually indicates a nominal feature.[6] For instance, the verb *sí* 'to respect' is reduplicated to form the noun *sísí* 'respect'. The same holds for the verb *sísɔ́* 'tremble' whose reduplicated form *sísɔ́sísɔ́* means 'trembling'. Further study in Gungbe as well as other Gbe languages is needed to determine the real nature of the adverbial-like elements in (18). For the sake of discussion, I continue to regard them as adverbs, bearing in mind that they differ both in form and distribution from the Gungbe monosyllabic adverbs, such as *tè* 'even', *kò* 'already', *sɔ́* 'again', which are excluded from the preverbal object position identified in the imperfective/ prospective sentences and the *gbé*-clauses (19).

(19) a. *Àsíbá   tò   tè / kò / sɔ́   (nà)   zɔ̃n
         Asiba   Imperf even/already/again Prosp   walk-NR
     b. *Àsíbá jà   tè / kò / sɔ́   (nà)   zɔ̀n   gbé
         Asiba come-Perf even/already/again Prosp walk   Purpose

Note in passing that a distinction should be made between the Gungbe reduplication process that serves as a morphological device to derive new words (e.g., *sí* 'to respect' *sísí* 'respect')[7] and the verb doubling strategy specific to the imperfective/ prospective sentences and the *gbé*-clauses. The former is unpredictable, while the latter is syntactically determined and occurs in well-defined contexts (Clements 1972; Fabb 1992b on reduplication in Ewegbe and Fongbe). The next section turns to the structure of OV constructions.

6.2 THE INTERNAL STRUCTURE OF OV CONSTRUCTIONS

On the account for the Gungbe imperfective and related constructions, I (1995) proposed that the imperfective marker *tò* creates an aspect domain that includes the verb and the object. Assuming that the Gungbe object necessarily moves leftward to [spec AgroP] and the verb to some aspect head position, sentence (3a) is thus analyzed by saying that the object moves to [spec AgroP] and the verb raises to Agr°. The order S- *tò* OV found in imperfective clauses is explained by suggesting that the verb cannot move higher to Asp° because the latter is already filled by the imperfective marker *tò*. The derivation is partially represented in (20).

(20)

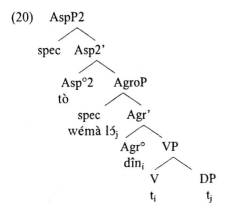

In the case of reduplication (5b), it is argued that Gungbe involves a copy strategy that allowed the insertion of a copy of the verb in Agr° leaving the genuine verb in its base position as exemplified in (21). The explanation for such a process is that the absence of object movement to [spec AgroP] results in a phonetically unrealized AgroP, whose head Agr° must be licensed otherwise by a phonetically realized element, or the copy of the verb.[8]

(21)

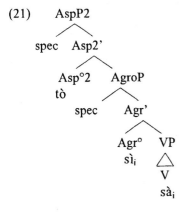

Similarly, the imperfective constructions involving clitic pronouns (7a) or lexical DP in postverbal position (8a) are accounted for by assuming that there is no case chain in Gungbe (Koopman 1992, 2000b). Assuming verb movement to Agr°, this amounts to saying that the trace of the Gungbe verb cannot guarantee for the DP object to survive in its base position, until it raises to [spec AgroP] at LF. Accordingly, the lexical verb must stay in its base position and a copy strategy applies (22).

(22)

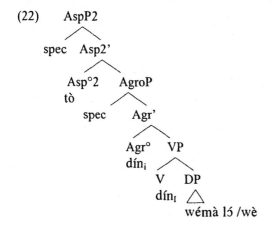

As for the prospective constructions, they are analyzed by assuming that the prospective marker *nà* is inserted in Agr°. As a consequence, verb movement is blocked and the verb remains in situ as illustrated by the ungrammatical sentence (23a). Being blocked in its base position, the verb can license clitic pronouns and DP objects that occur to its right as represented by (23c). Sentence (23b) is the unmarked case where the DP object precedes the prospective marker, which in turn precedes the verb.

(23) a. *Kòfí   tò   dín   nà   wémà   lɔ́
           Kofi   Imperf search Prosp   book   Spf[+def] -NR
      b. AspP2

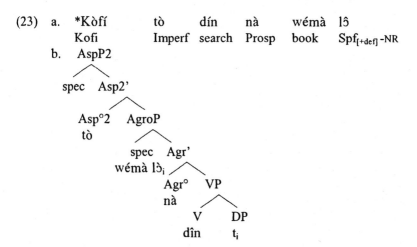

c. AspP2

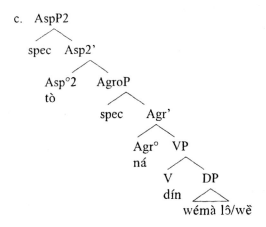

Though this analysis might look consistent with the Gungbe imperfective/ prospective constructions, it has several drawbacks. One such shortcoming is the question of clitic placement in the Gungbe imperfective/prospective sentences and the *gbé*-clauses. Let's assume, as traditionally proposed in the literature, that clitics are heads and must surface in a derived position in order to be licensed (Haegeman 1993, 1995a; Belletti 1993, 2001; Roberts 1993; Chomsky 1995; Friedemann & Siloni 1997; Cardinaletti & Starke 1999). The question then arises as to what position the object clitic occupies in a structure like (23c).

A priori, one could propose an analysis in terms of 'clitic in-situ' and postulate an LF clitic movement to a derived position in Gungbe. But I demonstrated in chapter 4 that this is an undesirable result. Indeed, such analysis suggests that the Gungbe clitics differ, for example, from the Romance and Germanic clitics, as the former must stay in their base positions but the latter necessarily move in some derived position. In addition, there is no strong evidence from Gungbe in support of such parametric variations with respect to clitic placement (or movement) in human languages. Instead, recent comparative studies indicate that clitic pronouns cannot survive in their base position and necessarily move in surface derived positions to be licensed.

From the empirical point of view, my 1995 article also falls short of accounting for the *gbé*-clauses. The structures under (20–23) provide no room for the purpose morpheme *gbé*. Similarly, it is impossible, on the basis of these structures, to account for the position that realizes the sentence-final floating low tone specific to the imperfective/prospective constructions. Recall from previous discussion (see also chapter 2) that I regard the final low tone as a quasi-null morpheme, that is, a toneme that is very much like the morpheme *gbé*. Both occupy similar syntactic positions and seem to play comparable functions in the sentence. The inadequacy of structures (20–23) becomes even more salient when it comes to Fongbe, Gengbe, and Ewegbe because these languages involve a sentence-final full morpheme in the imperfective constructions. Consider, for instance, the sentences under (24).

(24) a.   ún   *(ɖò)   nǔ   dù   *(wè)

          1sg   Imperf thing   eat   NR

          'I am eating'

      b.   mí   *(ɖò)   zìzé   è   *(wè)

          1pl   Imperf take-take 3sg   NR

          'We are taking it'   [Fongbe]

      c.   mù   *(lè)   núpó   pò   *(ɔ̀)

          1sg   Imperf word   speak NR

          'I am speaking'

      d.   mù   *(lè)   dódó   è   *(ɔ̀)

          1sg   Imperf planting 3sg   NR

          'I am planting it'   [Gengbe]

      e.   mè   *(lè)   nú   dù   *(ḿ)

          1sg   Imperf thing   eat   NR

          'I am eating'

      f.   mè   *(lè)   dzòdzó   *(ḿ)

          1sg   Imperf leave-leave   NR

          'I am leaving'   [Ewegbe]

As the reader can see, sentences (24) clearly show that, unlike Gungbe, other Gbe languages, such as Fongbe, Gengbe, and Ewegbe, exhibit imperfective constructions that involve both the imperfective marker and a sentence-final morpheme. In no circumstance can the imperfective marker or the sentence-final morpheme remain unrealized. Once again, the analysis proposed in previous paragraphs cannot account for these constructions. This is rather unwelcome, since the languages are closely related and the fact that they share similar properties with respect to imperfective constructions cannot be accidental (Capo 1988, 1991). It thus follows that the analysis proposed for one language of the cluster should also extend to other languages of the group.

6.2.1 Reanalyzing Aboh (1995)

As just emphasized in the preceding section, my 1995 article undesirably implied that Gungbe differed from other Gbe languages with regard to imperfective constructions. In the analysis developed here, I propose (as in Aboh 1996a, 1999),[9] that Gungbe, Fongbe, Gengbe, Ewegbe are all alike in the sense that they all exhibit imperfective constructions, which necessarily involve bipartite imperfective morphology including an imperfective marker (i.e., tò, ɖò, lè, lé) which obligatorily requires the presence of a sentence-final morpheme (i.e., ∅, wè, ɔ̀, ḿ).[10] In this respect, the only difference between Gungbe and other Gbe languages lies in the fact that the Gungbe sentence-final morpheme undergoes partial deletion, leaving only a low toneme that necessarily attaches to the preceding syllable.[11] In terms of the analysis presented in this study, the Gungbe sentence-final toneme is regarded as a 'quasi-null morpheme' that encodes the nominalizing feature [+n].

That is to say, the sentence-final morpheme or (toneme) specific to the Gbe imperfective/prospective sentences and the *gbé*-clauses has "gerundive characteristics like -*ing* in English" (Kinyalolo 1992: 44). In the terms of Tenny (1987), this would mean that the Gbe imperfective markers (or aspect verbs used in *gbé*-clauses) delimit a nominal environment. Granting this, the following hypotheses are in order to account for the Gungbe imperfective/prospective constructions (see also Kinyalolo 1992; Fabb 1992a, b; Ndayiragije 2000; Aboh 2000, in press b).

Hypothesis A

The imperfective marker *tò* selects a small clause, that is, a reduced clause lacking AgrP, NegP, and TP.[12] Assuming the imperfective marker requires a nominal environment, this small clause is introduced by a Nominalizer Phrase (NomP) whose head Nom° realizes the sentence-final quasi-null morpheme $\varnothing$[13] in Gungbe. In this analysis, NomP is the equivalent of CP in the clause or DP in the noun phrase. I further assume that there is a close relationship between Nom° (occupied by $\varnothing$) and the aspect head Asp°2 (manifested by *tò*) in the sense that Nom° must be the head of a constituent that is part of a chain governed by Asp°2.[14] On the other hand, Nom° dominates Asp°3, the locus of prospective marker *nà*, which in turn dominates AgroP, which in turn dominates VP by assumption. The internal structure of NomP is represented in (25):

(25)

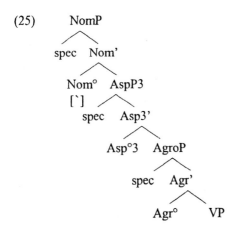

This hypothesis has three immediate consequences. First, I conclude that the sequence to the right of the imperfective marker *tò* is a constituent. Second, that constituent involves an articulated structure. Third, granting that this constituent involves a left periphery, the latter is expected to display certain properties common to the Gbe left periphery.

A strong piece of evidence in favor of the hypothesis that the complement of the Gungbe imperfective marker *tò* forms a syntactic unit is given by sentences under (26). It appears from these sentences that when focusing arises, the whole sequence must be moved to the appropriate left peripheral position.[15]

(26) a.
Àsíbá	tò	[gò	ló	nà	**dîn**]
Asiba	Imperf	bottle	Spf$_{[+def]}$	Prosp	search-NR

'Asiba is about to look for the specific bottle'

b.
[gò	ló	nà	**dîn**]	Àsíbá	tè
bottle	Spf$_{[+def]}$	Prosp	search-NR	Asiba	Imperf

Asiba is ABOUT TO LOOK FOR THE SPECIFIC BOTTLE'

Similarly, empirical evidence that the sequence [object-prospective-verb] is a constituent (i.e., a small clause) that might include other (intervening) positions is shown in the imperfective/prospective constructions involving ditransitive verbs. In these contexts, the direct and indirect objects are simultaneously focused along with the verb, as illustrated in (27).[16] In no circumstance can the verb be focused with the direct or indirect object independently. I return to focus constructions in chapter 7.

(27)
[gò	ló	nà	zé	nà	Rèmî]	Àsíbá	tè
bottle	Spf$_{[+def]}$	Prosp	take	for	Remi- NR	Asiba	Imperf

'Asiba is ABOUT TO GIVE THE SPECIFIC BOTTLE TO REMI'

Additional justification for claiming that the complement of *tò* involves a quite rich structure is found in the imperfective serial verb constructions.

(28) a.
yé	nyàn	yòkpó	lé	tón
3pl	chase-Perf	child	Num	go-out

'They chase the children out'

b.
yé	tò	[yòkpó	lé	nyàn	tón]
3pl	Imperf	child	Num	chase	go-out-NR

'They are chasing the children out'

c.
yé	tò	[yòkpó	lé	nà	nyàn	tón]
3pl	Imperf	child	Num	Prosp	chase	go-out-NR

'They are about to chase the children out'

d.
[yòkpó	lé	nà	nyàn	tón]	yé	tè
child	Num	Prosp	chase	go-out-NR	3pl	Imperf

'They are ABOUT TO CHASE THE CHILDREN OUT'

e.
[yòkpó	lέ]	wè	yé	tò	nà	nyàn	tón
child	Num	Foc	3pl	Imperf	Prosp	chase	go-out-NR

'They are about to chase THE CHILDREN out'

Sentence (28a) is an instantiation of serial verb construction in Gungbe. In example (28b), the occurrence of the imperfective marker leads to the preposing of the noun object in a position to the left of the first verb *nyàn*. Sentence (28c) shows that the object position is not left adjacent to the first verb since the object can be separated from the verb by the intervening prospective marker *nà*. Finally, example (28d) clearly indicates that when focalization applies, it must target the bracketed unit. There is no situation whereby each of the verbs contained in the unit can be focused individually with the object. This is so, even though it is always possible to focus the object independently, as illustrated in (28e).

Setting aside the appropriate analysis for serial verb constructions (Baker 1989; Lefebvre 1991b; da Cruz 1993; Tossa 1993, 1994; Veenstra 1996; Collins 1997; Stewart 1998; Aboh 2001b), the data in (28) suggest that the bracketed unit provides different positions to host the object, the prospective marker, and the two verbs in the series. On the assumption that free adjunction is impossible in natural languages (Kayne 1994), we are thus forced to say that each of these positions is associated with a functional projection within the small clause that is selected by *tò*. In addition, the fact that the so-called shared argument (i.e., the object) must precede both verbs in (28b) and the prospective marker in (28d–e) favors the hypothesis that the preverbal object position cannot be a case position. Put differently, object shift here cannot be motivated by case reasons. Instead, the object must have been assigned case to some position to the right of the first verb in the series. For example, Baker (1989) and Collins (1997), to cite only a few, accounted for the S-V1-O-V2 (XP) order assuming that the shared argument is assigned case in a position between V1 and V2. If this is the right characterization, then it cannot be claimed that the S-*tò*-(O)-*nà*-V1-V2 observed in (28d–e) is also motivated by case reasons. [17]

Finally, if true that NomP is the left periphery of the small clause, then it must show properties like the Gungbe markers of the C-type. Assuming that the sentence-final low tone is the reflex of a nominalizing morpheme that has been partially deleted, I argue that it belongs to the class of left peripheral markers, some of which may occur to the right edge. Recall from the discussion in chapter 3 that the Gungbe determiner and postnominal morphemes occur to the right edge because they force leftward movement on to their complements. The same holds of the Gungbe question marker *lò* that selects DPs (29c) (Aboh 2000, 2002, in press c).

(29) a. $[_{DP}$ òzàn$_i$ $[_{D°}$lɔ́ $[_{NP}$ t$_i$]]]
          bed   Spf$_{[+def]}$
          'The specific bed'

      b. $[_{PP}$ òzàn lɔ́$_i$ $[_{P°}$ glɔ́ $[_{DP}$ t$_i$]]]
          bed Spf$_{[+def]}$ under
          'Under the specific bed'

      c. $[_{InterP}$ òzàn lɔ́$_i$ $[_{Inter°}$ lò $[_{DP}$ t$_i$]]]
               bed   Spf$_{[+def]}$ QM
          'Where is the specific bed?'

On the clausal level, sentence (30a) shows that the Gungbe topic and focus markers occur to the left periphery. They surface to the right of the complementizer $ɖɔ̀$ in a presubject position. But in yes-no questions, they may occur to the right edge. Observe that sentence (30b) involves the Gungbe sentence-final yes-no question marker represented by the additional low tone on the topic marker. The fact that the topic and focus markers also occur sentence-finally suggests that there has been leftward movement of the clause to the specifier position of the projection whose head hosts the yes-no question marker. Notice that leftward movement of the clause is also responsible for the mirror image (*wè*; *yà*) in (30b) as opposed to the fixed order (*yà*; *wè*) in (30a); see chapters 7 and 8 for a careful discussion on the Gungbe left periphery.

(30) a. ùn   ɖɔ̀   ɖɔ̀   Kòfí$_j$ yà
         1sg   say-Perf that   Kofi   Top
         òzàn 1ɔ́$_i$ wè   é$_j$ xɔ̀   t$_i$
         bed   Spf$_{[+def]}$ Foc   3sg   buy-Perf
         'I said that as for Kofi he bought THE SPECIFIC BED'
     b. ùn   kánbíɔ́   ɖɔ̀   [Kòfí   xɔ̀   òzàn   1ɔ́]   wè   yǎ
         1sg   ask-Perf that   Kofi   buy-Perf bed   Spf$_{[+def]}$ Foc Top-QM
         'I asked whether KOFI BOUGHT THE SPECIFIC BED [as expected]?'

We now have a clear analogy between the Gungbe markers of the C-type: D, Num°, $P°$, Nom°, Inter°. They all force leftward movement on to their complement to their specifier positions. This would mean that the low tone specific to the imperfective and prospective constructions occurs sentence-finally due to the licensing conditions on the nominalized small clause, which requires that the strong features [+nominal] under Nom° be checked before spell-out. In the Gungbe imperfective and prospective constructions, this requirement is satisfied in overt syntax by leftward movement of AspP3 to [spec NomP]. [18]

Hypothesis B

With respect to the small clause inflectional system, I argue that the order S-*tò*-OV results from movement of the internal argument to [spec AspP3] in order to satisfy the EPP. In other words, [spec AspP3] is regarded as the subject position of the small clause whose left periphery is manifested by NomP. In this regard, [spec AspP3] is not linked to case assignment: it is the subject of predication. This analysis naturally accounts for the fact that not only case assigned elements appear in the preverbal position. As I mentioned earlier, this position also hosts reduplicated adverbs.

Hypothesis C

> Reduplication is a licensing process that applies whenever [spec AspP3] cannot be legitimated otherwise, either by leftward movement of the internal argument or a reduplicated adverb to [spec AspP3], or by licensing a null expletive in [spec AspP3] (e.g., in prospective constructions involving a clitic pronoun that cannot be moved to [spec AspP3]). In some sense, I consider verb reduplication a way of circumventing EPP violation by making Asp°3 stronger enabling as such the licensing of a null expletive in [spec AspP3].[19]

The idea here is that the Gungbe verb must move to an aspect position to check aspect features if it can, that is, if there is no aspect marker to encode the aspect head. It follows that the verb must move to Asp°3 in imperfective constructions, but this is not sufficient to license a null expletive in [spec AspP3] and verb reduplication must apply. An implicit consequence of this analysis is that the Gungbe aspect positions can be regarded as weak, whenever they are negatively set for the values [prospective], [imperfective], [habitual], that is, when they are not morphologically realized by the aspect markers. In other words, reduplication should be seen "a language-specific process contingent upon the weakness" of a [-prospective] Asp°3 (Chomsky 1995: 139).

Since Gungbe exhibits no agreement morphology, "a 'dummy' CV morpheme is inserted, which the verb attaches to, and which the phonological material from the verb spreads onto (in an analysis of reduplication like that of Pulleyblank 1988)" (Fabb 1992a: 15).[20] Needless to say, the word process that alternates vowels [a], [e], [o], [ɔ], [ɛ], and their nasal counterparts into [i] in verb reduplication is a phonological manifestation.[21]

The theory advocated for here straightforwardly accounts for the fact that prospective constructions involving clitic objects manifest no verb reduplication and the word order is S-tò-nà-V-CL. This is also consistent with the prospective constructions including intransitive verbs where the required order is S-tò-nà-V, as opposed to the imperfective sentences where the object is a clitic pronoun and the verb reduplicates yielding the order S-tò-VV-CL.

Granting structure (25) and the hypotheses under A, B, and C, I propose an analysis of the imperfective and prospective constructions in which a sentence like (31a) is assigned the partial derivation in (31b). Under Sportiche (1988), I assume that the DP-subject moves leftward to [spec AgrP] to be licensed for case. I further argue that the imperfective marker selects for a small clause whose subject position must satisfy the EPP. Consequently, the DP object moves to [spec AspP3], via [spec AgroP].[22] The verb raises cyclically to Agr° and Asp°3 for aspectual licensing (i.e., [-prospective]). Finally, the nominalization requirement on the imperfectives triggers the leftward movement of AspP3 to [spec NomP], creating the order S-tò-OV-∅.[23]

(31) a. Àsíbá   tò   àgán   lɔ́   dîn
         Asiba   Imperf stone   Spf[+def] search-NR
         'Asiba is looking for the specific stone'

   b. AspP2

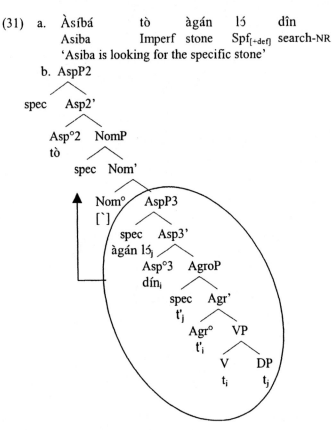

In a similar vein, the Gungbe prospective constructions can be accounted for by assuming that Asp°3 realizes the marker *nà*. Everything else being held constant, I propose that in prospective sentences, the verb is stuck in Agr°. It cannot move higher to Asp°3 as the latter is already occupied by the prospective marker. The object moves to [spec AspP3] via [spec AgroP]. Subsequently, AspP3 as a whole moves to [spec NomP] where it is nominalized. In this respect, sentence (32a) is attributed the representation (32b).

(32) a. Àsíbá   tò   [àgán   lɔ́   nà   dîn]
         Asiba   Imperf stone   Spf[+def] Prosp   search-NR
         'Asiba is about to look for the specific stone'

b. AspP2

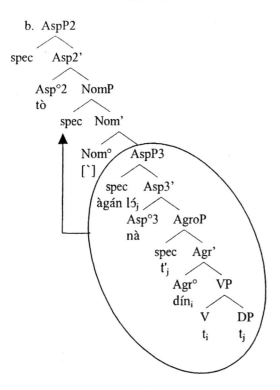

The same reasoning could be extended to the imperfective constructions that involve verb reduplication. It is argued here that verb reduplication is necessarily triggered in the case of intransitive verbs as a means of licensing a stronger Asp°3. As proposed in hypothesis C, when Asp°3 is not marked as [+prospective] (i.e., realized by the prospective marker), it must be made stronger in order to legitimate a null expletive in [spec AspP3]. The presence of this null expletive in [spec AspP] satisfies the EPP. I thus conclude that, in the Gungbe imperfective constructions involving intransitive verbs, the verb moves cyclically to Agr° and Asp°3 where it is doubled. AspP3 subsequently moves to [spec NomP] where it enters a spec-head relation with the nominalizing head. This is illustrated in structure (33b) as partial representation of sentence (33a).

(33) a. Kòfí tò   hìhɔ̀n
          Kofi Imperf flee-flee-NR
          'Kofi is fleeing'

b. AspP2

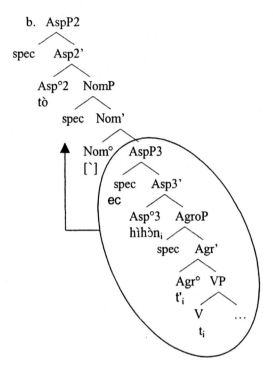

This analysis can also be extended to the reduplication cases involving object clitics. It is traditionally assumed that clitics are heads and must surface in derived positions. In this regard, it has been proposed that clitic movement includes two steps: the clitic first moves out from its VP internal position as a maximal projection and then second as a head to some agreement head positions in the clause (Kayne 1975; Siloni 1991; Belletti 1993; Rizzi 1993; Haegeman 1993; Longobardi 1994; Chomsky 1995; Friedemann & Siloni 1997; Cardinaletti & Starke 1999).

Building on this, I propose that the Gungbe clitic moves first as an X^{max} element from the VP-internal position (probably to the specifier position of a projection intermediate between AgroP and VP and labeled here as FP), and in a second step as an $X°$ element to $Agr°$ where it is licensed. The verb raises to $Agr°$ (via $F°$) and left-adjoins to the clitic. The complex verb-clitic moves to $Asp°3$. But as [spec AspP3] is not occupied, reduplication is triggered to license the null expletive, yielding the complex verb-verb-clitic as shown in (34a). Finally, AspP3 as a whole is moved to [spec NomP] for nominalization. Sentence (34a) can therefore be represented as in (34b):

(34) a. Àsíbá   tò   **díndín**   wè
          Asiba   Imperf search-search   2sg-NR
          'Asiba is looking for you'

b. AspP2

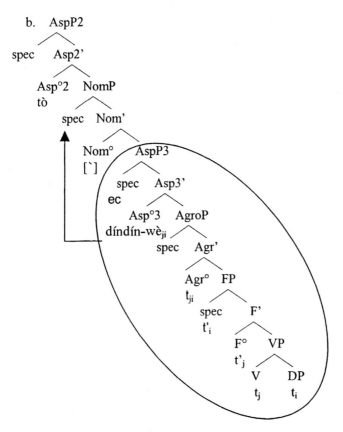

Under (34b), a sentence like *Àsíbá tò díndín wémà lʃ* 'Asiba is looking for the book', where the DP object follows the reduplicated verb, can be accounted for by proposing that the object moves to [spec AgroP] to be licensed for case. The verb moves cyclically to Agr° and Asp°3 where it doubles in order to license a null expletive in [spec AspP3]. If this is the right characterization, the marginality of such constructions can be seen as an instantiation of some 'economy principle' violation, in the sense that it might be costlier to license the argument in VP-internal position (or else in [spec AgroP]) and generate a null element in [spec AspP3] than moving the internal argument directly to [spec AspP3] to satisfy the EPP (see Chomsky 1993, 1995, 2000; Collins 1996, 2001; and references cited there for the discussion on economy of derivations).

The theory developed here also accounts for cases where the object is wh-extracted in a straightforward manner. The fact that the verb reduplicates, when the object has been wh-extracted, precludes an analysis in terms of [spec AspP3] as an escape hatch for wh-extraction. Reduplication of the verb in such constructions strongly suggests that the source of extraction is the base position. Consequently, [spec AspP3] remains empty and must be licensed otherwise to avoid EPP violation. This would mean that pure EPP positions should be distinguished from case- or agr-related EPP positions. I therefore conclude that verb reduplication follows the same path as that of intransitive verbs or those verbs whose complement has been cliticized. Here, I propose that the wh-phrase is preposed in a specifier position, say [spec FocP] (see chapter 7), and the verb moves cyclically to Agr° and Asp°3 where it doubles to license the null expletive in [spec AspP3]. AspP3 then moves to [spec NomP] to be nominalized. Sentence (35a) is assigned the partial representation in (35b).

(35) a.   ménù   wè   Àsíbá   tò   **díndîn** ?
           who   Foc   Asiba   Imperf   search-search-NR
           'Who is Asiba looking for?'

      b. AspP2

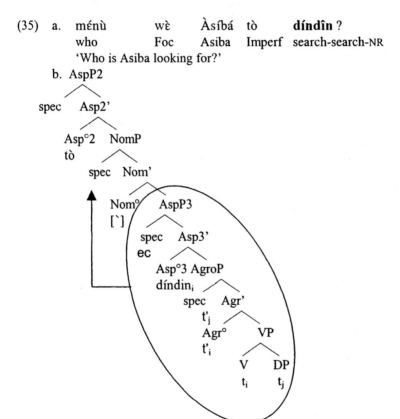

This analysis correctly predicts that reduplication never takes place in the prospective constructions (36a), since Asp°3 is filled by the prospective marker *nà* and a null expletive is licensed in [spec AspP3]. In addition, the verb is trapped (together with the clitic) in Agr° as exemplified in (36b).

(36) a.   Àsíbá   tò   nà   dín   wè
           Asiba   Imperf   Prosp   search   2sg-NR
           'Asiba is about to look for you'

b.   AspP2

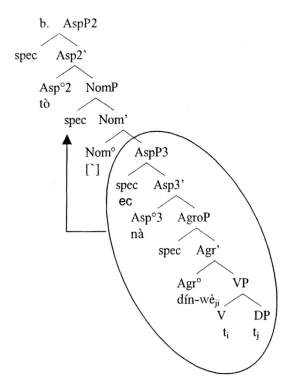

It follows that reduplication is also blocked in the prospective constructions involving intransitive verbs as illustrated in sentence (6) repeated here.

(37)   sìn   lɔ́   **tò**   nà   (*sì)-**sã̀**
       water   Spf[+def]   Imperf   Prosp   pour-NR
       'The specific water is about to pour'

6.2.2 The purpose morpheme *gbé* as an expression of Nom°

The Gungbe purpose sentences, or the *gbé*-clauses, are perfectly captured by the analysis proposed here for the imperfective/prospective sentences. The verbs *yì, wá, jà* are aspect verbs that occupy the same position as the imperfective marker selecting the small (or reduced) clause involved in imperfective constructions. An argument in favor of this hypothesis is that these verbs do not co-occur with *tò*, as suggested by the ungrammatical sentence (38a). On the other hand, the grammatical sentence (38b) shows that they can be realized simultaneously with the habitual marker. Building on the analysis put forward to account for the imperfective/ prospective constructions, I propose that the *gbé*-clauses resemble the imperfective/ prospective sentences in that they involve a similar syntactic structure. Accordingly, sentence (38c) can be accounted for if we assume that the morpheme *gbé* is inserted in Nom°. That *gbé* manifests the nominal left periphery need not be further demonstrated. Note that this marker occurs to the right edge like the Gungbe determiner, the postnominal morpheme, and the nominalizer, which all qualify as left peripheral markers (see chapters 2, 3, 7, 8). This naturally accounts for the fact that the *gbé*-clauses do not involve the nominalizer sentence-final low tone or any other left peripheral element within the selected small clause. Building on the analysis of the imperfective/prospective sentences, I argue that the object *hwèví* 'fish' moves to [spec AspP3] to satisfy the EPP. The verb *jrá* 'to sell' raises to Agr° and Asp°3, for aspectual licensing. Finally, the whole AspP3 moves leftward to [spec NomP] due to nominalization (38d).

(38) a. *Àsíbá   tò   yì   hwèví jrá   *(gbé)
          Asiba   Imperf   go   fish   sell   Purpose
      b. hwěnénu   Àsíbá   nò   yì   hwèví jrá   gbé
          at that time   Asiba   Hab   go   fish   sell   Purpose
          'At that time, Asiba habitually went out to sell fish'
      c. Àsíbá   *(yì)   hwèví jrá   *(gbé)
          Asiba   go   fish   sell   Purpose
          'Asiba went out to sell fish'
      d. AspP2

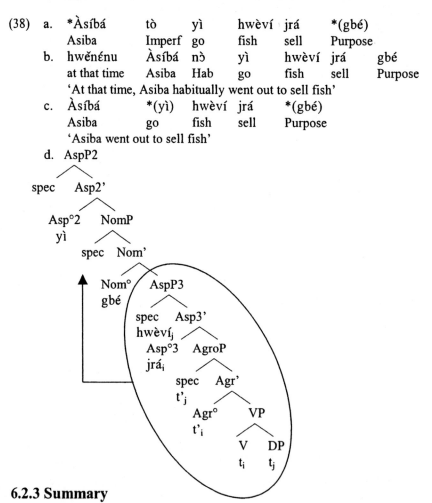

6.2.3 Summary

The preceding sections account for the Gungbe imperfective/prospective sentences and the *gbé*-clauses by assuming that the imperfective marker *tò* or the aspect verb of a *gbé*-clause selects a small clause. The latter involves both a left periphery and an inflectional system. The left periphery consists of a nominalizer phrase NomP whose head Nom° hosts the Gungbe sentence-final low tone or the purpose morpheme *gbé*. On the other hand, the inflectional system involves an aspect phrase AspP3 whose head Asp°3 is the locus of the prospective marker *nà*. AspP3 dominates AgroP whose specifier serves as accusative licensing position under spec-head agreement. AgroP in turn dominates the VP as represented in (39).

(39) ..... [$_{NomP}$ [$_{AspP3}$ [$_{AgroP}$[$_{VP}$]]]]

Under the representation (39), I argue that the Gungbe prospective constructions are parasitic on the imperfective sentences. Only a positively set Asp°2 (i.e., an Asp°2 that is overtly realized by the imperfective marker *tò* or by an aspect verb entering a purpose clause) can select for the nominalized (or purpose) small clause. The parasitic prospective marker is inserted in Asp°3 and encodes the feature [+prospective]. In this context, Asp° is strong and can license a null expletive in [spec AspP3], which satisfies the EPP (unless object movement applies). When Asp°3 is set as [-prospective], it is weak and EPP must be satisfied either by object movement to [spec AspP] when possible, or by licensing a null expletive in [spec AspP], provided Asp°3 is made strong (e.g., by means of reduplication).

　　In addition, the different word orders specific to the imperfective/ prospective sentences and the *gbé*-clauses are analyzed in terms of movement of the internal argument to [spec AspP3] (due to the EPP) and cyclic verb movement to Agr°-Asp°3, respectively (due to aspectual licensing). The low tone occurs sentence-finally due to leftward movement of the whole AspP3 to [spec NomP] where it is nominalized.[24]

　　I further draw a strong parallel between NomP and other left peripheral markers of the Gbe languages. Recall from the discussion in chapters 3 and 4 that I account for the ΣP-D-Num° order found in Gungbe in terms of movement of the complement ΣP to [spec NumP] and [spec DP] where it checks the features [±plural] and [±specific], respectively. The conclusion reached there is that the D°-Num° articulation represents the nominal left periphery.[25] It follows from the Gungbe data I have discussed so far that such licensing criterion can also force movement of the complement to the specifier position of its head. In chapter 8, I show that the Gungbe yes-no question marker triggers a similar process: the whole clause is moved to the specifier of the yes-no question marker to check the strong interrogative feature against the interrogative head realized by the question marker. In this regard, the yes-no question marker belongs to those left peripheral markers that force movement on to their complement and therefore occur to the right edge. This clearly suggests that a certain left peripheral feature, call it *force*, seems to trigger this type of complement-to-spec movement. As I show in chapters 7 and 8, for example, the Gungbe focus and topic marker do not trigger such movement freely. Assuming this is the right characterization, we now have strong evidence that movement of a complement to the specifier position of its head is a diagnostic for the left peripheral markers in the Gbe (and possibly Kwa) languages.

The analysis I develop here implies that complement-head orders cannot be taken as instances of head-final structures, assuming the directionality parameter is a valid one. Conversely, we now have additional evidence that the Gbe languages manifest head-complement orders underlyingly. Instances of complement-head orders must result from the leftward movement of the complement due to the satisfaction of some licensing condition that involves either some features of the inflectional system (e.g., EPP, agreement) or certain features of the left periphery (e.g., specificity, nominalization, interrogative, etc.).

6.3 THE VO ORDER AND THE NON-IMPERFECTIVE CLAUSES

Granting the analysis proposed for the Gungbe imperfective/prospective sentences and the *gbé*-clauses, the question arises about how to account for the word order manifested in the so-called non-imperfective constructions. In this study, the expression 'non-imperfective sentences' refers to the sentences that do not involve the imperfective marker or an aspect verb that may license the nominalized (or purpose) clause. For instance, the non-imperfective sentences include those constructions that involve the future marker *ná*, the habitual marker *nɔ̀*, the mood marker *ní*, and sentences read as perfective.

Compare, for example, the SVO order found in the sentences under (40) and the fixed order S-*tò*-O-(*nà*)-V-(CL-NR/*gbé*) specific to the imperfective/prospective sentences and the *gbé*-clauses discussed in the preceding sections.

(40) a. Kòfí   dín   gólù
          Kofi   look-Perf   gold
          'Kofi looked for gold'
      b. Kòfí   ná   dín   gólù
          Kofi   Fut   look   gold
          'Kofi will look for gold'
      c. Kòfí   nɔ̀   dín   gólù
          Kofi   Hab   look   gold
          'Kofi looks for gold habitually'

How can we account for the fact that in example (40) the verb always precedes the object while in the imperfective/prospective sentences and the *gbé*-clauses it necessarily follows?

6.3.1 Object placement and verb movement in non-imperfective clauses

In order to account for the S-(Fut)-(Hab)-VO word order manifested in the Gungbe non-imperfective sentences, I make the following hypotheses:

Hypothesis D
> Object movement to [spec AgroP] always applies

Hypothesis E
> Verb movement to Asp° always applies

Hypothesis F
> *Tò* and certain aspect verbs select for a nominalized (or purpose) small clause.

On the basis of these assumptions, I can now account for the S-*ná*-VO, S-*nɔ̀*-VO or SVO orders found in the non-imperfective constructions by proposing that when AspP2 is marked as [-imperfective], it selects a more reduced structure that lacks the higher projections NomP and AspP3. This means that an [-imperfective] Asp°2 takes AgroP as complement, which in turn dominates VP. Pursuing this idea, it can be argued that in a sentence of the type S-*ná*-VO (40b), the object moves to [spec AgroP] to be licensed (Chomsky 1993), and the verb moves cyclically to Agr°, Asp°2, and Asp°1, where it gets the features [-imperfective], and [-habitual], as represented in (41a).

(41)   a.   TP

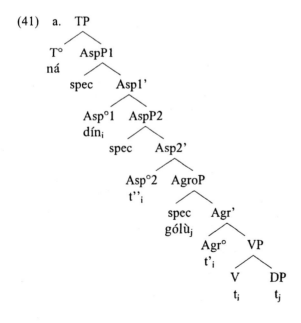

In a similar vein, clauses that exhibit an S-*nɔ̀*-VO word order (40c) are analyzed in terms of object movement to [spec AgroP]. In this case, however, verb movement is stopped in Asp°2, since Asp°1 is marked as [+habitual] and hosts the habitual marker *nɔ̀* as illustrated in (41b). In this context, the verb gets only the feature [-imperfective] but is associated with the feature [+habitual] realized by Asp°1 with whom it is in a local relation (Rizzi 1990). Note that in the imperfective/prospective and *gbé*-clauses, verb movement to Asp°2 and Asp°1 cannot hold since the verb is trapped in the small clause headed by Nom°.

(41) b. TP

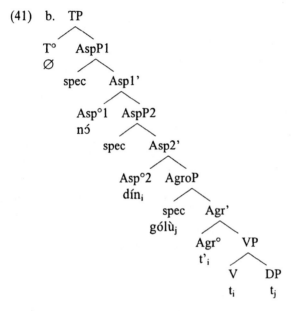

This analysis is consistent with the idea put forward in chapters 2 and 5 that verb movement in Gungbe does not target T°, since this position is always marked for features [± future] and is thus occupied either by the future marker *ná* or by a null morpheme Ø. In addition, the ungrammatical sentence (42a) forces me to the conclusion that adjunction to T° is not possible in Gungbe.

(42) a. *Kòfí   gbà   ná   xwé   lɔ́
          Kofi   build   Fut   house   Spf[+def]

The impossibility of V-to-T° movement in Gungbe is further confirmed by the fact that the language allows for certain adverbs to be inserted between the future marker and the verb, as exemplified in (42b).

(42) b. Kòfí ná   gbé   cɔ́   xwé   lɔ́   ná   yé
          Kofi Fut   at least watch   house   Spf[+def]   for   3pl
          'Kofi will at least watch the specific house for them'

Granting Cinque's (1999) proposal that adverbs occupy the specifier of a projection within the inflectional system, I can account for the grammaticality of sentence (42b) by assuming that there exists, between T° and the verb, another head position that blocks verb raising due to feature incompatibility. The idea here is that the verb cannot adjoin to an adverbial head on its way to T°.

A fundamental problem that arises at this stage is that of the perfective interpretation assigned to the sentences involving no preverbal tense or aspect marker. In other words, why is it that a sentence like (43), is read as perfective?

(43) Kòfí   xò   gbàdó
      Kofi   buy-Perf   maize
      'Kofi bought some maize'

6.3.2 Perfective constructions

The interpretation assigned to sentence (43) clearly indicates that contrary to habitual and imperfective aspects, the Gungbe perfective aspect is not morphologically realized in the sentence. Gungbe doesn't use any marker or affixation process to signify perfective aspect. In my account for sentence (43), I pursue the hypothesis put forward in previous sections that both object and verb movements apply in Gungbe, with the object moving to [spec AgroP] and the verb raising to some aspect head to check its aspect features. This leads me to the conclusion that in sentence (43) the verb must move successively to Asp°2 and Asp°1, where it checks the features [-imperfective], [-habitual] before spell-out as represented in (44).

(44)

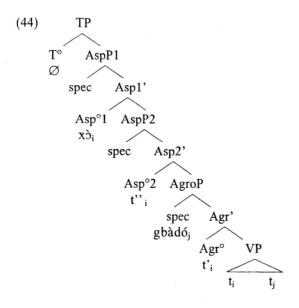

Since T° is specified as [-future], as expression of the null morpheme ∅, I propose that the raised verb associated with the features [-future], [-habitual], [-imperfective] is interpreted as perfective by default. In other words, I assume (contra Avolonto 1992a, b, c, 1995) that the grammar of Gungbe does not include any null morpheme indicating perfective aspect. I thus suggest that in sentences like (43), it is the combination of the features [-imperfective], [-habitual] associated with the verb, together with the feature [-future] manifested by T°, which triggers perfective aspect reading. This is an expression of the fact that a sentence that contains no adverbial specification (or tense/aspect markers) can never refer to an action or a scene whose reference time is the future, combined with habitual or imperfective aspects. Instead, it must be necessarily read as perfective (43).

Yet, everything being held constant, the realization of the future or habitual/imperfective markers automatically discards the perfective reading. A null perfective aspect morpheme hypothesis à la Avolonto would have to account for these facts by postulating that each time a tense or aspect marker occurs in the sentence, it has the immediate consequence of annihilating the perfective marker. This is rather an ad hoc analysis that falls short of accounting for the fact that the overt markers (i.e., tense, habitual, imperfective, prospective markers) do not exhibit such a property, since they are not mutually exclusive. Instead, they enter different combinations (see chapters 2 and 5). It therefore follows that the theory put forth in this study captures better the Gungbe facts, by assuming that no perfective marker is available in the language. This implies that the perfective aspect assigned to sentences involving no tense or aspect markers corresponds to the default aspect in the Gbe languages.

6.3.3 State versus dynamic verbs

As seen in sentence (43), the perfective interpretation is systematically assigned to the so-called dynamic verbs. On the other hand, state verbs are assigned a present time reading.[26] Consider, for example, the contrast between (45a) and (45b):

(45) a. Kòfí   zé   àmì   lɔ́
          Kofi   take-Perf   oil   Spf[+def]
          'Kofi took the specific oil'
      b. Kòfí   nyɔ́   hàn   lɔ́
          Kofi   know-Pres   song   Spf[+def]
          'Kofi knows the specific song'

Actually, the Gungbe state verbs are generally read as conveying a somewhat permanent state unless modified by time or aspect adverbs. For example, a verb like ɖì 'resemble' is generally interpreted as present as in é ɖì bàbà étɔ́n tàwùn 'he resemble father his really'. In this context only the intervention of an aspect adverb like kò 'already' or wáyì 'past' can assign a perfective (or non-permanent) reading to the verb as in *é dì bàbà étɔ́n wáyì* 'he resemble father his past', where the sentence could be understood as 'he used to resemble his father (but his appearance has changed as he grew up)'. It thus seems that the interpretation of state verbs in present rather results from the fact that they intrinsically imply a permanent state or modification (of the mind). Granting the correctness of this assumption, I can formulate the following speculation in accounting for the contrast in (45).

Let's consider that the situation of state verbs is the same as that of dynamic verbs. This would mean that both verb-types must move to an aspect head position to be licensed. I can therefore propose that a verb like *nyɔ̀* 'to know' in (45b) raises to Asp°2 and Asp°1, where it checks the features [-imperfective], [-habitual]. Since T° is specified as [-future] and hosts the null tense morpheme $\varnothing$, the verb ends up with a combination of features [-imperfective], [-habitual], [-future] that is interpreted as perfective by default. It can be argued that the perfective reading associated with the verb in (45b) signifies that the process of learning the song took place at a time t-1. However, such perfective reading conflicts with the permanent or lasting state that is normally associated with state verbs, such as *nyɔ́* 'to know'. That is, everything being held constant, the fact that the learning process ended at a time t-1 implies a modification that took place at t-1 but whose long-lasting consequence is effective at t0, t+1....t+n. A particularly telling Gungbe example is a sentence like (46):

(46)   ún   nyɔ́   hàn   lɔ́   gànjí,   ɖó   úwɔ̀   kéɖέ   wὲ
          1sg   know   song   Spf$_{[+def]}$ well   because 3S-sg   only   Foc
          ún   kplɔ́n   sɔ̀
          1sg   learn-Perf   yesterday
          'I know this song very well because it is the only one that I learned yesterday'

It clearly appears in this sentence that the verb *nyɔ́* 'to know', interpreted in present tense, denotes only the result (or consequence) of a process that took place the day before. An immediate prediction of this analysis is that the present tense reading is somehow promoted by default in case of state verbs. But the present tense reading can be overruled by means of time or aspect adverbs. This is exactly what occurs in constructions like (47) where the state verb is necessarily interpreted in the past (47a) or assigned a perfective aspect (47b).

(47)   a.   ún   nyɔ́   hàn   éhé   dáí
             1sg   know   song   this   once
             'I used to know this song'
      b.   ví   kpὲví   lɔ́   kò   nyɔ́   mὲ   étɔ́n   lé   kpó
             child   little   Spf$_{[+def]}$ already   know   people   his   Num   all
             'The little child has already known all his people'

I further conclude that the so-called Gbe dynamic verbs versus state verbs partition does not reflect a difference in syntax. In these languages, the verb must move in an aspect position due to aspectual licensing. In non-imperfective constructions, the verb must check (or eliminate) the features [-imperfective], [-habitual] before spell-out. As a consequence, sentences with no overt tense and aspect specification are assigned the default perfective aspect. In certain contexts, however, this default aspect may conflict with semantic properties (in this case, the notion of permanent state) that is normally associated with state verbs. A present tense (or a non-perfective) reading is therefore promoted, unless the sentence contains clear time or aspect adverbs that strengthen the perfective (or past) reading.

Though additional study is needed to confirm this analysis, there is no evidence against the assumption that the different behavior of dynamic and state verbs with respect to tense and aspect interpretation is lexical and does not result from difference in structure. The discussion so far suggests that the Gungbe I-system can be represented as in (48), where NomP and AspP3 are present only if needed, that is, when AspP2 is marked as [+imperfective] and hosts the imperfective marker *tò* or some aspectual verb.[27]

(48)

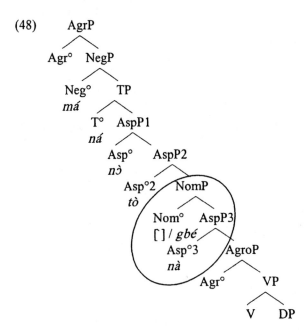

6.3.4 Some speculations on V-to-I movement

A particularly interesting point that arises from the discussion in this chapter is that there is a priori no direct relation between the strength of INFL and V-to-I movement. Contrary to what is generally assumed in the literature (e.g., Pollock 1989), I have shown that the poor inflectional morphology exhibited by Gungbe (and the Gbe languages) does not necessarily entail a poor or reduced structural make-up. Instead, I demonstrate that the language manifests a rather rich structure involving a series of functional heads that project within the I- and C-systems. In this regard, the discussion in the preceding paragraphs suggests that the idea that verb movement is driven by strong inflection is not tenable, if the strength of INFL is seen as some rich inflectional ending on the verb. On the other hand, the hypothesis is perfectly adequate if the strength of INFL is understood as an articulated structure involving a series of functional heads endowed with certain strong I-features that are not necessarily encoded on the raising verb. Recall from the discussion that the Gungbe perfective constructions involve V-to-Asp°1 movement even though there is no visible inflectional morpheme on the verb. This conclusion has consequences for understanding of verb movement cross-linguistically.

Observe, for example, that in terms of the traditional analysis (Pollock 1989; Belletti 1990; Vikner 1997; among others) English, though poorly inflected, has a richer inflectional morphology than the Gbe languages discussed here. Unlike the Gbe languages, English has both person and tense distinctions: the third person singular '-s' and the past morpheme '-ed'. A priori, this means that English should have verb-movement, which is not the case under Pollock (1989) and Vikner (1997). The contrast between English and Gbe naturally raises the question of how strong an INFL should be to trigger V-movement. With regard to this question, Vikner (1997) proposed that V-to-I movement arises in a language, if and only if all tenses are inflected for person. This formulation is motivated by data from Yiddish, a language that has no tense morphology but involves V-to-I movement. According to Vikner, this situation is expected because Yiddish displays clear person distinctions in the only tense it has (i.e., present). Compare, for example, the Yiddish data as opposed to the English examples in (49), adapted from Vikner (1997: 191)

(49)

	Yiddish	English
Infinitive	hern	hear
Present		
1sg.	her	hear
2sg.	herst	hear
3sg.	hert	hears
1pl.	hern	hear
2pl.	hert	hear
3pl.	hern	hear
Forms	4	2

Yiddish has four distinct forms as opposed to two in English. In addition, all persons are distinct in Yiddish, while in English only the third person singular is distinct from the infinitive. As the reader could see, Vikner's interpretation of the strength of INFL presupposes that person morphology is found in (all) tense(s). This analysis naturally excludes English and the Gbe languages from the V-to-I movement paradigm. But as I showed in the discussion on the VO versus OV asymmetry in Gungbe, this cannot be true for the Gbe languages. Recall also from the discussion in chapter 2 that the fact that the habitual marker precedes the verb in Gungbe and Fongbe, but follows the verb in Gengbe and Ewegbe, can be explained if and only if we assume verb-movement to the left of the habitual marker in Gengbe and Ewegbe but not in Gungbe and Fongbe (50– 51).

(50) Kòfí   **nò**   sà   àgásá   [Gungbe]
      Kofi   Hab   sell   crab
      'Kofi habitually sells crab(s)'
      Kòfí   **nò**   sà   àsón   [Fongbe]
      Kofi   Hab   sell   crab
      'Kofi habitually sells crab(s)'
(51) Kòfí   sà-**nà** àglán   [Gengbe]
      Kofi   sell-Hab crab
      'Kofi habitually sells crab(s)'
      Kòfí   jrà **(n) á**   àkòdú   [Ewegbe]
      Kofi   sell-Hab   banana
      'Kofi habitually sells banana(s)'

Recall, however, that the Gbe languages manifest no person distinction, since the verb always keeps the infinitive form. In this regard, the conclusion I reached in the preceding paragraphs is that verb movement arises due to aspectual licensing. In languages where the aspect markers are non-affixal (e.g., Fongbe, Gungbe), subsequent verb movement to T° is blocked and the verb surfaces to the right of the aspect markers (50). In these languages, verb movement is short; the verb moves to the next aspect head. On the other hand, in languages of the Gengbe/Ewegbe-type where the aspect marker is affixal, long verb movement to T° is allowed and the verb may surface to the left of the aspect markers (51).

Consider now additional facts from Bambara that also show that a rich inflectional morphology is not a necessity for V-to-I movement. The data discussed here are adapted from Koopman (1992, 2000b). According to the author, Bambara is a non-pro-drop language. It displays no person or gender distinction, nor subject-verb agreement. In addition, case is not morphologically marked, and the Bambara pronouns show no reflexes of abstract case relations. Like the Gbe languages, Bambara clearly appears to be what has been traditionally qualified as a poor INFL language. However, like the Gbe languages, Bambara has a quite rich system of morphologically distinct markers (or auxes) that realize the middle field (i.e., the position between [spec AgrP] and the verb) and express tense and aspect specifications. Among these elements, we find the morphemes *ye* and *ra* that encode the perfective aspect. In terms of Koopman (1992, 2000b), *ra* is affixal and selects only for intransitive and unaccusative verbs and transitive verbs that require a PP.

(52) a.   A   kasi-ra
           3sg   cry-Perf
           'S/he cried'
      b.   *A   ye   kasi
           s/he   Perf   drink
      c.   N   bò-ra   [PP i   ye]
           1sg   visit-Perf   2sg   at
           'I visited you'
      d.   * N   ye   bò   [PP i   ye]
           1sg   Perf   visit   2sg   at

On the other hand, *ye* is non-affixal. It selects for transitive verbs that take a DP complement.

(53) a.   Den   ye   ji   min
           child   Perf   water   drink
           'The child drank water'
      b.   *Den min-ra   ji
           child drink-Perf   water

It is interesting to see that the VO versus OV asymmetry found in the Gbe and Kwa languages also arises here. The verb precedes the complement (here a PP) in constructions involving the INFL element *ra*, while those sentences that include the element *ye* display the OV word order. Assuming that case is assigned to the left in Bambara,[28] Koopman (1992, 2000b) suggests that the two word orders can be explained on the basis of the structures under (54).

(54) a.   IP   b.   IP

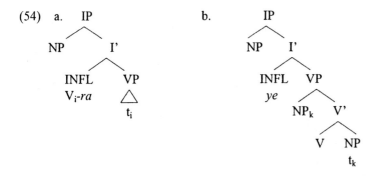

Situation (54a) corresponds to the *ra* constructions: the verb moves to INFL where it adjoins to the perfective marker. Situation (54b) matches with the *ye* constructions. In those constructions, verb movement to INFL is blocked due to case reasons: the verb must stay in situ to assign case to the DP that is located to its left.[29] As a consequence *ye*-insertion arises: it is like *do*-insertion, a language-particular device that allows the system to save an otherwise ungrammatical sentence.

It is clear from Koopman's description that the same data could be naturally analyzed in the theory I develop here for verb movement. Starting from an original VO, suppose that Bambara is like Gungbe, in the sense that the object is licensed in [spec AgroP], to the left of the VP. Suppose further that just as it is the case in the Gbe languages, the Bambara verb must move leftward to some aspect/tense head position due to aspect/tense licensing. If true, then the Bambara case can be reduced to the Gbe facts: in the perfective OV constructions, the verb is stuck in a position lower than the licensing position of the object. INFL, on the other hand, hosts a non-affixal perfective marker. In the perfective VO constructions, though, INFL hosts an affixal perfective marker. No blocking effect arises and the verb may move as high as to the position to the left of the perfective marker *ra*.[30] This analysis also extends to the Kru languages (e.g., Vata, Gbadi; Koopman 1984; Manfredi 1997). The important point here is that the languages under discussion here (i.e., Kwa, Kru, Mandekan) seem to involve V-to-I movement even though they do not fall in Vikner's formalization of what strong INFL languages should look like.

The data presented here provide additional evidence that there is no direct correlation between inflectional morphology and V-to-I movement.[31] Put another way, that verb movement can be traced thanks to inflectional morphology in certain languages (e.g., French, Italian, German, Dutch, etc.) does not necessarily mean that V-to-I movement is triggered by strong inflection, where the strength of INFL is encoded by rich inflectional morphology (i), and consequently that languages which show no such inflectional morphology prohibit verb raising (ii). In this regard, strong INFL in my terms, better qualifies as an articulated structure involving a series of functional heads endowed with certain (strong) I-features such as tense, aspect, mood, and negation. These features need not be morphologically realized. Recall from the discussion on the Gungbe perfective sentences that V-to-Asp°2 movement arises due to negatively set aspect heads [-imperfective], [-habitual], the combination of which is interpreted—together with the feature [-future] on T°—as perfective. In this respect, I argue that verb movement is forced by the licensing conditions on the verb that require that it check its features against the corresponding heads. Cross-linguistic evidence suggests that languages do not necessarily show reflexes of these licensing operations (i.e., V-to-I movement) by means of inflectional ending on the verb. Granting that languages invariably involve the category [V], I further argue that the licensing conditions on [V] should be the same for every language. This would mean that V-to-I movement is a universal process that occurs in overt syntax. This also holds of object shift, or movement of the object to [spec AgroP] due to case reasons.

This conclusion is not trivial, as it suggests (contra what is traditionally admitted in the literature) that English may have V-to-I movement. If true, we could eliminate the conflicting analyses of English in terms of affix lowering (a type of rightward movement) or covert verb movement, LF movement (Chomsky 1993; Haegeman 1994; Haegeman & Guéron 1999). In the theory developed here, there is no overt versus covert syntax with respect to verb movement. All languages involve V-to-I movement. The difference between English-type languages and the Romance languages is reducible to the fact that the former involves short V-to-I movement, while the latter involve long V-to-I movement. It seems that, in English, short V-to-I movement is masked by subsequent movement operations that might involve other components of the I-system. Recall, for instance, the Malagasy examples discussed in chapter 3 that appear to involve snowballing movement including the VP and certain classes of adverbs. In this respect, the analysis I propose here suggests that the middle field adverbs often cited in the literature may not be a diagnostic for V-to-I movement in English and all the relevant cases (e.g., Kwa, Kru). Whether adverb distribution may serve as diagnostic for V-to-I movement in a given language (e.g., French, Italian, German, Dutch) does not entail that all languages should be considered from that perspective. The middle field consists of several functional projections encoding tense, aspect, mood specifications whose specifiers or heads may signal V-to-I movement (Laenzlinger 1998; Cinque 1999). For instance, recall from the discussion that the Gbe languages involve a limited number of the middle field adverbs (e.g., só 'again', tè 'even', gbέ 'at least' in Gungbe), all of which necessarily precede the habitual marker and the verb. In this respect Cinque's (1999) seminal work on adverb placement and the middle field functional projections might provide a good starting point for a better analysis of which class of adverbs or (tense, aspect, mood, etc.) markers could serve as diagnostic for V-to-I movement in languages of the Gbe- or English-type.

6.4 CONCLUSION

This chapter accounts for the VO versus OV order found in the Gbe languages in terms of the interaction between object shift (i.e., movement of the object to some licensing specifier position) and verb movement. Under the hypothesis that the Gungbe aspect markers are the morphological realizations of the different aspect heads Asp°1, Asp°2, and Asp°3 that form the Gungbe aspect system, I propose that Asp°1 and Asp°2 host nɔ̀ [+habitual] and tò [+imperfective], which encode habitual and imperfective aspects, respectively. As the realization of the imperfective marker necessarily triggers a nominalization process as well as the potential occurrence of prospective aspect, I suggest that Asp°2 can select a small clause whose left periphery corresponds to the nominalizer phrase NomP, which is headed by Nom°, the locus of the floating low tone specific to imperfective constructions in Gungbe. I further assume that NomP dominates an aspect phrase AspP3, whose head Asp°3 hosts the prospective aspect marker nà. AspP3 in its turn dominates an object agreement phrase (AgroP) that dominates the verb phrase (VP). Under this articulated structure, I account for object preposing in the imperfective/prospective constructions in terms of object movement to [spec AspP3] due to the EPP. Reduplication, on the other hand, is analyzed as a means of licensing a null expletive in [spec AspP3] when object movement is blocked or unavailable, or else when the prospective aspect head Asp°3 is not properly filled by the prospective marker. Finally, that the nominalizer low tone occurs sentence-finally is explained in terms of movement of AspP3 as a whole to [spec NomP] for nominalization. I further argue that such comp-to-spec movement is typically triggered by the licensing condition on certain left peripheral markers. This analysis naturally extends to the Gungbe *gbé*-clauses.

Building on the analysis proposed for the Gungbe OV constructions, I take the absence of the floating low tone and the impossibility of having the prospective marker in the 'non-imperfective' constructions as a manifestation of the fact that those constructions involve a reduced structure. They are monoclausal and cannot include NomP and AspP3. These projections are exclusively licensed in an embedded small clause, which is selected only by a positively set Asp°2, that is, an Asp°2 filled either by the imperfective marker *tò* or by an aspect verb. Assuming this is the right characterization, the SVO order manifested in the non-imperfective constructions results from the fact that the object moves to [spec AgroP] to be licensed for case. On the other hand, the verb must move to the aspect heads to be licensed. In Gungbe, verb movement applies whenever an aspect head is not morphologically realized, as represented in (55). I assume that object shift (i.e., step I) and verb movement (i.e., steps II and III) are never optional. Asp°2 is negatively set in non-imperfective constructions. Yet step IV applies only and only if Asp°1 is negatively set.

(55)

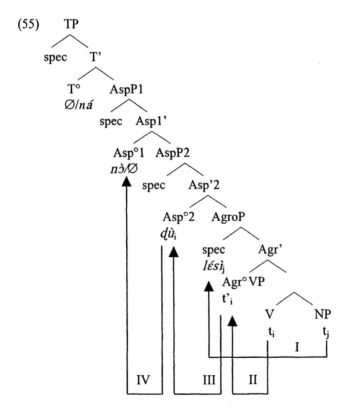

7

Focus and Wh Constructions

In section 5.3 of chapter 5, I discussed two manifestations of the Gungbe left periphery and proposed an analysis in terms of the split-C hypothesis (Rizzi 1997). In this respect, the conjunction *nɩ́* and the mood (i.e., injunctive/subjunctive) *nɩ́* are considered the expressions of Force° and Fin°, the heads of the functional projections ForceP and FinP that terminate the C-system upward and downward, respectively. This chapter investigates two other instantiations of the C-system: focalization and wh-questions.

Section 7.1 examines focus constructions in Gungbe and shows that this language involves a focus process that necessarily triggers leftward movement of the focused category (i.e., a maximal projection or a head) to a specific focus position. Sentences that contain a focused category present a number of syntactic, semantic, and phonological characteristics that distinguish them from other 'ordinary' Gungbe sentences. Consider, for example, sentence (1b)—derived from (1a)—where the focused subject immediately precedes the focus marker *wɛ̀* and sentence (1c) where the focused verb occurs sentence-initially and leaves a copy[1] in the IP-internal position.

(1) a. Sɛ́ná   xìá   wémà   lɔ́
         Sena   read-Perf   book   Spf$_{[+def]}$
         'Sena read the specific book'
     b. Sɛ́ná *(wɛ̀)   xìá   wémà   lɔ́
         Sena   Foc   read-Perf   book   Spf$_{[+def]}$
         'SENA read the specific book'
     c. xìá Sɛ́ná   xìá   wémà   lɔ́
         read Sena   read-Perf   book   Spf$_{[+def]}$
         'Sena READ the specific book'

235

In this work, the sentences of the type (1b–c) are called focus sentences and those that do not include a focused element (1a) are referred to as neutral sentences. Since focusing involves both maximal projections and heads in Gungbe, it is argued that the Gungbe focus strategy requires leftward movement of the focused category to the specifier or head positions of a functional projection FocP whose head Foc° is specified as [+f] (Ndayiragije 1993; Aboh 1995, 1998a, 1999). [2] I further propose that Gungbe focus constituents are subject to a licensing condition that is satisfied in overt syntax (i.e., at PF) and requires that every category specified as [+f] be in a spec-head configuration with a [+f] head and vice versa. Under such a symmetrical checking relation, the focused phrase must raise in syntax to check its focus features (see Brody 1990; Rizzi 1991, 1996, 1997; Puskás 1992, 1996; Chomsky 1995). This analysis extends to wh-questions. Note in example (2) that focus constructions and wh-questions are similar in Gbe. The focused phrase and the wh-phrase target the same position immediately to the left of the focus marker *wὲ*.

(2)   été   *(wὲ)   Sέná xìá ?
       What   Foc   Sena read-Perf
       'What did Sena read'

Section 7.2 argues that focus phrases and wh-phrases are licensed in the focus position, [spec FocP]. Granting that Foc° is endowed with the features [+f, +wh, . . .], it then follows that, in Gungbe, any [+wh] XP must move to the specifier position of the focus projection to check its [+wh] features against the head Foc° (Rizzi 1991, 1996; Puskás 1992, 1996, 2000; Aboh 1998a, 2001a, in press a, c). I further propose that focused elements and wh-phrases must appear immediately to the left of the focus marker *wὲ*, because the latter is the PF realization of the features [+f, +wh . . .] that are associated with the focus head Foc°. Section 7.3 concludes the chapter.

7.1 FOCUS

As I suggest in the previous paragraph, the Gungbe focus sentences reflect a syntactic process that moves the focused element to the left periphery. Focused maximal projections (i.e., elements of the type XP) surface to the left-adjacent position to the morpheme *wὲ* and leave an empty category in the IP-internal position (1b). On the other hand, verb focus moves a head (i.e., an element of the type X°) to a specific focus position, the IP-internal position being filled by a copy (1c). The following section further discusses non-verbal and verbal focus constructions.

7.1.1 Preliminary remarks

In this study, the occurrence of focused maximal projections to the left-adjacent position to the morpheme *wὲ* is analyzed as evidence that the Gungbe focus sentences cannot be accounted for in terms of cleft constructions.[3] In this respect, Ameka (1992: 3) suggests that

> focus constructions are different from cleft constructions in these languages. For example in Ewe and Akan, the focus marker may occur on a constituent in a cleft sentence, but a focus-marked construction does not have to be cleft. Obviously the two types of constructions are related in terms of their information structure, but I maintain that they should be distinguished because they have different grammatical, semantic and pragmatic properties. . . . One difference between such focus movement and cleft constructions, for example, in English is that the focused entity should be known but in focus movement constructions the focused entity should be thought to be salient. . . . The focused elements in the Kwa constructions are thought of as salient and they do not necessarily have a known information status in the discourse.

In this respect, the Gungbe focus constructions are equivalent to focus constructions in languages such as Hungarian (Brody 1990; Puskás 1992, 1996, 2000), Italian (Cinque 1990; Rizzi 1997), and Arabic (Ouhalla 1992). A superficial difference between Gbe, Arabic, Hungarian, and Italian is that the former allow for a C-type focus marker, while the latter don't. But the discussion in the following sections shows that these languages manifest the same left peripheral structure.

7.1.1.1 Some characteristics of focus in Gungbe

Sentence (4a) is a neutral sentence: it displays the SVO pattern and contains no focus marker. Sentence (4b) is an instance of a focus sentence. The subject *Séná* has moved leftward to the position immediately to the left of *wè* and the word order is S *wè* VO. In example (4c), the direct object *wémà lɔ́* is moved immediately to the left of *wè*, giving rise to the word order O-*wè*-SV. In both cases (4b–c), the sentence receives a focus interpretation and the moved element is seen as salient.

(4) a. Séná   xìá   wémà
        Sena   read-Perf   book
        'Sena read a book'
     b. Séná$_i$ *(wè)   t$_i$ xìá   wémà
        Sena   Foc   read-Perf   book
        'SENA read a book'
     c. wémà$_i$ *(wè) Séná   xìá   t$_i$
        book   Foc   Sena   read-Perf
        'Sena read A BOOK'

Example (5a) shows that the left adjacent position to *wè* must be realized at PF. Similarly, no leftward movement can occur in the absence of *wè*, as exemplified by sentence (5b).[4] Finally, the ungrammatical sentence (5c) shows that multiple foci are prohibited in Gungbe.

(5) a. *wè Séná   xìá   wémà   lɔ́
         Foc Sena   read-Perf book $Spf_{[+def]}$
     b. *[wémà lɔ́]   Séná   xìá
         book $Spf_{[+def]}$ Sena   read-Perf
     c. *[wémà lɔ́,   Kɔjó]   Séná   xìá   ná
         book $Spf_{[+def]}$ Kojo   Sena   read-Perf for
         'Sena read THE SPECIFIC BOOK for KOJO'

That one cannot assign a focus interpretation to sentences (6a–b) clearly indicates that Gungbe doesn't allow focus in situ strategy. In addition, unlike the English case *'JOHN likes beans'*, whereby the focused subject *John* bears focal stress, no stress mechanism arises in the Gungbe focus strategy. Focusing is realized only through movement of the focused element to the left-adjacent position to *wè*, as shown by examples (1b–c) and (4b–c), see Rochemont and Culicover (1990) for the discussion of focus in English.

(6) a. *Séná   xìá   wémà   lɔ́
         Sena   read-Perf book $Spf_{[+def]}$
         'SENA   read the specific book'
     b. *Séná   xìá   wémà lɔ́
         Sena   read-Perf book $Spf_{[+def]}$
         'Sena read THE SPECIFIC BOOK'

As one can see from the sentences under (7), focus movement is also available in subordinate clauses. Example (7a) is a neutral subordinate clause. It contains no focus and does not receive the interpretation of a focus phrase. On the contrary, sentences (7b–c) are instances of embedded focus sentences. In (7b) the subject *Séná* has moved to the position immediately to the left of *wè*, while in (7c) it is the direct object *wémà lɔ́* that has moved to the focus position.

(7) a. ùn   lèn   dɔ̀   Séná   xìá   wémà   lɔ́
         I   think-Perf that   Sena   read-Perf book $Spf_{[+def]}$
         'I think that Sena read the specific book'
     b. ùnlèn   dɔ̀ $Séná_i$ wè t_i xìá   wémà   lɔ́
         I think-Perf that   Sena Foc   read-Perf book $Spf_{[+def]}$
         'I think that SENA read the specific book'
     c. ùn   lèn   dɔ̀   wémà $lɔ́_i$ wè   Séna xìá t_i
         I   think-Perf that   book $Spf_{[+def]}$ Foc   Sena read-Perf
         'I think that Sena read THE SPECIFIC BOOK'

The examples presented in the sentences under (4–6) lead me to conclude that focusing in Gungbe requires the leftward movement of the focused element to a specific position, which I refer to as the focus site. This position appears to be immediately to the left of *wè*. As the morpheme *wè* necessarily occurs in focus sentences, I consider it to be a focus marker (FM), the morphological realization of the focus feature [+f] (see Ndayiragije 1993 for a similar proposal about Fongbe).

7.1.1.2 The analogy with wh-questions

Sentence (2), repeated here as (8a), shows that the Gungbe wh-question formation is very similar to the focus process, as it implies movement of the wh-phrase to the position immediately to the left of the FM *wè* (8b–c).[5] Like the focus sentences in (4–5), movement to the position to the left of the FM is obligatory and Gungbe doesn't allow wh in situ strategy, as illustrated by the ungrammatical (8d). This is, of course, with the exception of echo-questions, which I don't discuss.

(8) a. été   *(wè)   Séná   xìá?
         What   Foc   Sena   read-Perf
         'What did Sena read?'

     b. ménú$_i$ *(wè) t$_i$ xìá   wémà   ló ?
         who   Foc   read-Perf   book   Spf$_{[+def]}$
         'Who read the specific book?'

     c. wémà   té$_i$ *(wè)   Séná   xìá   t$_i$?
         book   which   Foc   Sena   read-Perf
         'Which book did Sena read?'

     d. *Séná   xìá   wémà   té ?
         Sena   read-Perf   book   which

Given the data in (8), a question that immediately arises is whether a focused category can co-occur with a wh-phrase in the same clause. The answer to this question is no, as shown by the ungrammatical sentences under (9).

(9) a. *wémà   ló$_j$ ménú$_i$ wè   t$_i$ zé   t$_j$?
         book   Spf$_{[+def]}$ who   Foc   take-Perf

     b. *ménú$_i$ wè   wémà   ló$_j$ t$_i$ zé   t$_j$?
         who   Foc   book   Spf$_{[+def]}$ take-Perf
         'Who took THE SPECIFIC BOOK?'

In sentence (9a), the focused object *wémà ló* 'book the' precedes the wh-phrase *ménú* 'who' left adjacent to the FM and the sentence is ungrammatical. In sentence (9b), the order is reversed, because the wh-phrase precedes the focused element, but the sentence is still ungrammatical. I conclude that the Gungbe focused and wh-elements compete for the same position: the focus site that lies immediately to the left of the FM *wè*. Under the X-bar theory, I can account for the ungrammatical sentences (9a–b) by saying that only one specifier position can be assigned to the focus head.[6] The same result obtains if we accept that movement is a last resort and adjunction to a maximal projection is not a freely available principle (Chomsky 1993; Kayne 1994). Accordingly, it is impossible to associate a focused element and a wh-phrase with only one head, the FM *wè*. The proposed analysis also accounts for the impossibility of multiple foci and multiple wh-questions in Gungbe.

7.1.1.3 Constituents that can be focused

The Gungbe focused categories may involve constituents of different types, as clearly illustrated by the sentences under (10). The bracketed elements in these examples show that the target of movement can be DPs, irrespective of whether they are indefinite and specific (10a), specific/definite (10b), or generic (10c). See chapter 3 for the discussion on specificity.

(10)   a.   [wémà   ɖé]   wè   Séná   xìá   bò   hù   àlè
            book   Spf$_{[-def]}$ Foc   Sena   read-Perf Coord   open-Perf madness
            'Sena read A SPECIFIC BOOK and became mad'

       b.   [wémà   lɔ́]   wè   Séná   xìá   bò   hù   àlè
            book   Spf$_{[+def]}$ Foc   Sena   read-Perf Coord   open-Perf madness
            'Sena read THE SPECIFIC BOOK and became mad'

       c.   [wémà]   wè   Séná   xìá   bò   hù   àlè
            book   Foc   Sena   read-Perf Coord   open-Perf madness
            'Sena read A BOOK/BOOK(S) and became mad'

Focusing also involves adverbs (11a), adjectives (11b), *P*Ps (11c), and verbal categories (11d–e). [7]

(11)   a.   [bléún]   wè   Séná   gbá   xwé   étɔ̀n
            quickly   Foc   Sena   build-Perf   house   his
            'Sena QUICKLY built his house'

       b.   [kpèvi]   wè   é   tè   bɔ̀   yé yí - ì
            small   Foc   3sg   be   and   3pl take-Perf-3sg-Acc
            'He was YOUNG when they adopted him'

       c.   [távò   lɔ́   jí]   wè   Séná   zé   gò   lé   ɖó
            table   Spf$_{[+def]}$ on   Foc   Sena   put-Perf   bottle   Num   Loc
            'Sena put the bottles ON THE SPECIFIC TABLE'

       d.   [xwé   lɔ́   gbá]   %wè   Séná   tè
            house   Spf$_{[+def]}$ build- NR   Foc   Sena   Imperf
            'Sena is BUILDING THE SPECIFIC HOUSE'

       e.   [gbá]   %wè   Séná   gbá   xwé   lɔ́
            build   Foc   Sena   build-Perf   house   Spf$_{[+def]}$
            'Sena BUILT the specific house'

The examples in (10–11) suggest that the focus position is not specified for a unique type of constituent, since it can host any focused XP. This is strong evidence that focus movement is not case-driven. Observe that focus movement involves both non-verbal categories (10; 11a–c) and verbal categories (11d–e). Focused non-verbal categories always appear to the position immediately to the left of the morpheme *wè*. The situation is more complex with respect to focused verbal categories. I return to this question in section 7.1.3. However, I draw the reader's attention to the fact that the diacritics in examples (11d–e) indicate that speakers tend to split in two groups when it comes to verbal category focusing. One group (including me) simply rejects the use of the focus marker in such constructions while the other considers it optional. For such speakers, the minimal pairs in (12a–b) are all grammatical.

(12)   a.   xwé lɔ́ gbâ   wè   Sɛ́ná tè
       b.   xwé lɔ́ gbâ   Sɛ́ná tè
            'Sena is BUILDING THE SPECIFIC HOUSE'
       a'. gbá wè   Sɛ́ná   gbá xwé lɔ́
       b'. gbá   Sɛ́ná   gbá xwé lɔ́
            'Sena BUILD the specific house'

However, some of my informants who accept such constructions mention that the interpretation they assign to a sentence without *wè* (12b–b') differs from the one assigned to a sentence with *wè* (12a–a'). Constructions of the (a)-type bear a kind of 'heavy focus' while those of the (b)-type are 'simple' verbal category focus. For those speakers, the (b)-type constructions represent the unmarked strategy. It is interesting to notice that this distinction might be an indication that the speakers who accept both the (a)-type and the (b)-type constructions have an additional focus strategy in their grammar. For the purpose of this study, I propose, following Ndayiragije (1993), that the Gungbe focused XPs must move to the specifier position of a focus phrase, [spec FocP]. On the other hand, verb focalization necessitates that the verb move (or adjoin) to Foc°.[8]

7.1.2 Non-verbal category focus as movement to [spec FocP]

So far, I have shown that the Gungbe focus strategy involves a syntactic process that necessarily triggers movement of the focused phrase to a preverbal position, immediately to the left of the FM *wè*. This position is unique and cannot be considered [spec ForceP]. Recall from example (7) that the focused elements occur in a position to the right of the complementizer *ɖɔ̀*, which is traditionally regarded as occurring in Force° (13a). Similarly the focus site cannot be associated with the I-system because focused elements are realized in a presubject position to the left of the FM *wè* (13b–c).

(13) a. ùnlèn   ɖɔ̀   xwé$_i$ wὲ   Rèmí gbá   t$_i$
      I   think-Perf that   house   Foc   Remi build-Perf
      'I think that Remi built A HOUSE'

     b. xwé$_i$ wὲ   Rèmí gbá   t$_i$
       house Foc   Remi build-Perf
       'Remi built A HOUSE'

     c. Rèmí$_i$ wὲ   t$_i$ gbá   xwé
       Remi   Foc   build-Perf house
       'REMI built a house'

I propose that the Gungbe focus constructions are manifestations of the left periphery. The focus domain corresponds to a projection FocP that is integrated to the C-system. Since focused non-verbal categories require the FM, I conclude that FocP is present in the structure only when there is a focus category to be sanctioned by spec-head requirement. Foc° hosts the feature [+f] that is morphologically realized in Gungbe as *wὲ*. On the other hand, [spec FocP] (i.e., the position immediately to the left of the FM *wὲ*) is taken to be the focus site. That position is not involved in case assignment and may therefore contain any focused element (Brody 1990; Rizzi 1991, 1996, 1997; Ndayiragije 1993; Puskás 1992, 1996, 2000; Aboh 1995, 1998a, 1999, 2001a, in press a, c). Put differently, the focused category in [spec FocP] and Foc° expressed by the FM *wὲ* are in spec-head configuration, and no element intervenes between them.

(14)   *xwé   lɔ́   sɔ̀   wὲ   Rèmí   ná   fó
       house Spf$_{[+def]}$ tomorrow Foc   Remi   Fut   finish

In the sentence (15a), FocP appears between Force°, expressed by *ɖɔ̀* 'that', and Fin°, realized by the injunctive marker *ní*. I provisionally conclude that when it is triggered, FocP projects as the complement of Force° and its head Foc° takes FinP as complement, as represented in (15b), but see chapter 8 for a refinement of this proposal.

(15) a. ún   ɖɔ̀   ɖɔ̀   Kɔ́jó   wὲ   yé   ní   yrɔ́
      1sg   say-Perf that   Kojo   Foc   3pl   Inj   call
      'I said that they should call KOJO'

b. ForceP

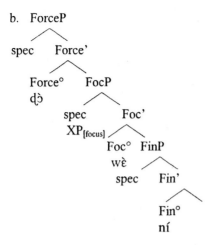

The fact that the subject *yé* 'they' intervenes between the FM and the injunctive marker *ní* in sentence (15a), precludes an analysis in terms of V-to-Fin-to-Foc movement. Put differently, it cannot be assumed that *wè* is generated in the I-system and moves to the focus head position, in a similar process to the verb-to-Foc movement found in Hungarian focus constructions (see Puskás 1992, 1995, 1996, 2000, and references cited there). Instead, the Gungbe situation is compatible with the idea that the FM is base-generated or first merged in Foc° (Chomsky 1995).

7.1.2.1 *Focusing in relative clauses*

Additional evidence that the focus domain should be distinguished from ForceP and FinP is that a relativized element cannot be focused. Sentences under (16) are instances of neutral relative clauses where the relativized element is the DP-object (16a) and the DP-subject (16b), respectively.[9] The ungrammatical sentences (16c–d) clearly indicate that neither the relativized DP-object nor the relativized DP-subject can be focused.[10]

(16) a.   dáwè$_i$ ɖě   Rɛ̀mí   mɔ̀   t$_i$
          man   that$_{[Rel]}$ Remi   see-Perf
          'The man that Remi saw'
      b.   dáwè$_i$ ɖě   t$_i$ wá   xwégbè
          man   that$_{[Rel]}$ come-Perf   house
          'The man who came into the house'
      c.   *dáwè   ɖě   wè   Rɛ̀mí   mɔ̀
          man   that$_{[Rel]}$ Foc   Remi   see-Perf
          'THE MAN that Remi saw'
      d.   *dáwè   ɖě   wè   wá   xwégbè
          man   that$_{[Rel]}$ Foc   come-Perf   house
          'THE MAN that came to the house'

Similarly, even though the relativized DP-subject can be freely extracted, leaving a gap in its base position (16b), no gap is allowed in that position when the relative clause also involves focusing of the DP-object (17a). Instead, such a construction requires the occurrence of a resumptive pronoun in the subject base position (17b).

(17) a. *dáwè$_i$ ɖě   hwèví ló   wè   t$_i$ hì
           man   that$_{[Rel]}$ fish   Spf$_{[+def]}$ Foc   smoke-Perf
           'The man who smoked THE SPECIFIC FISH'

      b. dáwè$_i$ ɖě   hwèví ló   wè   é$_i$ hì
           man   that$_{[Rel]}$ fish   Spf$_{[+def]}$ Foc   3sg   smoke-Perf
           'The man who smoked THE SPECIFIC FISH'

Under Kayne's (1994) analysis of relative clauses, sentence (17) involves simultaneous movement of the subject *dáwè* 'man' to [spec ForceP] and movement of the focused object *hwèví ló* 'the fish' to the focus position [spec FocP]. A priori, one could think that the ungrammaticality of sentence (17a) results from some minimality condition violation. A natural explanation for (17) is that the presence of a focus phrase in [spec FocP] triggers minimality effect on subsequent movement of the relativized subject. However, that (17a) could be saved by a resumptive pronoun in the IP-internal subject position suggests that this cannot be the right characterization. Alternatively, I propose that movement to the focus field leads to the occurrence of a head, Foc°, that blocks Force° from licensing the subject trace, as was the case in (16b). As a remedy to this problem, the language employs the resumptive pronoun strategy. This further supports the assumption that the focus domain depends on a specific projection that is integrated to the C-system. On the basis of sentence (18), I therefore propose that there is a hierarchy in the C-system whereby the focus domain necessarily follows the relative *ɖě* in ForceP and precedes FinP. Accordingly, I propose that a relativized element cannot be focused because relativization and focalization apply in distinct domains that correspond to a hierarchical order and cannot be crossed freely by movement.[11]

(18) [hwèví éhé]$_i$ ɖě   Rèmí$_j$ wè   t$_j$ ní   hì   t$_i$
       fish   Dem   that$_{[Rel]}$ Remi   Foc   Inj   smoke-Perf
       'This fish that REMI should smoke'

7.1.2.2 FocP recursion versus simultaneous focus

In discussing the analogy with wh-questions in section 7.1.1.2, I analyzed ungrammatical sentences (9a–b), repeated here as (19a–b), by assuming that multiple foci or wh-questions are not available in Gungbe. The reason for this incompatibility is that only one specifier position is allowed, and adjunction to a maximal projection is not freely allowed (Kayne 1994). But this analysis falls short in accounting for the ungrammatical sentence (19c) where each focused element is associated with an FM, that is, a head.

(19) a. *wémà   lɔ́ⱼ   ménúᵢ   wὲ   tᵢ   zé   tⱼ ?
          book   Spf₍₊def₎ who   Foc   take-Perf

      b. *ménúᵢ   wὲ   wémà   lɔ́ⱼ   tᵢ   zé   tⱼ ?
          who   Foc   book   Spf₍₊def₎   take-Perf
          'Who took THE SPECIFIC BOOK?'

      c. *wémà   lɔ́ⱼ   wὲ   Sénáᵢ   wὲ   tᵢ   zé   tⱼ
          book   Spf₍₊def₎ Foc   Sena   Foc   take-Perf
          'SENA took THE SPECIFIC BOOK'

A straightforward explanation for the ungrammatical sentence (19c) is that no focus recursion is possible in Gungbe. As Puskás (1995: 4) suggested for similar data in Hungarian, the impossibility of focus recursion may be seen as deriving from interpretational constraints on focusing: "if focusing is understood as selecting one individual in an identificational way . . . there can be no multiple occurrence of separate focusing, syntactically realized as separate focus projections." See also Rizzi (1997) for a similar proposal for a unique focus projection in Italian as opposed to recursive topic projections.[12]

Puskás' suggestion can be extended to the Italian constructions that exclude simultaneous focus in the main and the embedded clauses. Compare the ungrammatical sentence (20a) to the grammatical examples (20b–c) where only one focus constituent is allowed.

(20) a. *A GIANNI ho detto che IL TUO LIBRO dovremmo leggere
           'TO GIANNI I said that YOUR BOOK we should read'
      b. A GIANNI ho detto che dovremmo leggere il tuo libro
          'TO GIANNI I said that we should read your book'
      c. Ho detto a Gianni che IL TUO LIBRO dovremmo leggere
          'I said to Gianni that YOUR BOOK we should read'

                                                    Rizzi 1997: footnote 15

Unlike Italian, Gungbe does allow simultaneous occurrence of focused elements in both main and subordinate clauses[13] (see Puskás 1996 for similar facts in Hungarian).

(21) a. Sénáᵢ   wὲ   tᵢ   sὲ   dɔ̀ Rὲmíⱼ   wὲ tⱼ zé   hĭ   lɔ́
          Sena   Foc   hear-Perf that Remi   Foc   take-Perf knife Spf₍₊def₎
          'SENA heard that REMI took the specific knife'

      b   Sénáᵢ   wὲ   tᵢ   sὲ   dɔ̀ hĭ   lɔ́ⱼ   wὲ   Rὲmí   zé   tⱼ
          Sena   Foc   hear-Perf that knife Spf₍₊def₎ Foc   Remi   take-Perf
          'SENA heard that Remi took THE SPECIFIC KNIFE'

      c. hĭ   lɔ́ⱼ   wὲ Séná sὲ   dɔ̀ Rὲmíᵢ   wὲ tᵢ zé   tⱼ
          knife Spf₍₊def₎ Foc Sena hear-Perf that Remi   Foc   take-Perf
          'Sena heard that REMI took THE SPECIFIC KNIFE'

Sentences (21a–c) are instances of simultaneous focusing. They clearly show that the position immediately to the left of the FM can be activated in both main and embedded clauses. Sentence (21a) is an example of simultaneous focusing where the subjects of the main and the embedded clauses are focused. In sentence (21b) the subject of the main clause is focused simultaneously with the object of the embedded clause. Finally, sentence (21c) illustrates long focus-movement of the embedded object *hĭ lɔ́* 'knife the' to the main clause simultaneously with focusing of the subject of the embedded clause.

The availability of sentences under (21) leads us to conclude that the focus domains of the main and embedded clauses are autonomous: each can be activated separately. In addition, the grammatical sentence (21c) suggests that an intervening focus site (e.g., the embedded focus position) cannot serve as an escape hatch for long extraction. If that were the case, example (21c) could not be well formed because the embedded focus site would be occupied by the focused subject *Rèmí*, and there would be no room for the focused object *hĭ lɔ́* 'knife the' to pass through. Accordingly, there must be some other position, say [spec ForceP], through which focused elements may pass in order to reach the main clause focus point.

It is, however, interesting to notice that simultaneous focusing is excluded when long focus movement involves an adjunct, as shown by the interpretations assigned to the sentences under (22a–b).

(22) a. [gbɔjé   mè]ⱼ   wè   Séná   sè   dɔ̀
          holidays in   Foc   Sena   hear-Perf   that
          [hĭ   lɔ́]ᵢ   wè   Rèmí   xɔ̀   tᵢ   tⱼ
          knife Spf[+def] Foc   Remi   buy-Perf
          '*Sena heard that Remi bought THE SPECIFIC KNIFE DURING THE HOLIDAYS'
          'Sena heard DURING THE HOLIDAYS that Remi bought THE SPECIFIC KNIFE'

      b. [gbɔjé   mè]ⱼ   wè   Séná sè   dɔ̀
          holidays in   Foc   Sena hear-Perf   that
          [Rèmí]ᵢ wè tᵢ   xɔ̀   hĭ   lɔ́   tⱼ
          Remi   Foc   buy-Perf knife Spf[+def]
          '*Sena heard that REMI bought the specific knife DURING THE HOLIDAYS'
          'Sena heard DURING THE HOLIDAYS that REMI bought the specific knife'

      c. [gbɔjé   mè]ⱼ   wè   Séná   sè   dɔ̀
          holidays in   Foc   Sena   hear-Perf that
          Rèmí   xɔ̀   hĭ   lɔ́   tⱼ
          Remi   buy-Perf knife Spf[+def]
          'Sena heard DURING THE HOLIDAYS that Remi bought the specific knife'
          'Sena heard that Remi bought the specific knife DURING THE HOLIDAYS'

      d. [Sɔ̀]ⱼ   wè   Séná   sè   dɔ̀
          yesterday Foc   Sena   hear-Perf   that

Rèmí	ná	xɔ̀	hĭ	lɔ́	t$_j$
Remi	Fut	buy	knife	Spf$_{[+def]}$	

'Sena heard YESTERDAY that Remi bought the specific knife'
'Sena heard that Remi bought the specific knife TOMORROW'

In terms of Rizzi's (1990) Relativized Minimality, the argument versus adjunct asymmetry manifested in sentences under (21) and (22) can be explained by saying that sentences (22a–b) involve two A'-chains that interfere with each other. In sentence (22a), for example, the trace of the object *hĭ lɔ́* 'the knife' is licensed by the verb *xɔ̀* 'buy' (assuming head-government). As it is an argument, the focused object carries a referential index and the binding relation between *hĭ lɔ́* and its trace holds. This is not the case with *gbɔ̀jé mὲ* 'during the holidays', which does not bear a referential index, being a time adjunct. Its trace is thus subject to antecedent-government under Rizzi's approach. It follows that in a context like (22a), long construal is impossible because the antecedent-governor *gbɔ̀jé mὲ* is too far in the clause, and the intervening focused object *hĭ lɔ́* acts as potential governor. What seems to be the case here is that head government suffices to license A'-chains involving arguments, while antecedent government is required when focus movement includes an adjunct. That sentences (22a–b) can be interpreted only as involving local focus movements on the main and embedded clauses underscores this analysis. In a similar vein, I can explain the ambiguity that arises in examples (22c–d) by saying that long construal is made possible due to the fact that there is no potential governor in the embedded [spec FocP] that could block antecedent government from [spec FocP] of the main clause. Sentence (22d) is particularly interesting in this respect. Recall from the discussion in chapter 5 that the time adjunct *sɔ̀*, which literally means [± 1 day], is identified as 'yesterday' when T° is marked as [-future], or 'tomorrow' when T° is specified as [+future]. This clearly shows that the first interpretation of sentence (22d) associates the time adjunct with the [-future] T° of the main clause. The second interpretation combines the time adjunct with the embedded [+future] T°, suggesting that there has been long extraction.

The sentences under example (22') further illustrate the adjunct versus argument asymmetry. In the sentence (22'a), the adverb *bléún* occurs in [spec FocP] of the main clause, and the sentence is ambiguous. Both short and long construals are possible: the adverb is extracted from the embedded or from the main clause.

(22') a. [bléún]$_j$ wὲ yé ɖɔ̀ t$_j$ ɖɔ̀ Rèmí xɔ̀ hĭ lɔ́
 quickly Foc 3pl say-Perf that Remi buy-Perf knife Spf$_{[+def]}$
 'They QUICKLY said that Remi bought the specific knife'

 b. [bléún]$_j$ wὲ yé ɖɔ̀ ɖɔ̀ Rèmí xɔ̀ hĭ lɔ́ t$_j$
 quickly Foc 3pl say-Perf that Remi buy-Perf knife Spf$_{[+def]}$
 'They said that Remi bought the specific knife QUICKLY'

But when simultaneous focusing arises, both in the main and subordinate clauses, only local (or short) construal is possible. The adverb is understood as originating from the main clause (22'c).

(22') c.   [bléún]ⱼ wè yé ɖɔ̀ tⱼ   ɖɔ̀ [Rèmí]ᵢ wè tᵢ xɔ̀   hĭ   lɔ́
quickly Foc 3pl say-Perf that Remi   Foc   buy-Perf knife Spf[+def]
'They QUICKLY said that REMI bought the specific knife'
*'They said that REMI bought the specific knife QUICKLY'

As I showed in the preceding paragraphs, I can account for the data in (22') in terms of Rizzi's (1990) Relativized Minimality or some of its variants (see Rizzi 1990, 2001; Chomsky 1995; Collins 1996, 2001; Roberts 2001, and references cited there). In addition, the fact that the sentences under (22) and (22') manifest an argument versus adjunct asymmetry clearly suggests that the ability of activating the focus domains separately—in the main or embedded clauses—need not mean that no chain interference arises in long focus movement.

7.1.2.3 The focus criterion and the checking theory

Granting the hypothesis that the Gungbe non-verbal focus involves XP-movement to [spec FocP], the next step to take is to identify what motivation underlies this process. In this perspective, I assume, in line with Chomsky (1993) and Rizzi (1997), that

> syntactic movement is "last resort" in the precise sense that it must be triggered by the satisfaction of certain quasi-morphological requirement of heads. . . . Independently from the particular style of presentation, the "last resort" intuition provides the conceptual justification for postulating a rich and articulated structure to host the different kinds of phrases moved to the left periphery: no free preposing and adjunction to IP is permissible, all kinds of movements to the left periphery must be motivated by the satisfaction of some criterion, hence by the presence of a head entering into the required spec-head configuration with the preposed phrase. (Rizzi 1997: 282)[14]

With regard to focus constructions, this requirement is expressed in terms of the focus criterion as proposed by Brody (1990: 208)[15]

(23)   a.   At s-structure and LF the spec of an FP must contain a +f-phrase.
       b.   At LF all +f-phrases must be in an FP.

The focus criterion is an expression of the fact that at the appropriate level of representation, every +f-phrase must be in a spec-head relation with a head endowed with the feature [+f].[16] It can be regarded as a universal rule that necessarily applies to all languages: either in overt syntax in languages like Hungarian, Gungbe, or at LF in languages like classical Arabic (Ouhalla 1992). In this framework, focus movement to [spec FocP] is motivated by the satisfaction of the focus criterion. It has been suggested in the literature (e.g., Haegeman 1995) that a trace cannot satisfy the focus criterion because a focused element that lands in [spec FocP] is frozen and cannot move further.

This constraint correctly excludes a representation of the ungrammatical (16c) and (16d), where the focus criterion is satisfied by the trace of the relativized element.[17]

Under Chomsky's (1995) checking theory, the focus criterion can be reformulated in terms of a symmetrical checking relation between the phrase in [spec FocP] and the focus head. This would mean that the head Foc° is endowed with a strong feature [+f] that must be "checked" at PF (see also Carstens 2000). Building on this, I can now straightforwardly account for the ungrammaticality of sentences under (24). Sentence (24a) is ruled out because the feature [+f] under FM *wè* is not checked. More precisely, the FM is not in a spec-head relation with a [+f]-phrase. Similarly, (24b) is ungrammatical because the focused object *wémà lɔ́* is not in a spec-head relation with a [+f] head. Sentence (24c) is ungrammatical because it contains no FM with a feature [+f] to be checked. In addition, the sentence does not include any phrase that needs to check its focus feature. Granting that checking entails raising in Gungbe (i.e., occurs in overt syntax), I can explain the absence of focus in situ strategy in the language by saying that a non-raised [+f]-category will fail to check its focus features.

(24) a. *wè   Séná   xìá   wémà   lɔ́
         Foc   Sena   read-Perf book   Spf$_{[+def]}$
         'Sena read THE SPECIFIC BOOK'

     b. *wémà lɔ́   Séná xìá
         book   Spf$_{[+def]}$ Sena read-Perf
         'Sena read THE SPECIFIC BOOK'

     c. *Séná   xìá   wémà lɔ́
         Sena   read-Perf book Spf$_{[+def]}$
         'Sena read THE SPECIFIC BOOK'

It follows that the Gungbe focus movement involving a non-verbal category can be represented as in (25).

(25) $[_{ForceP}\ [_{Force°}\ \text{ɖɔ̀}\ [_{FocP}\ XP_{i\,[+f]}\ [_{Foc°}\ \text{wè}\ [_{FinP}\ ...t_i...\ ]]]]]$

This analysis is also compatible with the idea developed in previous paragraphs that the focus domain (i.e., FocP) can be activated separately or simultaneously in both the main and embedded clauses. This would mean that, when possible, the focus features are checked either within the embedded clause (26a), or the main clause (26b), or both simultaneously (26c).

(26) a. ùnlèn   ɖɔ̀   Séná$_i$ wè   t$_i$ xìá   wémà   lɔ́
         1sg think-Perf that   Sena   Foc   read-Perf book   Spf$_{[+def]}$
         'I think that SENA read the specific book'

     b. wémà lɔ́$_i$ wè   ùn   lèn   ɖɔ̀   Séna xìá   t$_i$
         book Spf$_{[+def]}$ Foc 1sg think-Perf that   Sena read-Perf
         'I think that Sena read THE SPECIFIC BOOK'

c.   Séna$_i$ wè   t$_i$ sè   ɖɔ̀ Rèmí$_j$ wè t$_j$ zé   hǐ   lɔ́
    Sena Foc   hear-Perf that Remi Foc take-Perf knife Spf$_{[+def]}$
    'SENA   heard that REMI took the specific knife'

7.1.3 Verbal category focus

As one can see in example (27), the Gungbe verbal category focus is characterized by two different strategies. The first strategy (call it verbal XP focus) moves the complement(s) of the verb and the verb itself—the verb in that sequence—to a presubject position (27a), while the second strategy (call it verb focus) moves the verb to a presubject position, leaving a copy in the IP-internal position (27b).

(27) a. [xwé   lɔ́   gbá]$_i$ %wè Séná tè t$_i$
        house Spf$_{[+def]}$ build- NR   Foc   Sena Imperf
        'Sena is BUILDING THE SPECIFIC HOUSE'
    b. [gbá] %wè Séná   gbá   xwé lɔ́
        build Foc Sena   build-Perf house Spf$_{[+def]}$
        'Sena BUILT the specific house'

Recall from the discussion in section 7.1.1.3 that the Gungbe speakers split in two groups with respect to the occurrence of the FM in focus constructions involving a verbal category. The diacritics in sentences (27a–b) indicate this tendency.

7.1.3.1 Verbal XP focus

The Gungbe verbal XP focus is specific to imperfective (and related) clauses, or constructions that typically involve preposing of the internal argument to a preverbal position and/or verb reduplication. Sentences under (28a–b) illustrate the Gungbe imperfective and gbé-clauses, respectively.

(28) a. Séná   tò   mótò lɔ́   dîn
        Sena   Imperf car   Spf$_{[+def]}$ search- NR
        'Sena is looking for the specific car'
    b. Séná   yì   mótò lɔ́   dîn   gbé
        Sena   Imperf car   Spf$_{[+def]}$ search   purpose
        'Sena went to look for the specific car'

As we saw in chapter 6, verb reduplication necessarily occurs in imperfective and related constructions in four major contexts:

1.   The object is a clitic pronoun (29a–b)

(29) a. Séná   tò   díndín   m̀
      Sena   Imperf search-search 1sg- NR
      'Sena is looking for me'

    b. Séná yì   díndín   mì   gbé
      Sena go-Perf   search-search 1sg Purpose
      'Sena went to look for me'

2. The object is wh-extracted (or focused) as shown in (30a–d)

(30) a. ménú$_i$ wè Séná tò   díndîn t$_i$?
      who   Foc Sena Imperf search-search- NR
      'Who is Sena looking for ?'

    b. Kòfí$_i$ wè Séná tò   díndîn t$_i$
      Kofi   Foc Sena Imperf search-search- NR
      'Sena looking for KOFI'

    c. ménú$_i$ wè Séná yì   díndín   t$_i$ gbé ?
      who   Foc Sena go-Perf search-search   Purpose
      'Who did Sena go looking for ?'

    d. Kòfí$_i$ wè Séná yì   díndín   t$_i$ gbé
      Kofi   Foc Sena go-Perf search-search   Purpose
      'Sena went to look for KOFI'

3. The object is a clause (31a–b)

(31) a. Séná tò ɖìɖɔ̀ ná Akìn [ɖɔ̀ kpònɔ̀ lɔ́   wá]
      Sena Imperf say-say to Akin- NR that   policeman Spf$_{[+def]}$ come-Perf
      'Sena is telling Akin that the specific policeman came'

    b. Séná   wá   ɖìɖɔ̀   ná   Kɔjó gbé
      Sena   come-Perf say-say to   Kojo Purpose
      [ɖɔ̀ kpònɔ̀   lɔ́   wá]
      that policeman   Spf$_{[+def]}$ come-Perf
      'Sena came to tell Kojo that the specific policeman came'

4. The verb is intransitive (32a–b)

(32) a. Séná   tò   hìhɔ̀n
      Sena   Imperf flee-flee- NR
      'Sena is fleeing'

    b. Séná jà   títɔ́n   gbé
      Sena arrive   go-out   Purpose
      'Sena is about to go out'

It appears from the description provided here that sentences involving object preposing (say type-1) manifest the word order S-*tò*-O-V-NR (28) while those including verb reduplication (say type-2) display the schema S-*tò*-V-V-(Cl)-NR; see the discussion in chapters 5 and 6. In my analysis of the Gungbe verbal XP focus, I discuss sentences of type-1, S-*tò*-O-V-NR, because only these imperfective constructions freely allow verbal XP focalization.

7.1.3.1.1 Verbal XP focus and verb reduplication

The ungrammatical sentence (33a) indicates that verbal XP focus is blocked when the sentence involves a reduplicated transitive verb followed by a clitic pronoun. In such contexts, the preferred strategy is shown in example (33b), whereby the preposed verbal XP includes a strong pronoun occurring in the preverbal object position. This gives rise to the OV S *tè* word order normally found in verbal XP focus involving a full DP-object, as example (33c) shows.

(33) a. *díndín   mì̀   Sɛ́ná   tè
           search-search   1sg- NR   Sena   Imperf
      b. nyɛ̀   dîn   Sɛ́ná   tè
           1sg-S   search- NR   Sena   Imperf
           'Sena is LOOKING FOR ME'
      c. Súrù   dîn   Sɛ́ná   tè
           Suru   search- NR   Sena   Imperf
           'Sena is LOOKING FOR SURU'

The sentences under (33) show that the [OV] word order found in the Gungbe imperfective and related constructions must be preserved even when focusing arises. As a result, the unique sequence that is allowed in a verbal XP focus involving transitive verbs is [OV] S *tè*.[18] Yet, the imperfective sentences containing intransitive verbs do allow for movement of the reduplicated complement of *tò*, as shown in (34).

(34) hìhɔ̀n   Sɛ́ná   tè
      flee-flee- NR   Sena   Imperf
      'Sena is FLEEING'

The analysis proposed here accounts for cases involving both transitive and intransitive verbs (33b–c; 34), as well as other related OV constructions (prospectives, *gbé*-clauses). But for the sake of clarity, the examples provided in this study are all instances of imperfective constructions containing transitive verbs.

7.1.3.1.2 Why tò must change into tè

As examples (33b–c) and (34) show, an outstanding property of verbal XP focus is that it necessarily triggers the alternation of the imperfective marker from *tò* into *tè* .

(35) Séná   dîn   %wὲ   mí   tὲ/*tò
      1sg   search- NR   Foc   1pl   Imperf
      'We are LOOKING FOR'

The alternation of *tò* into *tὲ* is not limited to verbal XP focus. Actually, a more accurate characterization would be to say that *tò* must change into *tὲ* whenever the complement, or more precisely the right-adjacent element, is fronted (i.e., by wh-extraction or focusing). This is exemplified by the sentences under (36).

(36) a. Séná   tò   yòvótòmὲ
          Sena   be   Europe
          'Sena is in Europe'
      b. *Séná   tò   dîn   yòvótòmὲ
          Sena   be   now   Europe
          'Sena is in Europe now'
      c. fíté   wὲ   Séná   tὲ ?
          Where   Foc Sena   be
          'where is Sena ?'
      d. yòvótòmὲ wὲ   Séná   tὲ
          Europe   Foc Sena   be
          'Sena is in EUROPE' (not in Africa)
      e. yòvótòmὲ wὲ   ùn   kpé   Séná   tὲ
          Europe   Foc 1sg   meet-Perf Sena   Prep
          'I met Sena in EUROPE'

In sentence (36a), *tò* surfaces as main predicate of the clause, though it cannot be reasonably analyzed on a par with the Gungbe lexical verbs (see chapter 5, section 5.2.2.1 for the discussion). The sentence (36b) shows that nothing can intervene between *tò* and the locational phrase immediately to its right. In sentences (36c–d), the locational phrase is wh-fronted and focused, respectively, triggering as such the necessary *tò/té* alternation. Finally, example (36e) indicates that this change also occurs in cases where *tò* surfaces as a preposition-like element that is stranded by its complement.

7.1.3.1.2.1 On the resumptive pronoun strategy

In accounting for similar facts in Fongbe, Ndayiragije (1993) proposed an analysis in terms of resumptive pronoun. Accordingly, the change of the Fongbe imperfective marker from *ɖò* into *ɖè* in sentence (37) (Ndayiragije's 149b) was seen as a reflex of 'vocalic harmony' between the imperfective marker and the resumptive pronoun *è* immediately to its right.

(37) àxì   mὲ   wὲ   Kɔ́kú ɖò   *(è)
      market   in   Foc Koku   be   3sg
      'Koku is at the market place'

Ndayiragije (1993) argues that the resumptive strategy involved in these constructions results from the fact that *ɖò* selects a KP whose complement is the locational phrase. When focusing applies, the locational phrase moves to [spec FocP] via [spec KP], leaving a trace in its base position (38) (Ndayiragije's 150). Assuming relativized minimality, Ndayiragije then concluded that, in this configuration, antecedent government is assured, but the trace fails to be head-governed due to the intervening head K°. Consequently, Fongbe adopts a resumptive pronoun strategy to avoid ungrammaticality, hence the occurrence of the third person singular clitic pronoun in the base position of the focused locational phrase (37).

(38)

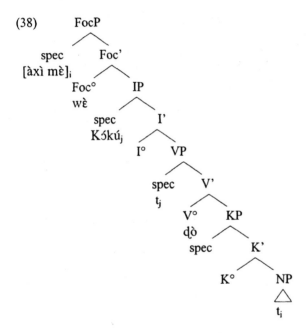

A problem with this analysis, though, is the obscure role of the projection KP. If we assume that the locational phrase is a nominal element (chapter 3, appendix) and KP a case phrase, as generally postulated in the literature, then it is not clear why the head K° fails to license the trace of the focused nominal complement. Also, Ndayiragije's analysis provides no explanation for the impossibility of the resumptive pronoun strategy in focus sentences where the habitual marker appears as main predicate, as shown by the Gungbe sentence (39a). This is an unwelcome situation, for both the imperfective and habitual markers belong to the class of the Gbe IP-markers. Notice also from the focus sentence (39b) that the resumptive strategy is not available in the Gungbe focus sentences involving lexical verbs. Put another way, those constructions do not involve a resumptive pronoun that occupies the IP-internal position of the moved (or focused) XP. This is of course with the exception of long subject extraction, where the subject position is necessarily occupied by a resumptive pronoun, due to that-trace effect (39c).[19]

(39) a. yòvótòmè   wὲ   Sɛ́ná   nɔ̀
          Europe   Foc   Sena   stay-Perf
          'Sena lived IN EUROPE'

      b. yòvótòmè   wὲ   Sɛ́ná   yì
          Europe   Foc   Sena   go-Perf
          'Sena went TO EUROPE'

      c. Sɛ́ná   wὲ   Kɔ̀kú   ɖɔ̀   ɖɔ̀   é   yì   yòvótòmè
          Sena   Foc   Koku   say-Perf that   3sg   go-Perf   Europe
          'Koku said that SENA went to Europe'

7.1.3.1.2.2 *Tὲ* as *tò* +agr

Given the inadequacies of Ndayiragije's analysis, I propose that the change from *tò* into *tὲ* is a manifestation of movement of the right-adjacent element through the spec of *tò*, used here as main predicate in (36), to [spec FocP]. The Gungbe situation is therefore similar to that of the French past participle agreement, where movement of the object through the specifier position of the past participle agreement phrase triggers agreement on to the verb[20] (see Kayne 1985, 1987, and references cited there, and Avolonto 1995 for a similar proposal in Fongbe). Suppose that, in sentences like (36a), *tò* heads a Predicate Phrase (PredP) that takes the locational phrase *P*P as complement (Zwart 1997a). Since those sentences do not contain any lexical verb, we can account for the word order *tò* - *P*P by proposing that *tò* must move to Asp°2 and Asp°1 successively to support aspect features [-imperfective, -habitual . . .] by default. Assuming this is the right characterization, we can attribute the partial representation (40a) to sentence (36a), (the 'bar level of PredP omitted).

(40) a. AspP1

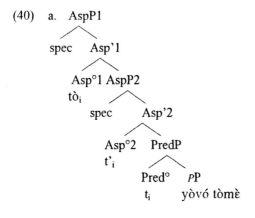

In sentences (36d), on the other hand, the *P*P-complement moves to [spec FocP] via [spec PredP], which is therefore filled by an intermediate trace (40b). As a result, *tò* must change into *tè* as a reflex of spec-head agreement.

(40) b.

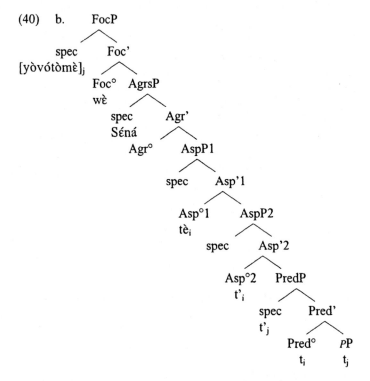

Notice that this special agreeing form (i.e., *tò* +agr) involves only cases where the right adjacent element has been extracted through the specifier of the projection headed by *tò*. This is exactly what we see in verbal XP focus, since the whole constituent immediately to the right of the imperfective marker is preposed, as shown by the partial representation (41).

(41) [$_{FocP}$ Sèná dín$_i$ [$_{Foc°}$ [$_{AgrsP}$ mí ......[$_{AspP2}$ t'$_i$ tè   [t$_i$]]]]]

On the surface level, it is quite interesting to notice that the conditions which trigger alternation from *tò* into *tè* are very similar to those underlying verb reduplication in Gungbe. In both cases, word alternation is triggered by some spec-head requirement.

7.1.3.1.3 Verbal XP focus as NomP focus

That verbal XP focus applies to the right-adjacent element to the imperfective marker (i.e., NomP) is supported by the fact that, in the Gungbe focus prospective constructions, the prospective marker *ná* moves along with the object and the verb in a fixed order [O *nà* V], as shown by example (42b) derived from (42a).

(42) a. Séná   tò   mótò ló   nà   kũ
        Sena Imperf   car $Spf_{[+def]}$ Prosp drive-NR
        'Sena is about to drive the specific car'

    b. [mótò ló   nà   kũ]   Séná tè
        car $Spf_{[+def]}$ Prosp drive-NR Sena Imperf
        'Sena is ABOUT TO DRIVE THE SPECIFIC CAR'

Building on the analysis proposed in chapter 6, section 6.2.1, for imperfective and related sentences, I conclude that the [OV-NR]-S-*tè* order required in verbal XP focus results from NomP movement to the specifier position of the focus phrase. In other words, verbal XP focus cannot be equated with VP fronting. Instead, it involves preposing of a maximal projection—different from the VP—that contains the verb and its complement(s). Sentences under (43) lend additional support to this hypothesis.

(43) a. Séná tò   [wémà ló   xò   ná   Kòfì]
        Sena Imperf book $Spf_{[+def]}$ buy   for   Kofi-NR
        'Sena is buying the specific book for Kofi'

    b. wémà ló   wè   Séná tò   xìxò   ná   Kòfì
        book $Spf_{[+def]}$ Foc Sena Imperf buy-buy for   Kofi-NR
        'Sena is buying THE SPECIFIC BOOK for Kofi'

    c. Kòfí wè   Séná tò   wémà ló   xò   nâ
        Kofi Foc Sena Imperf book $Spf_{[+def]}$ buy   for-NR
        'Sena is buying the specific book for KOFI'

    d. *wémà ló   xò   Séná tè   ná   Kòfí
        book $Spf_{[+def]}$ buy-NR Sena Imperf for   Kofi

    e. *Kòfí xò   Séná tè   wémà ló   ná
        Kofi buy-NR Sena Imperf book $Spf_{[+def]}$ for

    f. [wémà ló   xò   ná   Kòfì] Séná tè
        book $Spf_{[+def]}$ buy   for   Kofi-NR Sena Imperf
        'Sena is BUYING THE SPECIFIC BOOK FOR KOFI'

Sentence (43a) instantiates the Gungbe imperfective construction involving a ditransitive verb. Examples (43b–c) suggest that even though both the direct object and the indirect object can be focused individually, they can never be preposed separately with the verb, as illustrated by the ungrammatical sentences (43d–e). The unique word order exhibited in verbal XP focalization is [OVIO-NR]-(FM)-S-*tè*.

Since the S *tò* OV-NR pattern required in the imperfective results from movement of the object to [spec AspP3], I could not argue that the constituent involved in verbal XP focalization is the VP itself. It is rather a maximal projection that is higher than the object and the verb, but follows the imperfective aspect phrase (AspP2). Recall that the imperfective marker *tò* remains in situ and must change into *tè*, as a reflection of movement through its specifier position. If this line of reasoning is correct, we predict that, in languages where the nominalizer head (i.e., Nom°) is morphologically realized, the latter necessarily moves alongside with the object and the verb to the focus position. In those contexts, the required word order is O-V-NR-S-Imperf. This prediction is borne out as shown by the Ewegbe[21] and Gengbe data in (44a–b) and (44c–d), respectively.[22]

(44)   a.   Kɔjò lè   nú   dù   mí   [Ewegbe]
            Kojo Imperf thing   eat   NR
            'Kojo is eating'
       b.   nú   dù *(mí)   Kɔjò lè
            thing eat   NR   Kojo Imperf
            'Kojo is EATING'
       c.   Kɔjò lè   axwé   tù   ɔ   [Gengbe]
            Kojo Imperf   house   build   NR
            'Kojo is building a house'
       d.   axwé   tù   *(ɔ)   Kɔjò lè
            house   build   NR   Kojo Imperf
            'Kojo is BUILDING A HOUSE'

In section 6.2.1 of chapter 6, I analyze the Gungbe imperfective constructions in terms of biclausal structures. In this respect, I propose that the imperfective marker *tò* selects a small clause introduced by a nominalizer that is manifested by a sentence-final low tone in Gungbe or by the nominalizing morphemes *wὲ, mí, ɔ,* in Fongbe, Ewegbe, and Gengbe, respectively. Accordingly, I assume that the nominalizing head Nom° projects as the left periphery of the reduced clause (i.e., NomP). I further propose that NomP takes AspP3 as complement, which in turn immediately dominates AgroP, which in turn dominates VP, as partially represented in (45a).

(45)   a.

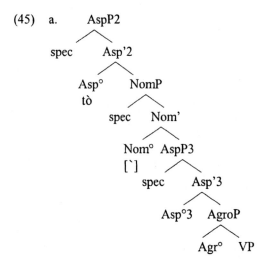

The S-*tò*-[OV-NR] order is thus accounted for in terms of object movement to [spec AspP3] (presumably via [spec AgroP]) to satisfy the EPP, while the verb moves cyclically to Agr° and Asp°3 to be licensed for aspect (i.e., [-prospective]). Finally, the low tone occurs sentence-finally as a manifestation of the nominalizing process that requires that AspP3 as a whole moves to [spec NomP], to be licensed for the feature [+n], as illustrated in (45b).

(45)   b.   AspP2

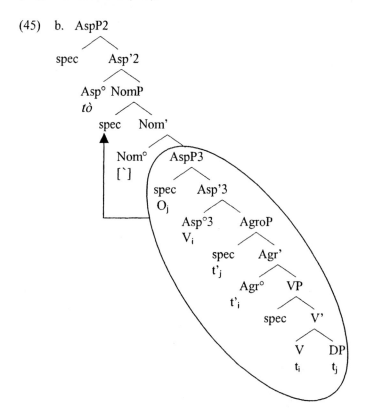

Assuming representations (45a–b), the only constituent that is higher than the VP but follows the AspP2 is NomP. We now have clear evidence to claim that verbal XP focus is NomP focus: a process that holds on the whole complement of the imperfective marker *tò*. In this respect, NomP focalization is similar to focusing of any maximal projection because it results from movement of a constituent to [spec FocP].

7.1.3.1.3.1 NomP focus and feature checking

Pursuing the idea developed in the previous section that verbal XP focus is NomP focus, I now draw a parallel between this type of focus movement and non-verbal focus. Both processes include movement of a maximal projection to [spec FocP].

Given that focus features under Foc° and the focused category must be checked before spell-out, I propose that a symmetrical checking relation is established between the head Foc° specified as [+f] and the focused NomP in its specifier. This amounts to saying that a sentence like (46a) can be represented as shown by (46b).

(46) a.   [wémà lɔ́   zê]   Sɛ́ná ná   nɔ̀   tè
           book   Spf[+defl] take-NR   Sena Fut   Hab   Imperf
           'Sena will be TAKING THE SPECIFIC BOOK habitually'

      b.   FocP

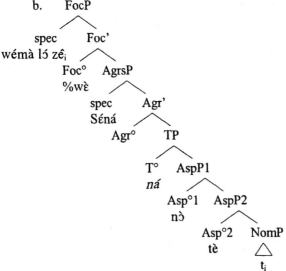

That certain speakers exclude the FM in such constructions can be analyzed by assuming that the verb encodes the feature [+f] under Foc°. Given that the verb is trapped in the nominalized constituent, the whole NomP must move in [spec FocP] to check the focus feature. Under (Chomsky 1995: 262) this would mean that NomP focus seeks to raise just feature [+f] on the verb, but "whatever extra baggage is required for convergence involves a kind of generalized pied-piping."[23] Observe, for instance, that imperfective constructions disallow both V and VP extraction out of the nominalized phrase. To see this, compare the ungrammatical sentences (47a–b) with the grammatical (47c). In the ungrammatical imperfective sentence (47a), the verb is preposed, leaving a copy inside NomP. Similarly, sentence (47b) is ungrammatical because it involves VP preposing: the verb and its internal argument are moved to the focus site leaving a trace in the NomP-internal position.[24] On the other hand, the grammatical sentence (47c) suggests that the Gungbe non-imperfective sentences allow for the V copy strategy.

(47) a.   *dín   mí   tò   Sɛ́ná dîn
            search 1pl   Imperf   Sena Search-NR
            'We are LOOKING for Sena'

b. *dín   Sɛ̂nâ   mí   tɛ̀
   search Sena- NR 2pl   Imperf
   'We are LOOKING for Sena'

c. gbá Sɛ́ná gbá   xwé   lɔ́
   build Sena build-Perf house Spf[+def]
   'Sena BUILT the specific house'

The contrast in sentences (47a–b) as opposed to (47c) indicates that NomP focus is specific to imperfective (and related) constructions (i.e., in OV sentences). Verb focus, however, is limited to non-imperfective contexts (i.e., in VO sentences). This seems to follow from the fact that the verb is stuck in NomP, in imperfective constructions, unlike non-imperfective sentences, which require no nominalizing process. This need not mean that in non-imperfective sentences the verb can be freely preposed. As we will see in section 7.1.3.2, the copy (or resumptive) strategy found in (47c) clearly indicates that focusing of a verbal element is not a free process.

7.1.3.1.3.2 NomP focus: A clause-bound process

So far, I suggested that NomP focus is similar to 'normal' focus movement in that it involves movement of a maximal projection into [spec FocP]. Yet a major difference between NomP and other types of maximal projections is that NomP focalization is clause-bound.

Sentence (48a) is an instance of long focus movement where a DP-object is moved from the embedded clause to the left periphery of the main clause. The ungrammatical sentence (48b), on the other hand, indicates that this strategy is not available in case of NomP focalization. NomP focus thus appears to be a local process that can target only the specifier position of the shortest FocP (48c). This amounts to saying that Gungbe disallows long or cyclic NomP-movement that could move NomP from an embedded clause to [spec FocP] of the main clause.

(48) a. [CP[FocP mótò lɔ́ᵢ [Foc° wɛ̀ [IP ùn lɛ̀n [CP t'ᵢ[C° ɖɔ̀ [FocP[IP Sɛ́ná kù tᵢ]]]]]]]
        car   Spf[+def] Foc 1sg think-Perf that   Sena drive-Perf
        'I thought Sena drove THE SPECIFIC CAR'

    b. *[CP[FP mótò lɔ́ kù]ᵢ   [IP ùn lɛ̀n [CP t'ᵢ[C° ɖɔ̀ [FocP[IP Sɛ́na tɛ̀ tᵢ]]]]]]
        car Spf[+def] drive- NR   1sg think-Perf that   Sena Imperf

    c. ùn lɛ̀n   [CP ɖɔ̀ [FocP [mótò lɔ́   kù]ᵢ   [IP Sɛ́na tɛ̀ tᵢ]]]
       1sg think-Perf that   car   Spf[+def] drive- NR Sena Imperf
       'I thought Sena was DRIVING THE SPECIFIC CAR'

In comparing the ungrammatical example (48b) to the grammatical English sentence (*I asked John to go home, and [go home] I think that he did*), one may be tempted to account for (48b) in terms of NomP/VP asymmetry, by claiming that ForceP is a barrier for maximal projections containing the VP, but not for the VP itself. In other words,

NomP focus is clause-bound because it consists in preposing a constituent involving the VP.

An analysis along those lines is hardly tenable, because there is empirical evidence from other languages that fronting of a maximal projection including VP is not necessarily clause-bound. In this respect, Haegeman (1995a, b) argues that the so-called VP topicalization in the Dutch literature probably concerns more than just the bare VP. Haegeman shows, for instance, that in West Flemish the preposed projection can contain *nie* (49a), an element she interprets as being [spec NegP]. As shown by (49b), the typical leftward movement of negative constituents, in the example *tegen niemand* ('against no one'), is also found in such preposed constituents. Haegeman assumes that this movement is triggered by the Neg-criterion and that the moved constituent attains a specifier head relation with Neg°, again suggesting that its landing site is not VP-internal.

(49)   a.   [Nie tegen Marie klapen] durven-k ook
             not against Marie talk dare I also
             'I also dare not to talk to Marie'
       b.   [Tegen niemand nie klapen] durven-k ook
             against noone not talk   dare I also
             'I also dare not to talk to anyone'

The moved constituent may also contain clitics (49c), which are known to move to a head position high in the clausal domain. The sentences under (49) suggest that the so-called VP topicalization involves a constituent that includes the VP itself and some higher categories. Yet, as shown by the grammatical (49d), VP topicalization is not clause-bound in West Flemish.

(49)   c.   [T an Valère al geven] meug-je nie
             it to Valère all give can you not
             'You should not give it all to Valère'
       d.   [T an Valère geven] peinzen-k [da-j nie goa meugen]
             it to Valère give think I(cl)   that you(cl)not go may
             'I don't think that you will be allowed to give it to V'

The West Flemish data are additional evidence that the Gungbe ungrammatical sentence (48b) cannot be simply accounted for in terms of an asymmetry between the preposing of a maximal projection including the VP, say NomP in Gungbe or some FP in West Flemish, versus VP-preposing in English. Instead, what seems to be the case is that NomP movement (i.e., movement of a verbal maximal projection) is sensitive to the minimality effect due to some intervening head of the C-system. On the other hand, VP-preposing in English and FP-preposing in West Flemish are normal A'-movements; they are expected to be sensitive to A'-interveners only. The schema (50) represents NomP movement, while (51) illustrates VP- (or FP-) preposing in English and West Flemish.

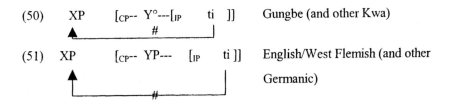

Following the discussion in chapter 3 with respect to snowballing movement (i.e., successive pied-piping of maximal projections when the targeted head cannot be extracted) and clitic movement (i.e., movement of a DP out of the VP, followed by subsequent movement of D°), we now face another situation where movement of a maximal projection is blocked by an intervening head, say Force°. This clearly suggests that NomP movement is actually a disguised head-movement and must therefore be sensitive to the locality constraints on such movement. This is consistent with the proposal in the preceding section that NomP focus seeks to raise just feature [+f] on the verb. Put differently, NomP focus is a disguised means to satisfy the requirements of a head, or the verb inside that sequence. This would mean that even though verbal XP focus requires movement to [spec FocP] (i.e., an instance of A'-movement), we cannot identify NomP as a normal maximal projection (e.g., DPs, PPs, *P*s). It shares the properties of both XP and X° elements. I will come back to the discussion in section 7.1.4 and show that NomP focus is also sensitive to the intervening negation marker, a fact that we can naturally account for if we assume an analysis in terms of head-movement. In a similar vein, this analysis also accounts for the fact that NomP focus excludes the Gungbe focus marker *wè*.

At this stage of the discussion, it suffices to say that NomP is clause-bound because the focused NomP is stuck in the lowest [spec FocP]. Assume, for example, that the null head Foc° checks verbal elements (whether XP or X°) with the feature [+f] (Brody 1990; Puskás 1996). Recall also from the discussion on the non-verbal XP focus that long focus extraction proceeds through [spec ForceP] (and not the lowest [spec FocP]; see section 7.1.2.2. Building on this, I conclude that when a verbal constituent tries to move, it is stopped in the lowest [spec FocP] because

1.   Movement cannot skip the active Foc°.
2.   The focused verb (i.e., the verb in the sequence) cannot undergo subsequent head to head movement out of the C-system, because Force° is necessarily occupied by the Gungbe complementizer *ɖɔ̀* 'that'.

Additional facts on the Gungbe verb focus in VO constructions strongly support this analysis.

7.1.3.2 Verb focus

So far, I have discussed the focalization process of both non-verbal and verbal XPs. What was revealed is that, in those cases, focusing requires movement of a constituent to [spec FocP]. This section investigates the Gungbe constructions involving verb focus, that is, sentences where the verb receives a focus interpretation. Sentence (52a) is an example of verb focus in the Gungbe main clauses. Here, the verb surfaces in a specific presubject position leaving a copy in the IP-internal position (52b). Verb focus is not limited to main clauses. Note in the examples (52c–d) that verb focus also arises in embedded contexts (52c) and in relative clauses (52d). In those cases, the preposed verb occurs in a position to the right of complementizer Force°, realized as ɖɔ̀ and ɖè, respectively.

(52) a. ɖù   Sɛ́ná ɖù   blέɖì lɔ́
          eat   Sena   eat-Perf bread Spf[+def]
          'Sena ATE the specific bread'

     b. ɖù_i   [_{IP} Sɛ́ná   ɖù_i blέɖì lɔ́]

     c. ùn ɖɔ̀   ɖɔ̀   fì   yé   fì   kwέ   étɔ̀ bléún
         I   say-Perf that   steal 3pl steal-Perf money   his   quickly
         'I said that they quickly STOLE his money'

     d. dáwè   ɖè   fì   yé   fì   kwέ   étɔ̀
         man   that steal 3pl steal-Perf money   his
         'The man that they STOLE his money'

7.1.3.2.1 Some characteristics of verb focus

Any verb can be focused in Gungbe, irrespective of its argument structure. Verbs that can be focused include both transitive and intransitive verbs (53a–b), double object construction verbs (53c), and ergative verbs in the sense of Burzio (1986), as shown by (53d).

(53) a. ɖù   Sɛ́ná ɖù   blέɖì lɔ́
          eat Sena   eat-Perf bread Spf[+def]
          'Sena ATE the specific bread'

     b. fɔ́n   yé   fɔ́n   hàɖòkpólɔ́
         stand 3pl stand-Perf immediately
         'They immediately STOOD UP'

     c. kplɔ̀n Sɛ́ná kplɔ̀n   hàn   vǐ   lé
         teach Sena   teach-Perf song   child Num
         'Sena TAUGHT the children a song'

     d. wá   yé   wá
         arrive 3pl arrive-Perf
         'They ARRIVED'

For the speakers who employ the FM in verb focus, nothing can intervene between the focused verb and the FM wè (54). Setting aside the status of the FM in such constructions, we can account for sentence (54) by proposing that the focused verb is realized under Foc° or adjoins to it (see Ndayiragije 1993 for a similar proposal for Fongbe).

(54)   *sà   bléú   wὲ   yé   sà   gbɔ́   lɔ́
        sell   quickly Foc   3pl   sell-Perf goat   Spf[+def]
        'They quickly SOLD the specific goat'

Assuming that the verb realizes Foc°, the question then arises whether the left-adjacent position to the verb is available for focused maximal projections. Put differently, could the focus projection be doubly filled? As seen from sentence (55), such double focusing is not possible in Gungbe, as the position immediately to the left of the focused verb is never morphologically realized.[25] Anticipating later discussion, the ungrammatical sentence (55) indicates that maximal projection focusing, as well as verb focusing, targets the same projection (FocP). Similarly, the fact that [spec FocP] is not available for further focusing when verb focalization arises could be considered an indication that this position might be filled by a null focus operator (see section 7.1.3.2.2).

(55)   *wémà lɔ́$_i$ xìá   Rὲmí   xìá t$_i$
        book Spf[+def] read   Remi   read-Perf

Contrary to observations made on Fongbe (Ndayiragije 1993), Gungbe manifests no specificity constraint on the arguments of the focused verb. This is illustrated by sentences under (56), which all involve focusing of a verb associated with non-specific arguments.

(56) a. nyàn   yé   nyàn   mὲ   sɔ́n   àlìò   jí
          chase   3pl   chase   one   from   road   on
          'People were CHASED from the road'
      b. xɔ̀   jíkù   xɔ̀   mὲ   kpédɛ́kpédɛ́
          beat   rain   beat   one   properly
          'One was really wet because of the rain'
      c. hù   xòvé   hù   gbὲtɔ́   tàù
          kill   hunger kill   human   very
          'One STARVED'

The ungrammatical sentence (57) indicates that, unlike XP focalization where the focused element moves leftward to [spec FocP] and leaves a gap in its base position, verb focusing involves a copy process where the fronted verb must leave a copy in its base position.[26]

(57)   *ɖù$_i$ Sέná   t$_i$ bléɖì   lɔ́
        eat   Sena   bread   Spf[+def]

It is interesting to notice that, just as NomP focalization, verb focus is a clause-bound process as exemplified by the ungrammatical sentence (58a). This example also shows that the same situation obtains with the so-called bridge verbs.[27]

(58) a. *ɖù   ún   sè   ɖɔ̀   yé   ɖù   blέɖì   lɔ́
        eat   1sg hear-Perf that 3pl eat-Perf bread Spf$_{[+def]}$
        'Eat I heard that they ate the specific bread'

    b. *ɖù ún ɖɔ̀   ɖɔ̀   yé   ɖù   blέɖì   lɔ́
        eat 1sg say-Perf that 3pl eat-Perf bread Spf$_{[+def]}$
        'Eat I said that they ate the specific bread'

Since verb focus requires that the verb leave a copy in its base position, the ungrammaticality of sentences under (58) cannot be reduced to an ECP violation. In terms of the analysis I proposed with respect to NomP focus, that verb focus is clause-bound is expected. If true that Foc° checks a verb with the feature [+f], then the focused verb will automatically be stopped in the lowest Foc° because long focus extraction of the verb cannot skip the intervening active Foc°. In addition, the moved verb cannot proceed through Force°, as the latter is occupied by the Gungbe complementizer. See also section 7.1.4 for the discussion on other Kwa.

    Partial justification for claiming that verb focus targets the verb itself is given by the facts already mentioned in section 7.1.3.1.3.1 with respect to NomP focus that Gungbe does not allow for VP preposing. Observe, for example, the ungrammatical sentences under (59), where it appears that the focused verb cannot co-occur with its complement(s).

(59) a. *ɖù   blέɖì   lɔ́   yé   nɔ̀
        eat   bread Spf$_{[+def]}$ 3pl   Hab
        'Eat the specific bread they habitually'

    b. *sà gbɔ́ lέ ná Kɔ̀jó yé nɔ̀
        sell goat Num to Kojo 3pl Hab
        'Sell the goats to Kojo they habitually'

This is strong evidence that verb focus does not involve VP or some other maximal projection dominating it. In a similar vein, verb focus cannot be accounted for in terms of cyclic verb movement through the different head positions (Asp°, T°, Agr°) between the focused verb and its copy. The ungrammatical sentences (60a–b) show that verb focus does not involve the Gungbe tense and aspect markers. Similar facts obtain with the Gungbe negation and mood markers, which must remain IP-internal when focus movement arises (60d–e). Observe from the sentence (60d) that the negative reading is neutralized, suggesting that verbal element focus and negation are incompatible. I will come back to this in sections 7.1.3.2.2 and 7.1.4.

(60) a. *ɖù-ná -nɔ̀ yé   ɖù   blέɖì   lɔ́
        eat-Fut-Hab 3pl   eat   bread Spf$_{[+def]}$

b. *ɖù- nɔ̀-ná yé   ɖù   blέɖì lɔ́
    eat-Hab-Fut 3pl eat   bread Spf[+def]

c. ɖù   yé   ná   nɔ̀   ɖù   blέɖì   lɔ́
    eat 3pl Fut Hab eat   bread   Spf[+def]
    'They will habitually EAT the specific bread'
    (i.e., each time I buy some bread, they eat it)

d. ɖù   yé   má   ɖù   blέɖì   lɔ́,
    eat 3pl Neg eat-Perf bread Spf[+def]
    yé   mì-ì   wὲ
    3pl   swallow-Perf-3sg Foc
    'They didn't only eat the specific bread, [they SWALLOWED it']
    *'The didn't EAT the bread'

e. ɖù   yé   ní   ɖù   blέɖì lɔ́
    eat 3pl Inj eat   bread Spf[+def]
    'They should EAT the specific bread'

7.1.3.2.2 Analysis of the data

The data discussed in the preceding section lead me to conclude that verb focalization is a process that enables the focused verb to occur in the focus domain FocP. It is argued here that the focused element is the verb itself, a head, and not a maximal projection as proposed by a number of authors (Lumsden & Lefebvre 1990; Law & Lefebvre 1995). Accordingly, contrary to XP focalization where the focused element is realized in [spec FocP], the focused verb is moved to a head position, Foc°. Sentence (53a) can therefore be represented as in (61).

(61) [FP[F° ɖù [IP Sέná ɖù   blέɖì   lɔ́]]]
           eat   Sena eat-Perf bread   Spf[+def]
      'Sena ATE the specific bread'

Building on this, I propose that symmetric focus checking occurs in overt syntax between the verb under Foc° and a [+f] empty focus operator in [spec FocP], as in (62). In this framework, a focus operator is defined as a *focus-phrase* in an A-bar position (Rizzi 1996; Puskás 1996).[28]

(62)   FocP
        ╱   ╲
    spec   Foc'
    Op[+f]   ╱   ╲
           Foc°   IP
           Vᵢ(wὲ)   △
                     Vᵢ

Alternatively, one could suggest that verb focus does not involve movement operations and simply claim that it is rather a process that enables the focused verb to be base-generated in Foc°. An argument in favor of this analysis could be that sentence (60a), repeated here as (63), is ruled out because the verb cannot move cyclically through the different head positions that separate it from Foc°.

(63) *ḍ̀ù-ná -nɔ̀   yé   ḍ̀ù   blɛ́ḍ̀ì   lɔ́
       eat-Fut-Hab 3pl   eat   bread   Spf$_{[+def]}$

It could also be argued that the verb cannot undergo long movement to Foc° because such a movement will violate the head movement constraint (assuming this is a valid principle; Chomsky 1995), or some minimality condition (see Rizzi 1990, 2001; Chomsky 1995; Collins 1996, 2001, and references cited there for various proposals about minimality conditions). Finally, the copy process that leads to verb reduplication could be interpreted as strong evidence that no movement is available in verb focalization. Instead, the language employs a copy strategy that allows for the verb to be base-generated (or first merged) in Foc° leaving a copy in the base position.

This explanation is weakened by the fact that it is not really clear why a process that enables the focused verb to be merged in Foc° should require a verb copy in the IP-internal position. That is to say, why is the focused verb incompatible with a gap in its base position (64a)?

(64) a. *ḍ̀ù$_i$ Sɛ́ná   t$_i$ blɛ́ḍ̀ì   lɔ́
          eat   Sena   bread   Spf$_{[+def]}$

Another drawback of this analysis is that the copy strategy is sensitive to the intervention of negation (64b). This is unwelcome since, in the literature, such a minimality effect is considered specific to movements (Klima 1964; Ross 1983; Travis 1984; Rizzi 1990, 2001; Chomsky 1991; Roberts 2001). Notice from the interpretation of (64b) that even though the sentence includes the Gungbe negative marker *má*, the focused event implies that *Sɛ́ná* ate the bread. In no circumstance can one interpret sentence (64d) as a negative focused verb. This clearly suggests that verb focus is sensitive to the intervention of certain heads of the middle field. See section 7.1.4 for the discussion.

(64) b. ḍ̀ù$_i$ Sɛ́ná   má   ḍ̀ù$_i$ blɛ́ḍ̀ì lɔ́
          eat   Sena   Neg°   eat   bread Spf$_{[+def]}$
          *'Sena didn't EAT the specific bread'
          'They didn't only eat the specific bread,
          [i.e., they SWALLOWED it, or greedily ATE it with]'

Taking these complications into account, I thus propose an analysis in terms of verb movement whereby the IP-internal copy functions as a resumptive verb or a copy in terms of Chomsky (1995) (see also Badejo 1983; Koopman 1984, 2000b; Manfredi

1991; Ndayiragije 1993; Aboh 1995, 1998b; Biloa 1997). In this regard, verb movement to the left periphery is seen as a last resort phenomenon.

At this stage, we can draw a parallel between the resumptive (or copy) verb and resumptive pronouns. Consider, for instance, the distribution of resumptive pronouns and gaps in Hebrew and Palestinian. The sentences under (65) show that resumptive pronouns are obligatory in oblique object positions and NP-internal positions. A gap is prohibited in these positions.[29]

(65) a. ha-ʔiš   še-   xašavti   ʕal-*(av)
        the-man   that- (I) thought about-(him)
        'The man that I thought about'

     b. ha-ʔis   še-   raʔiti ʔet   ʔišt-*(o)
        the-man   that- (I) saw-ACC wife-(his)
        'The man whose wife I saw'   [Hebrew]

     c. l-bint   ʔilli   fakkarti   fii-*(ha)
        the-girl that (you. F) thought   on-(her)
        'The girl that you thought about'

     d. l-bint   ʔilli   šufti   beet-*(ha)
        the-girl that (you. F) saw   house-(*her)
        'The girl whose house you saw'   [Palestinian]

In his account for these data, Shlonsky (1992) suggested that the obligatory occurrence of resumptive pronouns in the Hebrew (65a–b) and the Palestinian (65c–d) is a direct consequence of the fact that a gap in the same position would violate some grammatical constraint. According to Shlonsky, the grammars of Hebrew and Palestinian possess a constraint against preposition stranding that is reducible to the ECP. As a result, when an oblique object is relativized, a gap in the [NP/PP] position violates the ECP. This assumption enables the author to view the resumptive pronoun that occurs in place of the gap as a saving device for an otherwise ungrammatical sentence. In this respect, the Hebrew and the Palestinian relative clauses (65a) and (65c) are the only acceptable options for relativizing an oblique argument. Similarly, the resumptive pronoun strategy is obligatory in (65b) and (54d) because the extraction of elements internal to NP is completely ruled out in those languages for ECP-related reasons (see Shlonsky 1992 and references cited there for the discussion).

It appears, however, that the resumptive pronoun strategy is a rather general process that is not limited to oblique and NP-internal positions in Hebrew and Palestinian. Moreover, the English and the Gungbe sentences under (66) suggest that the resumptive strategy is not unique to Hebrew or Palestinian.

(66) a. the guy who we wondered whether *(he) was sane (Safir 1986)

     b. dáwè   ḍê   ún   sè   ḍɔ̀   *(é) hù   àlὲ
        man   that 1sg   hear-Perf   that 3sg   open-Perf   madness
        'The man that I heard that he became mad'

In order to capture the generality that seems to apply for resumptive pronoun strategy, Shlonsky (1992) proposes that this strategy be regarded as a last resort phenomenon. He argued that not only do relativized oblique objects and NP-internal arguments utilize resumptive pronouns to circumvent ungrammaticality.

The full distributional paradigm of resumptive pronouns in Hebrew and Palestinian can be assimilated to the last resort strategy. In other words, the resumptive pronoun strategy cannot be regarded as a freely available grammatical strategy since resumptive pronouns always occur in positions where gaps are illicit. Since the resumptive pronoun strategy is very similar to the copy strategy manifested by verbal focus in Gungbe, it is reasonable to think that languages may also possess a resumptive verb strategy that will allow the occurrence of a resumptive verb in a position where a gap is excluded. Such a resumptive verb may be either a pleonastic verb or a copy. Following Shlonsky's (1992) proposal for resumptive pronouns, I assume that the resumptive verb strategy is a last resort strategy. It is not a freely available grammatical strategy in its own right. In verb focus, a gap in the IP-internal position is illicit. Therefore, to avoid such a gap, a verb copy is necessary: it fills the gap and the result is a grammatical sentence. In terms of Chomsky's (1995) theory of 'traces as copy' we now have a new insight with respect to those traces that are spelled out versus those that are not. It seems to be the case that the traces that are spelled out (as copy or some resumptive element) are precisely those that are illicit, that is, traces that violate some licensing condition (e.g., ECP or HMC).

This analysis provides a straightforward account for sentence (67) because movement of V to Foc° (via Asp°) is ruled out and the presence of a gap in the base position will give rise to a minimality condition violation (Rizzi 1990, 2001; Chomsky 1995; Collins 1996, 2001). Since the language doesn't possess any pleonastic verb that may be inserted in the base position, verb movement to Foc° is blocked and hence the verb-trace is spelled out as a process of last resort.

(67) ɖu$_i$ Séná ná   *(ɖu$_i$) blédì   lɔ
      eat   Sena Fut   eat   bread   Spf$_{[+def]}$
      'They will EAT the specific bread'

In this respect, the Gungbe facts presented in this study are similar to verb focus in Madi.[30] In this language, verbal focus appears to be realized through a movement/copy rule that results in placing a copy of the verb (morphologically altered with a low final tone)[31] in the final position (Fabb & Blackings 1995). Here, again, the focused verb is incompatible with a gap, and the language employs the verb copy strategy as a last resort saving device for an otherwise ungrammatical sentence.

(68) má   mvü   érúá   rì   *(mvù)
      I   drink medicine the drink (Foc)
      'I DRANK the medicine (i.e., not injected it)

Though the focus position seems to be different in Gungbe and Madi sentences, both languages adopt the copy strategy as last resort. This process is triggered when verb movement is blocked by some syntactic constraint (e.g., HMC for the Gungbe case) and when the language allows the copy of the verb to be used resumptively. As such, the verb copy strategy represents a more general principle of the grammar, a last resort process that results from the impossibility of a gap. Here, the use of the copy can be explained by the fact that languages like Gungbe and Madi do not have a pleonastic verb that may be inserted to support tense and agreement morphemes.

The verb copy strategy observed in Gungbe and Madi reminds us of the *do*-support phenomenon in modern English. As proposed by Chomsky (1991), *do*-support occurs when two conditions are met. First, V-to-I movement is ruled out, and second, the language has a pleonastic verb that may be inserted to support tense and agreement morphemes. It is interesting to notice that just as the English *do* is associated with tense and aspect specifications, the Gungbe copy verb combines with tense and aspect markers of the I-system. See also Robert 1988 and Holmberg (1999) and the references cited there for the discussion on VP-fronting and the V copy strategy in Germanic and Scandinavian languages, respectively.

7.1.4 Some notes on the typology of verbal focus and the copy strategy in Kwa

The conclusion I reached in the previous sections is that there are basically two focus strategies in Gbe: non-verbal XP focus and verbal focus. The latter includes two strategies: verbal XP focus, where XP represents the VP or a sequence containing the VP, and verb focus, where the verb is extracted. Verbal XP focus is specific to the so-called OV constructions. It involves movement of a verbal maximal projection to [spec FocP] leaving a trace in the IP-internal position. On the other hand, verb focus occurs in VO constructions only. The focused verb raises to Foc° leaving a copy in the IP-internal position. The different situations are represented in (69).

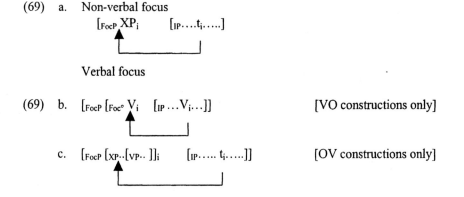

(69)   a.   Non-verbal focus

$[_{FocP} XP_i \quad [_{IP}....t_i.....]$

Verbal focus

(69)   b. $[_{FocP} [_{Foc°} V_i \quad [_{IP}...V_i...]]$ [VO constructions only]

c. $[_{FocP} [_{XP}..[_{VP}..]]_i \quad [_{IP}..... t_i.....]]$ [OV constructions only]

The situation I describe in (69a) is reducible to normal cases of A'-movement, the movement of a maximal projection to the left periphery. In terms of Cinque (1990), Rizzi (1990, 1997), Lasnik and Stowell (1991), and Puskás (1996), among others, this movement-type involves a quantificational chain, the tail of the chain being a variable (see chapter 8, section 8.1.3.2 for the discussion). On the other hand, the situations in (69b) and (69c) are more intricate: both cases are understood as instances of head-movement, even though (69c) involves movement of a maximal projection.

The V copy strategy specific to VO constructions is a last resort phenomenon. Observe, for example, that in Gungbe where the tense, aspect, mood markers are non-affixal, the focused verb must cross the different head positions occupied by those markers on its way to Foc°. In this respect, a gap in the IP-internal position will necessarily violate the HMC. The V copy strategy therefore helps circumvent this problem and appears a last resort strategy to save an otherwise ungrammatical sentence, as represented in (70).

(70) $[_{ForceP}[_{Force°}\textit{ɖɔ}\ [_{FocP}[_{Foc°}V_i\ \textit{-(wè)}\ [_{FinP}\ [_{Fin°}\ \textit{ní}\ [_{TP}[_{T°}\textit{ná}\ [_{AspP}[_{Asp°}\ \textit{nɔ}\ [_{VP}\ [V_i]]]]]]]]]]]]$

A theory that assumes that the V copy strategy is last resort (i.e., a costlier strategy) also accounts for those Kwa languages where verb focus requires that the fronted verb be nominalized. In Akan, Ewe, Edo, and Yoruba, for example, the focused verb is reduplicated, hence nominalized. In this context, verb focus resorts to what I referred to as non-verbal XP focus, as shown in (69a). A difference, though, is that the nominalized fronted verb must leave a copy in the IP-internal position, suggesting that even in those cases a gap is excluded in the IP-internal verb position.

(71)   a.   nkyerɛw   na   mekyerew
             NR -write   Foc   I-Hab-write
             'Writing I do'   [Akan; Ameka 1992: 8]

       b.   ɸo-ɸo-   é   wó-   ɸo-   é
             RED-hit   Foc   3sg   hit   3sg
             'Beating s/he beat him/her'   [Ewe; Ameka 1992: 12]

       c.   òtué   Ozó   tuè   mwè
             greeting Ozo   greet   me
             'It is greeting that Ozo greeted me'   [Edo; Omoruyi 1989: 288]

       d.   jíjí   ni   olè   jí   ìwé   ɔmɔ náà
             stealing Foc   thief   steal   book   child Dem
             'What the thief did is that he stole the child's book'
                                                        [Yoruba; Awóbùlúyì 1979: 131]

Contrary to the Gbe languages where verb focus does not require verb nominalization, languages of the Yoruba-type prohibit focusing without nominalization (i.e., reduplication). This is illustrated by the ungrammatical sentence (71e).

(71) e. *jí   ni   Dáda   á   jí   owó   Ojó
         steal Foc   Dada   Infl   steal money   Ojo
         'What Dada actually did is that he stole Ojo's money'   [Yoruba]

As the discussion proceeds, I will show that the Yoruba strategy—the requirement that
the focused verb be nominalized (i.e., reduplicated)—is also a device to circumvent the
minimality conditions that hold on head movement. In this particular case, it seems that
verb nominalization via reduplication creates genuine maximal projections (see
Manfredi 1991; Awóyalé 1997). This naturally suggests that, contrary to the cases of
disguised head movement described with respect to Gbe (e.g., the V copy strategy,
NomP focus), verb focus should not show any minimality effect that is reducible to the
HMC. This would mean that the movement of the reduplicated verb should not be
clause-bound nor should it be sensitive to an intervening head within the I-system (i.e.,
TAM markers). This prediction is realized. Note that long extraction is possible with
the reduplicated verb in Ewegbe (72a) but not in Gungbe, where the focused verb
cannot reduplicate (72b).

(72) a. FoFoe   me-se   be   wo-Fo   Devi-a
         RED-beat-Foc   1SG-hear   that   2SG-beat   child-DEF
         'I heard that beating the child he did'   [Ewegbe]
     b. *dù   ún   sè   dɔ̀   yé   dù   blέdì lɔ́
         eat   1sg   hear-Perf   that   3pl   eat-Perf   bread Spf$_{[+def]}$ [Gungbe]

In terms of the theory I develop here, the sentence (72a) is grammatical because long
extraction can proceed through [spec ForceP] on a par with the cases of long wh/focus
extractions discussed in section 7.1.2.2. The conclusion reached there was that the
lowest FocP cannot serve as an escape hatch for movement, since Gungbe allows for
simultaneous focusing in both the main and embedded clauses. As a result, long
extraction must proceed through ForceP. In this regard, the fact that long extraction of
the focused verbal element (i.e., V or NomP in Gungbe) is prohibited is taken as a sign
of some minimality condition violation (e.g., the HMC or some of its variants; Rizzi
1990, 2001; Chomsky 1995; Collins 1996, 2001; see also Ura 2001 for economy
conditions on generalized pied-piping). The focused (disguised) head cannot skip the
active Foc°, and there is no escape hatch for subsequent head-to-head movement out of
the C-system. This means that the focused verb should move through Force°, but this is
impossible since this position is always occupied by the Gungbe complementizer. As
discussed in chapter 3 with respect to snowballing movement, this is typical of head
movement, which involves an adjunction rule. In addition, the fact that the IP-internal
position is filled by the copy warrants that neither the ECP nor the HMC is violated.
This clearly shows that the copy strategy is not contingent on to head movements only.
As I proposed in previous paragraphs, it is a last resort phenomenon that helps
circumvent ungrammaticality where a gap is excluded (see Shlonsky 1992 and
references cited there).

This analysis clearly suggests that we can use long extraction to diagnose (disguised) head movement versus genuine XP-movement. According to Roberts (2001), another diagnostic test that we can use is the intervention of negation. The choice of negation here is grounded on the fact that negation may qualify as potential A'-binder and therefore may interact with certain constructions involving the left periphery, such as wh- and focus constructions (see Rizzi 1990, 1997; Haegeman & Zanuttini 1991; Zanuttini 1991; Haegeman 1995, and references cited there). Assume further that certain left peripheral constructions (e.g., wh/focus constructions) and sentence negation involve the same class of features, say those features of the type [+Q]. If true that minimality effects arise only within classes of features but not across them (Rizzi 2001), this would mean that negation might interact with certain left peripheral constructions.

Under this analysis, genuine non-verbal XP focus is neither clause-bound nor sensitive to the intervention of negation. Under relativized minimality, this is expected since the Gbe preverbal negative expresses Neg°. On the other hand, if focusing of a verbal category (i.e., V°, NomP) involves (disguised) head movement, therefore that movement operation must be clause-bound and sensitive to the intervention of a middle field head, as in negation. This prediction is fulfilled. The Gungbe sentence (73) indicates that non-verbal XP focus is neither clause-bound nor sensitive to the intervention of the middle field markers.

(73) hǐ   lɔ́ⱼ   wɛ̀   Sɛ́ná   ɖɔ̀   ɖɔ̀
      knife   Spf[+def]   Foc   Sena   say-Perf   that
      Rɛ̀mí   ní   má   nɔ̀   zé   blô   tⱼ
      Remi   Inj Neg Hab   take   anymore
      'Sena said that Remi should not take THE SPECIFIC KNIFE anymore'

On the contrary, the sentences under (74) show that the V copy strategy is clause-bound and sensitive to the intervention of negation.

(74) a. *ɖà   ún   sè   ɖɔ̀   yé   ɖà   blɛ́ɖì   lɔ́
             cook   1sg   hear-Perf   that   3pl   cook-Perf   bread   Spf[+def]
             'I heard that they BAKED the specific bread'
      b. *ɖà   yé   má   ɖà   blɛ́ɖì   lɔ́
             cook   3pl   Neg   cook-Perf   bread   Spf[+def]
             *'They didn't BAKE the specific bread'
             'They didn't just bake the specific bread, [e.g., they BAKED it with pleasure]

In a similar vein, NomP focus cannot involve long extraction. In addition, it is incompatible with negation.

(75) a. *[mótò lɔ́   kǔ]ᵢ   ùn   lèn   ɖɔ̀   Séna   tè   tᵢ
          car   Spf[+def]   drive- NR   1sg   think-Perf   that   Sena   Imperf
          'I think that Sena is DRIVING THE SPECIFIC CAR'

b. *[mótò   ló   kù]   Séna má   tè t$_i$
    car   Spf$_{[+def]}$ drive- NR Sena Neg   Imperf

The Yoruba facts under (76) lend further support to the analysis in terms of movement of a maximal projection versus (disguised) head movement. Starting from the original sentence (76a), Yoruba displays two alternatives: the preposed verb is reduplicated for nominalization, leaving a V copy in the IP-internal position (76b). Or else the whole nominalized sequence containing the verb and the object is moved to sentence-initial position, leaving an XP-copy in the IP-internal position (76c).[32] The fact that the preposed sequence may also include an aspect marker (76d) strongly suggests that what is being preposed is not just the VP, but involves a higher projection, say AspP (see Manfredi 1991, and references cited there).[33]

(76) a. Ajé   ra   ìwé
          Aje   buy-Perf   book
          'Aje bought books'
      b. [Rírà]   ni   Aje   [ra]   ìwé
          RED-buy   Foc   Aje   buy-Perf   book
          'Aje BOUGHT books' [e.g., he didn't go yam-selling]
      c. [Rírà- wé]   ni   Ajé   [ra   ìwé]
          RED-buy-book Foc   Ajé   buy-Perf book
          'Aje BOUGHT books' [e.g., he didn't go yam-selling]
      d. [Mi-máa rà   wé]   ni   Aje   [máa rà   ìwé]
          NR -Hab buy book   Foc   Aje   Hab   buy   book
          'Aje is BUYING a book' [e.g., he didn't go yam-selling]

Pursuing the discussion on verb reduplication, I naturally conclude that sentence (76b) involves movement of a nominal maximal projection. As suggested by the examples (77a–b), movement here is neither clause-bound nor sensitive to negation.

(77) a. [Rírà]   ni   mo   wí   kpé   Ajé   ra   ìwé
          RED-buy   Foc   1sg   say-Perf that   Aje   buy-Perf   book
          'I said that Aje BOUGHT books'
      b. [Rírà]   kọ́   ni   Ajé   ra   ìwé
          RED-buy   Neg   Foc   Ajé   buy-Perf   book
          'Aje DIDN'T BUY books'

That the bracketed constituent in (77a–b) is essentially nominal is further supported by the fact that the Yoruba negative marker kọ́ negates nouns only as suggested by the examples (77c–d).[34]

(77) c. Iyèn   kọ́   ni   a   wí
          that   not   Foc   2pl   said
          'That's not what we said'

    d.   Iwé   kọ́   ni   mo   rà
        book not   Foc 1sg buy
        'I didn't buy a BOOK'

However, the analysis of the sentences under (77) cannot be simply extended to all the constituents involving the reduplicated verb. Recall from the sentences (76c–d) that the preposed nominalized sequence contains an aspect marker, the verb, and its object. In those cases, Yoruba resorts to some sort of NomP focus of the Gungbe-type: focusing seeks to raise just the feature [+f] on the verb but whatever 'extra baggage' is required for convergence is pied-piped along with the verb. This would mean that the sentences (76c–d) are cases of disguised head movement. Consequently, these constructions should behave like verbal focused sentences involving verb extraction associated with the copy strategy. In section 7.1.3.2, it was shown that verb focus is, clause-bound and sensitive to sentential negation. This prediction is also realized with respect to the Yoruba focus constructions involving a sequence that includes an active verb associated with its arguments (and an aspect marker). Consider, for instance the sentences under (78) and (79). The sentences under (78) are the counterparts of (76c). The marginal examples (78a–b) involve the 'argument negation' in Yoruba. Notice that sentence (78b), which involves long extraction, is more degraded. On the other hand, the ungrammatical example (78c) shows that the Yoruba sentential negation *kò* is prohibited in those constructions.

(78) a. ?[Rírà-   wé] kọ́   ni   Ajé [ra   ìwé]
          RED-buy book Neg Foc   Ajé buy   book
     b. ??[Rírà- wé]   kọ́ ni   mo   wí   kpé Ajé [ra ìwé]
          Nom-buy book Neg Foc 1sgs ay-Perf that Aje buy book
     c. *[Rírà-   wé]   ni   Ajé   kò [ra   ìwé]
          RED-buy book   Foc Aje   Neg buy   book

The degradation is more severe in cases where the nominalized sequence includes the aspect marker, the verb, and its object. The sentences under (79) are the counterparts of (76d). Here, again, sentential negation *kò* leads to ungrammaticality (79c).

(79) a. ??[Mi-máa rà   wé] kọ́   ni   Aje [máa rà   ìwé]
          NR -Hab buy   book Neg Foc Aje Hab buy book
     b. ??[Mi-máa rà wé] kọ́ ni   mo wí   kpé Aje [máa rà ìwé]
          NR -Hab buy book Neg Foc 1sg say-Perf that Aje   Hab buy book
     c. *[Mi-máa rà wé]   ni   Aje kò [máa rà   ìwé]
          NR -Hab buy   book   Foc Aje Neg [Hab buy   book

The fact that the sentences under (78–79) exclude both the argument negation *kọ́* and the sentential negation *kò* (even though with a different degree of degradation) suggests that the preposed constituent does not qualify as a simple nominal phrase. Instead, I take this incompatibility to mean that the preposed constituent is verbal in nature. The

FOCUS AND WH CONSTRUCTIONS

verb inside the sequence is active and what focusing seeks to raise is just the feature [+f] associated with that verb. But the verb cannot be extracted, as nominalization creates an island for verbal extraction. As a result, the whole sequence is pied-piped to the relevant focus position.

Granting this, I conclude that the Kwa languages presented here do not differ with respect to focusing. They all involve non-verbal element focusing (i.e., DPs, AdjP, AdvP, etc.) where a quantificational A'-chain is created. In those cases, movement leaves a trace in the IP-internal position and focusing is neither clause-bound nor sensitive to negation. This situation was described in the representation (69a) repeated here as (80a).

(80)   a. $[_{FocP}$ XP$_i$ $[_{IP}$...... t$_i$.....]$ [Non-verbal focus]

On the other hand, we have crosslinguistic evidence that cases where the focused category is a verb or a nominalized sequence ΣP including the VP involve disguised head-movement. Focusing seeks to raise the feature [+f] on the verb but, because the later is inaccessible for movement, the whole nominalized ΣP is preposed to [spec FocP]. A difference, though, between situation (80a) and ΣP-focus is that the former is sensitive to the locality constraints traditionally attributed to cyclical specifier-to-specifier movement (e.g., long extraction), while the later is sensitive only to the locality conditions that hold for head movement (e.g., ΣP-movement is and sensitive to intervening heads). In addition, I show that, in certain languages, ΣP-focus leaves a trace in the IP-internal position. In those cases, the language must provide a device that guarantees that the trace does not violate the ECP (or the HMC). A case in point is Gungbe, where NomP focus requires that the imperfective marker *tò* change into the agreeing form *tè*, which properly licenses the trace in the IP-internal position under government (section 7.1.3.1.2.2 for the discussion). This is illustrated by the representation (80b).

(80)   b. $[_{FocP}$ $[_{ΣP}$..$[_{VP}$..]]$_i$ $[_{Foc}$ $[_{AspP}$ *tè* [t$_i$.....]]]]   [Verbal ΣP-focus]

On the contrary, where no licensing mechanism is provided (e.g., Yoruba, Ewegbe, Akan, Edo, also Gungbe in cases of verb focus) languages resort to what could be called the α-copy strategy, where α resumes the focused sequence in the IP-internal position. In this framework, α may spell out as V, in cases where V-focus requires V or [NomVV]-preposing (80c–d), or else as ΣP in those cases where verb focus results in ΣP-pied-piping (80e).

(80)   c. $[_{FocP}$ $[_{Foc°}$ V$_i$ $[_{AspP}$......... V$_i$...]]]   [Verbal Σ-focus]

d. $[_{FocP} [NR \text{ -V-V}]_i [_{Foc°} \quad [_{AspP} \ldots \ldots V_i \ldots]]]$ [Verbal Σ-focus]

e. $[_{FocP} [_{ΣP} \ldots [_{VP} \ldots]]_i [_{Foc°} [_{AspP} \ldots [_{ΣP} \ldots [_{VP} \ldots]]_i \ldots]]]$ [Verbal ΣP-focus]

The data discussed here clearly favor the idea that the α-copy strategy is a last resort phenomenon that necessarily occurs when there is no language device to license an illegitimate gap. At this stage, it is worth going back to long subject extraction and showing that even in those cases of non-verbal XP focus, the α-copy strategy (or resumptive pronoun strategy) must occur whenever a gap is excluded.

(81) a. hǐ   lɔ̃ⱼ   wὲ   Sɛ́ná sὲ   ɖɔ̃   Rὲmí   zé   tⱼ
          knife Spf$_{[+def]}$ Foc Sena hear-Perf that   Remi   take-Perf
          'Sena hear that Remi took THE SPECIFIC KNIFE'

      b. Rὲmíᵢ   wὲ   Sɛ́ná sὲ   ɖɔ̃   éᵢ zé   hǐ   lɔ̃
          Remi   Foc   Sena hear-Perf that   3sg take-Perf knife   Spf$_{[+def]}$
          'Sena hear that REMI took the specific knife'

      c. *Rὲmíᵢ   wὲ   Sɛ́ná sὲ   ɖɔ̃   tᵢ zé   hǐ   lɔ̃
          Remi   Foc   Sena hear-Perf that   take-Perf knife   Spf$_{[+def]}$

The sentences under (81) manifest a subject versus object asymmetry. In sentence (81a), the object of the verb *zé* 'take' is long extracted, leaving a trace in the IP-internal position. The sentence is grammatical because the trace is properly governed and long construal is possible (Rizzi 1990). As generally observed across languages, the contrast between the examples (81b) and (81c) suggests that long subject extraction excludes a trace in the lower [spec AgrP]. In terms of Rizzi (1990), a trace cannot occur in that position due to ECP violation. Observe that the lower [spec AgrP] is not accessible for government of the higher verb due to the intervention of the Gungbe complementizer *ɖɔ̃*. As Rizzi (1990: 61) proposes,

> The most radical way to resolve the problem is to eliminate the subject gap through the insertion of a resumptive pronoun; this can be a particular instance of a generalized resumptive strategy . . . for all the positions not head-governed in the proper way.

In this regard, the resumptive pronoun strategy in (81b) appears a variant of a general rule (i.e., the α-copy strategy) that necessarily applies to all cases where a gap is excluded. As I show in section 8.1.3 of chapter 8, the same holds of argument topic constructions where a gap is prohibited in the IP-internal position. In addition, the analysis of the copy strategy as last resort naturally accounts for the fact that the Kwa languages under study here allow for copying of large sequences (see the Yoruba examples).

7.1.5 Summary

In this section I show that focalization in Gungbe is a syntactic process that requires movement of the focused element to a focus domain, FocP. In this regard, I propose that focused constituents must check their focus feature against the focus head Foc°, in a spec-head configuration. In languages of the Gungbe-type, this requirement is satisfied in overt syntax. Consequently, Gungbe allows for movement of both non-verbal and verbal constituents that are specified as [+f]. With respect to non-verbal constituents, focalization involves movement of an XP element to the specifier position of the focus phrase, [spec FocP], and the focus feature of the fronted constituent is checked against the focus head Foc° manifested as *wὲ*. The Gungbe verbal elements focus is said to include two strategies. One, referred to as verbal XP focus, is specific to imperfective constructions and applies to a maximal category NomP, the complement of the Gungbe imperfective marker *tò*. It is therefore argued that the verb inside NomP is marked as [+f]. As a consequence, the whole NomP is affected and must move to [spec FocP], where it enters in a spec-head relation with the focus head Foc°. Under this analysis, NomP focus is a disguised head movement. It is sensitive to the locality conditions that normally hold of head movements. The other strategy, verb focus, triggers movement of the focused verb to Foc°, leaving a resumptive verb in the IP-internal position. The resumptive verb strategy is considered a last resort phenomenon to avoid ungrammaticality, since long movement of the verb to Foc° would yield HMC or minimality condition violation. Here the spec-head relation is established between the moved verb under Foc° and a null focus operator in [spec FocP]. In this framework a focus operator is defined as a [+f]-phrase in an A-bar position. While it accounts for the Gungbe data in an effective and attractive way, the analysis presented here also proves successful in unifying the Gbe and Kwa data in the sense that no further assumption or extra rule is needed to capture focus constructions in those languages.

7.2 WH-QUESTIONS IN GUNGBE

As already discussed in section 7.1.1.2, Gungbe displays wh-questions that are very similar to the non-verbal XP focus sentences. The preposed wh-phrase necessarily moves to the left-adjacent position to the FM *wὲ*, as illustrated in sentences under (72b–d) derived from (82a).

(82) a. Séná xìá   wémà   ló
          Sena read-Perf book $Spf_{[+def]}$
          'Sena read the specific book'
    b. été$_i$ *(wὲ)   Séná xìá t$_i$?
          What Foc   Sena   read-Perf
          'What did Sena read?'

c. ménú$_i$ *(wè) t$_i$ xìá   wémà   ló ?
    who   Foc   read-Perf book   Spf$_{[+def]}$
    'Who read the specific book?'

d. wémà   té$_i$ *(wè)   Séná   xìá t$_i$?
    book   which   Foc   Sena   read-Perf
    'Which book did Sena read?'

Movement to this position is obligatory since Gungbe doesn't allow wh in situ strategy, as illustrated by the ungrammatical sentences under (83a–b). This is, of course, with the exception of echo-questions, which I don't discuss here. Finally, the ungrammatical sentence (83c) indicates that multiple wh-questions are not possible in Gungbe.

(83) a. *Séná   xìá   été ?
          Sena   read-Perf   what
          'What did Sean read?'

      b. *ménù   xìá   wémà   ló ?
          who   read-Perf   book   Spf$_{[+def]}$
          'Who read the specific book?'

      c. *été$_j$ ménú$_i$ wè   t$_i$ zé   t$_j$?
          what   who   Foc   take-Perf
          'Who took what?'

7.2.1 The landing site of wh-phrases in Gungbe

Following the tradition, I assume that wh-movement is substitution. It allows for movement of a maximal projection to a specifier position (Chomsky 1986; Rizzi 1990; Cheng 1991). Sentence (84a) is an instance of a wh-question within an embedded clause. This example clearly shows that main and embedded clauses manifest the same word order with respect to wh-questions. In both cases, the wh-phrase is preposed in the position immediately to the left of the FM and to the right of the Gungbe complementizer ɖɔ̀ (82–84a). In addition, the ungrammatical sentence (84b) suggests that the wh-phrase and the FM are in spec-head relation: nothing can intervene between them.

(84) a. ùn   kànbió   ɖɔ̀   été   wè   Sùrù   ɖù ?
          1sg   ask-Perf that   what   Foc   Suru   eat-Perf
          'I asked what did Suru eat?'

      b. *ùn   kànbió   ɖɔ̀   été   sɔ̀   wè   Sùrù   ɖù ?
          1sg   ask-Perf that   what   yesterday   Foc   Suru   eat-Perf
          'I asked that what did Suru eat yesterday?'

That the wh-phrase occurs to the right of the Gungbe complementizer neatly indicates that [spec ForceP] cannot be considered the landing site for wh-elements. In previous sections, the position immediately to the left of the FM has been identified as [spec FocP]. Accordingly, we can reasonably assume that the Gungbe wh-phrases and the focused elements move to the specifier position of a focus projection FocP that projects within the C-system. As this position is not involved in case assignment, any XP that is specified [+f] or [+wh] must move to [spec FocP], where it enters in a spec-head relation with the head Foc°. This analysis is consistent with the otherwise unexplainable fact that focus and wh-phrases are mutually exclusive, as shown in (85).

(85)   ... *ɖɔ̀   Sùrù   wɛ̀   été   wɛ̀   ɖù ?
              that   Suru   Foc   what   Foc   eat-Perf

Additional evidence that focused and wh-elements occur in the same position is that they manifest the same distribution with respect to topic elements, which they must follow as shown in example (86).

(86)   a.   ún   ɖɔ̀   ɖɔ̀   [dàn lɔ́]   yà,
            1sg   say-Perf   that   snake Spf[+def]   Top
            [Kòfí]   wɛ̀   ún   hù - ì   ná
            Kofi   Foc   1sg   kill-Perf -3sg   for
            'I said that, as for the specific snake, I killed it for KOFI'
       b.   ún   ɖɔ̀   ɖɔ̀   [dàn lɔ́]   yà,
            1sg   say-Perf   that   snake Spf[+def]   Top
            [ménù]   wɛ̀   ún   hù - ì   ná ?
            whom   Foc   1sg   kill-Perf -3sg   for
            'I said that, as for the specific snake, whom did I kill it for?'

If true that [spec FocP] is the landing site for both focus- and wh-elements in Gungbe (and the Gbe languages in general), the question might arise as to what position wh-phrases occupy in other typologically different languages. The following sections discuss similar data in Hungarian and Italian, where it appears that focus and wh-elements target the same position (Puskás 1996; Rizzi 1997).

7.2.2 The landing site of wh-phrases in Hungarian

In Hungarian, wh-phrases occur in the left-adjacent position to the verb, as shown by sentence (87a). Example (87b) indicates that topic elements can precede wh-phrases, but nothing can intervene between the wh-phrase and the verb (87c). The ungrammatical sentence (87d) suggests that movement to this position is obligatory, since Hungarian does not allow wh in situ strategy (except for echo questions).

(87)   a.   Kit   keresett   Zeta ?
            who-ACC   look-for-Pas-3sg   Zeta-NOM
            'Who did Zeta look for?'

b. Zeta   kit   keresett ?
   Zeta-NOM   who-ACC   look-for-Pas-3sg
   'Zeta, who did he look for?'
c. *Kit   Zeta   keresett?
   who-ACC   Zeta-NOM   look-for-Pas-3sg
d. *Zeta   keresett   kit?
   Zeta-NOM   look-for-Pas-3sg who-ACC

In the embedded clauses, wh-phrases appear in the same position as in the main clauses, immediately to the left of the verb, but they must follow the Hungarian complementizer *hogy* 'that' as illustrated by sentence (88a). Sentence (88b) shows that in this context, too, the wh-phrase can be preceded by a topic element, but it cannot be separated from the verb (88c). In no circumstances can the wh-phrase remain in situ, as shown by the ungrammatical example (78d).

(88) a. Kiváncsi vagyok   hogy kit   keresett   Zeta
        curious be-Pres-1sg that who-ACC look-for-Pas-3sg Zeta-NOM
        'I wonder who Zeta looked for'
     b. Kiváncsi vagyok   hogy   Zeta   kit   keresett
        curious be-Pres-1sg that   Zeta-NOM who-ACC   look-for-Pas-3sg
        'I wonder who Zeta looked for'
     c. * Kiváncsi vagyok   hogy kit   Zeta   keresett
        curious   be-Pres-1sg that who-ACC Zeta-NOM look-for-Pas-3sg
     d. * Kiváncsi vagyok   hogy Zeta   keresett   kit
        curious   be-Pres-1sg that Zeta-NOM look-for-Pas-3sg who-ACC

In her account for sentences under (87–88), Puskás (1992, 1996) argues that the wh-phrase occurs in a position left adjacent to the verb, but lower than the complementizer *hogy*, because it occupies [spec FocP]. The adjacency requirement between the verb and the wh-phrase is thus analyzed in terms of verb movement to Foc°. Partial justification for this analysis is that the subject *Zeta* occurs postverbally when it is not topic, as shown by examples (87a) and (88a). Additional evidence in support of this analysis is given by the following contrast:

(89) a. Emöke   kit   láttot   Zetával?
        Emöke-NOM   who-ACC   see-Pas-3sg   Zeta-INSTR
        'Who did Emöke see with Zeta?'
     b. *EMOKE   kit   láttot   Zetával?
        Emöke-NOM   who-ACC   see-Pas-3sg   Zeta-INSTR
        'Who did EMOKE see with Zeta?'
     c. *kit   EMOKE   láttot   Zetával ?
        who-ACC   Emöke-NOM see-Pas-3sg   Zeta-INSTR
        'Who did EMOKE see with Zeta?'

In sentence (89a) the subject *Emöke* is topic and precedes the wh-phrase. But the ungrammatical sentences (89b–c) clearly indicate that the wh-phrase *kit* and the focused subject are mutually exclusive. This pattern obtains regardless of whether the focus precedes or follows the wh-phrase. These facts led Puskás (1996) to conclude that (89b–c) are ruled out because the focused phrase and the wh-phrase compete for the same position: [spec FocP].

Needless to say, the brief description provided here does not cover all aspects of the Hungarian wh-constructions, and the reader is referred to Puskás' own work for a detailed and careful discussion (see also Horvàth 1986, 1995; Kiss 1987; Brody 1990, 1995). Nevertheless, it is interesting to see that the Hungarian data perfectly match the Gungbe facts. Data from both languages underscore the analysis that the landing site of wh-phrases cannot be the specifier position of the complementizer (i.e., [spec ForceP]) as it is assumed in classical GB theory. Rizzi (1997) presents similar data from Italian focus- and wh-constructions that underscore this analysis.

7.2.3 The landing site of wh-phrases in Italian

The Italian wh-phrases display similar behavior to their Gungbe and Hungarian counterparts. As extensively discussed in Rizzi (1997, 1999), they can follow topics in both main and embedded questions. Observe, for instance, the contrast between sentences (90a–b) and sentences (91a–b).

(90) a.   *A chi, il premio Nobel, lo daranno?
           'To whom the Nobel prize, will they give it?'
      b.   Il premio Nobel, a chi lo daranno?
           'The Nobel prize, to whom will they give it?'

(91) a.   Mi domando, il premio Nobel, a chi lo potrebbero dare
           'I wonder, the Nobel prize, to whom they would give it'
      b.   ?Mi domando, a chi, il premio Nobel, lo potrebbero dare'
           'I wonder to whom, the Nobel prize, they could give'

That the Italian wh-phrase can marginally precede the topic in embedded questions (81b) but not in main questions (90a) remains to be explained. I will not discuss this matter here, and the reader is referred to Rizzi's own work. But it is interesting to notice that in sentences (90b) and (91a) the wh-phrase *a chi* seems to share the same surface position as its Gungbe and Hungarian counterparts. It is realized in the Topic/Focus area, in a position lower than the complementizer. This led Rizzi (1997) to conclude that the Italian wh-phrase occupies the same position as the focus phrase: [spec FocP]. Strong evidence in favor to this analysis is that the wh-phrase and the focus phrase are in complementary distribution in main clauses.

(92) a.   *A GIANNI che cosa hai detto (non a Piero)?
           'TO GIANNI, what did you tell (not to Piero)'

b. *che cosa A GIANNI hai detto (non a Piero)?
'What TO GIANNI did you tell (not to Piero)?

As proposed by Rizzi (1997), a natural explanation for the ungrammatical sentences (92a–b) is to say that the wh-phrase and the focused element compete for the same position.
        The data discussed in Puskás (1996), Rizzi (1997), and in this study confirm the hypothesis that, in Gungbe, Hungarian, Italian (and possibly all languages), wh-phrases necessarily occupy a position other than the specifier of the complementizer, that is, [spec ForceP]. In all these languages, wh-phrases surface in a position structurally lower than [spec ForceP] and [spec TopP], assuming topics realize the specifier position of a topic projection within the C-system (Rizzi 1997). Granting that in these languages the wh-phrases and the focused elements are mutually exclusive, we are left with the only option that they seek for the same position in the clause, [spec FocP]. Now the question arises as to what triggers movement to this position.

7.2.4 Wh-constructions in Gungbe: The wh-criterion and the checking theory

As the reader may see from the previous paragraphs, cross-linguistic evidence suggests that the wh-phrase moves out from its base position, to be licensed in the left periphery. This is further exemplified by the grammatical English sentence (93a) as opposed to the ungrammatical examples (93b–d).

(93) a. Who has Mary seen ?
      b. *Mary has seen who ?
      c. *Has Mary seen who ?
      d. *Who Mary has seen ?

In order to account for those facts, Rizzi (1991, 1996) proposes that the interrogative sentences are subject to the wh-criterion, a general principle that is responsible for the surface distribution of wh-operators in English and applies universally at LF. The wh-criterion was formulated as follows:

(94) a. a wh-operator must be in a spec-head configuration with a $X°_{[+wh]}$
      b. an $X°_{[+wh]}$ must be in a spec-head configuration with a wh-operator.
          (wh-operator = a wh-phrase in an A-bar position)

                                                          Rizzi 1996: 64

Under this theory, the ungrammaticality of sentences (93b–d) suggests that the wh-criterion is satisfied in overt syntax in English. Rizzi (1991, 1996) further assumed that, in main clauses, Infl (or some inflection head under Pollock 1989) is also specified [+wh]. Building on this, we can account for the ungrammatical sentences (93b–d) in a straightforward manner. Sentence (93b) is ruled out by clause B of the wh-criterion. There is no wh-operator in the specifier position of the main inflection carrying the feature [+wh], and the required spec-head configuration is not met. Sentence (93c) is ungrammatical for the same reason. In sentence (93d), wh-movement has applied, but the sentence is also ruled out by clause A. The wh-operator *who* is not in a spec-head configuration with a head that bears the feature [+wh]. In sentence (93a), however, the inflectional head associated with the feature [+wh] (i.e., *has*) moves to the C-system (i.e., Foc° in this framework; see also Rizzi 1997), the wh-operator lands in [spec FocP], and the required spec-head configuration is met. It follows from this analysis that both wh-movement and subject inversion in English (i.e., I-to-C movement) are a means of satisfying the wh-criterion (see also Puskás 1992, 1996).

As I have proposed in section 7.1.2.3, the focus- or wh-criterion could be reformulated in terms of a symmetrical checking relation between the [+wh]-phrase in [spec FocP] and the focus head that encodes the feature [+wh]. Put differently, the head Foc° is endowed with a strong feature [+wh] that must be checked before spell-out. The same holds true of any X^{max} category that is specified as [+wh].

The discussion on Gungbe has shown that wh-phrases must occur in the position immediately to the left or the FM *wè*, and no in situ strategy is allowed in the language (95a–c).

(95) a. été$_i$ wè   Séná xìá t$_i$?
      What   Foc   Sena read-Perf
      'What did Sena read?'

    b. *été$_i$ Séná   xìá t$_i$?
      what   Sena   read-Perf

    c. *wè Séná xìá   été ?
      Foc Sena read-Perf   what

In section 7.1, I proposed that the FM *wè* encodes the feature [+f] on Foc°. However, that the FM *wè* must also occur with the wh-phrases clearly suggests that that morpheme actually encodes a set of features [+f, +wh] that are associated with Foc° and must be checked in overt syntax. Under the symmetrical checking relation, this requirement is met by moving the appropriate category (i.e., a phrase with either or both of the features [+f, +wh]) to [spec FocP]. Put differently, symmetrical checking requires a spec-head configuration between the wh-phrase and the FM *wè* that encodes the sets of features under Foc°. This analysis is consistent with the idea that Gungbe manifests no I-to-C movement, since Foc° is already filled in syntax by the FM *wè*. Note, for instance, that the verb associated with the IP-markers must be realized within the I-system in a position lower than the subject (96a). In a similar vein, that the FM must occur in a structural position higher than the subject and *ní*—which I analyzed as the PF realization of Fin° (96b)—precludes an analysis in terms of V-to-Fin°-to-Foc° movement (see section 7.1).

(96) a. été   wè   Séná má   ná   nɔ̀   tò   nà   xìá ?
          what Foc Sena Neg Fut   Hab Imperf Prosp read
          'What is it that Sena will not be about to read?'
      b. été   wè   Séná ní xìá ?
          What Foc Sena Inj read-Perf
          'What should Sena read?'

Similarly, I can account for the ungrammatical sentences (95b–c) by arguing that, in sentence (95b) the wh-phrase *été* moves in sentence-initial position, but the sentence is ruled out because Foc° doesn't carry the feature [+wh] and the sentence doesn't contain the FM *wè*. Sentence (95c), on the other hand, is ruled out because there is no wh-operator in spec-head configuration with the [+wh] Foc° realized by *wè*.

The system developed in this study suggests that the Gungbe left periphery contains a focus projection FocP whose head Foc° is endowed with the features [+f, +wh], and is morphologically realized as *wè*. Given that [spec FocP] is not a homogeneous position and is not involved in case assignment, it is reasonable to assume that FocP is present only in sentences that include a focus- or wh-element that must be licensed under symmetrical checking. Granting that the focus field occurs to the right of the complementizer and follows topic (84–86) and given that it precedes the subject and the injunctive/subjective marker *ní* (96b), the Gungbe C-system can be partially represented as follows:

(97) [$_{ForceP}$ [$_{Force°}$ ɖɔ̀ [$_{TopP}$ [$_{FocP}$ XP$_{[+f/+wh]i}$ [$_{Foc°}$ wè [$_{FinP}$ [$_{Fin°}$ ní [$_{AgrP}$ ...t$_i$ ...]]]]]]]]]

7.2.5 On simultaneous wh-phrases in main and embedded clauses

So far, the discussion has shown that Gungbe does not manifest multiple-wh strategy or FocP recursion. Recall, for instance, that it is never possible to prepose more than one wh-phrase to the position immediately to the left of the FM (98a). In a similar vein, the occurrence of two FMs in the clause leads to ungrammaticality, as shown by sentence (98b).

(98) a. *été$_j$ ménú$_i$ wè   t$_i$ zé   t$_j$?
          what   who   Foc   take-Perf
          'Who took what?'
      b. *été$_j$ wè   ménú$_i$ wè   t$_i$ zé   t$_j$?
          what   Foc   who   Foc   take-Perf
          'Who took what?'

It is also interesting to notice that in sentence (98c), only one wh-phrase can move to [spec FocP], the second must remain in situ, and the sentence is necessarily interpreted as an echo question. The conclusion I reached there is that only one specifier position is allowed and there is no FocP recursion or free adjunction.

(98) c. ménú$_i$ wè   t$_i$ zé   été ?
          who   Foc   take-Perf what
          'Who took what?'

Yet the impossibility of preposing multiple wh-phrases to [spec FocP] of the same
clause, (or having recursive FocPs) does not exclude simultaneous occurrence of wh-
phrases in both main and embedded clauses (99a). Like focus constructions, long wh-
extraction is also compatible with simultaneous wh-movement in the embedded clause
(99b–c). In addition, sentences (99b–c) clearly suggest that the Gungbe wh-phrases do
not use the lower [spec FocP] as an escape hatch. If this were the case, the sentences
would be ungrammatical because there would be no landing site for the embedded wh-
phrase. The grammaticality of these sentences suggests that there must be some other
intermediate position for wh-phrases to move out from the embedded clause. Building
on the discussion in previous sections about focus constructions, I assume this position
to be the specifier position of the complementizer, [spec ForceP].[35]

(99) a. ménú$_i$ wè   t$_i$ kánbió   dò   été$_j$ wè   Rèmí zé   t$_j$?
          who   Foc   ask-Perf that   what   Foc   Remi take-Perf
          'Who asked what Remi took?'
      b. été$_j$ wè   Séná   kánbió   dò   ménú$_i$ wè t$_i$ zé   t$_j$?
          what   Foc   Sena   ask-Perf   that   who   Foc   take-Perf
          'What did Sena ask that who take?'
      c. ménú$_i$ wè   Séná   kánbió   dò   été$_j$ wè   é$_i$ zé   t$_j$?
          who   Foc   Sena   ask-Perf that   what   Foc   3sg take-Perf
          'What did Sena ask who took?'

Finally, the impossibility of interpreting sentence (99d) as in (99e) clearly indicates that
the argument versus adjunct asymmetry that I discussed with respect to the focus
constructions is also found in the wh-questions involving long extraction. Recall from
the discussion in section 7.1.2.2 that representation (99e) is ruled out under Relativized
Minimality. Under Rizzi's approach, the time adjunct *hwèténú* 'when' does not bear a
referential index. As a consequence, it cannot identify its trace by binding. It therefore
follows that adjunct traces are subject to antecedent government. However, antecedent
government fails in the representation (99e) due to the intervening wh-phrase *été*
'what'. In this regard, notice that the only possible interpretation for sentence (99d) is
that where the time adjunct *hwèténú* 'when' is extracted from the main clause, as
illustrated in (99f). As expected, such constructions manifest argument versus adjunct
asymmetry because long extraction of the internal argument is (marginally) possible
even when the embedded [spec FocP] is filled by the time adjunct *hwèténú* 'when'
(99g) (see Rizzi 1990, 1997; Cinque 1990, and references cited there for more details).

(99) d. hwèténú wè   Séná   kánbió   dò   été   wè   Kójó zé   ?
          when   Foc   Sena   ask-Perf that   what Foc   Kojo take-Perf
          'When did Sena ask what Kojo took?'

e. *hwèténú$_j$ wè Séná kánbió   ɖɔ̀ été$_i$ wè   Kɔ́jó zé   t$_i$ t$_j$?
   when   Foc Sena ask-Perf that what Foc   Kojo take-Perf

f. wèténú$_j$ wè Séná kánbió t$_j$ ɖɔ̀   été$_i$ wè   Kɔ́jó zé t$_i$?
   when   Foc Sena ask-Perf that   what Foc   Kojo take-Perf

g. %été$_i$ wè   Séná kánbió   ɖɔ̀   hwèténú$_j$ wè Kɔ́jó zé t$_i$ t$_j$?
   what Foc   Sena ask-Perf that when   Foc Kojo take-Perf
   'When did Sena ask what Kojo took?'

Interestingly enough, the argument versus adjunct asymmetry is maintained even when the intervening [spec FocP] is occupied by a focused element. As the reader may see, the only possible interpretation for the sentence (99h) is that which allows for the wh-adjunct to be extracted from the main clause. Long construal is impossible, as shown by the representation (99i).

(99) h. hwèténú wè Séná sè   ɖɔ̀ hǐ lɔ́ wè Kɔ́jó xɔ̀ ?
         when   Foc Sena hear-Perf that knife Spf$_{[+def]}$ Foc Kojo buy-Perf
         'When did Sena hear that Kojo bought the specific knife?'

      i. *[hwèténú$_j$] wè Séná sè   ɖɔ̀ [hǐ lɔ́$_i$]   wè Kɔ́jó xɔ̀ t$_i$ t$_j$?
         when   Foc Sena hear-Perf that knife Spf$_{[+def]}$ Foc Kojo buy-Perf

In terms of the analysis I propose here, the contrast in (99h–i) is expected since the wh-phrase and the focused constituents compete for the same position [spec FocP].

7.2.6 Summary

This section shows that the Gungbe wh-phrases occur in [spec FocP], to the left of the FM *wè*. In this respect, I propose that the Gungbe FM encodes the set of features [+wh, +f] that are associated with the head Foc°. I further argue that movement to [spec FocP] is motivated by the need of the [+wh]-phrase to check its [+wh]-features against the head Foc° before spell-out. Given that simultaneous wh-question associated with long wh-extraction is possible in this language, we conclude that [spec FocP] of the embedded clause does not serve as escape hatch for wh-phrases. A wh-phrase that undergoes long extraction moves through [spec ForceP] on its way to the focus site, [spec FocP] of the main clause.

7.3 CONCLUSION

In this chapter I have shown that, in addition to ForceP and FinP that are realized as conjunction and mood *ní* respectively, the Gungbe C-system also involves a focus projection.

    Under the split-C hypothesis, I suggest that the Gungbe focus constructions reflect a syntactic process that requires movement of the focused category to a focus domain, FocP headed by the focus marker *wὲ*. Under symmetrical checking, I further propose that the focus phrases must move in syntax in order to reach a spec-head configuration with a focus head. No focus in situ strategy is allowed in the language, and focus movement targets both non-verbal and verbal constituents that are specified as [+f]. The non-verbal constituents (i.e., elements of the type XP) move to [spec FocP] where they enter a spec-head configuration with the focus head Foc° manifested as *wὲ*.

Two types of verbal category focus are found in Gungbe. Verbal XP focus is typical to OV constructions, that is, imperfective and related clauses. In those constructions, focusing applies to NomP, the complement of the Gungbe imperfective marker *tò*. It is argued here that the verb inside NomP is marked as [+f], but the whole NomP is moved to [spec FocP] as a result of generalized pied-piping. In this regard, the verb inside NomP checks its focus features against the focus head Foc°. On the other hand, verb focus triggers movement of the focused verb to Foc°, leaving a resumptive verb or a V copy in the IP-internal position. Under last resort, the resumptive verb strategy is a way to avoid ungrammaticality: since a straight movement of the verb in Foc° would give rise to the HMC or some minimality condition violation. I argue that in such contexts, symmetrical checking is achieved due to the presence of a null focus operator in [spec FocP]. This operator is defined as a [+f]-phrase in an A-bar position. Extending the discussion to other Kwa languages, I showed that the copy strategy is not limited to verbs only. It is a generalized rule that applies to all the cases where a gap is prohibited. This naturally includes cases of verb focus that involve pied-piping of a maximal projection, say ΣP, the IP-internal position being filled by an ΣP-copy.

Granting that the Gungbe wh-phrases must occur to the left-adjacent position to the focus marker *wὲ*, I propose that the Gungbe focused and wh-phrases compete for the same position: [spec FocP]. Evidence in favor of this hypothesis is that focused categories and wh-phrases are mutually exclusive. In no circumstance can a focused category and a wh-phrase co-occur in the same domain. Yet simultaneous focus and/or wh-questions are possible in both main and embedded clauses. This indicates that [spec FocP] of the embedded clause does not serve as escape hatch for long extraction of focus or wh-phrases. I account for the distribution of the Gungbe wh-phrases by proposing that the focus marker encodes the set of features [+f, +wh] that characterize the head Foc°. Following Rizzi (1991, 1996), I assume that wh-movement to [spec FocP] is motivated by the need of the wh-phrase to check its [+wh] features against the head Foc° also bearing corresponding [+wh] features.

8

Argument Topics and Yes-No Questions

In chapter 7 I accounted for the sentences under (1) by arguing that the C-system involves a Focus Phrase (FocP) that projects between ForceP and FinP. The focus- and wh-phrases occur in [spec FocP], where they check their [+f, +wh] features in a spec-head relation with the focus head Foc° that also encodes the features [+f, +wh]. Those features are morphologically realized by the focus marker *wὲ* that occurs under Foc° (Rizzi 1990, 1996; Chomsky 1995; Aboh 1998a, 1999).

(1) a. [dàn   lɔ́]$_i$ wὲ   Kɔ̀fí   hù   t$_i$
          snake   Spf$_{[+def]}$ Foc   Kofi   kill-Perf
          'Kofi killed THE SPECIFIC   SNAKE'
    b. [été]$_i$ wὲ   Kɔ̀fí   hù   t$_i$?
          what   Foc   Kofi   kill-Perf
          'What did Kofi kill?'

I further showed that focusing of verbal elements involves two strategies. The first, call it NomP-focusing, is specific to OV constructions (2a). It forces movement of the maximal projection NomP to [spec FocP], where it checks its [+f] feature against the focus head Foc°, leaving a trace in the IP-internal position. The second strategy is typical of VO constructions. It involves a V copy strategy whereby the focused verb is moved to Foc°, leaving a copy in the IP-internal position.

(2) a. [xwé   lɔ́   gbá]$_i$ %wὲ   Sէná   tè   t$_i$
          house   Spf$_{[+def]}$ build-NR   Foc   Sena   Imperf
          'Sena is BUILDING THE   SPECIFIC HOUSE'

b. [gbá]ᵢ   %wὲ   Sέná   gbáᵢ   xwé   lɔ́
    build   Foc   Sena   build-Perf   house   Spf[+def]
    'Sena BUILT the specific house'

This chapter extends the analysis I proposed there to the Gungbe topic constructions and yes-no questions. Section 8.1 investigates the topic constructions exemplified in (3). In these two sentences, (a main clause in (3a) and an embedded clause in (3b)), the topic *dàn lɔ́* 'the snake' is left adjacent to the morpheme *yà*, in a position to the right of the complementizer *ɖɔ̀*, as illustrated in (3b). Sentences (3c–d) clearly indicate that topic and focused (or wh) elements are not mutually exclusive, though they must occur in a fixed order Topic-Focus/Wh-phrase.

(3) a. [dàn   lɔ́]   yà,   Kɔ̀fí   hù - ì
         snake   Spf[+def] Top   Kofi   kill-Perf-3sg
         'As for the specific snake, Kofi killed it'

     b. ún   ɖɔ̀   ɖɔ̀   [dàn   lɔ́]   yà,   Kɔ̀fí   hù - ì
         1sg   say-Perf that snake Spf[+def] Top   Kofi   kill-Perf-3sg
         'I said that, as for the specific snake, Kofi killed it'

     c. ún   ɖɔ̀   ɖɔ̀   [dàn   lɔ́]   yà,
         1sg   say-Perf   that   snake   Spf[+def] Top
         [Kɔ̀fí]   wὲ   ún   hù - ì   ná
         Kofi   Foc   1sg   kill-Perf-3sg   for
         'I said that, as for the specific snake, I killed it for KOFI'

     d. ún   ɖɔ̀   ɖɔ̀   [dàn   lɔ́]   yà,
         1sg   say-Perf that snake   Spf[+def] Top
         [ménù]   wὲ   ún   hù - ì   ná ?
         whom   Foc   1sg   kill-Perf -3sg   for
         'I said that, as for the specific snake, whom did I kill it for?'

Granting the impossibility of free adjunction to IP, I propose, in line with Culicover (1992), Müller and Sternefeld (1993), and Rizzi (1997), among others, that the topic occupies a specific position different from [spec ForceP], or [spec FocP]. In other words, the C-system necessarily consists of several projections whose specifier positions host topic and focus elements, respectively. Assuming Rizzi's (1997) analysis, it is argued that the C-system includes a topic projection (TopP) that projects between ForceP and FocP and whose specifier position hosts the topic. I further assume that *yà* is merged in Top° as the morphological realization of the feature [+topic]. Accordingly, I argue that movement to [spec TopP] is motivated by the necessity of the topic phrase to check its topic feature [+topic] against the topic head Top°. Section 8.2 focuses on the Gungbe yes-no questions as shown in (4).

(4)   a.   Kòfí   dù   nú
           Kofi   eat-Perf   thing
           'Kofi ate'

      b.   Kòfí   dù   nû ?
           Kofi   eat-Perf   thing-QM
           'Did Kofi eat?'

The sentences under (4) form a minimal pair. But the example (4b) is interpreted as a yes-no question because it involves the sentence-final low tone specific to the Gungbe yes-no questions (see chapter 2). In this respect, I argue that the sentence-final low tone is the reflex of a 'quasi-null' morpheme that functions as yes-no question marker (QM). Pursuing the discussion in section 8.1,[1] I conclude that this QM heads an interrogative projection InterP that projects within the C-system and whose specifier hosts the clause. In this context, the QM has scope over the whole clause, which is interpreted as a yes-no question. Section 8.3 concludes the chapter. The appendix extends the split-C hypothesis to the so-called clausal determiners in Gbe. A parallel is made between the clausal determiner that necessarily occurs sentence-finally and the Gungbe left peripheral markers that require that their complement be moved in their specifier position.

8.1 ARGUMENT TOPICS IN GUNGBE

The sentence (5) is an instance of a topic construction involving an embedded clause. In this context, we see that the topic, the bracketed element, surfaces in a presubject position where it is sandwiched between the complementizer ḍɔ 'that' and the morpheme yà specific to the topic sentences. Building on the discussion in chapter 7, I interpret the occurrence of the topic in this position as clear indication that the topic constructions involve the left periphery. But before getting on to the precise analysis of the topic constructions in Gungbe, a note on the theoretical background is in order.

(5)   ún ḍɔ   ḍɔ   [dàn   lɔ]   yà   Kòfí   hù   í
      1sg say-Perf that   snake Spf$_{[+def]}$ Top   Kofi   kill-Perf 3sg
      'I said that as for the specific snake, Kofi killed it'

8.1.1 The TopP analysis (Rizzi 1997)

It has been shown in the literature (Cinque 1977, 1990; Sternefeld 1991; Culicover 1992; Müller & Sternefeld 1993, 1996; Puskás 1995, 1996; Müller 1995, 1998; Rizzi 1997; Zwart 1997a; Poletto 2000; Benincà 2001) that besides focus- and wh-constructions, languages also manifest another construction that typically involves the left periphery: topicalization. As illustrated in sentences under (6), the topic (in boldface) is "a preposed element characteristically set off from the rest of the clause by comma intonation and normally expressing old information" (Rizzi 1997: 4).

(6)   a.   **Il tuo libro**, lo ho comprato   . [Italian]
            'Your book, I bought it'
      b.   **Your book**, I bought   [English]
      c.   **Jànos ezt a filmet** MARIVAL làtta   [Hungarian]
            John-NOM this film-ACC Mary-INSTR saw
            'This film, John saw with MARY'

In his account of the Italian topic constructions, that is, Clitic Left Dislocation (CLLD)[2] illustrated in example (6a), Rizzi (1997) proposes that topic elements occur in the specifier position of a projection, TopP, within the C-system. Accordingly, the topic-comment articulation that is expressed in topic constructions can be represented as in (7):[3]

(7)   TopP

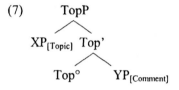

$XP_{[Topic]}$ Top'

    Top° $YP_{[Comment]}$

Top° is associated with the functional interpretation that its specifier is the topic and its complement the comment. In this regard, Rizzi (1997: 286) argues that the functional head Top° defines a higher domain of predication, that is,

> a predication within the Comp system; its function is thus analogous to the function of AgrS within the IP system, which also configurationally connects a subject and a predicate.

Granting that topic, focus and wh constructions are manifestations of the C-system, we can further conclude that they are instantiations of constructions involving A-bar chains. The question then becomes how can we distinguish between those chains. In this respect, Rizzi (1997) demonstrates that the Italian topic and focus constructions present distinct properties that help identify their fundamentally different nature. Three major properties determine these differences.

    First, the Italian topic constructions necessarily involve an IP-internal resumptive clitic when the topicalized constituent is the direct object. Compare, for example, the grammatical sentence (8a) and the ungrammatical example (8b). On the other hand, focus constructions never require the occurrence of the resumptive clitic. In the focus sentence (8c), the object clitic is present and the sentence is ruled out. Instead, the grammatical focus sentence (8c) involves no clitic.

(8)　a.　Il tuo libro, lo ho comprato
　　　　　'Your book, I bought it'
　　b.　*Il tuo libro, ho comprato t
　　　　　'Your book, I bought'
　　c.　*IL TUO LIBRO lo ho comprato (non il suo)
　　　　　'YOUR BOOK I bought it (not his)'
　　d.　IL TUO LIBRO ho comprato t (non il suo)
　　　　　'YOUR BOOK, I bought (not his)'

Second, granting that Weak Cross Over (WCO) effects are a diagnostic for Operator-chains, it is interesting to notice that a topic never yields any WCO effect, while a focus does. This is exemplified by the contrast in sentences (9a–b).

(9)　a.　Gianni, sua madre lo ha sempre apprezzato
　　　　　'Gianni, his mother always appreciated him'
　　b　??GIANNI sua madre ha sempre apprezzato (non Piero)
　　　　　'GIANNI his mother always appreciated, not Piero'

Third, unless they are linked to a lexical restriction within the DP, bare quantificational expressions like *no one*, or *all* cannot be topicalized (10a). But they can easily be focused as shown by example (10b).

(10)　a.　*Nessuno, lo ho visto
　　　　　'No one, I saw him'
　　b.　NESSUNO ho visto
　　　　　'NO ONE I saw'

In order to account for the three properties, Rizzi (1997) proposed an updated version of Cinque's (1990) analysis, that these characteristics reduce to one basic distinction: focus is quantificational; topic is not. Following Lasnik and Stowell's (1991) proposal that WCO is diagnostic for A-bar relations that involve true quantification, Rizzi (1997: 292) further proposes that

> A' dependencies, all sensitive to Strong Cross-Over (i.e., principle C), split into variable binding by a quantificational operator (assigning a range to the variable), and binding of a null constant by an anaphoric operator (whose role is to connect the null constant to an antecedent). The former, but not the latter, is sensitive to WCO.[4]

This leads Rizzi to conclude that the contrast in (9), the fact that focalization is sensitive to WCO while topicalization is not, can be explained if we assume that focus involves quantificational operator-variable binding. In contrast, topic allows for no such quantificational A'-binding.

Granting Chomsky's (1992) Full Interpretation, Rizzi's approach provides straightforward account for the first property illustrated by the sentences under (8): quantified expressions must bind syntactic variables, that is, a non-pronominal XP in an A-position (see Cinque 1990; Rizzi 1997). In other words, sentence (8d) is grammatical because the focused constituent *il tuo libro* binds a syntactic variable in the IP-internal position. But this is not the case in the ungrammatical example (8c), where none of the potential bindees (the clitic and its trace) qualifies as a syntactic variable.

Sentence (8b) is ruled out on the same ground. The topic is not quantificational; therefore, the empty category in the IP-internal position has no legitimate status. It cannot be a variable, since there is no quantificational element to bind it. Moreover, it does not fall under any typology of empty categories (e.g., PRO, pro, or DP-trace; see Rizzi 1997 and references cited there). On the other hand, sentence (8a) is grammatical because the empty category in the object position has the legitimate status of a clitic trace. In other words, the obligatory realization of the resumptive clitic in (8a) results from the fact that no other well-formed derivation could be associated with its cliticless variant (8b). If a clitic is present, no problems arise, the resulting configuration being a normal clitic-'trace' configuration, subject to antecedent government (Cinque 1990).

However, not all languages adopt the Italian strategy (i.e., the licensing of the empty category in the IP-internal position via a resumptive clitic pronoun). In English, for example, the empty category is a null constant licensed (i.e., A'-bound) by the topic via an empty operator (11).

(11)   Your book, [OP [I bought t]]

In terms of Rizzi's analysis, the null constant is not freely available in the language. It is legitimated by a unique type of A'-binder: the non-quantificational anaphoric operator that is defined as "an element inherently characterized as an operator but different from quantificational operators in that it does not assign a range to its bindee; rather, the anaphoric operator seeks for an antecedent to which it connects its bindee" (Rizzi 1997: 293). The licensing condition of the null constant is therefore expressed in principle (12):

(12)   A null constant is licensed by an anaphoric operator.

In this regard, language variations are accounted for in terms of parametric variations. Put differently, there is a parameter (e.g., similar to the pro-drop parameter) that determines whether a language involves the null anaphoric operator or not.[5] In languages of the English-type, this parameter is positively set. The topic constructions involve the null anaphoric operator that binds a null constant in the IP-internal position. In the languages of the Italian-type, however, the parameter is negatively set. As a result, the topic binds a clitic, which in turn licenses a clitic-trace in the IP-internal position. This amount to saying that, in the Italian and

English examples, the clitic and the empty operator have the same function. They establish a connection between the topic and the corresponding empty category in the IP-internal position.

Under such assumptions, I can explain the third difference illustrated in sentences (10) by proposing that topic is not quantificational and cannot allow for a variable in the IP-internal position. As a result, topic constructions are incompatible with quantified expressions. Sentence (10a) is ruled out because neither the clitic nor its trace qualifies as a variable. But sentence (10b) is grammatical because focus is quantificational and the variable in the IP-internal position is legitimated. If this analysis is correct, then the following generalization arises:

(13) a. focus is quantificational and topic is not
      b. the anaphoric operator parameter applies:
          A null constant is allowed in the IP-internal position only and only if the language allows for the anaphoric operator in topic constructions (Cinque 1990; Rizzi 1997).

Clause b necessarily implies that those languages that lack the anaphoric operator in topic constructions must adopt a strategy that helps circumvent ungrammaticality. Italian is such a language: it uses a resumptive clitic pronoun strategy that licenses the empty category in the IP-internal position. Not all languages choose the Italian strategy. A case in point is the Hungarian topic constructions where the IP-internal empty category is licensed via pro (Puskás 1995, 1996, 2000).

8.1.2 Hungarian topics

On her account of the Hungarian topic constructions, Puskás (1995) shows that they manifest the following properties.

First, the Hungarian topics do not yield WCO effect, unlike the focus constructions.

(14) a. Jànost$_i$ azt mondta az pro$_i$ anyja hogy szereti Mari e$_i$
          John that said the pro mother-his that likes Mary
          'John, his mother said that Mary likes him'
      b. *JANOST$_i$ mondta az pro$_i$ anyja hogy Mari szereti e$_i$
          who-ACC said the pro mother that Mary likes

Second, an overt pronominal element is excluded in the Hungarian topic constructions (15a–b). According to Puskás (1995), there is no clitic pronoun in Hungarian, and the language does not allow for the null anaphoric operator strategy adopted by English.

(15) a. Marit A MOZI ELOTT vàrta Peter
          Mary-ACC the cinema before waited Peter-NOM
          'Peter waited for Mary in front of the cinema'
      b. *Marit A MOZI ELOTT öt Peter
          Mary-ACC the cinema before waited her Peter-NOM

Third, the topic appears with the morphological case corresponding to that assigned in the IP-internal position (16a). No default case can be assigned to the topic (16b).

(16) a. Ezt az angol filmet MARIVAL làtta Peter
          this the English film-ACC Mary-INSTR saw Peter-NOM
          'This English film, Peter saw with Mary'
      b. * Ez as angol film MARIVAL làtta Peter
          'This the English film-NOM'

Following Cinque's (1990) and Rizzi's (1997) analysis of the Italian topic constructions, Puskás (1995, 1996) proposes that the first property is an indication that the Hungarian topic involves A'-movement, but no quantificational operator-variable chain is formed. In other words, Hungarian is like Italian and English in that it manifests topic constructions that give rise to A'-chains involving non-quantificational A'-binders.

On the other hand, the second and third properties indicate that the Hungarian topicalization displays neither the resumptive clitic strategy nor the null anaphoric strategy that were observed in Italian and English, respectively. Alternatively, Puskás (1995: 10) suggests that the Hungarian topic develops a third strategy that displays

> a null pro, which A-binds its trace in the base position. This pro is formally licensed by the relevant Agr head. It is identified by the rich morphological features realized on the constituent it is linked with via the non-quantificational A'-chain it forms with the constituent.

Consequently, sentence (15a) above could be represented as in (17):

(17) $[_{TopP}$ Marit$_i$ $[_{FP}$ A MOZI ELOTT vàrta [Peter pro$_i$ t$_i$]]]

8.1.3 Gungbe topics

Granting that the analysis presented in the previous paragraphs is correct, let's now focus on the Gungbe topic constructions. In this section, I show that, in this language, topic constructions and the focus/wh constructions are both similar and dissimilar in a number of respects. I further argue that those similarities and dissimilarities can be accounted for if we assume the analysis developed for English, Italian, and Hungarian that the topic constructions involve a non-quantificational chain whereby the topic element is moved to the specifier position of a topic projection that projects within the C-system.

8.1.3.1 Some similarities between topic and focus/wh constructions

The Gungbe topic constructions are similar to the focus and wh constructions: they necessarily involve preposing of the topic element to the left periphery (18a). The ungrammatical sentence (18b) indicates that Gungbe doesn't involve topic in situ strategy.

(18) a. dàn   ló   yà   Kòfí   hù   ì
          snake Spf[+def] Top   Kofi   kill-Perf   3sg
          'As for the specific snake, Kofi killed it'

      b. *yà Kòfí   hù   dàn   ló
          Top Kofi   kill-Perf   snake Spf[+def]
          'As for Kofi, he killed the specific snake'
          'As for the specific snake, Kofi killed it'

In embedded clauses, the topic occurs to the right of the complementizer ɖɔ̀ in a presubject position (19). Recall from chapter 7 that the same is true of focus and wh constructions.

(19) ùn   ɖɔ́   ɖɔ̀   dàn   ló   yà   Kòfí   hù   ì
      1sg say-Perf that snake Spf[+def] Top   Kofi   kill-Perf 3sg
      'I said that as for the specific snake, Kofi killed it'

Just as focused and wh elements must occur in the left-adjacent position to the FM wɛ̀, topics surface in a position immediately to the left of the morpheme yà that is analyzed as the topic marker (TM). For some speakers, the TM is optional. But as I will show in section 8.1.3.3.4, two different constructions underlie this apparently optional occurrence of the TM. It is thus argued that each construction manifests a distinct specification of the topic head Top°. At this stage of the discussion, it suffices to say that the TM expresses the fact that the left-adjacent element is topic (i.e., preestablished in discourse) and the predicate to its right is comment (Cinque 1990; Puskás 1995, 1996; Rizzi 1997). This is illustrated by the sentences under (20). In example (20a), the speaker makes a statement about Kòfí. But in his answer to that statement, the speaker of sentence (20b) tries to determine whether the statement is made about a specific Kòfí that is preestablished in discourse. This is why the noun Kòfí surfaces with a possessive cé 'my', a quantifier lòkpó 'the (only) one', and the specific marker ló. It is particularly interesting to see that the topic marker yà can be combined only with definite or specific (i.e., D-linked) DPs. In this respect, the contrast in (20c–d) shows that the topic marker cannot co-occur with a DP associated with the Gungbe indefinite specificity marker ɖé.

(20) a. ùn sè ɖɔ̀ Kòfí yì yòvótòmὲ
     1sg hear-Perf that Kofi go-Perf Europe
     'I heard that Kofi went to Europe'

b. Kòfí cé lòkpó lɔ́ yà fíté wὲ é ná hὲn kwέ sɔ́n ?
   Kofi my one Spf[+def] Top where Foc 3sg Fut take money from
   'You mean the one specific Kofi (that we both know) where will he find the money?'

c. *[Kòfí ɖé] yà é bí xúgán vǐ cé lέ kpó
   Kofi Spf[-def] Top 3sg intelligent than child my Num all
   'As for a certain Kofi, he is more intelligent than all my children'

d. [Kòfí lɔ́] yà é bí xúgán vǐ cé lέ kpó
   Kofi Spf[+def] Top 3sg intelligent than child my Num all
   'As for the specific Kofi, he is more intelligent than all my children'

The ungrammatical sentence (21a) shows that only one topic can be associated with the topic marker *yà*. In a similar vein, the morpheme *yà* can occur only once in the clause (21b). In terms of the topic phrase (TopP) analysis, sentences under (21) suggest that no TopP recursion is possible in Gungbe.[6] Recall from the discussion in chapter 7 that similar data about focus and wh constructions led me to conclude that FocP recursion does not exist in Gungbe.

(21) a. *gólù lɔ́ àgbá lɔ́ yà Kòfí zè-è ɖó é mὲ
     gold Spf[+def] box Spf[+def] Top Kofi put-Perf-3sg Loc 3sg in

b. *gólù lɔ́ yà àgbá lɔ́ yà Kòfí zè-è ɖó é mὲ
   gold Spf[+def] Top box Spf[+def] Top Kofi put-Perf-3sg Loc 3sg in

Such precedence requirement on the topic, focus, and wh elements suggests that the topic position is higher than the focus position, as shown by sentences (22a–b).

(22) a. Kòfí yà gànkpá mὲ wὲ kpònɔ̀n lέ sú - ì ɖó
     Kofi Top prison in Foc policeman Num shut-Perf-3sg Loc
     'As for Kofi, the policemen put him IN PRISON'

b. *gànkpá mὲ wὲ Kòfí yà kpònɔ̀n lέ sú- ì ɖó
   prison in Foc Kofi Top policeman Num shut-Perf-3sg Loc

I propose, in chapter 7, that focused and wh phrases target a focus projection (FocP) that projects within the C-system. Assuming Rizzi (1997), the same reasoning is extended to the Gungbe topics. The topic occurs in the specifier position of a topic projection TopP that dominates the focus projection FocP. I further propose that the TM *yà* is inserted in Top° where it encodes the feature [+topic]. Granting that movement is last resort, I assume, in line with Puskás (1995, 1996), and Rizzi (1997), that movement to [spec TopP] is triggered by the need of the topic phrase to check its topic features against the topic head. This would mean that the topic phrase and the topic head must be spec-head configuration in overt syntax. That nothing can intervene between the TM and the element immediately to its left suggests that the topic and the TM share a spec-head relation (23).

(23) *Kòfí   égbé   yà   é   nyàn   àzɔ́nwàtɔ́ cé lɛ́   kpó
       Kofi   today   Top   3sg chase-Perf workers   my Num all
       'As for Kofi, he fired all my workers today'

Granting this analysis, we can then straightforwardly account for the similarities discussed above. The fact that topic, focus, and wh phrases target distinct positions in the left periphery also follows (see examples 20–23). The markers *yà* and *wè* encode features [+topic] and [+focus, +wh] that are associated with Top° and Foc°, respectively. These heads project in the left periphery as components of the C-system. In this regard, the Gungbe left periphery can be attributed the partial representation in (24).

(24)

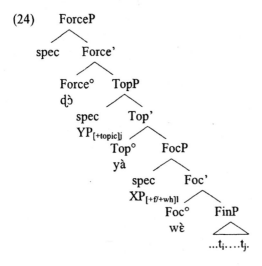

In a similar vein, properties 1, 2, and 4 follow immediately if we assume that the topic-focus system is triggered in a structure only when the clause contains a constituent that needs to check its topic, focus or wh feature. A consequence of this assumption is that TopP and FocP are two independent projections that can be triggered either separately (18–19) or simultaneously, as illustrated in (22a).

8.1.3.2 Some dissimilarities between topic and focus/wh constructions

Topic constructions necessarily involve an IP-internal resumptive element that is identified by the topic. In this respect, topicalization contrasts with focus and wh constructions in that the latter never include a resumptive pronoun strategy (except when an embedded subject is wh-extracted or focused).

(25) a. ùn ɖɔ́ ɖɔ̀ dàn lɔ́ yà Kòfí hù ì
        1sg say-Perf that snake Spf[+def] Top Kofi kill-Perf 3sg
        'I said that as for the specific snake, Kofi killed it'
     b. *ùn ɖɔ́ ɖɔ̀ [dàn lɔ́]ᵢ yà Kòfí hù tᵢ
        1sg say-Perf that snake Spf[+def] Top Kofi kill-Perf
     c. *[dàn lɔ́] wὲ Kòfí hù ì
        snake Spf[+def] Foc Kofi kill-Perf 3sg
     d. *[été] wὲ Kòfí hù ì
        what Foc Kofi kill-Perf 3sg

The Gungbe topic constructions also differ from the focus and wh constructions in that the latter can apply to different types of constituents (see chapter 7), while the former involves DPs essentially. For example, sentences (26a–b) show that when topicalization involves a *P*P, only the DP inside the *P*P can be topicalized, hence the grammatical sentence (26a). In those contexts, the *P*P-internal position is filled by the resumptive pronoun preceding the postnominal morpheme *P*. In no circumstance can the whole *P*P be preposed to [spec TopP], as illustrated by the ungrammatical sentence (26b). In the focus and wh constructions, however, the whole *P*P must be moved to [spec FocP], as shown by the grammatical sentences (26c–e), on the one hand, as opposed to the ungrammatical examples (26d–f), on the other.

(26) a. [DP xɔ̀ lɔ́]ᵢ yà Kòfí bíɔ́ [PP éᵢ mὲ]
        room Spf[+def] Top Kofi enter-Perf 3sg in
        'As for the room, Kofi entered it'
     b. *[PP xɔ̀ lɔ́ mὲ] yà Kòfí bíɔ́ é
        room Spf[+def] in Top Kofi enter-Perf -3sg
     c. [PP xɔ̀ lɔ́ mὲ] wὲ Kòfí bíɔ́
        room Spf[+def] in Foc Kofi enter-Perf
     d. *[DP xɔ̀ lɔ́] wὲ Kòfí bíɔ́ [PP é mὲ]
        room Spf[+def] Foc Kofi enter-Perf 3sg in
     e. [PP été mὲ] wὲ Kòfí bíɔ́ ?
        what in Foc Kofi enter-Perf
        'What was it that Kofi entered it?'
     f. *été wὲ Kòfí bíɔ́ [PP é mὲ] ?
        what Foc Kofi enter-Perf 3sg in
        'What was it that Kofi entered it?'

Bare quantificational expressions, for example, *nú lέ kpó* 'everything' and *nú ɖé* 'something', resist topicalization (27a), while they can be freely focused or wh-questioned, as illustrated in (27b–c).[7]

(27) a. *[nú lέ   kpó]   yà   Kòfí sìgán xò   yé
        thing Num   all   Top Kofi can   buy 3sg
     b. [nú lέ   kpó]   wὲ   Kòfí sìgán xò
        thing Num   all   Foc Kofi can   buy
        'Kofi can buy EVERYTHING'
     c. [nú té lέ kpó]   wὲ   Kòfí sìgán xò
        thing which Num all Foc Kofi can   buy
        'What is it that Kofi can buy all?'

The fact that bare quantificational elements cannot be topics (27a) underscores the analysis that topics do not involve a quantificational operator-variable chain (Cinque 1990; Puskás 1995, 1996; Rizzi 1997). Granting that topics necessarily manifest non-quantificational A'-binders, it follows that quantified expressions cannot be topicalized because they must bind a variable in the IP-internal position. Sentence (27a) is therefore ruled out because the resumptive pronominal element in the IP-internal position does not qualify as a syntactic variable.

If topic is not quantificational, therefore the first property illustrated under (25) also follows. Sentence (25b) is ungrammatical because the topicalized element is not quantificational, and the empty category in the IP-internal position is illegitimate. It cannot be a variable (there is no quantificational element to bind it), it cannot be PRO (the structure violates the binding theory), it cannot be pro (it is not properly identified (Rizzi 1986), it cannot be an NP-trace (it is A-free in its governing category), it cannot be a null constant since a null constant is licensed by an anaphoric operator (see section 8.1.1). Actually, there is no evidence of the existence of such null anaphoric operator in the topic-comment constructions. Consequently, no well-formed derivation can be associated with a sentence like (25b).

We are therefore left with one last strategy: the use of a resumptive pronoun in the IP-internal position, as illustrated by the grammatical (25a). In this respect, Gungbe differs from Italian and Hungarian because it displays a resumptive pronoun that is A'-bound by the topic. It is argued that the resumptive pronoun is subject to the same recoverability requirements as traces and must satisfy the identification requirement as proposed by Rizzi (1990): the resumptive pronoun must be identified by a local A'-antecedent (i.e., the topic).[8] Sentence (25a) can be represented as in example (28):

(28) [Force° ɖɔ̀ [TopP dàn lɔ́ᵢ [Top° yà [Kòfí hù ìᵢ]]]]

A conclusion that could be made here is that Gungbe is just another confirmation of generalization (13): it differs from languages like English because it lacks the anaphoric operator in topic constructions, but it is like Italian or Hungarian because they all seek for a specific strategy to circumvent ungrammaticality: the Italian topic uses a resumptive clitic pronoun, the Hungarian topic relies on pro, and the Gungbe topic depends on a resumptive pronoun.

Granting this analysis, the fact that the Gungbe topic constructions essentially involve definite and specific DPs in the topic constructions also follows: resumptive pronominalization is typical of DPs in A-positions. Since Gungbe lacks pronominal *P*Ps, the only option that is left, in case of *P*P topicalization, is the preposing of the DP inside the *P*P as illustrated in (26).[9] As the reader may notice, this is additional evidence for the analysis of the resumptive strategy as a last resort phenomenon. Recall from the discussion in chapter 7 and earlier sections that the resumptive strategy (more generally the α-copy strategy) arises only in cases where a gap is excluded.

8.1.3.3 Why the Gungbe topics are not hanging topics

The facts discussed in previous sections dealt with topic constructions involving extraction from an argument position. In this case, the topic moves to the specifier position of a topic phrase headed by the topic marker *yà*, leaving a resumptive pronoun in the IP-internal position. At first sight, one could believe that the Gungbe topic is similar to the Italian topics (also known as Clitic Left Dislocation, CLLD) discussed in section 8.1.1. But this cannot be the right characterization since the Gungbe topics manifest two major properties that could suggest that they might involve what Cinque (1977, 1990) referred to as hanging topics. In what follows, I show that the Gungbe topics are neither counterparts of the Italian CLLD constructions nor hanging topics.

8.1.3.3.1 Hanging topics

Cinque (1977) showed that even though they involve the left periphery, hanging topics differ from CLLD in many respects.[10] CLLD requires that the dislocated element be old information, while hanging topic constructions are a means of "promoting an NP to a topic status at a point in the discourse when it was not a topic" (Cinque 1977: 406). In this respect, assuming the questions (29a–b), the author proposed that only sentence (30a) can be paired with (29a), while (30b) is the normal reply to (29b).

(29) a. Sai che Maria è andata a stare da Giorgio a Roma [Maria is topic]?
          'You know that Maria has gone to live with Giorgio in Rome?'
      b. Sai che tuo cugino mi ha telefonato ieri per dirmi che ha trovato un bell'appartamento à Roma [tuo cugino is topic]?
          'Do you know that your cousin called me up yesterday to tell me that he found a nice apartment in Rome?

(30) a. Ah, Giorgio, sapevo che lui voleva andare a stare in campagna
          'Ah Giorgio, I used to know that he wanted to go and live in the country'

b.   Ah, Giorgio, sapevo che voleva andare a stare in campagna'
     'Ah Giorgio, I used to know that he wanted to go and live in the country'

In the example (30a), *Giorgio* is promoted as topic and substitutes for the real topic *Maria* that was introduced in question (29a). In sentence (30b), however, *Giorgio* is old information: it is introduced in question (29b) as *tuo cugino*.

CLLD and hanging topic constructions also differ with respect to the copy (or resumptive) element that appears in the IP-internal position. The sentences under (31) show that CLLD constructions require a clitic pronoun in the IP-internal position, as opposed to hanging topics that display a strong pronoun. Compare, for example, the sentences under (31).

(31)   a.   A Giorgio, sono sicuro che non **gli** ho mai scritto
            'To Giorgio, I am sure that I have never written to him'
       b.   Giorgio, sono sicuro che non ho mai scritto a **lui**
            'Giorgio, I am sure that I have never written to him'

Sentence (31a) is an instance of CLLD. It involves the clitic *gli*, as opposed to the hanging topic (31b) that displays the strong pronoun *lui*. It is also interesting to notice here that the two sentences have different entailments. In (31a) *Giorgio* is old information and the speaker's comment suggests that he has never written to *Giorgio* as opposed to other people he has certainly written to. In sentence (31b), on the contrary, *Giorgio* is understood as new topic (or new information), and nothing can be said as to whether the speaker has written to other people or has ever written to anyone.

Virtually any maximal projection can surface to the left periphery of a CLLD construction. Consider the following examples taken from Cinque (1990).

(32)   a.   [$_{PP}$ Al mare],   ci siamo già stati
            'To the seaside there-(we)-have already been'
       b.   [$_{AP}$ Bella]   non lo è mai stata.
            'Beautiful   not-it-(she) ever was'
       c.   [$_{VP}$ Messo da parte]   non lo è mai stato
            'Got out of the way   not-it-(he) ever was'
       d.   [$_{QP}$ Tutti],   non li ho visti ancora
            'All   not-them-(I) have seen yet'
       e.   [$_{CP}$ Che bevi],   lo dicono tutti
            'That (you) drink it says everybody'

On the contrary, hanging topics essentially involve DPs. Compare, for instance, the sentences under (32) to the hanging topic examples (30a) and (31b).

Unlike hanging topics, CLLD constructions are sensitive to island constraints.[11] The ungrammatical sentence (33a) shows that the clitic pronoun of a CLLD cannot occur inside an island. But this is not the case with respect to hanging topic construction (33b), where the resumptive pronoun surfaces in a complex NP island.

(33) a. *A Giorgio, ieri ho conosciuto [la ragazza che *gli* ha scritto quelle insolenze]
          'To Giorgio, yesterday I met the girl who wrote
          those insolent words to him'
      b. Giorgio, ieri ho conosciuto la ragazza che gli ha scritto quelle isonlenze
          'Giorgio, yesterday I met the girl who wrote those insolent words to him'

Another fact that distinguishes CLLD from hanging topics is that the former can occur in root and embedded contexts but the latter is restricted to root contexts only. Sentences under (34a–b) are instances of embedded CLLD. As shown by the ungrammatical sentences (34c–d) hanging topics are prohibited in such contexts.

(34) a. Ho paura che a Giorgio, Marco gli abbia già scritto
          'I fear that to Giorgio, Marco has already written to him'
      b. Non so proprio chi, questo libro, potrebbe recensirlo per domani
          'I don't know who this book could review it for tomorrow'
      c. *Sono sicuro che Mario, lui vuole andare al mare
          'I am sure that Mario he wants to go to the sea'
      d. *Ho l'impressione che Paolo, sappiate benissimo chi gli ha scritto
          'I've got the impression that Paolo you know very well who wrote to him'

Unlike hanging topics, CLLD constructions exclude cleft constituents. Observe, for instance, the contrast in (35).

(35) a. *A Giorgio, è a lui che ho scritto
          To Giorgio, it's to him that I wrote'
      b. Giorgio, è a lui che ho scritto
          'Giorgio, it's him that I wrote'

CLLD constructions can involve multiple topics in contrast to hanging topics, which allow for only one dislocated DP (36a–b).

(36) a. Di vestiti, a me, Gianni, in quel negozio, non mi ce ne ha mai comprati
          'Clothes to me Gianni in that shop (he) not-to-me-there-of-them ever bought'
      b. *Di libri, Giorgio, sapevo che lui voleva comprarne due
          'Of books, Giorgio, I-knew that he wanted to buy two of them'.

The contrasts illustrated under (29–36) indicate the differences between CLLD and hanging topics. In accounting for these facts, Cinque (1977) argued for Ross' (1967) analysis in terms of movement rule. He therefore proposed that those differences are better captured if we assume that CLLD involves movement of the topic to the left periphery. On the contrary, hanging topics are instances of base-generated topics. The following sections show that even though the Gungbe topic constructions share certain syntactic properties with hanging topics, they cannot be considered as such. Actually the Gungbe topics appear to share the properties of both CLLD and hanging topics.

8.1.3.3.2 The similarities between the Gungbe topic and hanging topic constructions

The Gungbe topics share certain properties with hanging topics in that they essentially involve DPs (30a, 31b, 32), they are not sensitive to island constraints (33), they may involve cleft constituents (35), and they allow for only one topic, as indicated in example (36).

As shown in section 8.1.3.2, the Gungbe topic constructions basically involve DPs. In this respect, the sentences under (26a–b)—repeated here as (37a–b) —show that when topicalization targets a postnominal phrase, the DP inside the PP must move to the left periphery, leaving a pronoun in the PP-internal position. In this context, it is impossible to pied-pipe the whole PP, as shown by the ungrammatical sentence (37b).

(37) a. [$_{DP}$ xɔ́ lɔ́]$_i$ yà   Kòfí   bíɔ́   [$_{PP}$ é$_i$ mὲ]
          room Spf$_{[+def]}$ Top   Kofi   enter-Perf   3sg   in
          'As for the specific room, Kofi entered it'
      b. *[$_{PP}$ xɔ́   lɔ́   mὲ]   yà   Kòfí   bíɔ́   é
          room   Spf$_{[+def]}$ in   Top   Kofi   enter-Perf   3sg

The Gungbe topics show no island constraints, at least if we consider Cinque's examples under (33). In this regard, the sentences under (38) indicate that the resumptive (or copy) element in the IP-internal position may surface in a complex NP-island or in a wh-island.

(38) a. [$_{DP}$ xwé   lɔ́]   yà   ùn   mɔ̀n
          house   Spf$_{[+def]}$ Top   1sg   see-Perf
          dáwè ɖĕ   gbê   ὲ   ná   Kòfí
          man   that$_{[Rel]}$ build-Perf-3sg   for   Kofi
          'As for the specific house, I saw the man who built it for Kofi'
      b. [$_{DP}$ xwé   lɔ́]   yà   ùn   kánbiɔ́   ɖɔ̀
          house   Spf$_{[+def]}$ Top   1sg   ask-Perf   that
          ménù wè   gbê   ὲ   ná   Kòfí ?
          who Foc   build-Perf-3sg   for   Kofi
          'As for the specific house, I asked who will build it for Kofi?'

The sentence (39b)—a comment on utterance (39a)—indicates that the Gungbe topic constructions can also involve cleft constituents. Notice, however, that in those cases, the left-dislocated constituents also bear the low tone specific to the Gungbe yes-no questions. That the bracketed sequence involves the yes-no question marker can be understood as a rhetorical question. Witness also that the reverse order FM-TM suggests that the cleft constituent here includes the whole FocP, assuming TopP dominates FocP, as shown in structure (24) (see also section 8.2).

(39) a. ùn sè   ɖɔ̀ Kòfí ɖù   gán   ná gbɛ́ lɔ́
         1sg hear-Perf that Kofi become-Perf chief   for club Spf[+def]
         'I heard that Kofi became president of the specific club'
    b. [Kòfí wè   yà]   é   bí   gbáú
         Kofi Foc   Top-QM 3sg   intelligent   very
         'You mean Kofi, he is very intelligent'

Just like hanging topics, the Gungbe topic constructions allow for only one topic. These facts were already discussed in section 8.1.3.1, where I show that there is not topic recursion in Gungbe. Consider again the ungrammatical examples (21a–b) repeated under (40a–b).

(40) a. *gólù lɔ́   àgbá   lɔ́   yà
         gold Spf[+def] box   Spf[+def] Top
         Kòfí zè-è   ɖó   é   mè
         Kofi put-Perf-3sg   Loc   3sg   in
    b. *gólù lɔ́   yà   àgbá   lɔ́   yà
         gold Spf[+def] Top   box   Spf[+def] Top
         Kòfí zè-è   ɖó   é   mè
         Kofi put-Perf-3sg   Loc   3sg   in

If we were to consider only these facts, we could simply conclude that the data discussed so far are evidence that the Gungbe topic constructions are hanging topics. But it turns out on close inspection that only properties illustrated under (35) and (36) are unquestionable in this respect. Put differently, the only real similarity between the Gungbe topic constructions and hanging topics (at least as Cinque 1977 described them) is that they allow for cleft constituents to be topics, but prohibit multiple topics (39b, 40). A priori, those two properties could favor an analysis along the lines of Cinque (1977) that the Gungbe topic constructions are instances of base-generated topics (or first merge in terms of Chomsky 1995, 1998). Such analysis seems to capture cases like (39b), where one may claim that the focused constituent *Kòfí wè* 'Kofi-FM' is base-generated in the position left adjacent to the topic marker *yà*. Observe, however, that this analysis has nothing to say about the obligatory presence of the Gungbe yes-no question marker (i.e., the additional low tone on *yà* (39b)) in those contexts (see section 8.2 for a possible analysis). In addition, I show that the other two similarities mentioned, the fact that the Gungbe topics essentially involve DPs and show no sensitivity to islands, are only apparent. In this regard, the Gungbe topic constructions differ radically from hanging topics. Some of the differences are illustrated next.

8.1.3.3.3 The differences between the Gungbe topic and hanging topic constructions

In his characterization of the constructions involving a left-dislocated constituent, Cinque (1977, 1990) argued that a crucial difference between hanging topics and CLLD is that the left-dislocated constituent of a CLLD is necessarily old information. Instead, no such requirement holds of hanging topics. When we look at the Gungbe topic constructions from this perspective, we see that they are similar to CLLD rather than hanging topics. As I showed in previous sections, the element immediately to the left of the TM must be old information. Consider again the following examples:

(41) a. *[vǐ ɖ́é]   yà   é   bí   xúgán wéxɔ̀mɛ̀-ví lɛ́ kpó
           child Spf[-def] Top   3sg   intelligent than   school-child Num all
           'As for a certain child, he is more intelligent than all the pupils'
      b. [vǐ   lɔ́]   yà   é   bí   xúgán wéxɔ̀mɛ̀-ví lɛ́ kpó
           child Spf[+def] Top   3sg   intelligent than   school-child Num all
           'As for the [specific] child, he is more intelligent than all the pupils'
      c. *vǐ   ɖ́é   lɔ́
           child   Spf[-def]   Spf[+def]

The contrast in (41a–b) strongly suggests that the topic marker cannot co-occur with a DP associated with the Gungbe indefinite specificity marker ɖ́é. I proposed in chapter 3 that the indefinite specificity marker and the definite specificity marker lɔ́ compete for the same position, as shown by the ungrammatical sequence (41c). Building on this, we can account for the grammatical sentence (41b) only if we assume that specific and definite sequences bear some referential feature because they select a pre-identified referent, or else as specific member of a set preestablished in discourse (i.e., D-linked in the sense of Pesetski 1987). This does not hold of the marker ɖ́é that only refers to a specific member of a set but does not necessarily select discourse-linked elements. In this regard the Gungbe indefinite specificity marker is like the French and English indefinite determiners un and a respectively. Consider the following examples.

(42) a. J'ai vu une femme dans le bar hier, je crois bien que c'était Marie
           'I saw a woman in the pub yesterday, I'm sure it was Mary'
      b. Nous cherchons un jeune pour ce travail
           'We need a young person for this job'

In example (42a), the indefinite pronoun *une* can refer to a specific woman (i.e., Mary). But in sentence (42b), *un* simply selects any person that qualifies as 'young'. Notice that in this case the selected person could be either female or male. Under this characterization, the Gungbe indefinite specificity marker *ɖé* corresponds to *un(e)* in example (42a).[12]

Another property of the Gungbe topic constructions is that they require a deficient pronoun (i.e., weak or clitic pronouns) in the IP-internal position. Instead, hanging topics seem to favor the so-called tonic or strong pronouns (see chapter 4 for the discussion on the Gungbe pronominal system). Granting that the Gungbe topics involve a deficient pronoun, we can further assume that the IP-internal copy surfaces in a derived position.[13] This would mean that the gap in the base position corresponds to a pronoun-trace similar to the clitic-trace of the Italian CLLD.

(43) a.   [vǐ   lɔ́]   yà   é   yì   wéxɔmè
            child   Spf$_{[+def]}$Top   3W-sg   go-Perf   school
            'As for the specific child, he went to school'
      b.   *[vǐ lɔ́]   yà   úɔ́   yì   wéxɔmè
            child   Spf$_{[+def]}$Top   3S-sg   go-Perf   school

I indicated in section 8.1.3.3.2 that the Gungbe topic constructions essentially involve DPs. But it is worth mentioning that those constructions may also involve certain adjuncts or clauses. Sentence (44a) is an instance of locational adjunct fronting; I return to the discussion of adjunct preposing in section 8.1.3.3.4. In sentence (44b), a full clause is topicalized and surfaces to the left of the topic marker *yà*. Sentence (44c), on the other hand, is some kind of be-located predicate preposing where the progressive marker *tò* merges as the head of the predicate phrase (PredP), but may move out to some higher aspect position as discussed in chapter 7, section 7.1.3.1.2.2 in regard to the *tò/tè* alternation.[14]

(44) a.   [$_{PP}$àtín lɔ́   sá]   yà   mí ná   nɔ̀   flén   còcɔ́ !
            tree   Spf$_{[+def]}$under   Top 1pl Fut stay   there   for sure
            'As for [under] the specific tree, we will sit there whether you like it or not!'
      b.   [$_{CP}$ ɖɔ̀   Sàgbó ná   fìn   nǔ   dó   mì]   yà
            that   Sagbo Fut   steal   thing   from   1sg   Top
            ùn   má   lèn   nú   mɔ́nkɔ̀tɔ̀   kpɔ́n   gbèɖé
            1sg   Neg   think-Perf   thing of the sort   look   never
            'That Sagbo would steal my things [as we now know], I never thought of anything of the sort'
      c.   [tò fí dìn]   yà   mè   ɖɔkpó má   wà   àzɔ́n   énɛ̀
            be here now   Top   person   one   Neg   do   work   that
            'As for here now, no one will do that work'

That heterogeneous elements can be topicalized, provided the relevant context, clearly suggests that a generalization that will regard Gungbe topicalization as typical of DPs cannot be right.

In a similar vein, that the Gungbe topics are not sensitive to complex NP-island cannot be taken to mean that those constructions show no locality constraint. Instead, the sentences under (45) indicate that those constructions are sensitive to subject islands, on the one hand (45a–b), and topic islands, on the other (45c–d). For instance the contrast under (45a–b) suggests that topic extraction out of a clausal subject is prohibited.

(45) a. [Kòfí ní   yì   yòvótòmὲ]   má   jró   mì
        Kofi Inj   go   Europe   Neg   please-Perf 1sg
        'That Kofi should go to Europe I didn't like'
     b. *Kòfí yà   [é   ní   yì yòvótòmὲ] má   jró   mì
        Kofi Top   3sg   Inj   go Europe   Neg please 1sg
        'As for Kofi, that he should go to Europe, I didn't like'

Similarly, the sentences under (45c–d) clearly indicate that topic extraction across an embedded topic is also prohibited in Gungbe. For instance, sentence (45c) is ungrammatical because the embedded topic position is already filled by a topic that blocks long extraction. But this is not the case in the grammatical sentence (45d). I return to topic islands in section 8.1.3.3.5; see also Müller and Sternefeld 1993.

(45) c. *Kòfí yà   ùn   sè   ɖɔ̀ mótò   lɔ́   yà é xɔ̀-ὲ
        Kofi Top 1sg hear-Perf that car   Spf[+def] Top 3sg buy-Perf-3sg
        'As for Kofi, I heard that As for the specific car he bought it'
     d. mótò lɔ́   yà   ùn   sè   ɖɔ̀   Kòfí   xɔ̀-ὲ
        car Spf[+def] Top 1sg hear-Perf that   Kofi   buy-Perf-3sg
        'As for the specific car, I heard that Kofi bought it'

The fact that topicalization in Gungbe is sensitive to island effects strongly favors the movement analysis proposed in this study.

Another fact that differentiates Gungbe topic constructions from hanging topics is that the topic phrase may occur in both root and embedded contexts. This is illustrated by the sentences under (46) where topicalization involves a root (46a), extraction to the embedded CP-layer (46b) and long extraction of the subject and the object to the matrix clause (46c–d).

(46) a. mótò lɔ́   yà   Kòfí   xɔ̀-ὲ
        car Spf[+def] Top   Kofi   buy-Perf-3sg
        'As for the specific car Kofi bought it'
     b. ùn   sè   ɖɔ̀   mótò lɔ́   yà   Kòfí   xɔ̀-ὲ
        1sg hear-Perf that car   Spf[+def] Top Kofi   buy-Perf-3sg
        'I heard that' as for the specific car' Kofi bought it'

c. Kòfí yà   ùn   sè   dɔ̀   é   xɔ̀   mótò   lɔ́
    Kofi Top   1sg   hear-Perf   that   3sg   buy-Perf   car   Spf[+def]
    'As for Kofi, I heard that he bought the specific car'

d. mótò lɔ́   yà   ùn   sè   dɔ̀   Kòfí   xɔ̀-è
    car Spf[+def] Top   1sg   hear-Perf   that   Kofi   buy-Perf-3sg
    'As for the specific car I heard that Kofi bought it'

The data discussed here suggest that the Gungbe topic constructions are not the counterparts of the Italian hanging topics. Similarly, the data implicitly suggest that the Gungbe topic constructions are similar to the Italian CLLD or topic constructions in terms of Cinque (1977, 1990) and Rizzi (1997). Accordingly, the Gungbe topic constructions belong to a class of topics that intersects with hanging topics and CLLD. Recall from the discussion that the Gungbe topic constructions exclude multiple topics, but include cleft constituents and show no sensitivity to complex NP islands on a par with hanging topics. On the other hand, the Gungbe topics are like their Italian CLLD counterparts in that they occur in root and embedded contexts, they require that the topic be old information, they necessitate a deficient pronoun in the IP-internal position, and they are sensitive to topic islands.

Under the movement analysis, we can account for those facts naturally by assuming that the Gungbe topic constituent moves to the left periphery in a topic position to the left of the TM. In section 8.1.3.1, I identified that position as [spec TopP], the specifier of a Topic Phrase, whose head hosts the TM *yà* in Gungbe. In terms of Rizzi's multiple topic phrases, this would mean that the Gungbe topic constructions target a specific topic phrase within the topic field. This could imply that the successive topic positions in Rizzi's framework are not interchangeable. More precisely, there might be a hierarchical order with respect to the elements that may occur as topics in languages that manifest multiple topics (e.g., Italian). In this respect, the Italian data suggest that only the sequence [hanging topic]-[CLLD (topic)] is allowed and not vice versa (Cinque 1977).

(47) a. Ah, Giorgio, di libri, sapevo che lui voleva comprarne due
          'Ah Giorgio, of books, I-knew that he wanted to buy two of them'
      b. *Di libri, Giorgio, sapevo che lui voleva comprarne due
          'Of books, Giorgio, I-knew that he wanted to buy two of them'
      c. Di libri, Giorgio, sapevo che voleva comprarne due
          'Of books, Giorgio, I-knew that he-wanted to buy two of them'

In a similar vein, Rizzi (1999) shows on independent ground that the Italian wh-elements like *perché, come mai*, target a different left peripheral position than ordinary wh-elements. For example, ordinary wh-elements and focus constituents are mutually exclusive in root contexts. But this is not the case with *perché* and *come mai* that must precede focus.

(48)   a.   *A chi QUESTO hanno detto (non qualcos'altro)?
          'To whom THIS they said (not something else)'
      b.   Perché QUESTO avremmo dovuto dirgli, non qualcos'altro?
          'Why THIS we should have said to him, not something else?'

In terms of Rizzi (1997, 1999), the contrast in (48) can be accounted for if we assume that focused constituents and normal wh-elements target the same position [spec FocP], in root contexts, while wh-elements of the *perché*-type are first merged in [spec INT] the specifier position of a projection whose head is the locus of the feature [+interrogative].[15]

    In addition to the examples in (47–48), what the Gungbe situation suggests is that there is, within the topic field, a distinct head that is endowed with the features [±topic, ± referential] and whose specifier hosts the type of topics Gungbe and, more generally, the Gbe languages manifest. The following facts are additional support to this hypothesis.

8.1.3.3.4 More on adjunct preposing in Gungbe

A close look at the Gungbe topic constructions involving adjuncts shows that things might be more intricate than the situation described in (44). Not all types of adjunct freely prepose in Gungbe. As illustrated by the ungrammatical sentence (49a), the locational adjunct *xɔ̀ kpá* 'beside the room' cannot occur as topic. But the grammatical sentence (49b) indicates that it is perfectly possible for the time adjunct *gbɔ̀jé mè* 'in the holidays' to surface in the position immediately to the left of the TM. I leave the question open as to which factors (whether pragmatic, semantic, or syntactic) account for such differences. It is interesting, though, to notice that, unlike argument topics, adjunct topics do not require the occurrence of a resumptive pronoun in the IP-internal position (49b).

(49)   a.   *[xɔ̀ kpá]$_i$ yà   Kòfí   zé   kèké   étɔ̀n   ɖó t$_i$
           house beside Top   Kofi   take-Perf bicycle his   Loc
           'Beside the house, Kofi put his bicycle'
      b.   [gbɔ̀jé mè]$_i$ yà yɔ̀kpɔ́ lɛ́   nɔ̀   yì   sɔ̀ndèskùl   t$_i$
           holidays in Top child Num   Hab   go   Sunday school
           'As for the holidays, children habitually go to Sunday school'

Since Gungbe does not have any pronominal form that could resume time, locational, or similar adjuncts, we can explain the impossibility of having a resumptive pronoun in sentence (49b) by saying that where no pronoun "exists that corresponds to a certain topic element, none is required" (Cinque 1990: 68). Accordingly, we can account for sentence (49b) by assuming that the topic is moved to [spec TopP], where it antecedent-governs the empty category in the IP-internal position, and the identification requirement is met.

A problem that obscures the description outlined here is that certain time adjuncts do surface in sentence-initial position without the TM. Generally, such constructions do not have a topic reading because they are interpreted as new information and may well be instances of hanging topics (50a–b).

(50) a. [gbɔ̀jé mὲ]ᵢ yɔ̀kpɔ́ lέ   ná   yì   sɔ̀ndὲskùl   tᵢ
           holidays in   child Num Fut   go   Sunday school
           'During the holidays, children will go to Sunday school'

      b. [égbé]ᵢ   yɔ̀kpɔ́ lέ   ná   yì   sɔ̀ndὲskùl   tᵢ
           today   child Num Fut   go   Sunday school
           'Today, children will go to Sunday school'

It is interesting to notice that such preposed adjuncts can precede focus but not topics as shown in sentences (51a–b).

(51) a. [gbɔ̀jé mὲ]ᵢ [yɔ̀kpɔ́ lέ]ⱼ   wὲ tⱼ ná yì sɔ̀ndὲskùl   tᵢ
           holidays in   child Num   Foc   Fut go Sunday school
           'During the holidays, CHILDREN will go to Sunday school'

      b. *[gbɔ̀jé mὲ]ᵢ [yɔ̀kpɔ́ lέ]ⱼ yà yéⱼ ná yì sɔ̀ndὲskùl tᵢ
           holidays in   child Num Top 3pl Fut go Sunday school
           'As for children, they will go to Sunday school during the holidays'

One possible interpretation of the contrast in (51) could be that the preposed adjuncts occur in [spec TopP]. Accordingly, sentence (51b) is ruled out because the two elements compete for the same position. I can thus characterize the absence of *yà* in sentences like (51a) by saying that the Gungbe TM is also referential: it expresses the fact that the element immediately to its left refers to specific member(s) of a set in the mind of the speaker or preestablished in discourse (see Pesetsky 1987; Cinque 1990; Enç 1991; Puskás 2000). This correctly predicts that sentences involving the TM can manifest only the topic-comment articulation (49) (see also Rizzi 1997), while those including simple adjunct preposing are interpreted as new information. In this respect, we can say that the time adjunct *gbɔ̀jé mὲ* in sentence (49) is definite and therefore referential: it refers to a pre-identified moment of time (e.g., within the period of holidays), but this is impossible in example (49a) because *xɔ̀ kpá* does not bear such a referential index and could refer to the vicinity of any house. The same holds of the grammatical examples under (50) where the time adjuncts simply introduce new information.

It is therefore reasonable to assume that even elements that do not co-occur with the TM are in [spec TopP], where TopP is headed by a null Top° specified as [-referential]. An immediate implication of this analysis is that Top° can be described as bearing features [± referential, ± topic]. When the feature [+referential, + topic] is triggered, Top° is morphologically realized as *yà*, unlike a null Top°, which is identified as [-referential, -topic] and hosts a null morpheme ∅.

An interesting parallel arises here. We now have additional evidence that both the TM and the Gungbe specificity marker *lɔ́* are left peripheral elements. The former belongs to the C-system of the clause structure while the latter manifests the left periphery of the nominal system (see chapters 3 and 4). In addition to the fact that they are left peripheral elements, both the topic marker and the specificity marker express the notion that certain constituents in the clause or the sequence are D-linked. For instance, recall from chapter 3 that the NPs that occur with the specificity marker are read as specific (i.e., preestablished in discourse). On the contrary, bare NPs do not trigger such reading. If referentiality means the ability of selecting specific members of a set preestablished in discourse, then we could conclude that the notion of specificity and referentiality as discussed here is one and the same thing. A particularly intriguing example in support of this analysis is that one can prepose the locational adjunct *xɔ̀ kpa* as long as the latter is specific (52). As the reader can see, preposing in this context requires the occurrence of the TM and the intervention of the resumptive *flèn* 'there' in the IP-internal position.

(52) [xɔ̀ lɔ́   kpá]$_i$ yà Kòfí zé kèké étɔ̀n ɖó flèn$_i$
      house Spf$_{[+def]}$ beside Top Kofi take-Perf bicycle his Loc there
      'As for beside the specific house, Kofi put his bicycle there'

8.1.3.3.5 Simultaneous topic and topic islands in Gungbe

In chapter 7, I showed that the Gungbe focus and wh constructions allow for simultaneous focus and wh phrases in main and embedded clauses. In sentence (53a), for instance, the object of the embedded clause, *hǐ lɔ́* 'the knife' is moved to [spec FocP] of the main clause, followed by subsequent focus movement of the subject of the embedded clause *Rèmí* to [spec FocP] of the embedded clause. The same holds of sentence (53b), where the wh-phrase *été* 'what' is moved to [spec FocP] of the main clause, with the wh-phrase *ménú* 'who' being moved to [spec FocP] of the embedded clause. The conclusion reached there was that the lower [spec FocP] does not serve as escape hatch for the focus or wh phrases. Instead, those elements proceed through [spec Force] on their way to the higher [spec FocP].

(53) a. hǐ   lɔ́$_j$ wè Séná sè   ɖɔ̀ Rèmí$_i$ wè t$_i$ zé t$_j$
          knife Spf$_{[+def]}$ Foc Sena hear-Perf that Remi Foc take-Perf
          'Sena heard that REMI took THE SPECIFIC KNIFE'
      b. été$_j$ wè   Séná kánbiɔ́ ɖɔ̀   ménú$_i$ wè t$_i$ zé   t$_j$
          what Foc Sena ask-Perf that who   Foc take-Perf
          'What did Sena ask that who take?'

It also appeared in the discussion there that focus and wh constructions manifest an argument versus adjunct asymmetry. For example, sentence (54) indicates that long construal of the adjunct is impossible when the lower [spec FocP] is already filled.

Accordingly, the sentence can be interpreted only as involving local focus movements in the main and embedded clauses.

(54) [gbɔ̀jé mɛ̀]ⱼ   wɛ̀   Séná   sè   tⱼ   ɖɔ̀
      holidays in   Foc   Sena   hear-Perf   that
      [hǐ   lɔ́]ᵢ   wɛ̀   Rɛ̀mí   xɔ̀   tᵢ
      knife   Spf[+def] Foc   Remi   buy-Perf
      '*Sena heard that Remi bought THE SPECIFIC KNIFE DURING THE HOLIDAYS'
      'Sena heard DURING THE HOLIDAYS that Remi bought THE SPECIFIC KNIFE

Building on this, one might expect to find the same situation with respect to topic constructions. Yet, for some reasons that remain to be explained, the Gungbe topic constructions seem to resist simultaneous activation of the topic domains in the main and embedded clauses. For instance, the sentences under (55a–b) show that it is possible to have a topic in [spec TopP] of the matrix clause followed by focus or wh phrases in the main and embedded clauses or vice versa.

(55) a. Sénáⱼ yà   ménùₖ wɛ̀ tₖ kànbíɔ́
          Sena   Top   who   Foc   ask-Perf
          ɖɔ̀   fítéᵢ   wɛ̀ éⱼ zé   kèké étɔ̀n   ɖó tᵢ?
          that   where   Foc 3sg put-Perf bicycle his   Loc
          'As for Sena, who asked where he put his bicycle?'
      b. ménùₖ wɛ̀ tₖ kànbíɔ́ ɖɔ̀   Sénáⱼ yà
          who   Foc   ask-Perf that   Sena   Top
          fítéᵢ   wɛ̀ éⱼ zé   kèké étɔ̀n ɖó tᵢ ?
          where   Foc 3sg put-Perf bicycle his Loc
          'Who asked that as for Sena, where he put his bicycle?'

The sentences under (56), on the other hand, indicate that a Gungbe sentence involving simultaneous topics in the main and embedded clauses is marginal.

(56) a. ??Sénáⱼ   yà   éⱼ   ɖɔ̀   ɖɔ̀
          Sena   Top   3sg   say-Perf that
          Rɛ̀míᵢ   yà   éᵢ zé   kèké lɔ́
          Remi   Top   3sg put-Perf   bicycle Spf[+def]
          'As for Sena, he said that as for Remi, he took the specific bicycle'
      b. ??Sénáⱼ   yà   éⱼ   ɖɔ̀
          Sena   Top   3sg   say-Perf
          ɖɔ̀   kèké lɔ́ᵢ   yà   Rɛ̀mí zé   éᵢ
          that   bicycle Spf[+def] Top   Remi   put-Perf 3sg
          'As for Sena, he said that as for Remi, he took the specific bicycle'

A priori, we cannot explain the marginal status of the sentences under (56) by invoking the impossibility of activating two topic domains in the sentence. As shown by the example (57), a sentence may involve a topic in the main clause in combination with a non-referential preposed adjunct (e.g., a time adjunct) in the embedded clause or vice versa.

(57) a. Sénáⱼ   yà   éⱼ ɖɔ̀   ɖɔ̀
       Sena   Top   3sg say-Perf   that
       [gbɔ̀jé mɛ̀]ᵢ Rɛ̀mí   ná   zé   kɛ̀ké lɔ́ tᵢ
       holiday in Remi   Fut   put   bicycle Spf$_{[+def]}$
       'As for Sena, he said that during the holidays Remi will take the specific bicycle'

   b. [gbɔ̀jé mɛ̀] Sénà   ɖɔ̀   ɖɔ̀
       holidays in Sena   say-Perf   that
       Rɛ̀míⱼ   yà   éⱼ   nà   zé kɛ̀ké   lɔ́
       Remi   Top   3sg Fut   take bicycle   Spf$_{[+def]}$
       'Sena said that as for Remi, he will take the specific bicycle during the holiday$_{[topic]}$'
       'During the holidays, Sena said that as for Remi, he will take the specific bicycle'

Granting the proposed analysis, both the topic, the element immediately to the left of the TM *yà*, and the preposed adjunct target [spec TopP]. With respect to the sentence (57a), this would mean that *Séna* occurs in [spec TopP] of the main clause, while the preposed time adjunct *gbɔ̀jé mɛ̀* 'during the holidays' targets the lower [spec TopP]. A difference, though, is that Top° in the main clause is specified as [+referential] as opposed to the lower Top°, which is not.

    The situation is reversed in sentence (57b), where [spec TopP] of the main clause is occupied by the preposed non-referential adjunct, while the lower [spec TopP] hosts the referential topic *Rɛ̀mí*. In addition, the fact that sentence (57b) is ambiguous and can be interpreted as involving either long construal (i.e., extraction of the preposed adjunct from the embedded clause) or local topic movement on the main clause clearly suggests that there is no argument versus non-referential adjunct asymmetry in the Gungbe topic constructions. However, it is interesting to see that simultaneous topicalization of referential adjuncts in main and in embedded clauses is degraded, on a par with simultaneous argument topicalization (58a). In addition, the ungrammatical sentence (58b) shows that topic constructions create islands for topic extraction. No such island effect arises in sentence (58c), where the focused constituent is extracted from an embedded clause introduced by a topic.

(58) a. ??gbɔ̀jé   mɛ̀   yà   Sénà   ɖɔ̀   ɖɔ̀
       holidays   in   Top   Sena   say-Perf   that
       sɛ̀gbé lɛ́   yà   Rɛ̀mí nà   nɔ̀   zé kɛ̀ké lɔ́
       Sunday Num   Top   Remi   Fut   Hab take bicycle Spf$_{[+def]}$
       'As for the holidays, Sena said that as for Sundays, Remi will habitually take the specific bicycle'

b. *kèké ló$_i$ yà Séna sè   ɖɔ̀ Rèmí$_j$ yà é$_j$ zé-è$_i$
   bicycle Spf$_{[+def]}$ Top Sena hear-Perf that Remi   Top 3sg take-Perf-3sg
   'As for the specific bicycle, Sena heard that as for Remi he took it'

c. kèké   ló$_i$ wè   Séna   sè
   bicycle   Spf$_{[+def]}$ Foc   Sena   hear-Perf
   ɖɔ̀ Rèmí$_j$ yà   é$_j$ ná   zé-è$_i$ gbáú
   that Remi   Top   3sg   Fut   take-3sg indeed
   'Sena heard that As for Remi, he will take THE SPECIFIC BICYCLE indeed'

The fact that simultaneous topicalization involving the topic marker is prohibited with both argument and referential adjuncts clearly suggests that referentiality is a condition on topicalization (Puskás 2000). As suggested before, this would explain why only DPs and elements that can bear the feature [+referential] can be topicalized in Gungbe. The question now arises why referentiality should block simultaneous topicalization. This is unexpected since simultaneous topicalization does occur cross-linguistically. A case in point is the Italian example in (59), where both the main clause and the embedded clause involve a topic.[16]

(59)   A Gianni, gli ho detto che il tuo libro, lo dovremmo leggere
       'To Gianni, I said to him that your book, we should read it' (Rizzi 1997: 329).

In this respect, I propose, as a first attempt, that what blocks simultaneous topicalization in the main clause and the embedded clause in Gungbe is feature competition. If topicalization requires the selection of one specific member of a set preestablished in discourse, therefore there cannot be multiple realizations of distinct topics, in separate topic positions in the sentence. This correctly predicts that the Gungbe topics differ from the Italian topics, because they target a different position in the topic field.

8.1.4 Summary

In this section, I show that, alongside focus and wh constructions, Gungbe also uses another construction that involves the left periphery: topicalization. In order to account for the syntactic aspects of such constructions, I adopt Rizzi's (1997) analysis that topic elements occur in the specifier position of a Topic phrase. TopP is considered a component of the C-system, and movement to [spec TopP] is motivated by the need of the topic phrase to check its topic feature against the topic head. I further show that the topic, focus, and wh constructions are similar in a number of respects because they all involve A'-chains. However, they differ sharply in that the focus and wh constructions are quantificational, whereas topic construction is not. Accordingly, I propose that topics manifest a different A'-chain involving a resumptive pronoun A'-bound by the topic. The discussion about adjunct preposing has led me to conclude that, among other things, the Gungbe topic head is specified for features [± referential] and therefore manifests a specific position within the topic field other than the projections that host CLLD phrases or hanging topics.

8.2 YES-NO QUESTIONS: ON THE SENTENCE-FINAL CP-MARKERS

In chapter 7, also section 8.1 here, I showed that the Gungbe focus, wh, and topic constructions involve a FM *wè* and a TM *yà* that immediately follow focus, wh, and topic elements, respectively. I further assume that the focus and topic markers are the PF realizations of Foc° and Top°, respectively, two components of the C-system. Since these two markers manifest the left periphery, one predicts that they must occur in a preverbal position (i.e., to the left of the subject). But as I show in this section, this is not always the case: both the TM and the FM are found in sentence-final position in Gungbe direct yes-no questions.

8.2.1 The sentence-final low tone as the yes-no question marker (QM)

Gungbe displays a yes-no question formation that arises from a sentence-final low tone represented here by an additional stroke [ ] (see chapter 2, section 2.3.2, for the discussion on syntactic tones). Consider, for example, the following sentences:

(60)   a.   Kòfí ɖù   nú
            Kofi   eat-Perf thing
            'Kofi ate'
       b.   Kòfí ɖù   nû ?
            Kofi   eat-Perf thing-QM
            'Did Kofi eat?'

Sentences (60a–b) form a minimal pair. From the surface level, the only difference between them is the intervention of the low tone in (60b), which triggers question reading, as opposed to sentence (60a), which is a statement. In discussing these facts in chapter 2, I propose that the low tone specific to the Gungbe yes-no questions is regarded as the reflex of a question marker (QM) that encodes the interrogative force.[17] I further assume that the Gungbe question marking toneme originates from a morpheme that has been partially deleted as the language evolved. Indirect evidence in support of this analysis comes, for instance, from Fongbe, which exhibits the sentence-final QM *à* in yes-no questions (61).

(61)   Kòkú   yró   Kòfí   à ?   [Fongbe]
       Koku   call-Perf   Kofi   QM
       'Did Koku call Kofi?'

Under the hypothesis that interrogative force is a specification of the C-system, the fact that the Gungbe QM occurs sentence-finally apparently contradicts the split-C analysis put forward in this study. But as I show, the Gungbe data are perfectly consistent with an analysis in terms of movement of the whole sentence in the specifier position of the projection headed by the QM (i.e., the low tone). Put differently, that the QM occurs sentence-finally underscores the analysis I developed in chapters 2, 3, and 6 that certain left peripheral markers (whether of the D- or C-type) force movement on to their complement to their specifier position. Movement of the complement creates the required spec-head relationship that sanctions the distribution of those left peripheral markers.

Granting Rizzi's (1997) analysis that ForceP is the locus of interrogative, declarative, and other specifications that are associated with the C-system, one could believe that the Gungbe QM is a manifestation of the head Force°. An immediate prediction of this hypothesis is that the QM must be in complementary distribution with the complementizer ɖɔ̀ 'that', which is traditionally assumed to occupy Force°. Put differently, the QM should never occur in an embedded clause introduced by the complementizer ɖɔ̀. As shown by example (62), this prediction is not borne out. In this sentence, the QM is realized in the final position of the embedded clause, hence the additional low tone on nǔ 'thing'.

(62) ùn   kànbíɔ́ ɖɔ̀   Kòfí   ɖù   nû ?
      1sg   ask-Perf that   Kofi   eat-Perf thing-QM
      'I asked whether Kofi ate'

Sentence (62) leads me to conclude that the complementizer ɖɔ̀ 'that' and the QM do not compete for the same position. Pursuing the split-C hypothesis, I thus propose that the QM encodes the interrogative force that is associated with a head Inter°, which projects within the C-system and whose specifier hosts interrogative phrases. Given that the interrogative phrase (or sentence) is sandwiched between the complementizer and the QM (62), I conclude that ForceP (the highest projection of the C-system) immediately dominates the interrogative projection, InterP.[18] This amounts to saying that the Gungbe interrogative constructions necessarily involve leftward movement of the whole sentence to the specifier position of the QM. As a result, the Gungbe QM must surface in sentence-final position, as partially represented in (63) (see Ndayragije 2000 for extending this analysis to Fongbe; Haddican 2000 for Gengbe. See also Szabolsci 1987 and Puskás 1996 for the discussion on the Hungarian yes-no QM).

(63)   ForceP

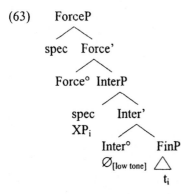

As I mentioned before, the system advocated here is similar to that discussed in previous chapters with respect to the D-system and the nominalization process, respectively. The theory I develop here in terms of the spec-head-complement structure provides a clear typology of those elements that occur to the right edge in Gbe and more generally in Kwa. We now have clear evidence that those elements that occur to the right edge in Gbe and other Kwa (e.g., D°, Nom°, *P*°, and Inter°) belong to the class of left peripheral markers. Those markers are sanctioned by a spec-head requirement that necessarily involves their complement. In this respect, they differ from other components of the left periphery, say Force°, Foc°, Top°, Fin°, whose specifiers need not be filled by their complement. Assuming this is the right characterization, it is interesting to notice that the Gungbe topic and focus markers are simultaneously realized in sentence-final position only and only if the sentence also involves the yes-no question marker. I consider those cases in the next section.

8.2.2 The use of the FM *wè* and the TM *yà* in yes-no questions

Building on the discussion in previous sections, one may wonder whether Gungbe (and more generally the Gbe languages) manifests yes-no questions where a full sentence relates to the TM, to the FM, or to both. This situation is illustrated by the sentences under (64). It appears in these sentences that it is perfectly possible (under certain pragmatic conditions) to produce yes-no questions that manifest the linear word order XP-(*wè*)-(*yà*)- ∅[low tone] (64a–c). Sentence (64d) indicates that this strategy is also available in embedded contexts.

(64) a. Kòfí ḍù   nú   wè ?
          Kofi eat-Perf thing   Foc-QM
          'DID KOFI EAT?'
      b. Kòfí ḍù   nú   yà ?
          Kofi eat-Perf thing   Top-QM
          'Did Kofi eat [as it was planned]?

c. Kòfí ɖù   nú   wὲ   yã̀ ?
   Kofi eat-Perf thing Foc   Top-QM
   'DID KOFI EAT?' (as it was planned)

d. ùn kànbíɔ́ ɖɔ̀ Kòfí ɖù   nú   wὲ   yã̀ ?
   1sg ask-Perf that Kofi eat-Perf thing Foc   Top-QM
   'I asked whether KOFI ATE [as it was planned]'

As seen from the glosses, sentences (64a–c) arise under different pragmatic
conditions. For example, sentence (64a) is a combination of yes-no question
formation and focusing of the clause *Kòfí ɖù nú*. On the other hand, question (64b)
expresses the fact that *Kòfí* will (or must) eat for some reason is preestablished in
discourse. Finally, sentence (64c) is a combination of both strategies associated with
question formation.

     Setting aside the different pragmatic conditions that trigger those
utterances, we can account for the data by assuming an analysis in terms of leftward
movement, as proposed earlier with respect to simple yes-no questions.

8.2.2.1 Evidence for snowballing movement

Building on the analysis proposed for simple yes-no questions, we might analyze
sentences (64a–b) by assuming that the whole sentence, including the TM and the
FM, is moved to [spec InterP]. But such analysis is not tenable, as we see in
sentence (64c) that the FM necessarily precedes the TM. This is evidence that there
has been successive movement of the whole sentence to [spec FocP] and then the
whole FocP moves to [spec TopP], followed by movement of TopP to [spec InterP].
This gives rise to the Force°- XP-(*wὲ*)-(*yà*)- $\emptyset_{[low\ tone]}$ word order found in
sentence (64c) and partially represented in (65). That the topic and focus markers
occur in the reverse order *wὲ-yà* as opposed to the fixed order *yà-wὲ* underscores
this analysis. Recall from chapter 7 and this discussion that the Gungbe left
periphery manifests the following hierarchy: Force > Inter > Topic > Focus >
Finiteness.

(65)   [ForceP [Force° ɖɔ̀ [InterP [Inter° ∅ [TopP [Top° yà [FocP[Foc° wὲ [FinP XP]]]]]]]]]

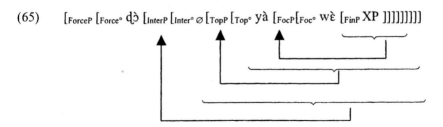

This analysis also extends to the cases of yes-no questions where the TM and FM
occur individually or in non-adjacent positions. For example, topicalization and/or

focalization may apply prior to yes-no question formation. The sentences under (66) illustrate some of those realizations.

(66) a. làn ló   yà   Kòfí   dù   ì   wĚ ?
         meat Spf[+def] Top   Kofi   eat-Perf 3sg   Foc-QM
         'As for the specific meat did KOFI EAT IT?'

     b. Kòfí wĚ   dù   làn   yà ?
         Kofi Foc   eat-Perf meat   Top-QM
         'Did KOFI eat the meat?'

In sentence (66a), topicalization applies to *làn ló* 'the meat' followed by focusing of the comment *Kòfí dù ì* 'Kofi ate it', which moves to [spec FocP]. Finally, the whole complement of the Gungbe QM, the derived clause, is moved to [spec InterP] giving rise to the order topic-clause-focus-QM. In this framework, such order can be achieved only if we assume movement of the whole TopP to [spec InterP]. In examples (66b), the situation is reversed since the subject *Kòfí* is focused, followed by topicalization of the whole clause. Finally, the clause is moved in [spec InterP] when yes-no question formation arises.

Assuming this is the right characterization, I further conclude that the Gungbe yes-no questions involve snowballing movement because movement seeks to raise the event expressed by the proposition. As a result, the whole FinP is pied-piped to the appropriate specifier position, [spec InterP].

8.2.2.2 *Against XP-movement associated with head-to-head movement*

Alternatively, it could be proposed that sentence (64c) does not involve snowballing movement to [spec FocP], [spec TopP], and finally [spec InterP] as discussed. Instead, it can be argued that such constructions require movement of the whole sentence to [spec InterP], followed by successive Foc°-to-Top°-to-Inter° movement, as illustrated in (67). An argument in favor of this analysis could be that successive head-movement leads to the mirror image Focus-Topic found in yes-no questions (64c–d).

(67) [ForceP [Force° dó [InterP [Inter° ∅   [TopP [Top° yà [FocP[Foc° wĚ [FinP XP]]]]]]]]]

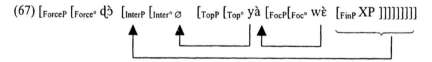

Though it might appear reasonable, this analysis wrongly predicts that when they co-occur in yes-no questions, the Gungbe TM and FM must be adjacent and must co-occur sentence-finally in the fixed order focus-topic. The sentences under (66) clearly show that this is not the right characterization.

8.3 CONCLUSION

In this chapter, I show that alongside focus and wh constructions, Gungbe also exhibits argument topic constructions. Following Rizzi (1997), I propose an analysis of these realizations that assumes that the topic element targets the specifier position of a topic phrase. TopP projects within the C-system, and its head Top° hosts the topic marker *yà*. When the focus, wh, and topic elements co-occur, the topic immediately precedes the focus and wh elements, suggesting that there is a hierarchy whereby TopP immediately dominates FocP. Pursuing the discussion on the focus and wh constructions, I therefore argue that movement to [spec TopP] arises because the topic phrase must check its topic feature before spell-out. This leads us to the conclusion that, the topic, focus, and wh constructions are similar: they all involve A'-chains. However, those constructions differ in a number of respects. The focus and wh elements are quantificational, while topics are not. The focus and wh constructions involve an A'-chain whereby the IP-internal position is filled by a gap, or a variable. On the other hand, the topic construction necessarily gives rise to an A'-chain involving a resumptive pronoun A'-bound by the topic. Contexts where the pronoun is not realized are those where the language displays no pronominal form that could resume the topic.

In addition, the Gungbe data on adjunct preposing show that topic constructions may be sensitive to referentiality. It therefore appears that the head Top° is actually specified for the features [±referential]. Building on the analysis I provide for the Gungbe specificity marker of the D-system, I propose that when Top° manifests the feature [+referential], it is overtly realized as *yà*, but when it encodes the feature [-referential], it is occupied by a null morpheme. This correctly explains why certain topics (e.g., adverbial adjunct) exclude the Gungbe topic marker.

The split-C hypothesis also helps account for the Gungbe yes-no question marker. In this respect, I suggest that the sentence-final low tone specific to the Gungbe yes-no question is a 'quasi-null' morpheme (or a toneme) that encodes the interrogative force associated with the interrogative projection (InterP) that projects within the C-system. This projection is headed by Inter°, the locus of the Gungbe yes-no question marker, that is, the sentence-final low tone. I interpret the fact that this toneme necessarily occurs sentence-finally and has scope over the sentence as strong evidence that the Gungbe yes-no questions involve leftward movement. The whole sentence moves leftward to [spec InterP], a position immediately to the right of the complementizer under Force°. In addition, the occurrence of the Gungbe topic and focus markers in the mirror image order *wè - yà* rather than *yà - wè* indicates that these constructions involve some sort of snowballing movement, or pied-piping of bigger chunks. FinP moves to [spec FocP]; then the whole FocP moves to the [spec TopP], followed by subsequent movement of TopP to [spec InterP]. On the basis of the analysis developed in chapters 5, 7, and the sections here, I attribute representation (68) to the Gungbe C-system.

(68)

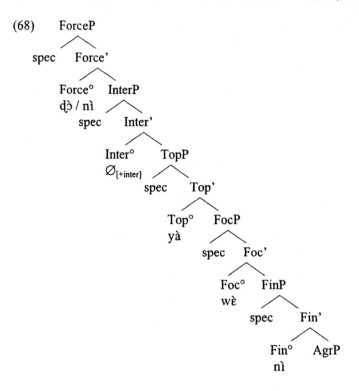

APPENDIX: SOME SPECULATIONS ABOUT THE SO-CALLED CLAUSAL DETERMINERS

In this chapter, I have shown that the left periphery is highly articulated, as each of the Force, Topic, Focus, and Finiteness features heads a projection within the C-system. In order to account for the Gungbe yes-no questions, I further assume that the C-system includes an interrogative projection (InterP) intermediate between ForceP and TopP and whose specifier hosts the whole clause, leaving the Gungbe question-marking low toneme in sentence-final position. As already mentioned, movement of the clause to [spec InterP] is quite similar to the type of movement found in the D-system (chapters 3 and 4) or in NomP (chapter 6). The conclusion I reached there was that these left peripheral markers that occur to the right edge, $D°$, $P°$, Nom°, and Inter°, force movement on to their complements to their specifier position: [spec DP], [spec PP], [spec NomP], [spec InterP], respectively.

This appendix discusses another left peripheral element that apparently requires such movement: the Gungbe clausal determiner. Certain Gbe languages of the Fon cluster (chapter 2) display a clausal determiner that occurs sentence-finally and indicates that the information being conveyed is preestablished in discourse and/or specific. In this respect, it is interesting to notice that the clausal determiner is morphologically and semantically identical to the Gungbe specificity marker *lɔ́* discussed in chapters 3 and 4. Examples from Fongbe and Gungbe are given in (1) and (2), respectively. The Fongbe examples are taken from Lefebvre (1992) (see also Law and Lefebvre 1995 and references cited there).

(1) Súnù   ɔ́   gbà   mɔ́tɔ̀   ɔ́   ɔ́
     man   Spf[+def] destroy-Perf car   Spf[+def] Det_CL
     'The specific man destroyed the specific car [as expected / as we knew]

(2) ɖĕ   Kòfí   hɔ̀n   lɔ́   vé   ná   yé
     that[Rel] Kofi   flee-Perf   Spf[+def] hurt-Perf   for   3pl
     'As Kofi specifically fled [instead of waiting] hurt them'

In her account for these constructions in Fongbe, Lefebvre (1992) showed that the occurrence of the clausal determiner is sensitive to features [±deictic] (i.e., specific in my term) in Fongbe. The clausal determiner appears only if the subject, or the object, or both are specified as [+deictic], as illustrated by the contrast in sentence (3a) and (3b–c).

(3) a. *Súnù   ɖé   gbà   mɔ́tɔ̀   ɖé   ɔ́
         man   Spf[-def] destroy-Perf car   Spf[-def] Det_CL
     b. Súnù   ɔ́   gbà   mɔ́tɔ̀   ɖé   ɔ́
         man   Spf[+def] destroy-Perf car   Spf[-def] Det_CL
         'The specific man destroyed a certain car [as expected]'
     c. Súnù   ɖé   gbà   mɔ́tɔ̀   ɔ́   ɔ́
         man   Spf[-def] destroy-Perf car   Spf[+def] Det_CL
         'A certain man destroyed the specific car [as expected]'

The facts in (3) led Lefebvre (1992) to conclude that argument sensitivity to feature [deictic] can be interpreted as manifestation of agreement domain AgrP that is headed by the clausal determiner. Given that both the subject and the object[19] determine the agreement facts, Lefebvre (1992) proposed that there are two agreement domains, that is, two available syntactic positions for the clausal determiner: AgrsP and AgroP. This amounts to saying that Agr is defined only for features [±deictic] in Fongbe. Under a split-IP analysis, Lefebvre (1992) suggested that the Fongbe facts can be partially represented as in (4) (Lefebvre's 31), assuming AgrsP and AgroP are head-final, and both the subject and object move out from their VP-internal position to [spec AgrsP] and [spec AgroP] to be licensed.

(4)

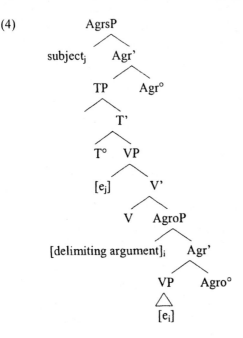

Setting aside the question of whether or not this structure is adequate for Fongbe, an analysis à la Lefebvre is not tenable in the framework adopted in this study. First, recall from chapter 2 that I argued extensively against the ambivalent structure. I thus assumed that Gungbe and other Gbe languages are head-initial: the head must precede the complement, and sequences where it follows are analyzed as instances of movement of the complement to some specifier position to the left.

Second, under the assumption that the clausal determiner realizes Agro when the sentence involves a [+specific] delimiting argument, one implies that Agro necessarily hosts the clausal determiner in imperfective clauses (5a). As shown by the ungrammatical sentence (5b), this analysis wrongly predicts that NomP focusing results in a generalized pied-piping that moves the [O-V] sequence, together with the clausal determiner in sentence-initial position. Instead, the marginal sentence (5c) clearly indicates that the clausal determiner must appear to the right of the imperfective marker tè. Assuming my analysis of the Gungbe imperfective constructions (chapters 5 and 6), the occurrence of the clausal determiner in this position clearly suggests that it does not occupy Agro. It cannot be reasonably argued that the clausal determiner manifests Agrs either, because it is clear from the sentences under (5) that it is not associated with a position between the subject and the verb.

(5)   a.   ɖě   Kòfí   tó   nú   ɖù   lɔ́
              that[Rel]   Kofi   Imperf thing   eat   Det_CL
              'As Kofi was eating'

b. *ḍě   nú   dù   lɔ́   Kòfí   tè
    that[Rel]   thing   eat   Spf[+def]   Kofi   Imperf
    'As Kofi was EATING'

c. ? ḍě   nú   dù   Kòfí   tè   lɔ́
    that[Rel]   thing   eat   Kofi   Imperf   Det_CL
    'As Kofi was EATING'

Given the data in (5), it seems natural to assume that the clausal determiner does not occupy a position internal to the Gungbe I-system. Since in sentence (5c) the clausal determiner is somehow set off from the rest of the clause, I propose that it actually manifests the left periphery. This analysis is consistent with Lefebvre (1991: 22) that the Haitian clausal determiner *an* manifests the left periphery (6).

(6)   M   di   ou   [li   vini   an]
       je   dire   toi   il   venir   Det
       'Je te dis qu'il est venu' [de cette venue qu'on savait qu'il devait faire]

With regard to the Gbe languages, the fact that it is the verb *dù* 'eat' that bears the sentence-final low tone specific to the Gungbe imperfective clauses (5) strongly favors an analysis of the clausal determiner as a left peripheral element. In terms of the split-C hypothesis, this would mean that there is, within the C-system, a projection SpfP whose head Spf° is the locus of the clausal determiner and whose specifier [spec Spf] hosts the whole sentence. I provisionally assume that SpfP immediately dominates FinP headed by the Gungbe injunctive/subjunctive marker *ní*. This correctly predicts that in an injunctive sentence that also includes the Gungbe CP-markers, the injunctive marker must intervene between the subject and the verb of the clause, the latter appearing to the left of the clausal determiner, the FM, the TM, and the QM, as shown in sentence (7).

(7)   ḍé ún   ḍɔ̀   ḍɔ̀   [Kòfí   ní   hɔ̀n]   lɔ́   wɛ̀ yǎ
       as 1sg   say-Perf that   Kofi   Inj   flee   Det_CL   Foc Top-QM
       'As I say that Kofi should run away?'

The fact that the clause involving the determiner occurs lower than the complementizer *ḍɔ̀* is strong evidence that the clausal determiner does not manifest Force°, the highest head of the C-system. In addition, the comp-[*ní*-clause]-*lɔ́-wɛ̀-yà-∅* format observed here precludes an analysis in terms of a D selecting a CP complement. Instead, these facts favor the analysis proposed in section 8.2.2.1 that movement of the clause to [spec InterP] involves snowballing movement. For instance, I can propose that the whole FinP moves to [spec SpfP] and the complex SpfP moves to [spec FocP], followed by movement of FocP to [spec TopP], which finally moves to [spec InterP].

This analysis casts a new light on facts about negation in the Gbe languages. In chapter 2 I proposed that the Fongbe, Gengbe, and Ewegbe sentence-final negative morphemes in (8) could be analyzed as negative adverbials of the type of French *pas*. That analysis suggests that those negative morphemes could realize some specifier position within the inflectional domain. However, the analysis that I develop here for the QM, the clausal determiner, and other typing morphemes suggests that the sentence-final negative morpheme could manifest some designated head position located in the C-system (8) (Ouhalla 1993; Progovac 1993). This would mean that, like other typing markers that surface to the right edge, the Gbe sentence-final negative morphemes force movement of the clause into their specifier position.

(8)   a.   Kòfí   ɖù   nú   á   [Fongbe]
           Kofi   eat-Perf thing   Neg
           'Kofi did not eat'

      b.   Kòfí   mú   plè   àvɔ̀   ò   [Gengbe]
           Kofi   Neg   buy-Perfcloth   Neg
           'Kofi didn't buy a cloth'

      c.   Kòfí   me   fle   gasɔ   o   [Ewegbe]
           Kofi   Neg   buy   bicycle Neg
           'Kofi didn't buy a bicycle'

I will not further develop this analysis here. However, the idea that the whole sentence moves to the specifier of a functional projection expressing some negative feature within the C-system is consistent with certain scope properties mentioned to me by Avolonto (p.c.).

(9)   a.   Kòfí yì   [ɖé   ún   ɖɔ̀   nú   wè   ɔ́]   á
           Kofi leave-Perf as   1sg   say-Perf to   2sg   Det_CL Neg
           'Kofi left as I didn't tell you'

      b.   Kòfí yì   á   [ɖé   ún   ɖɔ̀   nú   wè   ɔ́]
           Kofi leave-PerfNeg as   1sg   say-Perf to   2sg   Det_CL
           'Kofi didn't leave as I told you'

According to Avolonto, that the bracketed clause is within the scope of the Fongbe negative morpheme *á* in sentence (9a) but not in (9b) is strong evidence that there is movement of the clause to the left-adjacent position to the negative morpheme in example (9a) but not in (9b). Regardless of the proper analysis of such constructions and the position that the Fongbe negative morpheme occupies, it is interesting to notice that the kind of movement I postulate for the Gungbe yes-no questions seems to operate within negative constructions. Granting this, I now draw another parallel between negation and certain constructions that typically involve the left periphery, such as interrogation (Haegeman 1995a, b, 1996a). Moreover, if it is true that leftward movement of the complement to the specifier position of its head is a diagnostic for those left peripheral markers that occur to the right edge, therefore the

Fongbe, Gengbe, and Ewegbe data clearly suggest that the C-system also involves certain negative markers.

9

Conclusion

In writing this book, I have tried to contribute to the discussion on word order patterns in Gbe and Kwa languages by providing a careful analysis of the syntax of Gungbe, while demonstrating that the close relationship that exists between this language and other Gbe languages (e.g., Fongbe, Gengbe, Ewegbe) is not just accidental but rather results from their common origin. In this perspective, the data presented here clearly indicate that the surface differences that may arise between these languages cannot be analyzed in terms of opposing underlying structures. Instead, it is argued here that all the Gbe languages are of the type S-H-C, and every case where the complement precedes the head must be seen as instantiation of comp-movement to the specifier of the head or to some other specifier position in the clause (Kayne 1994; Aboh 1999). The theory developed here naturally extends to Kwa languages, as well as typologically different languages that manifest complement-head sequences.

This basic hypothesis sheds a new light on our understanding of the D-system. Granting that comp-movement gives rise to the complement-Det order found in Gungbe, it clearly appears that the nominal system involves an articulated structure that allows for both the specificity and the number markers to co-occur freely with nominal modifying elements such as adjectives, demonstratives, and numerals. In this regard, I propose that the D-system involves discrete projections NumP and DP whose heads (Num°, D°) encode the features [±plural] and [±specific] that are morphologically realized by the markers. Under this analysis, D° and Num° form the nominal left periphery. D° manifests the higher projection of the D-system as the interface between the nominal sequence and the discourse, while Num° expresses the lower projection intermediate between the nominal left periphery and the nominal inflectional system. This would mean that D° and Num° are the counterparts of Force° and Fin° that manifest the clausal left periphery. I further propose that the nominal inflectional domain consists of discrete functional projections (labeled as DemP, NralP, AP, etc.), whose specifiers host demonstratives, numerals, and adjectives. Building on the parallels between these noun modifiers and adverbs, I conclude that nominal modifiers manifest distinct positions within the nominal infection, that is, the nominal counterpart of I within the clause.

Under this approach, the Gbe languages provide evidence for three-way distinction within the pronominal system: strong, weak, and clitic pronouns. Strong pronouns are like full DPs and involve a similar underlying structure. On the other hand, weak pronouns lack some of the categories that are present in strong pronouns. They project only the categories DP and NumP whose heads are specified for person and number, respectively. The weak pronoun is generated in Num°, where it is specified for number and then moves to D° to get person specification. With respect to object clitics, it is proposed that they are the weakest of all. They are intransitive Ds in the sense of Abney (1987): they manifest a DP that includes only the head D°, the anchorage of person specifications.

On my account of the Gungbe sentence-internal structure, I propose an analysis of the Gungbe IP-markers by assuming that each of the so-called I-features (e.g., agreement, negation, tense, aspect) is a syntactic head that projects within the I-system (Pollock 1989, and references cited there). In this perspective, the Gungbe negation marker is associated with Neg°, the head of a functional projection NegP that dominates the tense phrase TP. In a similar vein, the Gungbe future is inserted in T° where it encodes the feature [+future]. This marker is in complementary distribution with the Gungbe default tense specification [-future] that is expressed by a null morpheme. Extending this analysis to the Gungbe aspect markers, I propose that they are the morphological realizations of the different aspect heads [habitual] Asp°1, [imperfective] Asp°2, and finally [prospective] Asp°3 that form the aspect system. When they are positively set, these aspect heads are morphologically realized in the language by the corresponding aspect markers. The Gungbe aspect system manifests a hierarchy whereby AspP1 precedes AspP2, which in turn precedes AspP3. Asp°1 hosts the habitual marker, Asp°2 the imperfective marker, and finally Asp°3 the prospective marker. Given that imperfective constructions necessarily involve a nominalizing process that may include the prospective marker, I further assume that Asp°2 can select a small clause headed by the nominalizer head Nom°, which projects as NomP and dominates AspP3, which in turn dominates AgroP, which dominates VP. On the other hand, no such small clause is available in the Gungbe non-imperfective sentences that involve neither nominalization nor prospective aspect. It thus follows that, in such structures, Asp°2 dominates AgroP, which in turn dominates VP. The existence of these two different structures in Gungbe and the kind of interactions they trigger with respect to object shift and verb movement help to account for the SVO versus SOV word order variation. In this regard, I propose that the SVO order is typical of the non-imperfective clauses because those constructions involve subsequent verb movement to the left of the shifted object. This would mean that, in those constructions, subsequent verb movement to the left masks object. But this is not the case in the SOV imperfective and related constructions where subsequent verb movement is blocked due to nominalization.

Extending Pollock's split-I hypothesis to the CP domain, I propose, following Rizzi (1997) and subsequent work, that each of the force, topic, focus, and finiteness features that are associated with the Comp-domain is a syntactic head that projects within the C-system. Evidence from Gungbe is in favor of this analysis, since the language manifests a conjunction and an injunctive marker, which all appear to manifest the left-periphery. In terms of Rizzi (1997) I propose that conjunction *ní*, the Gungbe counterpart of English *if* or French *si*, encodes Force°, the topmost head of the C-system, where it indicates conditional specifications, while mood *ní* manifests Fin°, the lowest head that terminates the C-system, where it expresses injunctive/subjunctive mood. In addition to these two markers that encode the external and internal projections of the C-system, the left-periphery also involves a question marker, a topic marker, and a focus marker that head an interrogative phrase (InterP), a topic phrase (TopP), and a focus phrase (FocP). Given that the Gungbe QM, TM, and FM are not mutually exclusive, it is reasonable to say that InterP, TopP, and FocP can project in the structure when needed. The Gungbe CP-markers manifest the following hierarchy: Force-Interrogation-Topic-Focus-Finiteness.

The richness of the Gungbe D-, I-, and C-systems leads me to the conclusion that the absence of agreement/inflectional morphology in the Gbe languages does not result from a 'poor' underlying structure. Instead, the numerous markers available in those languages suggest their highly articulated structure. Accordingly, the conclusions achieved in this book should also extend to other Kwa languages, taking into account language specificities that could result in surface variation. As proposed in this study, such variation should not necessarily be seen as the reflex of opposing underlying structures. Instead, such differences may result from certain limited parametric variations (e.g., the neg-parameter) or simply from the length and/or target of movement operations.

There are open questions, though, about language acquisition in the Gbe, Kwa context. For instance, given the analysis I develop here with respect to the Gungbe CP- and IP-markers, two question arise: how do the Gbe learners acquire those markers, and the structure they manifest, knowing that Gbe languages display no agreement morphology and that some of the markers are non-overt, homophonous with other words, or simply reduced to a toneme (i) and what will such study tell us about language acquisition in general (ii). This is a completely new field in the Kwa context, and I hope to return to those problems in future research.

Notes

Chapter 2

    1. In this study, the term 'father tongue' is preferable to 'mother tongue'. Considered in its traditional sense, the term 'mother tongue' is inadequate in a multilingual context where the language one speaks is not necessarily one's mother's native language. As discussed in Aboh (1994), it is often the case in Africa that the native tongue of an individual is his father's tongue, his mother's tongue, his community tongue, or a combination of these languages (see also Jobe 1992 for the discussion for the Gambian situation).

    2. See Capo (1991) and references cited there.

    3. See chapter 3 for the discussion on DPs in Gbe.

    4. Essegbey (1999) also adopted this analysis for the Ewegbe argument structure.

    5. This is consistent with Houngues (1997), who proposes that the Gengbe marker *lá* marks future and is inserted under T°. In his framework, T° is specified in Gbe as [+future] or [+past]. The feature [+past] has no morphological realization. On the contrary, some authors (e.g., Avolonto 1992a, b, c, 1995; Kinyalolo 1992, 1997; da Cruz 1993; Tossa 1994; Manfredi 1997) have argued that the element expressing futurity is actually an irrealis aspect marker. In this perspective, the Gbe languages are considered aspect languages: tense is derived from aspect. On the other hand, Essegbey (1999) suggests that the Ewegbe *á* does not encode tense. It expresses potentiality, which the author considers a mood specification. As I discuss in chapters 5 and 6, the analysis developed in this book departs radically from the proposals sketched here by assuming that both tense and aspect are fully expressed in Gbe, by means of IP-markers that encode the tense and aspect features on T° and Asp°, respectively. The future marker encodes the feature [+future] but past and present tenses are derived from the null [-future] as default values.

    6. See Lefebvre (1990, 1995a) and da Cruz (1993) for a discussion on the existence of PPs in Fongbe. The analysis proposed there could be easily adopted for Gbe as a whole.

    7. See section 2.5.1.3. for a brief discussion of Tossa's work.

    8. The reader is also referred to Manfredi (1991), Déchaine (1993), and references cited there for a similar analysis of other Kwa languages.

    9. Tossa's (1994) proposal that the SVO order is derived from the underlying SOV reminds us of Koster's (1975) analysis of the Continental West Germanic languages that the main

clause VO order is derived from the embedded OV order via a process of leftward verb-movement (see also Ross 1970; Maling 1972; Zwart 1997a, b; and references cited there).

10. See chapter 6 for the discussion.

11. This is in contradiction to Lefebvre's (1992, 1998) analysis that the Fongbe preverbal negation marker *má* is in [spec NegP] while the sentence-final marker *á* manifests Neg°. In her framework, NegP is head-final. As the reader may see, this analysis presupposes that Fongbe and possibly the Gbe languages involve mixed structures. But as I show here, such a proposal cannot be maintained for the Gbe languages.

12. In an approach that assumes Rizzi's split-C hypothesis, the C-system may also be the locus of negative specifications (Ouhalla 1993; Progovac 1993). That the Fongbe negation marker occurs sentence-finally on a par with other Gbe left peripheral markers can be considered an indication that it manifests some head position within the left periphery (see chapter 8). If this is true, we can therefore assume that these markers occur sentence-finally as a result of movement of the whole sentence to their specifier positions. This would not be surprising, though, since this book shows that the Gbe left peripheral elements do trigger such movement.

13. Agbedor (1993) reached a similar conclusion on his account for the Ewegbe bipartite negation marker.

14. For the discussion on serial verb constructions, see Westermann 1930; Ansre 1966a; Bámgbósé 1974; Sebba 1987; Baker 1989; Lefebvre 1991b; Manfredi 1991; Tossa 1993, 1994; da Cruz 1993, 1995, 1997; Déchaine 1993, 1997; Veenstra 1996; Collins 1997; Stewart 1997, 1998; Aboh 2001b, to cite only a few.

15. It is interesting to notice that Avolonto (1995) and Kinyalolo (1995), respectively proposed a reanalysis of Fongbe I- and D-systems as involving head-initial underlying structure.

16. See also Koopman (1984) for a similar proposal for Vata and Gbadi, two Kru languages spoken in Ivory Coast.

17. See Sportiche (1988) where it is argued that subjects are base-generated in [spec VP].

18. The term *subjunctive* is used here in a loose sense to refer to Gungbe sentences like (43d), which involve the marker *ní* that is also found in Gungbe conditionals. But see chapter 5 for the discussion on those constructions.

19. See section 2.5.2 and references cited there for the discussion.

20. See Manfredi (1997) for the discussion of similar facts in the Niger-Congo languages.

21. Similar facts are found with the Gbe control verbs (Fabb 1992a, b; Kinyalolo 1992; Aboh 1999).

22. These similarities underscore Koopman's (1984) analysis of Kru in terms of V2.

23. See Zwart (1997a) and references cited there for the discussion of embedded SVO order in Dutch.

24. See also Roberts (1985); Rohrbacher (1994); and references cited there.

25. Dutch main clauses may be introduced by other elements than the subject. In such contexts, the verb is right adjacent to the sentence-initial phrase (see Zwart 1997a for the discussion):

(i) a. Weer   kust   Jan   Marie
         again kisses John   Mary
         'Again John kisses Mary'

b. Waarom   kust   Jan   Marie?
   Why   kisses   John   Mary
   'Why does John kiss Mary?'

26. But see Zwart (1997a) and references cited there for an alternative.

27. Alternatively, it has been proposed that DP-arguments and CP-arguments have different base positions. DP-arguments are generated to the left of the V while CP-arguments are generated to the right. See Koster (1989) and references cited there.

28. See also Müller (1997) where it is argued that extraposition can be seen as an instance of remnant movement.

29. Alternatively, one could adopt Zwart's (1997a) minimalist view that V-to-I movement is an instance of Feature movement.

30. See Haider (1997) and Haegeman (1998a) for an alternative in terms of leftward movement of the verb.

31. See also Mahajan (1997), who argues for an analysis of rightward scrambling in terms of leftward movement of the verb and some of its arguments.

Chapter 3

1. In certain contexts, the Gungbe bare noun can also be interpreted as generic.

(i)   ùn   nɔ̀   sà   távò
      1sg   Hab   sell   table
      'I habitually sell tables'

2. See also Bickerton (1981), Bruyn (1995), and references cited there for the specific versus non-specific opposition in Creole languages.

3. In his account for Fongbe D-system, Kinyalolo (1995) argues against Brousseau and Lumsden's (1992) first proposal that Fongbe (and, by implication, other Gbe languages) exhibits a head-final DP projection in that the surface word order found in determiner phrases matches the DP underlying structure of these languages (see also Lefebvre 1992). He then adopts a head-initial hypothesis and proposes that the surface Noun-Det order results from the satisfaction of Sportiche's Generalized Licensing Criterion, which requires that the complement of D be moved in [spec DP].

4. This analysis is compatible with Ihsane and Puskás' (2001) proposal that the nominal periphery involves a Definite Projection (DefP), the head of which encodes definiteness. In that framework, DefP projects as the lowest projection of the system. In the analysis proposed in this book, however, I assume that the head Num encodes both plurality and definiteness.

5. See also chapter 4 for the discussion of the Gungbe plural strong pronouns as involving the number marker lɛ́.

6. But see Zribi-Hertz and Hanne (1995) for the discussion on the category Spf° (specific) as a component of the D-system, which projects between D° and NP in Bambara. In their account for specificity marking in Bambara, Zribi-Hertz and Hanne (1995) proposed that, in this language, the D-system involves a Specificity Phrase, which is the locus of features [± specific]. SpfP projects between D° and Num° as represented in (ii); see also note 4.

(ii) $[_{DP}$ .... $[_{SpfP}$ .... $[_{NumP}$.... $[_{NP}$.....$]]]]$

7. See also Panagiotidis (2000) for a similar proposal.

8. This analysis is compatible with Carstens' (2000) proposal that in the Italian examples '*le mie case belle*' the determiner is merged under D°. The genitive pronoun is merged NP-internally in some position lower than adjectives, but raises to [spec NumP], followed by N-raising to Num°. Interestingly, the Italian examples discussed by Bernstein (1997, 2001a, b) show that in demonstrative reinforcer constructions the preposed noun occurs with its modifiers as in '*questo [libro vecchio] qui*' (Bernstein 2001b: 17). This is evidence that such constructions might allow for NP-raising.

9. See for instance Ihsane and Puskás (2001).

10. In terms of Carstens (2000), this structural relationship could be accounted for by assuming that D° subcategorizes for Num°. This is actually an updated version of Abney's (1987) 'f-selection': "there are syntactic relations between all heads and their complements or adjuncts, by which those complements and adjuncts are licensed— a minimal condition on a well-formed syntactic structure is that every node be licensed by some such relation" (Abney 1987: 55).

11. Gungbe actually displays two genitive case markers: *sín* and *tòn*. An argument case marked by *sín* occurs prenominally as in ((iii)a) and postnominally when it is case marked by *tòn* as in ((iii)b). See Aboh (2002) for the discussion on Gungbe, and Brousseau and Lumsden (1992) and Kinyalolo (1995) for the analysis of Fongbe genitive markers.

(iii)   a.   Kɔ́jó   sín   mótò
             Kojo   Pos   car
             'Kojo's car'
        b.   mótò   Kɔ́jó   tòn
             car   Kojo   Pos
             'Kojo's car

12. See Kinyalolo (1995) for a similar proposal for Fongbe.

13. See also Hawkins (1990) on the theory of word order universals.

14. In this framework, we assume, following Ritter (1991) and subsequent work, that the functional projection NumP is universally present in the D-system even though it is not morphologically realized in all languages. An alternative would be to suggest that languages that lack an overt number marker possess a syncretic D head that encodes, among other features, the feature specification [±plural], but I don't follow this line here.

15. See Panagiotidis (2000) who proposes that not all demonstratives are of the type XP. According to him, certain demonstratives are generated as heads.

16. In terms of Giusti (1994, 1997), DemP and NralP are considered AgrPs that project between D° and NP.

17. Thanks to Guglielmo Cinque for discussing previous versions of the analysis presented here.

18. As suggested to me by Michal Starke (p.c.), an alternative could be that the head N° first moves via Nral° to the head position Y°, immediately to the left of the numeral. Then the projection YP as a whole moves to [spec XP] to the left of the demonstrative. Finally, XP moves cyclically to [spec NumP] and [spec DP] to satisfy the GLC. A priori the result is the same as the one proposed.

19. See Rizzi (2001) for the discussion and a similar account for adverb placement within the I-system.

20. Jun (1999) proposes a similar analysis for the distribution of demonstratives and adjectives in Korean.

21. I thank Anne Zribi-Hertz and Victor Manfredi for their suggestions.

22. Noni has both the orders D (ii) and D (iv).

23. See Longobardi (1994) on the licensing of null Ds.

24. See Shlonsky (2000) for the discussion of snowballing movement and remnant NP-movement in Semitic.

25. The reader is referred to Cinque's own work for a very careful and detailed discussion.

26. See Baker 1989; da Cruz 1993; Tossa 1993, 1994; Collins 1997; Stewart 1998; Aboh 2002, and references cited there for the discussion on the serial verb constructions.

27. This differs from topic constructions where it appears that the postnominal morpheme remains in situ but is obligatorily preceded by an IP-internal resumptive pronoun whose antecedent is the moved DP.

(iv)	mótò	lɔ́	yà	Àsíbá	bɪ́ɔ́	é	mὲ
	car	Spf[+def]	Top	Asiba	enter-Perf	3sg	P2
	'as for the car, Asiba entered it'						

28. This reminds us the English verb/object adjacency facts as extensively discussed in the literature. See, for example, Pollock (1989) for an analysis of the contrast between English and French (see the introductory chapter and the references cited there).

Chapter 4

1. For example, German *es* and *ihn* are weak, but their reduced forms *'s* and *'n* lack the ΣP layer and are considered clitic pronouns (see Cardinaletti 1994; Cardinaletti & Starke 1999 for the discussion).

2. Da Cruz and Avolonto (1993) discuss such cliticization process in Fongbe. See section 3.2.7.

3. Notice that in topic constructions where the full DP is left-dislocated, a sentence corresponding to (47g') is grammatical:

(i)	Kòfí	yà,	éɔ̀	ná	yì
	Kofi	Top	3S-sg	Fut	leave
	'As for Kofi, he will leave'				

In such constructions, the strong pronoun is necessarily read as emphatic.

4. Sentences (21d–e) can be uttered in a situation where Kofi pretends to have headache, but behaves like someone who is not sick. The speaker therefore wonders whether he is really sick or is just pretending to be sick.

5. But see Cardinaletti 1994; Giusti 1994; Cinque 1994; Longobardi 1994, 2001, where an N-to-D movement is assumed in order to account for the distribution of (pre and post) nominal modifiers.

6. See also Nash (1997) for the status of first and second person singular in ergative languages.

7. See also Postal (1966), Kayne (1998), and references cited there for the discussion.

8. See Larson (1988) and references cited there for the discussion on double object constructions.

9. Alternatively, one could assume that the theme is merged higher than the goal and that situations where the goal precedes derive from movement to the left of the theme, but I will not develop this analysis here.

Chapter 5

1. See also the introductory chapter for the discussion of Pollock's (1989) analysis that the I-system involves a more complex structure where each of the set of so-called I-features (i.e., tense, agreement, negation etc.) is anchored on a functional head, say T°, Neg°, Agr°, which projects as a component of I.

2. See chapter 2, section 2.4, for the discussion on similar properties in Fongbe, Gengbe, and Ewegbe.

3. See Vikner (1997) for the discussion of 'rich inflection' in the Germanic languages.

4. Except for second person singular imperatives ((i)a–a') and certain serial constructions ((i)b); see Tossa (1993) for the discussion.

(i) a. ___   tón
     get-out
 a'. mì   tón
     2pl   get-out
     'get out'
 b. Kòfí xò   mótò dé   bó   kù - ì   bíó tò   mè
    Kofi buy-Perf car Spf[-def] Coord   drive-Perf-3sg enter country Post
    'Kofi bought a car and drove it down town'

5. This is in exception to imperfective clauses where the verb may be affected by a low tone and must reduplicate in case there is no phonetic material intervening between the imperfective marker and the verb. See chapter 6 for the discussion.

6. I draw the reader's attention to the fact that the future marker *ná* and the preposition *ná* glossed as 'for' can be a priori considered two distinct elements that have different distributions. The former always occurs in a preverbal position between the subject and the verb ((ii)a–a'), while the latter obligatorily occurs in a postverbal position and selects benefactive DP or locational *P*P complements ((ii)b–c). Observe also that the two elements can co-occur in a sentence ((ii)c).

(ii) a. Kòfí   ná   sà   hwéví
      Kofi   Fut   sell   fish
      'Kofi will sell some fish'
 a'. *Kòfí   sà   ná   hwéví
      Kofi   sell   Fut   fish
 b. Kòfí   sà   hwéví   ná   Kòjó
    Kofi   sell-Perf fish   for   Kojo
    'Kofi sold fish for/to Kojo'

c. Kòfí   ná   sà   hwéví   ná   Kɔjó
   Kofi   Fut   sell   fish   for   Kojo
   'Kofi will sell fish for/to Kojo'

Alternatively, we could assume that the preverbal and postverbal *ná* express one and the same thing: an abstract category P that may occur under T° to express tense or to the right of the verb to encode location, beneficiary, and so on. This reminds us of the English preposition 'to' that occurs under T° in non-finite clauses (e.g., For John to come would be difficult) or in postverbal position (e.g., I gave the book to John).

7. See section 3.2.3. for the discussion on other possible elements that may occur between the subject and the verb in Gungbe.

8. See Stowell (1981) for the discussion of similar adjacency facts in English.

9. I discuss the stative versus dynamic asymmetry in chapter 6, section 4.3.

10. See Avolonto (1992a, b, c, 1995) for an alternative.

11. According to Ouhalla (1990), three language groups obtain with respect to negation marking: (i) languages that mark sentential negation by means of a preverbal marker that encodes the head of NegP (e.g., Gungbe), (ii) languages where sentential negation is expressed by a postverbal marker (e.g., Fongbe, Occitan dialects, etc.) that is licensed in [spec NegP], and (iii) languages that allow for a simultaneous realization of preverbal and postverbal negation markers (e.g., Gengbe, Ewegbe, French) that realize [spec NegP] and Neg°, respectively.

12. Chomsky (1995) develops a different analysis of case assignment by assuming that the "function of Agr is to provide a structural configuration in which features can be checked: Case and Φ-features, and categorial features ([V-] and [T-] by adjunction, [D-] by substitution). The Case-assigning feature is intrinsic to the heads (V, T) that raise to Agr for checking of DP in [Spec, Agr], so there is no reason to assign it to Agr as well" (Chomsky 1995: 351). In this respect Ndayiragije (2000) proposes that there is no Agr projection in Gbe and that nominative case is a property of T. The question arises, though, how nominative case is assigned in the Gbe languages, since they seem not to manifest V-to-T-to-Agr movement (see chapters 2 and 6).

13. A priori, that English subjunctive sentences can contain the negative marker *not* precludes this analysis. But the reader is referred to Zanuttini (1996), where it is proposed that the English embedded subjunctive involves an impoverished structure that lacks certain functional categories that are normally present in other types of finite clauses, that is, the functional projection containing tense and modal elements. This hypothesis is supported by the fact that lexical verbs in subjunctive do not exhibit inflectional morphology ((iii)a), auxiliary *be* and *have* cannot raise to pick up inflectional morphology ((iii)b), and negation can be expressed only by the negative marker *not* ((iii)c–d).

(iii)   a. I insist that she go /*goes
         b. I demand that everybody be admitted
         c. I insist that she not stay
         d. *I insist that she don't stay

Zanuttini interprets the impossibility of realizing the negative morpheme *n't* in such constructions as manifestation of the fact that the functional category TP, which is necessary for the presence of NegP, is missing. As a result, negation in expressed in subjunctive constructions by use of the adverbial negative marker *not*, which realizes the specifier position of some functional projection other than NegP.

14. The reader is referred to Rizzi (1997) and references cited there for a detailed discussion on the left periphery.

15. See chapter 6, also Aboh (in press b), and references cited there for the discussion on the Gungbe imperfective constructions and verb reduplication.

16. See also the discussion in the preceding paragraphs and in chapter 2.

17. See chapter 6 for the discussion of features [-habitual], [-imperfective].

18. The term 'biclausal' is used here to refer to the fact that an aspect marker or an aspectual verb may select a lower small clause. Notice, however, that the situation here differs from that of standardly assumed biclausal structures that involve two lexical verbs associated with their own extended projections.

19. See also Lefebvre (1995a).

20. See Avolonto (1992c) for a detailed discussion on Fongbe mood morphemes.

21. This indirectly supports the idea that there is no null perfective aspect morpheme in Gungbe since, as I showed in example (52), *ní* does not have such blocking effect on other Gungbe aspect markers.

22. I do not consider imperative-like sentences involving a null subject interpreted as 3sg.

(iv)	ní	ɖà	àgásá	ná	Kòfí
	Inj	cook	crab	for	Kofi

'S/he should cook crabs for Kofi'

23. See Cowper (1991) for a similar analysis of imperatives.

24. In this respect, Kayne (1992) proposed that the usage of infinitival forms in second person Italian imperative constructions results from the realization of a null mood morpheme in the structure (see also Roberts 1985 and Pollock 1997 for an alternative).

25. See Motapanyane (1995) for a similar proposal in terms of movement of the Romanian subject to [spec MP] where MP immediately dominates AgrP and M° is morphologically realized as *sa*.

26. I leave open the question of the application of subject movement to [spec FinP] in sentences where there is no overt manifestation of mood. In other words, does this movement always apply in Gungbe? Notice that this is linked to a more general question of whether the CP layer is always present in a clause even if not needed. (See Avolonto 1992c for an alternative).

27. See also Haegeman (1996b) for a similar analysis of V2 phenomenon in Germanic.

28. Beukema and Coopmans (1989) propose that imperative and subjunctive forms are similar in the sense that they are specified as [-tense; +Agr]. In other words, injunctive and subjunctive constructions lack TP projection but contain an Agreement projection that can license the subject when needed. However, since Gungbe displays no agreement or inflectional morphology, there is no empirical evidence for or against Beukema and Coopman's proposal. Granting that AgrsP is responsible for nominative case in Gungbe, the fact that pronominal elements that appear to the left of mood *ní* bear nominative case and are necessarily interpreted as subject of the clause can be said to be a manifestation of the [-tense, +agr] specification of subjunctive/injunctive clauses.

Chapter 6

1. See Essegbey (1999) for the discussion on argument structure in Gbe.

2. For completeness, it is worth mentioning that the Gungbe verb doubling system follows a rather rigid pattern where the base vowel of the derived verb is always changed into [i]. This is with the exception of verbs that have [u] as base vowel. In other word, reduplication also involves a phonological process that changes mid and low vowels (as well as their nasalized counterparts) into high-front [i] (or its nasalized correspondent), as the following examples show.

(i)   a. xɔ̀ (buy)   tò   xìxɔ̀ ...
      b. zé (take)   tò   zízè̀ ...
      c. ɖà (cook)   tò   ɖìɖà ...
      d. fìn (steal)   tò   fìnfìn ...
      e. ɖù (eat) tò   ɖùɖù ...

3. Not all Gungbe speakers accept these constructions. While some find them quite marginal, others consider them ungrammatical. However, regardless of the judgments of the Gungbe speakers with respect to the S-*tò*-VV-NP-NR object schema (8a), an analysis of the Gungbe imperfectives should also account for the order S-*tò*-VV-Clitic (object) -NR found in (7a).

4. The OV sequence is also found in contexts involving the verb *bɛ́* 'start' or its complex counterpart *jè...jí* 'begin...on' or other verbs like *gbɛ́* 'refuse', *gbɔ̀* 'stop', specific to injunctives, *nyɔ́* 'know', as the following examples show:

(ii) a. yé   bɛ́   nú   ɖù
          3pl   start-Perf   thing   eat
          'They started eating'

      b. yé   jè   nú   ɖù   jí
          3pl   start-Perf   thing   eat   on
          'They started eating'

      c. yé   gbɛ́   nú   ɖù
          3pl   refuse-Perf   thing   eat
          'They refused to eat'

      d. mì   gbɔ̀   nú   ɖù
          2pl   stop   thing   eat
          'You stop eating!'

      e. yé   nyɔ́n   wè   ɖú
          3pl   know-Perf   dance   dance
          'They can dance'

As correctly mentioned by Fabb (1992a), a complication with these sentences is that they can optionally be expressed by constructions where the object precedes a reduplicated verb, as exemplified in (ii):

(ii) f. yé   gbɛ́   nú   ɖùɖù
          3pl   refuse-Perf   thing   eat-eat
          'They refused to eat'

But see Aboh (in press b) for extending the analysis proposed here to these constructions.

5. See also Aboh (1996a, 1999).

6. Though it might be reasonable to analyze these adverbs as nominal elements targeting argument positions (e.g., see example ((iii)a), where the reduplicated adverb surfaces in a subject position), they cannot be regarded as full nominals as they never co-occur with the Gungbe adjectives, numerals, and specificity or plural markers (b). But see Plann (1986) on the discussion of so-called substantives in Spanish, also Carstens (1997) on empty nouns in Bantu locatives for a possible extension to the reduplicated adverbs.

(iii)   a.   dédé   ní   kpé   mì
             slowly Inj   impregnate   2pl
             'Be prudent'
        b.   dédé   *àtòn   *éhé   *lɔ́   *lɛ́
             slowly three   Dem   Spf[+def]   Num

7. A more correct way to analyze non-syntactic word reduplication in Gbe is to regard it as a process of word derivation, since it generally leads to the creation of a new word from an existing one. For example, the state verb *kló* 'to be big' becomes an adjective-type word *kíkló* 'big size' by reduplication. Similarly, the verb *zè* 'cleave' can be doubled as in *zìzè* 'cleft' to form a modifier as illustrated in *àgbán zìzè* 'broken plate'.

8. See Kinyalolo (1992) for a slightly different proposal for verb reduplication in the Fongbe imperfective/prospective and *gbé*-clauses.

9. The analysis proposed here differs minimally from Aboh (1996a) in postulating that this small clause involves an additional functional projection AspP3 that hosts the prospective marker and dominates AgroP, which in turn dominates VP (see also Kinyalolo 1992; Fabb 1992a, b for an interesting discussion of imperfective constructions in Fongbe and Ewegbe, respectively).

10. Some authors (e.g., Essegbey 1999) have argued that the sentence-final morphemes (i.e., Ø, wè, ɔ̀, m̄) are aspect markers while the preverbal ones (i.e., tò, ɖò, lè, lè) must be considered auxiliaries.

11. Similar facts are found in imperfective constructions in Ayizogbe another Gbe language (Capo 1988, 1991).

12. But see Starke (1995), where it is proposed that small clauses are full-fledged clauses.

13. This means that in Fongbe, Gengbe, and Ewegbe, the nominalizer heads are realized by wè, ɔ̀, m̄, respectively. In this respect, Fabb (1992a: 13) proposed an adaptation of Kangni (1989): "the final particles in these cases are locational noun 'possessed' by the embedded progressive constituents. (Location is expressed in Gbe languages not generally by prepositions but by nouns referring to location which are possessed by the things they locate; hence 'inside hut' would be expressed as 'hut's inside': xɔ̀ mɛ̀.) The final particles sometimes are actual locational nouns; Fon wè and Ewe m̄ are not, but might be argued to be derived diachronically from locational nouns."

14. The suggestion that there is a close relationship between Nom° and Asp° is a reinterpretation of Fabb (1992a), who proposed that the upper verb (the imperfective marker in my term) licenses the sentence-final morpheme (just as progressive *ing* must be licensed by a higher governing verb in English; Fabb 1992a: 11).

15. See also Kinyalolo (1992) for a similar proposal for Fongbe.

16. Notice, however, that with respect to imperfective constructions containing a clausal complement ((iv)a), it is completely impossible to prepose the sequence [VV-IO-CP-complement] as shown in ((iv)b).

(iv) a. Kɔjó tò d̀ìdɔ̀ ná Kɔkú [dɔ̀ Báyɔ́ xɔ̀ kèkɛ́]
      Kojo Imperf say-say to Koku that Bayo buy-Perf bike
      'Kojo is telling Koku that Bayo bought a bike'

   b. *[d̀ìdɔ̀ ná Kɔkú [dɔ̀ Báyɔ́ xɔ̀ kèkɛ́]] Kɔjó tè
       say-say to Koku that Bayo buy-Perf bike Kojo Imperf

17. With respect to the nature of the preverbal position, see also the discussion in example (18). Also relevant is the discussion in Aboh (2001b), where it is proposed that argument sharing is not a condition on verb serialization.

18. Observe also that, granting the correctness of this hypothesis, the facts discussed here are perfectly consistent with the data described in chapter 3 on the Gungbe DPs and *P*Ps that also require that nominal complements be moved to their spec positions, as an instance of spec-head relation.

19. Thanks to Chris Collins for discussing previous versions of this analysis.

20. This is consistent with the fact that only the first syllable of the verb reduplicates. For example, a disyllabic verb *sísé* 'push', *sínsín* 'melt', *sísɔ́* 'tremble' is reduplicated as *sísísé, sínsínsín, sísísɔ́*.

21. An alternative would be to say that reduplication makes it possible to insert a dummy element or an expletive in [spec AspP3]. In this perspective, the reduplicated part of the verb could be seen as a 'dummy CV' occupying [spec AspP3] the subject position of the small clause. A problem with this analysis, though, is that the prospective marker excludes such a 'dummy CV', since *nà* never undergoes reduplication. In this study, I assume that the Gungbe imperfective/prospective verb reduplication is a strategy of making Asp°3 stronger. In other words, reduplication can be seen as a strategy parallel to the *do-support* phenomenon in English in terms of Chomsky (1995).

22. See also Ndayiragije (2000), Holmberg (2000) for similar analyses.

23. See chapter 2 section 2.4.8.5 for the analysis of CP-complements.

24. The analysis proposed here will have to face the fact that contrary to Gungbe and Fongbe, where the sequence [O-(Prosp)-V-IO] is moved to [spec NomP], Gengbe seems to adopt another strategy since the nominalizer head must intervene between the verb and the indirect object. This leads to the sequence [O-V- NR]-IO, as illustrated in sentence ((v)a). In this case, the object combined with the verb and the nominalizer head form a cluster because only that sequence can be focused, leaving the indirect object in some IP-internal position ((v)b–c). That nothing can intervene between the verb and the nominalizer head ((v)d) clearly suggests that both elements form a complex head. According to my Ewe informants, the situation described here also holds for Ewegbe. Notice finally that Ewegbe and Gengbe do not have the corresponding prospective constructions, suggesting that in those languages AspP3 is not overtly realized. I leave the question open as to whether this projection is absent or transparent. That reduplication applies in both Gengbe and Ewegbe suggests that (some equivalent of) AspP3 might exist in the structural make-up of these languages (Aboh in press b). But see Fabb 1992a for a slightly different approach.

(v) a. Kɔjó lè núpó pò-ɔ̀ nɛ́ Apàn
      Kojo Imperf word say- NR to Apan
      'Kojo is speaking to Apan'

   b. núpó pò-ɔ̀ yé Kɔjó lè nɛ́ Apàn...
      word say- NR Foc Kojo Imperf to Apan

344

'Kojo is SPEAKING to Apan'

c.	*núpó	pò-ò	né	Apàn	yé	Kòjó	lè
	word	say-NR	to	Apan	Foc	Kojo	Imperf
d.	Kòjó	lè	núpó	pò	(*útó)	ò	útó
	Kojo	Imperf	word	say	a lot	NR	

'Kojo is speaking a lot'

At first sight, these facts preclude my analysis of the Gbe imperfectives in terms of NomP, but I see no problem here, since the fact that the indirect object does not belong to the sequence [O-V-Nom°] could be an indication that it has moved to some other position in the clause before verbal XP-focusing arises. Though an analysis along this line awaits further development, I nevertheless maintain my fundamental hypothesis that Gbe languages basically involve the same underlying structure. The surface order differences are taken to be a consequence of either some limited parametric variation (e.g., with respect to negation, see chapter 2) or the interaction between object shift and verb movement.

25. In a representational framework, this would mean that movement to [spec NumP] and [spec DP] is sanctioned by a licensing criterion that requires that a maximal projection endowed with a certain feature [f] be in a spec-head relationship with a head bearing the same feature and vice versa (Rizzi 1996).

26. The distinction between state and dynamic verbs is informal: these terms are used here to refer to verbs that express a state (or the state of affairs) on the one hand as opposed to verbs that express an action or a movement. See Avolonto (1992a, 1995) for a detailed discussion on similar verbs in Fongbe.

27. That NomP and AspP3 are present only if needed can be seen as a manifestation of some economic principle (e.g., avoid structure). Alternatively, it could be assumed that only NomP is subject to that requirement as a left periphery. This would mean that in the non-imperfective constructions, Asp°2 dominates an AspP3 whose head is negatively set, or [-prospective]. Accordingly, the verb must move to Asp°2 via Agr°, Asp°3, respectively. On the other hand, the object moves [spec AgroP]. The problem with this analysis is that it fails to explain naturally why reduplication is absent from the non-imperfective constructions.

28. This would mean that Bambara is a head-final language, but as I have shown, these facts can be perfectly captured in a theory that does not assume the directionality parameter (i.e., head-initial vs. head final languages).

29. Koopman's analysis is simplified here for the sake of the discussion. The reader is referred to Koopman's own work for a detailed and careful discussion.

30. That the Bambara verbs may select *ra* or *ye* depending on their argument structure is not a problem. For instance recall from Burzio (1986) that the Italian ergative verbs are assigned the auxiliary *essere* 'be', while the intransitive verbs are associated with the auxiliary *avere* 'have'. Compare the following examples:

(vi) a. Giovanni è arrivato   a'. *Giovanni ha arrivato
     Giovanni is arrived   Giovanni has arrived
   b. Giovanni ha telefonato   b'. *Giovanni è telefonato
     Giovanni has telephoned   Giovanni is telephoned

31. See Ackema (2001) for a similar conclusion.

Chapter 7

1. At this stage of the discussion, the term copy is used informally to express the semantic and morphological identity between the focused verb and its counterpart in the IP-internal position. See sections 7.1.3.2 and 7.1.4 for a more formal discussion.

2. But see McCloskey (1992) and Suñer (1993) for an analysis in terms of CP-recursion.

3. In accounting for the English cleft sentence *'it is John who read the book'*, it is commonly assumed in the literature (Chomsky 1977) that the cleft NP is base-generated in an adjoined position to CP, triggering as such movement of a wh-operator in the specifier of CP; $[_{IP}$ Expl Be $[_{CP}$ XP$_i$ $[_{CP}$ OP$_i$ $[_{IP}$...t$_i$]]]]. It will become clear in the discussion that this analysis cannot capture the Gungbe focus process that requires that the focused element be moved to the specifier position of a Focus Phrase. Many linguists working on the Gbe languages use the terms focusing and clefting interchangeably. Ndayiragije (1992, 1993), for example, refers to Fongbe focus movement as clefting. Yet he extensively argued against an analysis of Fongbe focus constructions in terms of operator movement, concluding that Fongbe clefts involve a focus marker *wè*, which heads a focus projection whose specifier hosts cleft constituents.

4. For some speakers, example (5b) is grammatical, as the occurrence of the focus marker is optional, except in case of subject focalization, where it is obligatory. But over the ten people that I consulted, seven found examples like (5b) marginal, two found them totally ungrammatical, and one considered them as grammatical as examples involving the focus marker. Similar facts in Fongbe led Ndayiragije (1993) to the conclusion that the Fongbe focus constructions manifest subject/object asymmetry. As the optional status of the focus marker *wè* is rather controversial, I will not consider examples like (5b) in this study.

5. See Puskás (1992, 1996) for a careful discussion on similar facts in Hungarian.

6. But see Chomsky (1995) for an analysis in terms of multiple specifiers.

7. For the sake of description, I define a verbal category as either a constituent that contains the verb and its complement(s) or the verb itself.

8. It has been suggested to me that, granting Chomsky's (1995) analysis of head adjunction, the problem arises how to account for the fact that verb focusing of the (b)-type excludes the focus marker, unlike XP focusing, where the focused category necessarily occurs to the left of the FM *wè*. This asymmetry can be captured by assuming that in verb focusing of the (b)-type, the verb itself encodes the feature [+f] as it appears in the left periphery to check the focus features present on Foc°. A similar fact is found in Hungarian, where the verb surfaces in focus position and bears the primary stress normally assigned to focused constituents (Puskás 1992, 1995, 1996).

(i) SZERETI Jànos Màriàt
     love-3sg-PRES John-NOM Mary-ACC
     'John LOVES Mary'

The Gungbe sentences involving both the focused verb and the FM can therefore be analyzed as types of double realization of feature [+f] by the moved verb and the FM. This may be the reason why speakers who allow this strategy seem to interpret it as 'heavy focus'. In a similar vein, the fact that some speakers reject such constructions or consider them as marginal could be interpreted as manifestation of some economy principle violation.

9. See Aboh (2002) for the analysis of relative clauses in Gbe.

10. Notice that sentences (16c–d) improve with the insertion of a resumptive pronoun in the focus position, as illustrated by examples ((ii)a–b).

(ii) a. ɖáwè   ɖê   éɔ̀   wè   Rɛ̀mí   mɔ̀
        man   that   3sg   Foc   Remi   see-Perf
        'The man that Remi saw HIM'

     b. ɖáwè   ɖê   éɔ̀   wè   wá   xwégbè
        man   that   3sg   Foc   come-Perf   house
        'The man that HE came to the house'

11. See Bianchi (1995) and Aboh (2002) for implementing Kayne's (1994) analysis of relative clauses in terms of split-C.

12. The facts that have been discussed so far are not limited to Gungbe. Recall from chapter 2 that focus constructions are attested in many other Gbe and Kwa languages (e.g., Gengbe, Yoruba). See Ameka (1992), Ndayiragije (1993), Adesola (1998), Ajiboye (1998), Manfredi (1993). In the examples, the focus phrase is moved to the position immediately to the left of a morphologically realized FM, written here in bold. Given the similarity between these constructions and those found in Gungbe, the analysis presented in this study should also be extended to other Kwa languages.

(iii) a. [àxwé wán]$_i$ yé   é   tù   t$_i$ [Gengbe]
         house that   Foc   he   build-Perf
         'He built THAT HOUSE'

      b. [Iwé]$_i$ ni   Kúnlé   rà   t$_i$ [Yoruba]
         book   Foc   Kunle   buy-Perf
         'Kunle bought A BOOK'

In his account for the Fongbe focus constructions, Ndayiragije (1993) proposed an analysis in terms of FocP, a functional projection that projects between CP and IP and whose specifier [spec FocP] hosts the focused elements. Brody (1990) made similar proposals for Hungarian. But see Puskás (1992, 1995, 1996) and Rizzi (1997) for a slightly different proposal in terms of split-C.

13. According to my Ewegbe informants, simultaneous focusing in the main and embedded clauses is impossible in Ewegbe, though the language allows for simultaneous wh-extractions in the embedded clause when there has been focusing in the main clause.

14. See also Kayne (1994) for a restrictive theory of adjunction.

15. Brody's proposal is in line with Rizzi's (1991) wh-criterion or the Neg-criterion, as proposed by Haegeman and Zanuttini (1991), Haegeman (1995a).

16. I have been assuming that the category in [spec FocP] must have the feature [+f]. But the feature [f] differs, for example, from the feature [±wh], because categories do not have it inherently. According to Brody (1990), the minimal hypothesis is that, in principle, this feature is assigned freely. He also proposed that this minimal hypothesis holds in the domain of the propositional part of the sentence, VP in Hungarian and IP in English. In this study, however, I assume [+f] is assigned freely.

17. See Rizzi 1991, 1996; Haegeman & Zanuttini 1991; Haegeman 1995a, 1996a for the discussion on the Wh- and Neg-criterion.

18. It is interesting to notice that under certain pragmatic conditions (which are still unclear to me), sentences like (33a) may improve. Compare the grammatical example ((iv)a) as

opposed to the marginal sentence ((iv)b). For the time being, I do not see how to capture this contrast in this framework.

(iv) a. díndín   mĩ   Séná   té   bɔ̀   ùn ɖó   mɔ̃-ὲ
           search-search   2pl-Nom   Sena   Imperf   Coord I did   see-him
           'Sena was LOOKING FOR YOU when I saw him'
      b. ??díndín   mĩ   Séná   té   bó bú
           search-search   2pl-Nom   Sena   Imperf   Coord disappear-Perf
           'Sena WAS LOOKING FOR YOU when he disappeared'

19. See Rizzi (1990) for the discussion of the that-t effect.
20. I thank Chris Collins for drawing my attention to this.
21. I thank Felix Ameka for discussing and providing me with these examples.
22. Verbal XP focusing in Fongbe obscures the analysis proposed here. Recall from chapters 2 and 6 that the Fongbe focus marker and the nominalizer head are homophones: they are both realized as wὲ ((v)a–b).

(v) a. Dòsà   ɖò   xwé   gbá   *(wὲ)
          Dosa   Imperf   house   build   Nom
          'Dosa IS BUILDING A HOUSE'
     b. xwé   wὲ   Dòsà   gbá
          house   Foc   Dosa   build-Perf
          'Dosa built a HOUSE (not a hut)'

Granting the analysis proposed, and taking into account speakers who accept the occurrence of the FM in verbal XP focusing, both the FM and the nominalizer head should be realized simultaneously when focusing arises. It is, however, surprising that this is never the case, as illustrated by the ungrammatical ((v)c). Instead, Fongbe speakers utter either sentence ((v)d) or ((v)e). Sentence ((v)d) is the unmarked strategy, while sentence ((v)e) is interpreted as bearing heavy focus. Notice that in both cases, speakers necessarily drop the nominalizer head.

(v) c. *xwé   gbá   wὲ   wὲ   Dòsà   ɖè
          house   build   Nom   Foc   Dosa   Imperf
     d. xwé   gbá   Dòsà   ɖè
          house   build   Dosa   Imperf
          'Dosa IS BUILDING A HOUSE'
     e. xwé   gbá   wὲ   Dòsà   ɖè
          house   build   Foc   Dosa   Imperf
          'Dosa is building a house'

To account for these data, it has been proposed (Law & Lefebvre 1992; Kinyalolo 1992) that Fongbe might involve a filter that blocks the realization of two adjacent homophonous functional heads (e.g., *wὲ wὲ). But as extensively discussed in Ndayiragije (1993), this analysis falls short in accounting for the simultaneous occurrence of the homophonous clausal and nominal determiners ɔ́ in Fongbe ((v)f).

(v) f. [dé   Dòsà   gbá   [xwé   ɔ́]]   ɔ́]
         that   Dosa   build-Perf   house   Spf[+def] Det_CL
     'That Dosa built the house'

These complications led Avolonto (1995) to conclude that the Fongbe imperfective constructions involve focusing. In that framework, the sentence-final morpheme wɛ̀ is identified as the Fongbe focus marker. Avolonto thus analyzed the apparent optional status of the element wɛ̀ in Fongbe verbal XP focusing (d–e) on a par with non-verbal XP focusing, where it was also claimed that the focus marker is optional. But if this is true, then the question immediately arises as to why the focus marker is obligatory in imperfective constructions (a). For the time being, I do not see how to properly capture the Fongbe data within the present framework and hope to return to it in future research.

23. The idea that NomP focusing is a means of focusing the nominalized verb reminds us of the discussion about clitic movement. Under the DP hypothesis, clitics are Ds (see chapters 4, 6, and references cited there). But it is traditionally assumed that clitic movement involves two steps. First, the clitic moves from its VP internal position as a maximal projection and then as a head to some agreement head positions in the clause. Yet clitic movement is considered the manifestation of some requirements on the head D (Belletti 1993; Rizzi 1993; Haegeman 1993; Chomsky 1995; Friedeman & Siloni 1997; and references cited there). In this regard, NomP movement could be equated to the first step of clitic movement. I thus assume that NomP shares both XP and X° properties just as clitics do.

24. See section 7.1.4, where it is shown that the Yoruba version of sentence (47b) is grammatical.

25. Notice that such realizations are perfectly grammatical in case of topicalization (see chapter 8 for the discussion).

(vi) blɛ́dì lɔ́   yà   dù   Rɛ̀mí   dù -   *(i)
      bread the   Top   eat   Remi   eat-Perf-it
      'As for the bread, Remi ATE it'

26. These facts could be reasonably interpreted as expressions of Chomsky's analysis of traces as copy. I can therefore propose that verb focusing differs from other types of focus movement in that it requires that the copy be spelled out at PF. There are, though, open questions as to why the copy is only spelled out in verb focusing and why the Verb copy chain should be clause-bound. See section 7.1.3.2.2 for the discussion.

27. This is in contradiction with Ndayiragije (1993), who proposed that long extraction is possible with bridge verbs in Fongbe. However, some of my Fon informants find the examples proposed by the author unacceptable or at least marginal.

(vii) gbà   (wɛ̀) Báyí   dì   dɔ̀ Kɔ̀kú   gbà   xwé   ɔ́
       destroy Foc Bayi   believe-Perf that Koku   destroy-Perf house Spf[+def]
       'Bayi believed that Koku DESTROYED the house'

See also Koopman (1984) for a similar proposal for Vata and Biloa (1997) for Tuki.

28. See section 7.2 for the functional definition of wh-operators.

29. I thank Shlonsky for discussing this analysis and helping with the Hebrew and the Palestinian data.

30. Madi is an Eastern Central Sudanic language spoken in southern Sudan and northern Uganda.

31. Note that there is no such modification in Gungbe.

32. See Williamson (1999) for the discussion of similar facts in the Izon focus constructions.

33. These data, adapted from Manfredi (1991), were submitted to the judgment of several Yoruba native speakers. As it is presented in the text, the Yoruba paradigm has been simplified for the sake of the discussion. Actually the judgments are rather subtle and may vary from one speaker to another quite significantly. For example, some speakers show the following contrast:

(viii)	a.	[Mi-maa-n-ra-iwe]	ni	Aje	maa	n	ra	iwe
		Nom-Prog-Agr-buy-book	Foc Aje	Prog	Agr buy book			
		'Aje is BUYING a book'						
	b.	??[Mi-maa-ra-iwe]	ni	Aje	maa	ra		iwe
		Nom-Prog-buy-book ni	Aje	Prog	buy	book		
		'Aje is BUYING a book'						

In addition, some speakers allow for some sort of partial AspP focusing, where the preposed sequence contains only the aspect marker and the verb:

(ix)	[Mi-maa-ra]	ni		Aje	maa	ra		iwe
	Nom-Prog-buy	Foc	Aje	Prog	buy	book		
	'Aje is BUYING a book'							

The data presented here suggest that things might be more intricate and that further research in the Yoruba focus constructions is needed. I thank Oluseye Adesola for providing these data.

34. Thanks to Prof. Oyelaran for his comments on negation in Yoruba.

35. See Puskás (1996), where it is argued that [spec ForceP] does not count as an intervening position for focus chains.

Chapter 8

1. See also chapters 2, 5, and 7 for the discussion of other markers of the Gungbe C-system.

2. See Cinque (1977, 1990); Müller and Sternefeld (1993); Haider (1990); Rizzi (1997); and references cited there for the discussion on Clitic Left Dislocation and topic constructions in the Romance and the Germanic languages.

3. See Gundel (1974) for the discussion on the topic-comment articulation.

4. Though the judgement is somewhat difficult, it is interesting to see that the Gungbe equivalents of the classical WCO examples appear to be grammatical:

(i)	a.	ménú$_i$	wè	íyá	étɔ̀n$_i$	nɔ̀	yró	t$_i$	hwɛ̀hwɛ̀ ?
		who	Foc	mother	his	Hab	call		often
		'Who his mother often called'							

b. Asíba_i wè   íyá   étòn_i   nò   yrɔ́   t_i   hwèhwè
    Asiba Foc   mother his   Hab   call   often
    'ASIBA, her mother often called'

5. Rizzi (1997) further proposed that languages may choose whether the anaphoric operator is overt or null. For example, some Germanic languages involve an overt counterpart of the English null anaphoric operator:

(ii)   Den Hans, den kenne ich seit langem
        'the Hans whom I have known for a long time'

6. The situation is different in Italian, which allows for more than one topic preceding and following focused elements, as shown in (iii), but see Rizzi (1997) for the discussion:

(iii)   a. Credo che a Gianni, QUESTO, domani, gli dovremmo dire
            'I believe that to Gianni, THIS, tomorrow we should say'
        b. Credo che QUESTO, a Gianni, domani, gli dovremmo dire
            I believe that THIS to Gianni, tomorrow, we should say

7. Irrelevant to the discussion is the fact that (27c) can also have a specific reading in the sense that *nú lé kpó* refers to a specific set of things that Kofi can buy.

8. See also Georgopoulos (1992) for the discussion on resumptive pronouns.

9. See also the examples under (20).

10. All the Italian examples discussed here are adapted from Cinque (1977, 1990).

11. See Ross (1967, 1970, 1983) for the discussion of island effects.

12. See chapter 3 where I proposed that non-specific indefinite DPs surface as 'bare nouns'.

13. See chapters 4 and 6 for a possible analysis of the structure of the Gungbe deficient pronouns and the position of object clitics in the clause. But see also Georgopoulos (1992); Shlonsky (1992); and references cited there for the discussion on resumptive pronouns.

14. Thanks to F. Ameka and J. Essegbey for drawing my attention to this.

15. See Aboh (1999) and section 8.2 for the existence of InterP in Gungbe.

16. See also Puskás (2000) for the discussion on simultaneous topicalization in Hungarian.

17. See also Cheng 1991 for the discussion on clausal typing.

18. This is consistent with Rizzi (1999), who proposes that the Italian interrogative complementizer *se* heads an interrogative projection (INT), which projects lower than ForceP between two series of topic projections, as shown in (iv):

(iv)   Force   (Top*)   Int   (Top*)   Foc   (Top*)   Fin   IP

As I said, a crucial difference between Italian and Gungbe topic constructions is that the latter only allow for one topic projection per clause. However, a quite strong generalization that arises on the basis of the Gungbe and Italian data is that the projection whose head encodes the feature [± interrogative] follows Force° but precedes a sequence of topics, which in turn precede focus: Force >Topic > Inter > Focus.

19. In terms of Tenny (1987), the subject and the object constitute the delimiting arguments.

References

Abney, Paul S. 1987. The English Noun Phrase in its Sentential Aspect. Ph.D. dissertation, MIT.

Aboh, Enoch O. 1992. Wh-movement in Gun. Petit mémoire, University of Geneva.

———. 1993. Théorie syntaxique et syntaxe du gun. Mémoire de lincense, University of Geneva.

———. 1994. "Plurilinguisme et développement." *Africa Diasporama* 3/4: 62–72.

———. 1995. "Notes on Focalization in Gungbe." *GenGenP* 1: 5–21.

———. 1996a. "A propos de la syntaxe du Gungbe." *Rivista di Grammatica Generativa* 21: 3–56.

———. 1996b. "On Argumental Topicalization in Gungbe." *GenGenP* 2: 80–93.

———. 1998a. "Focus Constructions and the Wh-criterion in Gungbe." *Linguistique Africaine* 20: 5–50.

———. 1998b. "On the Syntax of Gungbe Noun Phrases." *GenGenP* 6: 1–28.

———. 1999. *From the Syntax of Gungbe to the Grammar of Gbe*. Editions à la carte S.A., Sierre, Switzerland.

———. 2000. "Object Shift and Verb Movement in Gbe." *Generative Grammar in Geneva* 2: 1-13.

———. 2001a. "Complementation in Gbe and Saramaccan." Ms. University of Amsterdam. Paper presented at the annual meeting of the SPCL, San Francisco, Jan. 3–6, 2002.

———. 2001b. "Object Shift and Verb Serialization." Ms. University of Amsterdam. Paper presented at the research seminars in Venice and Leiden.

———. 2001c. "Review of Brousseau 1998." *Lingua* 111/10: 759–769.

———. 2001d. "Clitiques phonétiques ou clitiques tout court." In Claude Muller, Paulo de Carvalho, Laurence Labrune, Frédéric Lambert, & Katja Ploog, eds., *Clitiques et cliticisation*. H. Champion, Paris.

————. 2002. "Morphosyntaxe de la péripherie gauche nominale." In Anne Zribi-Hertz & Anne Daladier, eds., *Recherches linguistiques de Vincennes* 31: 9–26, La syntaxe de la definitude 2002. PUV, Paris.

————. in press a. "Focus Constructions across Kwa." In Cege Githiora, Heather Littlefield & Victor Manfredi, eds., *Trends in African Linguistics* 5. Africa World Press, Trenton, New Jersey

————. in press b. "Object Shift, Verb Movement and Verb Reduplication." In Guglielmo Cinque & Richard Kayne, eds., *Handbook of Syntax*. Oxford University Press, New York.

————. in press c. "Left or Right? A View from the Kwa Peripheral Positions." In David Adger, Cécile De Cat, & George Tsoulas, eds., *Volume on Peripheral Positions*. Kluwer, Dordrecht.

————. in preperation. "The Architecture of the Nominal Left Periphery: Deriving Relative and Factive Clauses." In Enoch O. Aboh, James Essegbey, & Juvénal Ndayiragije, eds., *Issues in the Syntax of Kwa*.

Ackema, Peter. 2001. "On the Relation between V-to-I and the Structure of the Inflectional Paradigm." *The Linguistic Review* 18: 233–263.

Adesola, P. Oluseye. 1998. "Sentence-final ni." In Sáàh, Kofi K. ed., *Niger-Congo Syntax & Semantics 9*. Boston University African Studies Center.

Agbedor, Paul. 1993. "Negation in Eve." In V. Manfredi & Karl Reynolds, eds., *Niger-Congo Syntax and Semantics 6*. Boston University African Studies Center.

————. 1996. "The Syntax of Ewe Personal Pronouns." *Linguistique Africaine* 16: 19–53.

Ajiboye, Oladiipo. 1998. "Ni in Moba Yoruba." In Kofi K. Sáàh, ed., *Niger-Congo Syntax & Semantics 9*. Boston University African Studies Center.

Alexiadou, Artemis, & Elena Anagnostopoulou. 2001. "The Subject-in-situ Generalization and the Role of Case in Driving Computations." *Linguistic Inquiry* 32:193–231.

Alexiadou, Artemis, & Chris Wilder. 1998. "Adjectival Modification and Multiple Determiners." In A. Alexiadou & C. Wilder, eds., *Possessors, Predicates and Movement in the Determiner Phrase*. Benjamins, Amsterdam.

Aljovic, Nadira. 2000. Recherches sur la morpho-syntaxe du groupe nominal en serbo-croate. Ph.D. dissertation, Paris 8.

Ameka, Felix. 1991. Ewe: Its Grammatical and Illocutionary Devices. Ph.D. dissertation, Australian National University, Canberra.

————. 1992. "Focus Constructions in Ewe and Akan: A Comparative Perspective." *MIT Working Papers in Linguistics* 17: 1–25.

Ansre, Gilbert. 1961. "The Tonal Structure of Ewe." *Hartford Studies in Linguistics*. Hartford Seminary Foundation.

————. 1966a. "The Verbid—A Caveat to Serial Verbs." *The Journal of West African Languages* 1: 29–32.

————. 1966b. The Grammatical Units of Ewe: A Study of Their Structure Clauses and Systems. Ph.D. dissertation, University of London.

Avolonto, Aimé. 1992a. De l'étude sémantico-syntaxique des marqueurs pré-verbaux à la structure de la phrase en fongbe. Ms. University of Quebec at Montreal.

————. 1992b. "AspP et la catégorie INFL en fongbe." *The Journal of West African Languages* 22: 97–113.

————. 1992c. "Les particules modales en fongbe et la nature de INFL dans les phrases injonctives." *MIT Working Papers in Linguistics* 17: 1–25.

————. 1995. Pour une approche minimaliste des verbes à objets inhérents en Fongbe. Ph.D. dissertation, University of Quebec at Montreal.

Awóbùlúyì, Oládélé. 1979. *Essentials of Yoruba Grammar*. Oxford University Press. Ibadan, Nigeria.

Awóyalé, Yíwolá. 1974. Studies in the Syntax and Semantics of Yoruba Nominalisations. Ph.D. dissertation, University of Illinois, Urbana-Champaign.

————. 1997. "Object Positions in Yoruba." In Rose-Marie Déchaine & Victor Manfredi, eds., *Object Position in Benue-Kwa*. The Holland Academic Graphics, The Hague.

Baker, C. Mark. 1989. "Object Sharing and Projection in Serial Verb Constructions." *Linguistic Inquiry* 20: 513–553.

Baltin, Mark Rueben. 1982. "A Landing Site Theory of Movement Rules." *Linguistic Inquiry* 13: 1–38.

Bámgbósé, Ayo. 1971. "The Verb-infinitive Phrase in Yoruba." *Journal of West African Linguistics* 8: 37–52.

————. 1974. "On Serial Verbs and Verbal Status." *Journal of West African Languages* 9: 17–48.

Badejo, B. Rotimi. 1983. "La topicalisation en yoruba." *Current Approach to African Linguistics*. Foris, Dordrecht.

Bayer, Josef. 1997. "CP-Extraposition as Argument Shift." In Dorothee Beerman, David LeBlanc, & Henk van Riemsdijk, eds., *Rightward Movement*. Benjamins, Amsterdam.

Belletti, Adriana. 1990. *Generalized Verb Movement*. Rosenberg & Sellier, Turin.

————. 1993. "Case Checking and Clitic Placement." *GenGenP* 1: 101–118.

————. 2001. "Agreement Projections." In Mark Baltin & Chris Collins, eds., *The Contemporary Handbook of Syntactic Theory*. Blackwell, Oxford.

Benincà, Paola. 2001. "The position of Topic and Focus in the left periphery." In Guglielmo Cinque & Giampaolo Salvi, eds., *Current Studies in Italian Syntax, Essays Offered to Lorenzo Renzi*. Foris, Dordrecht.

Benveniste, Emile. 1966. "La nature des pronoms." *Problèmes de linguistique générale 1*. Gallimard, Paris.

Bernstein, Judy. 1991. Nominal Enclitics in Romance. *MIT Working Papers in Linguistics* 14: 51–66.

————. 1993. Topics in the Syntax of Nominal Structure across Romance. Ph.D. dissertation, City University of New York.

————. 1997. "Demonstratives and Reinforcers in Romance and Germanic languages." *Lingua* 102: 87–113.

————. 2001a. "Focusing the 'Right' Way in Romance Determiner Phrases." *Probus* 13–1: 1–29.

————. 2001b. "The DP Hypothesis: Identifying Clausal Properties in the Nominal Domain." In M. Baltin & C. Collins, eds., *The Handbook of Contemporary Syntactic Theory*. Blackwell, Oxford.

Beukema, Frits, & Peter Coopmans. 1989. "A Government-Binding Perspective on the Imperative in English." *Journal of Linguistics* 25: 417–436.

Bianchi, Valentina. 1995. Consequences of Antisymmetry for the Syntax of Headed Relative Clauses. Ph.D. dissertation, Scuola Normale Superiore, Pisa.

Bickerton, Derek. 1981. *Roots of Language*. Karoma, Ann Arbor.

Biloa, Edmond. 1997. *Functional Categories and the Syntax of Focus in Tuki*. Lincom Studies in African Linguistics 02. Lincom Europa, München, Newcastle.

Bitjaa Kody, Z. D. 1993. "Le système tonal du bassa." *The Journal of West African Languages* 23: 65–73.

Bole-Richard, Remy. 1983. *Systématique Phonologique et Grammatical d'un Parler Ewe: le Gen-Mina du Sud-Togo et Sud-Bénin*. L'Harmattan, Paris.

Bresnan, Joan, & Sam A. Mchombo. 1987. "Topic, Pronoun and Agreement in Chichewa." *Language* 63: 741–782.

Brody, Michael. 1990. "Some Remarks on the Focus Field in Hungarian." *UCL Working Papers in Linguistics* 201–25.

————. 1995. "Focus and Checking Theory." In István Kenesei, ed., *Approaches to Hungarian* vol 5. JATE, Szeged.

Brousseau, Anne-Marie, & John S. Lumsden. 1992. "Nominal Structure in Fongbe." *The Journal of West African Languages* 22: 5–25.

Brugè, Laura. 1996. "Demonstrative Movement in Spanish: A Comparative approach." *University of Venice Working Papers in Linguistics* 6.

Bruyn, Adrienne. 1995. *Grammaticalization in Creoles: The Development of Determiners and Relative Clauses in Sranan*. Studies in Language and Language Use 21. IFOTT, Amsterdam.

Büring, Daniel, & Katharina Hartmann. 1997. "The Kayne Mutiny." In Dorothee Beerman, David LeBlanc, & Henk van Riemsdijk, eds., *Rightward Movement*. Benjamins, Amsterdam.

Burzio, Luigi. 1986. *Italian Syntax, A Government and Binding Approach*. Reidel, Dordrecht.

Campbell, Richard. 1996. "Specificity Operators in SpecDP." *Studia Linguistica* 2: 161–188.

Capo, Hounkpati B. C. 1983. "Nasal Vowels and Nasalized Consonants in Gbe." *Current Approach to African Linguistics*.

————. 1988. *Renaissance du Gbe: Réflexions critiques et constructives sur l'Eve, le Fon, le Gen, l'Aja, le Gun etc.* Helmut Buske, Hamburg.

————. 1991. *A Comparative Phonology of Gbe*. Publications in African Languages and Linguistics. Foris, Berlin, New York.

————. Forthcoming. De l'évolution du proto-Gbe au gungbe actuel. Ms. Université Nationale du Bénin, Labo Gbe.

Cardinaletti, Anna. 1994. "On the Internal Structure of Pronominal DPs." *The Linguistic Review* 31: 319–355.

————. 1997. "Subjects and Clause Structure." In Liliane Haegeman, ed., *The New Comparative Syntax*. Longman Linguistics Library, London.

Cardinaletti, Anna, & Ian Robert. 1991. "Clause Structure and X-second." In Wynn Chao and Geoffrey Horrocks, eds., *Levels of Representation*. Foris, Dordrecht.

Cardinaletti, Anna, & Michal Starke. 1996. "Deficient Pronouns: A View from Germanic. A Study in the Unified Description of Germanic and Romance." In Höskuldur Thráinsson, Samuel David Epstein, & Steve Peter, eds., *Studies in Comparative Germanic Syntax. Studies in Natural Language & Linguistic Theory* 38. Kluwer, Dordrecht.

Cardinaletti, Anna, & Michal Starke. 1999. "The Typology of Structural Deficiency: A Case Study of the Three Classes of Pronouns." In Henk Van Riemsdijk, ed., *Clitics in the Languages of Europe*. Mouton de Gruyter, Berlin.

Carstens, M. Vicky. 1988. "Serial Verbs in Yoruba." Paper presented at the 2nd workshop in Niger-Congo Syntax and Semantics. MIT, Cambridge, Mass.

————. 1991. The Morphology and Syntax of Determiner Phrases in Kiswahili. Ph.D. dissertation, UCLA.

————. 1997. "Empty Nouns in Bantu Locatives." *The Linguistic Review* 14: 361–410.

————. 2000. "Concord in Minimalist Theory." *Linguistic Inquiry* 31: 319–355.

CENALA. 1990. "Alphabet des Langues nationales." CENALA, Bénin.

Cheng, Lisa Lai-Shen. 1991. On the Typology of Wh-questions. Ph.D. dissertation, MIT.

Chomsky, Noam. 1977. "On Wh-movement." In Peter W. Culicover, ed., *Formal Syntax*. Academic Press, New York, San Francisco.

————. 1981. *Lectures on Government and Binding*. Foris, Dordrecht.

————. 1986. *Barriers*. MIT Press, Cambridge, Mass.

————. 1991. "Some Notes on Economy of Derivation and Representation." In Robert Freidin, ed., *Principles and Parameters in Comparative Grammar*. MIT Press, Cambridge, Mass.

————. 1992. *A Minimalist Program for Linguistic Theory*. MIT Occasional Papers in Linguistics, Cambridge, Mass.

————. 1993. "A Minimalist Program for Linguistic Theory." In Kenneth Hale and Samuel J. Keyser, eds., *The View from Building 20: Essays in Linguistics in Honor of Sylvain Bromberger*. MIT Press, Cambridge, Mass.

————. 1995. *The minimalist Program*. MIT Press, Cambridge, Mass.

————. 1999. "Derivation by Phase." In Michael Kenstowicz, ed., *Ken Hale: A Life in Languages*. MIT Press, Cambridge, Mass.

————. 2000. "Minimalist Inquiries: The Framework." In Robert Martin, David Michaels, & Juan Uriagereka, eds., *Step by Step: Essays in Honor of Howard Lasnik*. MIT Press, Cambridge, Mass.

————. 2001. Beyond Explanatory Adequacy. Ms. MIT.

Chomsky, Noam, & Howard Lasnik. 1977. "Filters and Control." *Linguistic Inquiry* 8: 425–504.

————. 1993. "Principles and Parameters Theory." In Joachim Jacobs, Arnim von Stechow, Wolfgang Sternefeld, & Theo Vennemann, eds., *Syntax: An*

International Handbook of Contemporary Research, Walter de Gruyter, Berlin, New York.

Cinque, Guglielmo. 1977. "The Movement Nature of Left Dislocation." *Linguistic Inquiry* 8: 397–412.

———. 1990. *Types of A'-Dependencies.* MIT Press, Cambridge, Mass.

———. 1993. "A Null Theory of Phrase and Compound Stress." *Linguistic Inquiry* 24: 239–297.

———. 1994. "On the Evidence for Partial N-movement in the Romance DP." In Guglielmo Cinque, Jan Koster, Jean-Yves Pollock, Luigi Rizzi, & Raffaella Zanuttini, eds., *Paths towards Universal Grammar.* Georgetown University Press, Washington, D. C.

———. 1996. "The "Antisymmetric" Program: Theoretical and Typological Implications." *Journal of Linguistics* 32: 447–464.

———. 1999. *Adverbs and Functional Heads, A Cross-linguistic Perspective.* Oxford University Press, New York.

Clements, Georges N. 1972. The Verbal Syntax of Ewe. Ph.D. dissertation, University of London.

———. 1975. "Analogical Reanalysis in Syntax: The Case of Ewe Tree-Grafting." *Linguistic Inquiry* 6: 3–51.

———. 1978. "Tone and Syntax in Ewe." In Donna Jo Napoli, ed., *Elements of Tone, Stress and Intonation.* Georgetown University Press, Washington, D.C.

———. 1983. "The Hierarchical Representation of Tone Features." In Ivan R. Dihoff, ed., *Current Approaches to African Linguistics.* Foris, Dordrecht.

Collins, Chris. 1993. Topic in Ewe Syntax. Ph.D. dissertation, MIT.

———. 1994a. Argument Sharing in Serial Verb Constructions. Ms. Cornell University.

———. 1994b. The Factive Construction in Kwa. Ms. Cornell University.

———. 1996. *Local Economy.* MIT Press, Cambridge, Mass.

———. 1997. "Argument Sharing in Serial Verb Constructions." *Linguistic Inquiry* 28: 461–497.

———. 2001. "Economy Conditions in Syntax." In Mark Baltin & Chris Collins, eds., *The Contemporary Handbook of Syntactic Theory.* Blackwell, Oxford.

Cowper, Elizabeth. 1991. "Infinitival Complements of Have." In Claire Lefebvre, John Lumsden & Lisa Travis, eds., *Functional Categories.* McGill/Queen's University Press.

Crisma, Paola. 1991. Functional Categories inside the Noun Phrase: A study on the Distribution of Nominal Modifiers. Ph.D. dissertation, University of Venice.

———. 1996. "On the Configurational Nature of Adjectival Modification." In Karen Zagona, ed., *Grammatical Theory and Romance Languages.* Benjamins, Amsterdam.

Culicover, Peter. 1992. "Topicalisation, Inversion and Complementizers in English." In D. Delfitto et al., eds., *Going Romance and Beyond.* OTS Working Papers. University of Utrecht.

———. 1996. "On Distinguishing A'-Movements." *Linguistic Inquiry* 27: 445–463.

Culicover, Peter W., & Michael S. Rochemont. 1990. "Extraposition and the Complement Principle." *Linguistic Inquiry* 21: 23–47.

da Cruz, Maxime. 1992. "ECP et l"alternance nu/na en fongbe." Ms. University of Quebec at Montreal.

————. 1993. Les constructions sérielles du fongbe: approches sémantique et syntaxique. Ph.D. dissertation, University of Quebec at Montreal.

————. 1995. "Aspectual Verbs fó, vɔ̀ 'finish' in Fongbe." *The Linguistic Review* 12: 361–380.

————. 1997. "Serial Verb Constructions and Null Arguments in Fon." In Rose-Marie Déchaine & Victor Manfredi, eds., *Object Positions in Benue-Kwa*. The Holland Academic Graphics. The Hague.

da Cruz, Maxime, & Aimé Avolonto. 1993. "Un cas d"harmonie vocalique en fongbe." In Khim Alain & Claire Lefebvre, eds., *Aspects de la grammaire du fongbe, Etude de phonologie, de syntaxe et de sémantique*. Langues et Cultures Africaines 18. Peeters, Paris.

Damonte, Frederico. 2002. The Syntax and Semantics of Salentino *ku*. Paper presented at the 28th Incontro di Grammatica Generativa, March 2002, Lecce, Italy.

DAPR. 1984. "Initiation a la transcription et l'enseignement du Gun." Direction de l'Alphabétisation et de la Presse Rurale. Rep. of Bénin.

Déchaine, Rose-Marie. 1993. *Predicates across categories; towards a category-neutral syntax*. PhD. Dissertation, University of Massachusetts, Amherst.

————. 1997. "Event Serialisation and Event Composition." In Rose-Marie Déchaine & Victor Manfredi, eds., *Object Positions in Benue-Kwa*. The Holland Academic Graphics, The Hague.

Den Besten, Hans. 1977. "On the Interaction of Root Transformations and Lexical Deletive Rules." In *Studies in West Germanic Syntax*. Ph.D. dissertation, University of Tilburg.

Diesing, Molly. 1992. *Indefinites*. MIT Press, Cambridge, Mass.

Dobrovie-Sorin, Carmen. 1987. "A propos de la structure du groupe nominal en roumain." *Rivista di Grammatica Generativa* 12: 123–152.

————. 1994. *The Syntax of Romanian: Comparative Studies in Romance*. Mouton de Gruyter, Berlin, New York.

Duffield, Nigel. 1993. "On Case Checking and NPI Licensing in Hiberno-English." *Rivista di Linguistica* 5: 215–244.

Durrleman, Stephanie. 1999. The Architecture of the Clause in Jamaican Creole. Mémoire de licence, University of Geneva.

Enç, Mürvet. 1991. "The Semantics of Specificity." *Linguistic Inquiry* 22: 1–26.

Epstein, Samuel, D., Höskuldur Thráinsson, & Jan Wouter Zwart, eds. 1996. *Minimal Ideas*. John Benjamins, Amsterdam.

Essegbey, James. 1999. *Inherent Complement Verbs Revisited: Towards an Understanding of Argument Structure in Ewe*. MPI series, Ponsen & Looijen bv, Wageningen.

Fabb, Nigel. 1992a. "Reduplication and Object Movement in Ewe and Fon." *Journal of African Languages and Linguistics* 13: 1–39.

————. 1992b. "The Licensing of Fon Verbs." *Journal of West African Languages* 22: 27–34.

Fabb, Nigel, & Mairi Blackings. 1995. Verb Movement in Madi. Ms. University of Strathclyde.

Frechet, Anne-Lise. 1990. "Le Downdrift en Gungbe." *Cahier d'Etudes Linguistiques* 3: 6–28. Université Nationale du Bénin.

Friedemann, Marc-Ariel, & Tal Siloni. 1997. "Agr_{object} is not $Agr_{participle}$." *The Linguistic Review* 14: 69–96.

Georgopoulos, Carol. 1992. *Syntactic Variables, Resumptive Pronouns and A' Binding in Palauan. Studies in Natural Language & Linguistic Theory.* Kluwer, Dordrecht, Boston, London.

Giusti, Giuliana. 1991. "The Categorial Status of Quantified Nominals." *Linguistische Berichte* 136: 438–452.

———. 1994. "Heads and Modifiers across Determiners: Evidence from Rumanian." In G. Cinque & G. Giusti, eds., *Advances in Rumanian. Linguistics Today* 10, Benjamins, Amsterdam.

———. 1997. "The Categorial Status of Determiners." In Liliane Haegeman ed., *The New Comparative Syntax.* Longman Linguistics Library, London.

Giusti, Giuliana, & Nedzad Leko. 1995. "Definite and Indefinite Expressions in Bosnian." *Problemi di morfosintassi delle lingue slave* 5: 127–145.

Givón, Talmy. 1979. "Language Typology in Africa: A Critical Review." *Journal of African Languages and Linguistics* 1: 199–224.

Greenberg, Joseph Harold. 1966. "Some Universals of Grammar with Particular Reference to the Order of Meaningful Elements." In J. H. Greenberg, ed., *Universals of Language*, 2nd ed. MIT Press, Cambridge, Mass.

Grimshaw, Jane. 1991. Extended Projections. Ms. Rutgers University.

Grosu, Alexander. 1973. "On the Status of the So-called Right Roof Constraint." *Language* 49: 294–311.

———. 1988. "On the Distribution of Genitive Phrases in Rumanian." *Linguistics* 26: 931–949.

Gundel, Jeanette K. 1974. *The Role of Topic and Comment in Linguistic Theory.* Indiana University Linguistic Club, Bloomington, Indiana.

Haddican, Bill. 2001. Gengbe Typing Morphemes and Determiners. Ms. New York University.

Haeberli, Eric. 1993. "Scrambling and Feature Checking." *GenGenP* 2: 26–47.

Haegeman, Liliane. 1993. "Object clitics in West Flemish and the identification of A/A" positions." *GenGenP* 1: 1–30.

———. 1994. *Introduction to Government and Binding Theory*, 2nd ed. Blackwell, Oxford, UK, and Cambridge, Mass.

———. 1995a. *The Syntax of Negation.* Cambridge University Press, Cambridge.

———. 1995b. "IPP constructions and V-movement in West Flemish." *GenGenP* 3: 50–76.

———. 1996a. "Negative Inversion, the Neg-Criterion and the Structure of CP." *GenGenP* 4: 94–118.

———. 1996b. "Verb Second, the Split CP and Null Subjects in Early Dutch Finite Clauses." *GenGenP* 4: 133–175.

———. 1996c. "Finite V-movement in Embedded Clauses in West Flemish." *South African Journal of Linguistics.* Special Issue on Minimalism 29: 69–104.

————. 1998a. Extraposed Clauses in the West Germanic SOV Languages. Ms. University of Geneva.

————. 1998b. "Verb Movement in Embedded Clauses in West Flemish." *Linguistic Inquiry* 29: 631–656.

————. 1998c. Embedded Verb Positions and Remnant Movement in the West Germanic SOV languages. Ms. University of Geneva.

————. 1998d. "V-positions and the Middle Field in West Flemish." *Syntax* 1: 259–999.

Haegeman, Liliane, & Jacqueline Guéron. 1999. *English Grammar. A Generative Perspective*. Blackwell, Oxford.

Haegeman, Liliane, & Raffaella Zanuttini. 1991. "Negative Heads and the NEG Criterion." *The Linguistic Review* 8: 233–251.

Haider, Hubert. 1990. "Topicalization and other Puzzles of German Syntax." In Günther Grewendorf & Wolfgang Sternefeld, eds., *Scrambling and Barriers*. Benjamins, Amsterdam.

————. 1997. "Extraposition." In Dorothee Beerman, David LeBlanc, & Henk van Riemsdijk, eds., *Rightward Movement*. Benjamins, Amsterdam.

Hawkins, John A. 1983. *Word Order Universals*. Academic Press, New York, London.

————. 1990. "A Parsing Theory of Word Order Universals." *Linguistic Inquiry* 21: 223–261.

Hazoumè, Marc Laurent. 1978. "Etude descriptive du Gungbe: phonologie, grammaire, suivie d'un essai sur la segmentation." Institut National des langues et civilisations orientales, Paris.

————. 1990. *Essai de classification synchronique*. Centre National de Linguistique Appliquée, Cotonou, Bénin.

Heim, Irene R. 1982. The Semantics of Definite and Indefinite Noun Phrases. Ph.D. dissertation, University of Massachusetts, Amherst.

Heine, Bernd. 1980. "Language Typology and Linguistic Reconstruction: The Niger-Congo Case." *Journal of Languages and Linguistics* 2: 95–112.

Hoekstra, Eric. 1997. "Analysing Linear Asymmetries in the Verb Clusters of Dutch and Frisian and their Dialects." In Dorothee Beerman, David LeBlanc, & Henk van Riemsdijk, eds., *Rightward Movement*. Benjamins, Amsterdam.

Holmberg, Anders. 1986. Word Order and Syntactic Features in the Scandinavian Languages and English. Ph.D. dissertation, University of Stockholm.

————. 1999. "Remarks on Holmberg's Generalization." *Studia Linguistica* 53: 1–39.

————. 2000. "Scandinavian Stylistic Fronting: How Any Category Can Become an Expletive." *Linguistic Inquiry* 31: 445–483.

————. 2001. "The Syntax of Yes and No in Finnish." *Studia Linguistica* 55: 140–174.

Houngues, Désiré M. K. 1997. Topics in the Syntax of Mina. Ph.D. dissertation, Boston University Graduate School of Arts and Sciences, Boston.

Horvàth, Julia. 1986. *Focus in the Theory of Grammar and the Syntax of Hungarian*. Foris, Dordrecht.

————. 1995. "Structural Focus, Structural Case and the Notion of Feature Assignment." In Katalin E. Kiss, ed., *Discourse Configurational Languages*. Oxford University Press, London.

Ihsane, Tabea, & Genoveva Puskás. 2001. "Specific Is not Definite." *Generative Grammar in Geneva* 2: 39–54

Inkelas, Sharon & Draga Zec, eds. 1990. *The Phonology-Syntax Connection*. University of Chicago Press, Chicago.

Jobe, Alieu. 1992. "Le répertoire linguistique de l'enfant gambien." Presses Universitaires de Grenoble.

Jondoh, E. Edina. 1981. Some Aspects of the Predicate Phrase in Gengbe. U.M.I. Dissertation Series.

Johnson, Kyle. 1991. "Object Positions." *Natural Language and Linguistic Theory* 9: 577–635.

Jun, Jae-yeon. 1999. Recherches sur le nombre en coréen: syntaxe, sémantique et morphologie. Ph.D. dissertation, Université Paris 8.

Kamp, Hans. 1981. "A Theory of Truth and Semantic Representation." In Jeroen A. G. Groenendijk, Theodoor M. V. Janssen, & Martin J. B. Stockhof, eds., *Formal Methods in the Study of Language*. Mathematisch Centrum, Amsterdam.

Kangni, Atah-Ekou. 1989. *La syntaxe du Gɛ. Etude syntaxique d'un parler Gbe (Ewe). Le Gen du Sud-Togo*. Peter Lang, Frankfurt.

Kato, Yasuhiko. 1993. "Negative Polarity, Feature Checking, and an Inflection Parameter." *Sophia Linguistica* 33: 85–99.

Kayne, Richard S. 1975. *French Syntax*, MIT Press, Cambridge, Mass.

————. 1992. "Italian Negative Infinitival Imperatives and Clitic Climbing." In Liliane Tasmowski, & Anne Zribi-Hertz, eds., *De la musique à la linguistique: Hommages à Nicolas Ruwet*. Communication & Cognition, Ghent.

————. 1985. "L'accord du participe passé en français et en italien." *Modèles linguistiques* 7: 73–89.

————. 1986. "Connexité et inversion du sujet." In Mitsou Ronat & Daniel Couquaux, eds., *La grammaire modulaire*. Editions de Minuit, Paris.

————. 1989. "Facets of Romance Past Participle Agreement." In Paola Beninca, ed., *Dialect variation & the theory of grammar*. Foris, Dordrecht.

————. 1991. "Romance Clitics, Verb Movement and PRO." *Linguistic Inquiry* 22: 647–686.

————. 1994. *The Antisymmetry of Syntax*. MIT Press, Cambridge, Mass.

————. 1998. Person Morphemes and Reflexives. Ms. NYU.

Kinyalolo, Kasangati K. W. 1991. Syntactic Dependencies and the Spec-head Agreement Hypothesis in Kigela. Ph.D. dissertation, University of California, at Los Angeles.

————. 1992. "A Note on Word Order in the Progressive and Prospective in Fon." *The Journal of West African Languages* 22: 35–51.

————. 1993. "On Some Syntactic Properties of ɖò in Fon." *Lingua* 91: 201–233.

————. 1995. "Licensing in DP in Fɔn." *Linguistique Africaine* 14: 61–92.

————. 1997. "The Verbal Gerund in Fon." In Rose-Marie Déchaine & Victor Manfredi, eds., *Object Position in Benue-Kwa*. The Holland Academic Graphics, The Hague.

Kiss, Katalin E. 1987. *Configurationality in Hungarian*. Reidel, Dordrecht.

Kitagawa, Yoshihisa. 1986. Subject in Japanese and English. Ph.D. dissertation, University of Massachusetts, Amherst.

Klima, Edward S. 1964. "Negation in English." In Jerry A. Fodor & Jerrold Katz, eds., *The Structure of Language*. Prentice Hall, Englewood, Cliffs, NJ.

Knittel, Marie-Laurence. 1998. "La structure morphosyntaxique des syntagmes nominaux possessivés du Hongrois." In Jacqueline Guéron & Anne Zribi-Hertz, eds., *La grammaire de la possession*. Pulidix, Paris, Nanterre.

Koopman, Hilda. 1984. *The Syntax of Verbs: From Verb Movement Rules in the Kru Languages to Universal Grammar*. Foris, Dordrecht.

————. 1992. "On the Absence of Case Chains in Bambara." *Natural Language and Linguistics Theory* 10: 555–594.

————. 1993. The Internal Structure of the Pronominal DP, and the Syntactic Distribution of Pronouns. Paper read at the research seminar, University of Geneva.

————. 2000a. "The Internal and External Distribution of Pronominal DPs." In *The Syntax of Specifier and Heads*. Routledge, London.

————. 2000b. *The Syntax of Specifier and Heads*. Routledge, London.

Koopman, Hilda, & Dominique Sportiche. 1991. "The Position of Subjects." *Lingua* 85: 211–258.

Koster, Jan. 1975. "Dutch as an SOV Language." *Linguistic Analysis* 1: 111–136.

————. 1989. "Left-right Asymmetries in the Dutch Complementizer System." In Dany Jaspers, Wim Klooster, Yvan Putseys, & Pieter Seuren, eds., *Sentential Complementation and the Lexicon. Studies in Honour of Wim de Geest*. Foris, Dordrecht.

Kuroda, Yuki. 1986. Whether We Agree or Not. Ms. UCSD.

Laenzlinger Christopher. 1998. *Comparative Studies in Word Order Variation. Adverbs, Pronouns, and Clause Structure in Romance and Germanic*. Benjamins, Amsterdam.

Laka, Itziar. 1990. Negation in Syntax: On the Nature of Functional Categories and Projections. Ph.D. dissertation, MIT.

————. 1993. "Negation in Syntax: the View from Basque." *Rivista di Linguistica* 5: 245–273.

Larson, Richard K. 1988. "On the Double Object Construction." *Linguistic Inquiry* 19: 335–391.

Lasnik, Howard, & Tim Stowell. 1991. "Weakest Cross-Over." *Linguistic Inquiry* 22: 687–720.

Law, Paul, & Claire Lefebvre. 1992. "On Predicate Cleft." Glow, Madrid, Spain.

————. 1995. "On the Relationship Between Event and Predicate Cleft in the Kwa Languages: The Case of Fongbe." *Linguistique Africaine* 14: 7– 47.

Lefebvre, Claire. 1990. "Establishing a Syntactic Category of P in Fon." *The Journal of West African Languages* 1: 45–65.

————. 1991. "On the Distribution of Clausal wè in Fongbe." *The Journal of West African Languages* 2: 21–35.

————. 1991a. "La distribution du déterminant et des complémenteurs en créole Haïtien." *Recherches Linguistiques* 20: 21–43.

————. 1991b. *Serial Verbs: Grammatical, Comparative and Cognitive Approaches.* Benjamins, Amsterdam.

————. 1992. "Agr in Languages Without Person and Number Agreement: The case of the Clausal Determiner in Haitian and Fon." *Canadian Journal of Linguistics* 37:137–156.

————. 1995a. "Les marqueurs préverbaux du Fongbe et du créole haïtien: étude de sémantique comparative." *Linguistique Africaine* 14: 155–180.

————. 1995b. "PPs Headed by the Fon Preposition nÚ 'to' Are Syntactic Adjuncts." *Linguistique Africaine* 14: 93–105.

————. 1998. *Creole Genesis and the Acquisition of Grammar: The Case of Haitian Creole.* Cambridge University Press, Cambridge.

Longobardi, Giuseppe. 1994. "Reference and Proper Names: A Theory of N-Movement in Syntax and Logical Form." *Linguistic Inquiry* 25: 609–665.

————. 2001. "The Structure of DPs: Some Principles, Parameters and Problems." In M. Baltin & C. Collins, eds., *Handbook of Syntactic Theory.* Blackwell, Oxford.

Lord, Carol. 1973. "Serial Verbs in Transition." *Studies in African Linguistics* 4: 269–295.

Lumsden, John, & Claire Lefebvre. 1990. "On the Haitian Predicate Cleft Construction." In John P. Hutchison & Victor Manfredi, eds., *Current Issues in African Linguistics* 7. Foris, Dordrecht.

Maling, Joan. 1972. "On Gapping and the Order of Constituents." *Linguistic Inquiry* 3: 101–108.

Mahajan, Anoop. 1997. "Rightward Scrambling." In Dorothee Beerman, David LeBlanc, & Henk van Riemsdijk, eds., *Rightward Movement.* Benjamins, Amsterdam.

Manfredi, Victor. 1991. Agbo and Ehungbo: Igbo Linguistic Consciousness, Its Origins and Limits. Ph.D. dissertation, Havard University.

————. 1993. "Verb Focus in the Typology of Kwa/Kru and Haitian. In Francis Byrne & Don Winford, eds., *Focus and Grammatical Relations in Creole Languages.* Benjamins, Amsterdam.

————. 1997. "Aspectual Licensing and Object Shift." In Rose-Marie Déchaine & Victor Manfredi, eds., *Object Position in Benue-Kwa.* The Holland Academic Graphics, The Hague.

May, Robert. 1985. *Logical Form, Its Structure and Derivation.* MIT Press, Cambridge, Mass.

Mboua, Clarisse. 1999. Le système aspecto-modal de l'ogbru: de la description des marqueurs préverbaux à la structure de la phrase en ogbru. Mémoire de DES, University of Geneva.

McCloskey, James. 1992. "Adjunction, Selection and Embedded Verb Second." Working Paper LRC-92–07, Linguistics Research Center, University of California, Santa Cruz.

Motapanyane, Virgina. 1995. *Theoretical Implications of Complementation in Romanian*. Padova Unipress.

Müller, Gereon. 1995. *A-bar Syntax*. Mouton de Gruyter, Berlin.

———. 1997. "Extraposition as Remnant Movement." In Dorothee Beerman, David LeBlanc, & Henk van Riemsdijk, eds., *Rightward Movement*. Benjamins, Amsterdam.

———. 1998. *A Derivational Approach to Remnant Movement in German*. Studies in Natural Language and Linguistic Theory. Kluwer, Dordrecht.

Müller, Gereon, & Wolfgang Sternefeld. 1993. "Improper Movement and Unambiguous Binding." *Linguistic Inquiry* 24: 461–507.

———. 1996. "A-bar Chain Formation and Economy of Derivation." *Linguistic Inquiry* 27: 480–511.

Nash, Léa. 1997. "La partition personnelle dans les langues ergatives." In Anne Zribi-Hertz ed., *Les pronoms: morphologie, syntaxe et typologie*. PUV, Paris 8.

Ndayiragije, Juvénal. 1992. "Structure syntaxique des clivées en Fɔn." *The Journal of West African Languages* 22: 63–95.

———. 1993. Syntaxe et sémantique du clivage du prédicat en fongbe. Ph.D. dissertation, University of Quebec at Montreal.

———. 2000. "Strenghening PF." *Linguistic Inquiry* 31: 485–512.

Omoruyi, Thomas, O. 1989. "Focus and Question Formation in Edo." Studies in African Linguistics 20: 279–299.

Ouhalla, Jamal. 1990. "Sentential Negation, Relativized Minimality and the Aspectual status of Auxiliaries." *Linguistic Review* 7: 183–231.

———. 1992. "Focus in Standard Arabic: the Identification Requirement and the Principles of Economy." Ms. Queen Mary and Westfield College, London.

———. 1993. "Negation, Focus and Tense: the Arabic *maa* and *laa*." *Rivista di Linguistica* 5: 275–298.

Panagiotidis, Phoevos. 2000. "Demonstrative Determiners and Operators: The Case of Greek. *Lingua* 110: 717–742.

———. 2001. Pronominals, Empty Nouns & φ Features. Paper read at the ULCL seminar, Leiden University.

Pattanaik, Umesh Prasad. 1996. The Nature and Function of the Question Words: Ka'an and Ki in Oriya. Ms. University of Geneva.

Pearson, Matthew. 1998. Two Types of VO Languages. Ms. UCLA.

———. 2000. "Two Types of VO Languages." In Peter Svenonius, ed. *The Derivation of VO and OV*. Benjamins, Amsterdam.

Pesetsky, David. 1987. "Wh-in-situ: Movement and Unselective Binding." In Eric Reuland, & Alice ter Meulen, eds., *The Representation of (In)definiteness*. MIT Press, Cambridge, Mass.

Picallo, Carme M. 1984. "The INFL Node and the Null Subject Parameter." *Linguistic Inquiry* 15: 75–102.

Plann, Susan. 1986. "Substantive: A Neutralized Syntactic Category in Spanish." In Ivonne Bordelois, Heles Contreras, & Karen Zagona, eds., *Generative Studies in Spanish Syntax*. Foris, Dordrecht.

Poletto, Cecilia. 2000. *The Higher Functional Field*. Oxford University Press, New York.

Pollock, Jean-Yves. 1989. "Verb Movement, Universal Grammar, and the Structure of IP." *Linguistic Inquiry* 20: 356–424.

———. 1997. "Notes on Clause Structure." In Liliane Haegeman, ed., *Elements of Grammar*. Kluwer, Dordrecht.

Postal, Paul Martin. 1966. "On Coreferential Complement Subject Deletion." *Linguistic Inquiry* 1: 439–500.

Progovac, Ljiljana. 1993. "Negation and Comp." *Rivista di Linguistica* 5: 329–347.

Pulleyblank, Douglas. 1988. "Vocalic Underspecification in Yoruba." *Linguistic Inquiry* 19: 233– 270.

Puskás, Genoveva. 1992. "The Wh-criterion in Hungarian." *Rivista di grammatica generativa* 17: 141–186.

———. 1995. "A Split CP Approach: Evidence from Hungarian." *GenGenP* 3: 1–12.

———. 1996. Word Order in Hungarian, the Syntax of A'-positions. Ph.D. dissertation, University of Geneva.

———. 2000. *Word Order in Hungarian: The Syntax of A'-positions*. Benjamins, Amsterdam.

Railland, Annie. 1988. Systèmes prosodiques africains ou fondements empiriques pour un modèle multilinéaire. Ph.D. dissertation, University of Nice.

Reinhart, Tanya. 1995. Interface Strategies. Ms. Faculty of Arts, Utrecht University, Research Institute for Language and Speech, OTS.

Ritter, Elizabeth. 1991. "Two Functional Categories in Noun Phrases: Evidence from Modern Hebrew. Perspective on Phrase Structure." *Syntax and Semantics* 25. Academic Press, Rothstein, New York.

———. 1992. "Cross-Linguistic Evidence for Number Phrase." *Canadian Linguistics Review* 37: 197–218 [special ed.].

———. 1995. "On Syntactic Category of Pronouns and Agreement." *Natural Languages and Linguistics Theory* 13: 405–443.

Rizzi, Luigi. 1986. "Null Objects in Italian and the Theory of pro." *Linguistic Inquiry* 17: 501–557.

———. 1990. *Relativized Minimality*. MIT Press, Cambridge, Mass.

———. 1991. Residual Verb Second and the Wh-criterion. Ms. University of Geneva.

———. 1993. Some Issues on Cliticization. Ms. University of Geneva.

———. 1996. "Residual Verb Second and the wh-criterion." In Adriana Belletti & Luigi Rizzi, eds., *Parameters and Functional Heads: Essays in Comparative Syntax*. Oxford University Press, New York.

———. 1997. "The Fine Structure of the Left Periphery." In Liliane Haegeman, ed., *Elements of Grammar*. Kluwer, Dordrecht, Boston, London.

———. 1999. On the Position "Int(errogative)" in the Left Periphery of the Clause. Ms. University of Siena.

———. 2001. "Relativized Minimality Effects." In Mark Baltin & Chris Collins, eds., *The Contemporary Handbook of Syntactic Theory*. Blackwell, Oxford.

Roberts, Ian. 1985. "Agreement Parameters and the Development of English Modal Auxiliaries." *Natural Language & Linguistic Theory* 3: 21–58.

———. 1988. Some Notes on VP-fronting and Head Movement. Ms. University of Geneva.

———. 1993. "Agreement and Object Clitics in Franco-Provençal Valdôtain." *GenGenP* 1: 31–41.

———. 2001. "Head Movement." In Mark Baltin & Chris Collins, eds., *The Contemporary Handbook of Syntactic Theory*. Blackwell, Oxford.

Rochemont, Michael S. 1992. "Bounding Rightward A-bar Dependencies." In Helen Goodluck & Michael S. Rochemont, eds., *Island Constraints: Theory, Acquisition and Processing*. Kluwer, Dordrecht.

Rochemont, Michael S., & Peter W. Culicover. 1990. *English Focus Constructions and the Theory of Grammar*. Cambridge University Press, Cambridge, New York.

———. 1997. "Deriving Dependent Right Adjuncts in English." In Dorothee Beerman, David LeBlanc, & Henk van Riemsdijk, eds., *Rightward Movement*. Benjamins, Amsterdam.

Rohrbacher, Bernhard W. 1994. The Germanic Languages and the Full Paradigm: a Theory of V to I Raising. Ph.D. dissertation, University of Massachusetts, Amherst, Mass.

Ross, John Robert. 1967. Constraints on Variables in Syntax. Ph.D. dissertation, MIT, Cambridge, Massachusetts. Appeared in 1986 as *Infinite Syntax*. Ablex, Norwood, New Jersey.

———. 1970. "Gapping and the Order of Constituents." In Manfred Bierwisch & Karl Erich Heidolph, eds., *Language and Cognition* 5: 179–194. Yearbook 1995 of the Research Group for Theoretical and Experimental Linguistics, University of Groningen.

———. 1983. Inner Islands. Ms. MIT.

Sáàh, Kofi K. 1993. "Negation in Akan." In V. Manfredi & Karl Reynolds, eds., *Niger-Congo Syntax and Semantics 6*. Boston University African Studies Center.

Sáàh, K. Kofi, & Ejiké Ezè. 1997. "Double Objects in Akan and Igbo." In Rose-Marie Déchaine & V. Manfredi, eds., *Object Positions in Benue-Kwa*. Holland Academic Graphics, The Hague.

Safir, Kenneth. 1986. "Relative Clauses in a Theory of Binding and Levels." *Linguistic Inquiry* 17: 663–690.

Sebba, Mark. 1987. *The Syntax of Serial Verbs*. Benjamins, Amsterdam.

Shlonsky, Ur. 1992. "Resumptive Pronouns as a Last Resort." *Linguistic Inquiry* 23: 443–468.

———. 1994. "Agreement in Comp." *The Linguistic Review* 11: 351–375.

———. 1995. Constituent Questions in Palestinian Arabic. Ms. University of Geneva.

———. 2000. The Form of Semitic Noun Phrases. Ms. University of Geneva.

Siloni, Tal. 1991. "Noun Raising and the Structure of Noun Phrases." *MIT Working Papers in Linguistics* 14: 255–270.

————. 1996. "Hebrew Noun Phrases: Generalized Noun Raising." In Adriana Belletti & Luigi Rizzi, eds., *Parameters and Functional Heads: Essays in Comparative Syntax*. Oxford University Press, New York.

————. 1997. "Event Nominals and the Construct State." In L. Haegeman, ed., *The New Comparative Syntax*. Longman Linguistics Library, London.

Sportiche, Dominique. 1988. "A Theory of Floating Quantifiers and its Corollaries for Constituent Structure." *Linguistic Inquiry* 19: 425–449.

————. 1992. Clitic Constructions. Ms. UCLA.

————. 1993. Movement, Agreement and Case. Ms. UCLA.

Starke, Michal. 1993. En deuxième position en Europe Centrale. Ms. University of Geneva.

————. 1995. "On the Format for Small Clauses." *Syntax and Semantics* 28: 237–269.

Sternefeld, Wolfgang. 1991. "Chain Formation, Reanalysis, and the Economy of Levels." In Hubert Haider & Klaus Netter, eds., *Derivation and Representation in the Theory of Grammar*. Kluwer, Dordrecht.

Stewart, Osamuyimen Thompson. 1997. "Object Agreement and the Serial Verb Construction: Some Minimalist Considerations." In Rose-Marie Déchaine & Victor Manfredi, eds., *Object Position in Benue-Kwa*. The Holland Academic Graphics, The Hague.

————. 1998. The Serial Verb Construction Parameter. Ph.D. dissertation, McGill University, Montréal.

Stowell, Timothy A. 1981. Origins of Phrase Structure. Ph.D. dissertation, MIT.

Suñer, Margarita. 1993. "About Indirect Questions and Semi-Questions." *Linguistics and Philosophy* 16: 45–77.

Szabolcsi, Anna. 1987. "Functional Categories in the Noun Phrase." In István Kenesei ed., *Approaches to Hungarian*. JATE, Szeged.

————. 1994. "The Noun Phrase." In Ferenc Kiefer & Katalin E. Kiss, eds., *Syntax and Semantics. The Syntactic Structure of Hungarian* 27: 179–274.

Tenny, Carol L. 1987. Grammaticalizing Aspect and Affectedness. Ph.D. dissertation, MIT.

Tossa, Comlan Z. 1993. "Auxiliaires et séries verbales dans les langues Gbe." *Canadian Journal of Linguistics* 38: 331–352.

————. 1994. "Adjonctions et séries verbales dans les langues Gbe." Ph.D. dissertation, University of Ottawa.

Travis, Lisa de Mena. 1984. Parameters and Effects of Word Order Variation. Ph.D. dissertation, MIT, Cambridge, Massachusetts.

Ura, Hiroyuki. 2001. "Local Economy and Generalized Pied-Piping." *The Linguistic Review* 18: 169–191.

Valois, Daniel. 1991. The Syntax of DP. PhD dissertation, UCLA, Los Angeles, California.

Veenstra, Tonjes. 1996. Serial Verbs in Saramaccan: Predication and Creole Genesis. HIL dissertation 17. The Holland Academic Graphics, The Hague.

Vikner, Sten. 1995. *Verb Movement and Expletive Subjects in the Germanic Languages*. Oxford University Press, New York.

————. 1997. "V-to-I Movement and Inflection for Person in all Tenses." In Liliane Haegeman, ed., *The New Comparative Syntax*. Longman Linguistics Library, Longman, London, New York.

Vikner, Sten, & Schwartz, Bonnie D. 1991. The Verb Always Leaves IP in V2 Clauses. Ms. Stuttgart University & Boston University.

Welmers, William Everett. 1973. *African Languages Structures*. University of California Press, Berkeley.

Westermann, Diedrich. 1930. *A Study of the Ewe language*. Oxford University Press, London.

Williamson, Kay. 1965. *A Grammar of the Kolokuma Dialect of Ijo*. Cambridge University Press.

————. 1986. "Niger-Congo: SVO or SOV?" *Journal of West African Languages* 16: 5–14.

————. 1999. The Izon Focus Marker ki/ki; what does it focus? Paper read at the 29th CALL, Leiden University.

Zagona, Karen. 1982. Government and Proper Government of Verbal Projections. Ph.D. dissertation, University of Washington at Seattle.

Zanuttini, Raffaella. 1991. Syntactic Properties of Sentential Negation. A Comparative Study of Romance Languages. Ph.D. dissertation, University of Pennsylvania.

————. 1996. "On the Relevance of Tense for Sentential Negation." In Adriana Belletti & Luigi Rizzi, eds., *Parameters and Functional Heads: Essays in Comparative Syntax*. Oxford University Press, New York.

————. 1997. *Negation and Clausal Structure: A Comparative Study of Romance Languages*. Oxford University Press, New York.

Zribi-Hertz, Anne, & Jean-François Hanne. 1995. "Pronoms, déterminants et relatives Bambara de Bamako." *Linguistique Africaine* 15: 91–135.

Zribi-Hertz, Anne. 1998. "Les syntagmes nominaux possessifs en français moderne: syntaxe et morphologie." In Jacqueline Guéron, & Anne Zribi-Hertz, eds., *La grammaire de la possession*. Publidix, Université Paris X, Nanterre.

Zribi-Hertz, Anne, & Liliane Mbolatianavalona. 1997. "De la structure à la référence: les pronoms du malgache." In Anne Zribi-Hertz ed., *Les Pronoms: Morphologie, syntaxe et typologie*. Sciences du Langage. PUV, Paris 8.

————. 1999. "Toward a Modular Theory of Linguistic Deficiency: Evidence from Malagasy Personal Pronouns." *Natural Language & Linguistic Theory* 17: 161–218.

Zwart, C. Jan-Wouter. 1993. *Dutch Syntax: A Minimalist Approach*. Groningen Dissertation in Linguistics 10, University of Groningen.

————. 1997a. *Morphosyntax of Verb Movement. A Minimalist Approach to the Syntax of Dutch*. Kluwer, Dordrecht.

————. 1997b. "The Germanic SOV languages and the Universal Base Hypothesis." In Liliane Haegeman, ed., *The New Comparative Syntax*. Longman Linguistics Library, London, New York.

Name Index

Subject Index

A'-movement, 21, 83, 262, 263, 272, 297
Adangbe, 30
Adjective, 99
  in Gbe. *See* noun modifiers
Adjunct preposing, 309, 312–314, 316, 317
Adverb placement, 111, 174, 175, 233
Akan, 50, 237, 272, 277
Akyé, 66
A-movement, 21, 61
Antisymmetry, 8
Argument structure, 9
Argument topic, 290
  hanging topic, 308
  topic marker, 51, 138, 177, 178, 180, 212, 298, 307, 309, 317, 323
  topic and focus/wh, 298–303
Aspect licensing, 34
  habitual, 34, 37–42, 156, 158, 160, 161, 168–173, 175, 224–228, 230
  imperfective, 34, 35–37, 55, 156, 159, 160
  perfective, 34, 35, 65, 163, 164, 225, 228, 230–233
    state versus dynamic verbs, 226
  prospective, 170, 196–198
Ayizogbe, 342n11
Bambara, 230–233

Case. *See* pronouns
C-command, 7, 8, 12
Chains, 11
  A-chains, 11
  A'-chains, 11, 247, 297, 317, 323
  quantificational, 50, 51, 277, 302
Clausal determiner, 324–329
Clause structure, 6–17, 190
Copy
  V-copy, 260, 263–279
  XP-copy, 275–279
Demonstrative-reinforcer, 85–87
Demonstratives. *See* noun modifiers
Double object constructions, 149–151, 203
Dutch, 67–73, 334–335n25
Edo, 272
Empty Category Principle, 10
English, 7, 9, 10, 12–14, 16, 17, 19, 85, 86, 101, 104, 109, 154, 176, 180, 209, 229, 238, 261, 263, 269, 271, 284, 293, 295, 308, 339n13
EPP, 143, 185, 193, 202, 212–221
Ewegbe, 24, 25, 31–39, 46, 47, 49, 50, 51, 81, 135, 147, 208, 230
Finiteness, 15–16, 82, 153, 154, 186, 190
  finiteness projection, 181
Focus, 47–50, 138, 236–250
  focus criterion and checking theory, 248

Printed in the United States
46362LVS00003B/31

9 780195 159905